JACQUES RANCIÈRE

HISTORY,

POLITICS,

AESTHETICS

JACQUES RANCIÈRE

GABRIEL ROCKHILL and

PHILIP WATTS, eds.

DUKE UNIVERSITY PRESS   DURHAM AND LONDON   2009

Typeset in Minion by Keystone Typesetting, Inc.

Library of Congress Cataloging-in-Publication Data

appear on the last printed page of this book.

Contents

Acknowledgments

This collection of essays has its earliest origins in a conference organized by Philip Watts at the University of Pittsburgh in March 2005 entitled *Jacques Rancière: Politics and Aesthetics*. We would like to thank the Department of French and Italian at the University of Pittsburgh, and in particular Monika Losagio, as well as Dean John Cooper and Associate Dean Jim Knapp for their generous support. We would also like to thank the graduate students in French at the University of Pittsburgh for their participation, and Melissa Deininger for her design of the conference program.

Given the high quality of the presentations and the growing interest in Rancière's work, we began discussing the possibility of editing a volume of essays. This idea was bolstered by the success of the conference organized at the Centre Culturel International de Cerisy la Salle in May 2005, where Alain Badiou and Jean-Luc Nancy presented the papers included in this collection. After the conference we contacted Étienne Balibar, who kindly agreed to let us translate one of his essays that examines Rancière's arguments in *Dis-agreement*. In order to include an essay on Rancière's important contribution to film theory, we also contacted Tom Conley for his well-known work in this area. Finally, Rancière himself was kind enough to write the afterword. We would like to express our immense gratitude to him for his support and generosity in helping complete this project. As all of those who have had the pleasure to work with him already know, his intellectual prowess goes hand in hand with a profound benevolence.

We would like to thank all of the contributors to this collection as well as all of those who have helped bring this longstanding project to completion, including Courtney Berger and Ken Wissoker at Duke University Press, and the translators who graciously agreed to work with us on this project: John Hulsey, Philip E. Lewis, Catherine Porter, and Tzuchien Tho.

Introduction

Jacques Rancière: *Thinker of Dissensus*

GABRIEL ROCKHILL and PHILIP WATTS

Jacques Rancière has written some of the most significant philosophic work to be published in French in the last forty years. His corpus to date extends well beyond traditional philosophic boundaries, and includes engagements with the fields of history, politics, sociology, literary theory, literary history, art, psychoanalysis, and film theory. Although he has an explicit aversion to systematic philosophies, it is clear that he has developed a unique and robust project that is helping reshape academic disciplines and contemporary thought about the complex relationship between politics and aesthetics.

If his reception in the English-speaking world has not kept apace with his rise to prominence in France and other parts of the world, it is in part due to the fact that his idiosyncratic work does not fit comfortably within the dominant models of intellectual importation. Although he is still sometimes mistakenly classified as a structuralist because of his early contribution to Louis Althusser's *Lire le Capital* (1965), his first book was a virulent collection of essays upbraiding his former *maître*

(*La leçon d'Althusser*, 1974), and he has repeatedly criticized the discourse of mastery and the logic of hidden truths, which he identifies with the structuralist project reaching back to Marx.[1] At the same time, there are a number of patent markers that differentiate his work from that of his "poststructuralist" compatriots, including his aversion to compulsive textualism (visible in the general lack of direct quotations and his allergy to etymology), his angst-free relationship to Hegel, his general indifference toward phenomenology, his lack of deference to ethico-religious forms of alterity, his criticisms of the ethical turn in politics, his disregard for the supposed specters of metaphysics and the project of deconstruction, and his intense commitment to history that has led him beyond the canonical writers of the philosophic tradition. His distance from what is called poststructuralism should have been visible in the opening lines of his very first book, where he not only rejected the structuralist distinction between science and ideology, but where he also forcefully declared his distance from Gilles Deleuze and Jean-François Lyotard, often identified as members of the "poststructuralist" avant-garde. From the very beginning, Rancière was interested in developing a research agenda that broke with the dominant intellectual paradigm of his student years—structuralism—without following the lead of the "philosophers of difference."

One of the fundamental objectives of this collection of essays is to show that Rancière does not fit comfortably within either of these identifiable movements, and that this is precisely one of the reasons why his work should be of interest today. Rather than rehearsing what have now become the familiar arguments of his immediate predecessors or simply exercising a form of exegetical thinking by updating the work of a single grand master from the past, Rancière has patiently elaborated a distinct project with its own conceptual vocabulary and analytic strategies. His work also maintains a sharp polemical edge, as he regularly attacks prevailing assumptions and tenaciously dismantles their underlying theoretical framework. He is a veritable *thinker of dissensus* who is constantly undermining what is easily taken to be the solid footing of previous philosophic work in order to resist the consensual systems of discourse and action that are in place.

The second major goal of this collection is to emphasize the breadth of Rancière's project and its relevance to a large number of current debates. For organizational purposes, we have chosen to divide the book into three sections, each one corresponding to the three principal areas of research Rancière has contributed to: history, politics, and aesthetics. Given the richness and depth of his work, as well as his distrust of institutional and disciplinary boundaries, it should come as no surprise that the essays grouped together in each of these sections touch on a myriad of different domains, ranging from the history of philosophy, art, and literature to political theory, aesthetics, historiography, psychoanalysis, ethics, and film. They also elucidate and explore the relationships between Rancière and the various authors and artists he has analyzed, ranging from Plato and Aristotle to Mallarmé, Auerbach, Bourdieu, Deleuze, and Badiou.

The third and final goal of this collection is to critically engage with Rancière's work. Rather than waning into laudatory hagiography or sectarian repetitions of Rancière's lyrical style, the authors take his work as a crucial reference point in current debates, whose force comes not only from providing answers but also from proposing methods and raising important questions. In other words, the contributors to this collection aim not only at elucidating Rancière's project but also at critically responding to it from their own perspectives.

HISTORY

Jacques Rancière has consistently engaged with the writing of history, with institutional and narrative constructions of time, and with the ways in which individuals and communities can disrupt what he has called the distribution of the sensible (*le partage du sensible*).[2] Seeking to draw attention to these ruptures and their potential for producing social change, Rancière has frequently argued with historians and social theorists who, even as they seemed to take on the role of workers' advocates, systematically erased from their scholarship the voices and names of these workers. One of Rancière's initial claims, a paraphrase of Marx defiantly maintained against Althusser's version of Marxism, articulates the stakes of much of his early work: "It is not Man who makes history, but *men*, that is to say concrete individuals, those who produce their means of existence, those who fight in the class struggle."[3] *The Nights of Labor* (1981) and *The Philosopher and His Poor* (1983) are histories of labor, dedicated to, among many other things, countering forms of historiography and sociology grounded in narratives that seem to exclude the men and women who make history. Hence, for Rancière, the importance of understanding history in terms of what he calls a "poetics of knowledge." History is based on a poetics with certain norms, but it is also a discipline constructed from voices, documents, and gestures borrowed from common thought, and because of this, one can never create a stable hierarchy that would distinguish the voice of a discipline from that of the object of its study. In his dialogue with historiography, Rancière's fundamental gesture is to put into question the historian's position as a scientist perched high above the events and the individuals he is studying. In spite of his deep admiration for Foucault—Rancière sat in on his lectures at the Collège de France in the mid-1970s—he has always voiced concerns about analyses of the machineries of power that leave little room for the voices and forces that disrupt the order of things. In his own work, words, images, objects, and names are potential events capable of shaking all of the certitudes on which forms of domination rest. Thus in *The Names of History* (1992), Rancière argues that the *Annales* school, in moving away from the history of the acts of great men, also erased the possibility of acknowledging the actions of anyone whatsoever. What Rancière calls a heretical history, on the other hand, gives life to events that *longue durée* historiography papered over. Heretical history restores the disorder of democracy and the egalitarian *bavardage* of the masses. As Alain Badiou writes in his contribution to this book, Ranciére is not a "spontaneous vitalist," but he has nonetheless always maintained that politics, that is to say the dissensual declaration of the equality of anyone with anyone else is an event that is brought about by, "democratic individuals." This is why at the core of Rancière's work we find a multitude of individuals such as Louis Gauny, Joseph Jacotot, Jeanne Deroin, or even Irène Girard, the main character of Rossellini's *Europa '51*, who by their declarations, their greivances, and their acts transform the distribution of the sensible. Rancière's attempt to free history from structural constraints that foreclose the emergence of transformative events may, in part, account for the interest that his work is generating today. This question is at the heart of a number of essays collected in this book.

In her contribution "Historicizing Untimeliness," Kristin Ross points to the importance of Rancière's polemics with various forms of historical determinism. Ross first brought Rancière's work to the attention of many of us in the United States with her translation of *The Ignorant Schoolmaster* in 1991, and in her essay for this book, she returns to this early moment when Rancière was taking on the rising tide of the social sciences that, in his own words, "tended to turn [sociocultural difference] into destiny."[4] One of his most significant contributions, Ross argues, is his insistence on the existence of events and agents that disrupt the reigning structures of historical time and social order. In his personal and analytic essay, Alain Badiou also poses the question of history and untimeliness, but with an emphasis on the transmission of knowledge. He retraces Rancière's itinerary, starting in the 1960s when he studied at the École Normale Supérieure in Paris and began to question institutional authority and the figure of the master. Badiou's essay is an excursion into the French intellectual field around May 1968, with Althusser, Lacan, and the Chinese Cultural Revolution making brief appearances. The essay is also an exploration of Badiou's own similarities and differences with Rancière's struggle on two fronts against institutionalized authority and spontaneous vitalism.

Eric Méchoulan begins his essay by questioning a tension in Rancière's work between his rejection of systematic philosophy and synthetic historiography, and his reliance on the analysis of "great masters" in his political work. An exemplary moment of this tension occurs in Rancière's reading of the ancients, and Méchoulan looks to the *Protagoras*, a Platonic dialogue about sophism. He reminds us that Rancière's own dialogues with Plato may have much in common with sophism's early attempts at egalitarianism. However, rather than establishing a simple historical continuity and classifying Rancière as a contemporary sophist, he examines the way in which the unique starting point of equality is shared by Socrates in the very same dialogue. The question of continuity and discontinuity is also at the center of Giuseppina Mecchia's essay on *Dis-agreement*. According to Mecchia, Rancière's work is characterized, at least in part, by a series of returns: a return to the archives of worker-poets in *The Nights of Labor*, a return to canonical literary texts, and a return to classical antiquity in his later writings. The following statement, which opens Rancière's essay on politics and racism, guides Mecchia's analysis: "In politics, everything depends on certain founding utterances. We still have to decide how such utterances are to be understood."[5] She takes Rancière's commentaries on Greek philosophy and Roman historiography to be a continuation of French theory since the 1960s but also, and perhaps more importantly, an attempt to question the foundation of political philosophy and use the presupposition of equality as a way of calling into question what Rancière refers to as the police order of contemporary society.

Jean-Luc Nancy's essay, which concludes this section, broadens the scope of properly historical analysis by inquiring into the relationship between Rancière and the history of metaphysics. Opening his essay with a definition of metaphysics as the discipline that concerns itself with the excesses of rational civilization, Nancy explores the ways in which Rancière's rejection of consensus maintains a conflictual and contradictory relationship to metaphysics. His ensuing investigation into the status of the "remainder" in acts of foundation is not only an examination of the role of the "nondivided *archē*" in the work of Rancière, but also an important contribution to Nancy's own thinking about the excesses of metaphysics. The fact that he explores these questions against the backdrop of the intertwining relationship between politics and art serves, moreover, as an appropriate transition into the next two sections.

POLITICS

It should be clear to anyone who has read Rancière that one of his most important contributions has been his questioning of disciplinary boundaries precisely because, according to him, institutional divisions of labor often mirror the partitions and hierarchies operative in society. In organizing this book along three major axes—history, politics, and aesthetics—we were not looking to reify specific categories of thought, but rather to point to the ways in which Rancière has tied together problems that institutional practices often tend to separate. Since at least *The Nights of Labor*, he has made the imbrications of history, politics, and aesthetics central to his work. "The modern political animal," Rancière tells us, "is first a literary animal," in part because the social order has been founded upon distinctions of who can speak in the public sphere and who cannot, of who is visible and who is not.[6]

Rancière has sought to demarcate what he calls "politics" (*la poli-*

tique) from what is commonly understood as the political life of a community. Politics, in his understanding of the term, occurs in intermittent acts of dissensus, when an individual or a group brings forth a wrong that has been done to them and proclaims the equality of anyone and everyone. *La politique* implies putting equality first, not as something that the state owes its citizens but as a presupposition to be verified. Politics is what happens when an improper manifestation disrupts the hierarchies, the divisions, and the partitions of the social order, or what Rancière calls "the police" (*la police*). Focusing on his engagement with politics in books such as *La leçon d'Althusser* (1974), *On the Shores of Politics* (1992 and 1998), *Dis-agreement* (1995), and in his essays published in *Révoltes Logiques*, the contributors to this section question how Rancière's understanding of politics compares with that of other writers of his generation.

The first essay is an article by Étienne Balibar that appeared five years after the publication of Rancière's *Dis-agreement* (1995). Much like the contributions by Ross and Badiou in the previous section, Balibar's essay situates Rancière's work in its immediate context, which in this case is the return of political philosophy in contemporary Europe, as visible most notably in the work of Jean-Luc Nancy, Giorgio Agamben, and Roberto Esposito (not to mention Balibar himself). In addition to this delicate work of contextualization, Balibar also explores the ways in which Esposito's category of the "impolitical" serves as a fruitful point of comparison with Rancière's democratic politics and his radical critique of consensus.

The starting point for the philosopher Todd May is the death of the young African American man, Kashef White, who was hit by a car in Clemson, South Carolina, in 2001. The death, and more specifically the mishandling of the incident by the police, greatly disturbed Clemson's African American community. Through a careful analysis of Rancière's writings on politics, May demonstrates how his thought remains fundamental to activists precisely because it helps negotiate the dividing line between two forces visible in the unfolding of the Kashef White case: a local government that generally denied the existence of racism and reaffirmed the status quo of the "police order," and the arguments for justice by members of a community who had been wronged and whose claims could constitute what Rancière calls "politics." May puts Rancière in relation to other theorists of equality such as John Rawls, Robert Nozick, and Amartya Sen and argues that his thought puts forth a novel account of equality that steers clear of the dangers of identity politics and provides hope for engaging in the pursuit of social justice.

Yves Citton, in his essay, takes on Rancière's category of "the sensible" in order to think through the question of political agency. Pointing to some of the differences that have separated his project from the work of neo-Spinozists such as Gilles Deleuze, Toni Negri, and the collective at the journal *Multitudes*, Citton argues for a possible "complementarity" between active and passive politics, between cognition of the sensible world and political activism. What Citton calls "membrane politics" aims at avoiding the pitfalls of a metaphysics of free will while at the same time offering the possibility of a reconciliation between a politics of the multitude and Rancière's politics of the people.

In an essay that explores the role of the theater in Rancière's writings on politics, Peter Hallward both praises the latter's contribution to thinking anarchic equality and warns that his frequent recourse to metaphors of theatricality might very well risk emptying his political theses of their potential for instigating concrete change. For Hallward, one of Rancière's fundamental contributions is his axiomatic conception of equality and his insistence on the primacy of subjective commitments in the politics of emancipation. But he also raises questions about the relation between his "theatrocracy" and sustainable political change in the contemporary world. Bruno Bosteels, in his article, questions the relation between politics and aesthetics in Rancière's work and points to an asymmetry in his treatment of these two practices, insofar as the latter is historicized and the former is not. Reading Rancière, and in particular his work *Dis-agreement*, alongside the work of Alain Badiou in an attempt to pinpoint some of his fundamental strategies, Bosteels explores the role of nominalism and the risks of speculative leftism in Rancière's attempts to identify the "there is" of politics. Solange Guénoun opens her essay where Bosteels ends his, by putting Rancière's thought in relation to the ethical turn of the last twenty years. As Guénoun shows, Rancière has developed in his most recent writings an increasingly radical, and at times problematic, critique of contemporary ethics and of Jean-François Lyotard's writings on the sublime, both of which he sees as being linked to the American crusade against the "axis of evil" and the suppression of democratic aspirations around the globe.

Since the late 1990s, Rancière has put forth one of the most novel and powerful accounts of aesthetics. Instead of taking art to be a historical constant and attempting to unveil its fundamental essence, he maintains that there is no "art in general" but only historically constituted "regimes" that establish a given distribution of the sensible and determine the framework of possibility for artistic production and theoretical reflection on art.

There are three regimes of art according to the account Rancière has outlined in books such as *La parole muette* (1998), *The Flesh of Words* (1998), *The Politics of Aesthetics* (2000), *L'inconscient esthétique* (2001), *Film Fables* (2001), *The Future of the Image* (2003), *Malaise dans l'esthé-tique* (2004), *Politique de la littérature* (2007), and *The Emancipated Spectator* (2009). The *ethical regime of images* came into being in ancient Greece and is exemplified by Plato's writings on the distribution of images that would best serve the ethos of the community. The ethical regime is preoccupied with distinguishing true art—meaning art that is both true to its origin and to its telos of moral education—from artistic simulacra that distance the community from truth and the good life. The *representative regime of the arts* has its roots in Aristotle's *Poetics*, but only came into full fruition in the seventeenth and eighteenth centuries. This regime freed the arts from the moral imperatives of the ethical regime by identifying a unique domain of fiction with its own set of guiding principles: the hierarchical distribution of subject matter and genres, the principle of appropriateness by which action and modes of expression are adapted to the subject matter represented and the genre employed, and the elevation of speech-as-act over action and visual imagery. Although both the ethical and the representative regimes continue to be operative in the modern age, it is the *aesthetic regime of art* that has left its mark on the last two centuries of artistic production. By abolishing the hierarchical rules of representation, the aesthetic regime has promoted the equality of subjects, the dissolution of genres, the indifference of style in relationship to content, and the power of writing and other "mute" things over the presence of speech. It is only in this "egalitarian" regime that art is identified in the singular. However, this occurs at the precise moment at which the hierarchical delimitation between art and life disappears, meaning that art in the modern world is caught in a contradiction: it only exists in the singular insofar as it loses its singularity-qua-art by dissolving itself into life. According to Rancière, it is precisely this contradiction between art and life that has been the driving force behind artistic production since the end of the eighteenth century.

Gabriel Rockhill's contribution to this collection picks up where the last section left off by outlining the relationship between Rancière's work and the writings of his immediate predecessors on the connection between art and politics. Highlighting Rancière's apparent "Copernican revolution," he charts out the evolution of his position in his most recent work. In particular, he tries to make sense of the traces of a surprising convergence between politics (*la politique*) and the police, which he relates to Rancière's key notion for thinking the politics of aesthetics: the distribution of the sensible. In the remainder of his essay, he raises a series of critical questions regarding Rancière's ahistorical account of politics and the "hermeneutic *epochē*" required by his aesthetic ontology. In both cases, he ballasts his criticisms with a set of counterclaims by disputing Rancière's image of the history of democracy and his claim that a new age of filmmaking has emerged with the release of *Mystic River, Dogville*, and *Elephant*.

Tom Conley's essay engages directly with Rancière's contribution to film studies. He emphasizes his unique position in the world of film theory by indicating how his heterodox approach distinguishes his writings from the now canonical works of André Bazin, Christian Metz, Serge Daney, and Gilles Deleuze. In analyzing Rancière's assiduous attention to detail and his proclivity for unearthing contradictions, Conley relates Rancière's singular methodology to his novel account of film history and his rejection of the "great divide" between classical and modern cinema. Rancière's major contribution, it would seem, is to have provided an unprecedented map of film history, replete with a contradictory temporality in which the "old" is no less modern than the "new," and in which the heritage of film reaches back to an era before the very birth of the medium.

The next two contributions both act as case studies by taking particular elements in Rancière's project on aesthetics and comparing them to rival accounts by his immediate predecessors. Raji Vallury examines Rancière's critical assessment of Deleuze and situates it within the broader framework of his analysis of the aesthetic regime of art. She shows how the author of *Essays Critical and Clinical* illustrates, for

Rancière, the contradictions inherent in this regime. At the same time, she attempts to draw out an unsuspected convergence between Deleuze's ontology and Rancière's conception of politics, which she does in part through an analysis of a form of literary discourse largely at the periphery of their respective aesthetic interests: the writings of Algerian novelist Tahar Djaout. Andrew Parker examines Rancière's engagement with the work of Erich Auerbach by comparing and contrasting it with the well-known account provided by Edward Said. He outlines their rival conceptions of alterity, which are rooted in two alternative approaches to the politics of poetics, and he suggests that there are grounds for believing that the lesson Rancière has learned from Auerbach is more politically compelling than Said's subjective identification with the exiled author of *Mimesis*.

The final essay in this section, James Swenson's "*Style indirect libre*," explores the relationship between Rancière's project and his idiosyncratic stylistics. Arguing that Rancière's work has always been driven by the fundamental axiom of intellectual equality, Swenson analyzes his attempt to construct a narrative that breaks with the assumption that there are those who think and those who need someone to think for them, or that there is a surface of ideological mystification and a deep truth behind appearances (only accessible to "those who think"). At the core of this break with what Rancière calls the "discourse of mastery" is his use of free indirect discourse, which blurs the lines between the narrator's voice and the voices narrated, or between the one who speaks and the one who is spoken for. By carefully studying a selection of passages and examining Rancière's use of *style indirect libre* as well as other rhetorical strategies, Swenson shows to what extent Rancière's intellectual project is premised on developing a unique mode of enunciation, which all readers of Rancière will immediately recognize.

AFTERWORD

In the final essay, Rancière addresses some of the questions of method and style raised by the essays in this collection. Returning to a passage from *The Nights of Labor* on a joiner, he reexamines his foundational insights regarding the relation between ideology and the distribution of the sensible, politics and the passions of literature, history and the power of equality. This reflective essay ties together a number of fundamental themes that traverse his entire corpus and relates his most recent concerns in the fields of aesthetics and politics to his earlier work on history. It also sheds light on his long-standing emancipatory method of using concepts as tools to displace existing topographies and undermine consensual regimes by thinking through the far side of the police order of discourse and action.

HISTORY

1.

Historicizing Untimeliness

KRISTIN ROSS

In an essay written shortly after the American war in Iraq began, Jacques Rancière wrote about the seamless integration of capital, state, military, and media power achieved in the United States during the months preceding the invasion. He called the fusion "a perfecting of the plutocratic system."[1] Certainly, those of us who lived through those months in the United States (or—again—the months preceding the 2004 presidential election) can testify to the background noise we heard. It wasn't bombs—these we saw and heard very little of—but rather the media's relentless litany of repeated phrases: "weapons of mass destruction," "Afghani women voting," "evil dictator," and one or two others. But I want to begin by evoking an earlier moment in the history of that seamless integration: the moment in 1983 when Ronald Reagan set up a covert CIA operation bearing a name I think Rancière might appreciate: "Perception Management." Perception Management, unlike other CIA operations, was directed domestically and was, for all intents and purposes, the now-forgotten origin of the media techniques later to be perfected by the George W. Bush administration. Reagan wanted to swing public opinion to support his Central American policies in Nicaragua and El Salvador, and to that end polling was conducted to determine which precise buzzwords and concepts would best turn U.S. citizens against the Sandanistas and get them to support the Contras and the Salvadoran government. In the face of the latest great "third-worldist" cause, the solidarity movements with the peoples of Nicaragua and El Salvador, the idea was to saturate the media with phrases repeated over and over like mantras: the Sandanistas are anti-Semitic, they're drug runners, they discriminate against indigenous peoples, they're terrorists, and so forth—to enormous effect.[2] It is during these years, I think—the early 1980s—that consensus first comes to be taken for granted as the optimum political gesture or goal, with "Perception Management" its more than adequate figure. And it was around this time that I first began to read Rancière's work. Against this ideological backdrop, the untimeliness of his project was strongly perceptible. This is why I'll not focus on *Dis-agreement* and the recent intellectual developments which, as conferences held in the United Kingdom, Berlin, Cérisy, and elsewhere suggest, are now placing Rancière's work at the center of contemporary discussions. I want to go back, rather, to the earlier stages of the project: to Jacotot and *The Names of History*. For it was in the late 1970s and early 1980s that a generalized offensive against equality, under the cover of a critique of egalitarianism, began to make of equality a synonym for uniformity, for the constraint or alienation of liberty, or for an assault on the free functioning of the market.[3] It is in this context that Rancière's preoccupation with, or recurrent staging of, equality and its verification could be called untimely, or that my own experience reading a book like *The Ignorant Schoolmaster* could be one of delighted shock—only initially really graspable for me, teaching in central California, as a kind of echo of certain Latin American utopian pedagogical experiments of the 1960s. So although the introduction I wrote to my translation of *The Ignorant Schoolmaster* created a kind of context for the book out of the French educational policies and debates of the first period of Mitterrand, my own enthusiasm, what made me want to do the translation, was the way Rancière's book seemed to me to resonate, however slightly, with earlier interventions like Ivan Illich's *Deschooling Society* or Paolo Friere's *Pedagogy of the Oppressed*.[4]

Now France, of course, like Germany, had no Reagan or Thatcher, which is to say no full-scale ultraconservative restructuring of its economy in the 1980s. Then, as now, a difference can be detected between governments where systems of social protection and solidarity have not been completely dismantled and those, like the United States, where they have. But the 1980s in France were nevertheless what Serge Halimi might call an intensely philo-American time,[5] as France began to accommodate itself to the ascendancy of an American liberal orthodoxy, an orthodoxy in which equality came to be seen as a body of principles which, at best, can be interpreted by a court rather than what Rancière's work insisted on showing it to be: a profoundly political problem, *the* problem, in fact, of politics per se.

Perhaps the best way to talk about Rancière's untimeliness in those years, though, is to remember how the interdisciplinary terrain had begun to be taken over and inundated, then, with a kind of cobbled-together "spatiality," as the human sciences came to embrace insights, perspectives, and methodologies imported from the "spatial sciences" of urbanism, architecture, ethnology, and geography. The spatial turn was reinforced by an appeal to culturalism, based on the category of culture as a static, spatial countenance—culture that cannot be seen as an agent of time. This spatial turn—the imbalance in humanistic and cultural studies that consisted in a privileging of space over considerations of temporality or change—is apparent in the still-manifest preoccupation in the critical literature (in its popular forms as much as in its more scientific uses) with the description of territories, movements, and relations in space. Students today—and not only students—shy away from large diachronic questions and from any attempt to conceptualize change, preferring instead to nest within a set of spatially determined cultural units of comparison. From the outset I think it's fair to say that Rancière's project worked against the grain of this spatial turn, both thematically and in its polemical attacks on the inherent functionalism that undergirded some of the principle thinkers associated with the turn. Functionalism, in all its guises, affirms the status quo by presenting a social system that is complete, achieved, from which nothing is lacking. Social systems or cultures appear as fixed and complete—fully formed. In the case of critics concerned with postmodernism and the spatial fix, such as David Harvey or Fredric Jameson, neither of whom figure in Rancière's polemics—(though Lyotard, another postmodernist, does)—the static fixity of the contemporary "postmodern" social system means some sort of arrival of what Marx called "real subsumption." Rancière's polemics have targeted a hyphenated structuralism-functionalism whose powerful hold on not only social anthropology and sociology, but also history and the social sciences generally, testifies to a kind of unbroken reign of evolutionist epistemology. Polemics, after all, is just a synonym for untimeliness. And to be untimely means to be about time, not outside of it, or beyond it. Rather than participating in the spatial fix, Rancière preferred to think the way time gives form to relations of power and inequality and how its denaturalization shatters those relations: his thinking concerns itself with both the temporal rhythms and schedules of work and ideology, as well as the temporality of emancipation. "Ideology," he wrote in *The Philosopher and His Poor*, "is just another name for work."[6] Rancière is not alone, of course, in being a thinker of differential temporalities. But to characterize him this way is to place him in a constellation of thinkers that might at first seem incongruous and that I'm not entirely sure he'd appreciate: in the company of the Marx of *Zeitwidrig* or contretemps, of his old teacher Louis Althusser's articulation of multiple times and the irreducibility of various levels to a single common history, of Ernst Bloch's "contemporaneity of the non-contemporaneous," of Maurice Halbwach's plurality of social times, or even of a conservative thinker like Reinhart Koselleck's recurrent insistence that the archaic persists, and even thrives, at the core of the most advanced modernity.

But if we return to the dominant spatial discourse of the period, we can see how a kind of all-pervasive functionalism informed the work of even those progressive thinkers who were called upon to form the bridge, so to speak, between an earlier linguistic/structural moment and the new explicit focus on exploring the mechanisms of living societies. I'm thinking of Pierre Bourdieu and Michel de Certeau, two thinkers whose principle works, *Distinction* and *The Practice of Everyday Life*, were translated into English during the 1980s and frequently assigned in classes, in the States at least. In the United States and Australia, critics attuned to developments in British cultural studies and weary of poststructuralism were looking for works they hoped would help them break out of the corral of epistemology to reach the social, and these books seemed to respond to that demand. These critics were particularly drawn to the spatialized dynamics of power and resistance that de Certeau derived from Foucault, and to the figure of his wily pedestrian, twisting and turning along backstreets and by-ways, "turns" that were tropological as well as geographic—de Certeau conflating the two in a whole celebratory rhetoric of nonconformist walking.[7] Here all the liberatory values and frissons of mobility associated, in the earlier moment of the linguistic paradigm, with the slippage of meaning in a literary text are attributed to the pedestrian's cunning tactics: the maneuvers and resistance of the relatively powerless. Leaving considerations of power to the center—where, like all good functionalists, de Certeau believes it belongs in the interest of social stability—what remains is life in the margins, which is allowed to exist precisely because it poses no threat to the center's hold. In a striking formulation that reading Rancière makes us alert to, de Certeau writes, "Their bodies follow the thick and thins of an urban text they write without being able to read."[8] A popular text is being written, in other words, but only on the condition that its authors cannot read or understand it. These, then, are the maneuvers of a more-or-less authentic urban folk, the authenticity of whose daily practices derives from their sheer, unknowing ordinariness, as well as their sheer unknowingness. "The actual order of things," de Certeau writes, "is precisely what popular tactics turn to their own ends, without any illusion that it is about to change."[9] Unlike, say, a more nuanced thinker of the everyday like Henri Lefebvre, de Certeau cannot imagine how the everyday can be about history—any tension between experience and anticipation for him has been erased. Change having been precluded and temporality effectively frozen, the way is now cleared for a socially cohesive, consensus portrait of what de Certeau called "ordinary culture"—unchanging, repetitive customs, hobbies, and dispositions that form what might at best be called a culture of consolation.[10] And the historian's role is completely assimilated to that of the ethnologist. "For the historian," he writes, "as for the ethnologist, the goal is to make function a cultural whole, to make its laws appear, to structure a landscape."[11]

It is easy, now, to see how such a mechanistic see-saw of power and resistance could go on to form the backbone of Anglo-American cultural studies' celebration of ludic resistance through consumption. Here, too, there is the presumption of a fully formed commodity relation, or "real subsumption." But already in 1977 the *Révoltes Logiques* collective, in an interview with Foucault, asked questions they and Nicos Poulantzas were alone in formulating at that time, questions that showed how power, in Foucault's schema, operates like full subsumption. For in such a schema, wasn't power, presupposed to be always already there, locked in the grip of a battle with equally unchanging mass-resistance tactics—wasn't power thus rendered absolute? Wasn't it better to begin a discussion of power with the question of whom it serves, in whose interests?[12]

De Certeau arrives at the same ratio of unknowingness and repetitive motion as Pierre Bourdieu, whose guiding concept of *habitus* houses both humans and their habitual dispositions. *Habitus* is that which allows us to practice an accumulation of collective experiences without knowing we are doing so. For Bourdieu, it goes without saying because it comes without saying. Once again, the *Révoltes Logiques* collective was alone at the time, in the early 1980s, in showing the way in which Bourdieu represented a powerful afterlife to Durkheimian sociology and its logic of social cohesion.[13] What is eternalized and internalized—the aptly named "second nature"—becomes what is forgotten in history. And a once-lively history filled with agents and eventfulness subsides into the stable representations of the habitus—where no horizon other than being in perfect conformity to one's condition is visible.

I wanted to revisit these widely read thinkers whose concerns with popular culture bore at least a passing resemblance to those of Rancière in order to highlight how different, in fact, his own questions were. Beginnings, points of departure, are more important for Rancière than for most thinkers, and the gesture of throwing the engine into reverse is one way he likes to begin. What happens if you begin not with culture conceived of as one's proper allotment of symbolic capital, nor with culture conceived of as a set of consoling rituals? What happens if you don't begin with culture at all, but instead with emancipation? "The concept of culture," Rancière noted in his book on history, "whether one applies it to knowledge of the classics or to the manufacture of shoes, has the sole effect of effacing this movement of subjectivization that operates in the interval between several nominations and its constitutive fragility."[14] The concept of culture presupposes an identity tied to a way of speaking, being, and doing that is itself tied to a situation, a name, a body, assigned to a place, a life station. Culture is inherently functionalist, noncontingent.

Arlette Farge has written very eloquently about the antiethnological dimension of Rancière's work on history writing, and the disquiet with which social historians initially greeted it, only to have their hostility subside into a willed forgetting.[15] What I take from her remarks is this: as long as space—territory or *terroir*—is the departure point for an analysis, if you begin with space, whether it be the space of the region, ghetto, island, factory, or *banlieue*, then peoples' voices, their subjectivities, can be nothing more than the naturalized, homogenized expression of those spaces. Rancière's project, in this sense, could be said to be at the forefront of one kind of cultural studies—but only an anti-identitarian one: a cultural studies where the concept of culture has been banished from the outset and identitarian matters twisted into a fluid and unscheduled nonsystem of significant misrecognitions.

It was when I taught a recent seminar on the various ways eventfulness is constructed and perceived that I began to get a full sense of the untimeliness of Rancière's project. For one way of characterizing the intellectual labor of the late 1970s and early 1980s is to see it as a massive and relentless dismantling of the event or eventfulness, at the hands not only of progressives like Bourdieu and de Certeau, but of virtually everyone in the vicinity. First and foremost, of course, there was the *Annales* school's preoccupation with summoning up the full weight and inertia of centuries of ways of doing, with reaffirming the whole circularity of nature and function. The New Philosophers, in another corner, wielded the weapon of scale, rendering every action negligible or suspect, dwarfed or criminalized in the face of the twin catastrophes of the Gulag and the Holocaust, and the various endisms to which these gave rise. In a not unrelated enterprise, François Furet set his sights on dismantling the event par excellence, anchoring his attempt to turn the French Revolution into the American Revolution squarely within the ideology of the present and the wish to provide a different genealogy for the liberalism (in the French sense) of the 1980s. An opportunistic but talented journalist, and a powerful model for followers like Tony Judt in the United States, Furet's reign as *roi des historiens* in France was no less long lived or far reaching than was Bourdieu's as *roi des sociologues*. It is not, I think, an exaggeration, to say that these two academics—with the various associates, journals, and *équipes de travail* each presided over, and the institutional privileges each was granted—virtually controlled the production and direction of countless French intellectual careers in and beyond their respective disciplines throughout the 1980s. In the case of Bourdieu, his own trajectory took an existential turn, if not a theoretical one, after 1995, with his increasingly militant political activities. In the case of Furet, his work was enormously facilitated by the emergence of American-style think tanks in the 1980s, including the Fondation Saint-Simon, over which he presided until his death. This foundation, whose history has yet to be written, brought together for the first time in France a mix of government leaders, academics, industrialists, and media people in a kind of dinner club organized around a nebulous "modernizing project," with modernity being understood to mean conformity to the economic constraints of the neoliberal order. The goal was to bring the social sciences into direct service to the state, and the result was, clearly, a further consolidation of the intellectual's position as expert or consultant to the state, clear eyed and cognizant of hard economic realities. The idea was that intellectuals, liberated from abstraction and engaged in pragmatic problem solving, would encounter social problems unbiased by ideological considerations. The model here had, of course, been provided by the American "servants of power": social scientists who were early on enlisted in the service of the state. The American ideal of Weberian-Parsonian "value-free" social science found a home at the Fondation Saint-Simon, where Furet, deeply engaged in a recuperation of the American model, attempted to bring France in line with the kind of seamless integration of media, capital, and state power I evoked earlier under the figure of "perception management." Any adversaries—critical intellectuals or those engaged in social movements —could be disqualified in advance as flaming ideologues, irresponsible, hellbent on swimming against the tide of history, or, in a favorite accusation of the time, "anti-American." And to be called anti-American in France in the 1980s was tantamount to being accused of fascist tendencies, Stalinist tendencies, or both at the same time—a kind of post-Arendtian Red-Brown fusion.

Rancière's battle, in this sense, was and, I believe, continues to be a battle with strategies whose aim is the suppression of time. After the *Révoltes Logiques* experiment came to an end in 1981, he was sustained in his fight, I think, by an abiding loyalty to what is perhaps an unlikely source:

to a certain reading of Benveniste, from whom he derived his insistence on the ways in which eventfulness depends upon speech. In Rancière's writing all of the startling and expansive emancipatory power Benveniste attributed to the production of the first instance of enunciation is retained and dramatized. "Language," wrote Benveniste in a famous formulation, "is so organized that it permits each speaker to appropriate to himself an entire language by designating himself as 'I.'"[16] Something of the enormous potentiality of the moment of subjectivity, the appropriation of an entire language—and not the crablike, sideways entry into subjectivity that Monique Wittig, in her reading of Benveniste, would later say is allotted to women—is retained in Rancière's version of the event. And something of the conscious framing or staging, as well: subjectivization in Rancière's texts never takes on the consistency of a theory of the subject, let alone a fixed or coherent subject, just as no underlying ontology to his analyses is ever explicitly designated as such. Yet the instance of appropriation is invariably, for him, at one and the same time a moment of disidentification, the creation of an *écart* or fissure in whatever had previously secured identity. Adrian Rifkin, commenting on the recurrent thematics of the *écart* throughout Rancière's work, has suggested that *écartement* (setting aside, deflection, displacement) is deployed there in several ways: It is a way of using images or themes in his writing, moving them around so that other figures become visible or recede from view. It is a strategy he deploys in the positioning of his writing vis-à-vis the current intellectual ambiance (what I am calling here his untimeliness) on the one hand, and in deflecting his reader from any doctrinal readings of materials on the other. It is even related to the kind of thought-effect he creates in his readers.[17] These delineations are extremely illuminating. Yet Rancière is a thinker whose first major work, *The Nights of Labor*, drew our attention very powerfully to the act of stealing time. His study relocated workers into another kind of time, outside the temporal regime established by Marx. Marx's "workday," he showed, was actually exceeded by night and all its possibilities. In this astonishing critique, what becomes clear for the first time is how closely aligned Marx's own perspective was: not with that of the worker, but rather with that of capital—the perspective of "the production of surplus value." Taking our lead from this early text, I think it may be useful to think of Rancière's *écartement* as first and foremost a fissure or wrinkle in time: a *décalage*, a moment of nonsynchronicity or fracture, an interval, as in "the rift or the interval through which subjects of history pass."[18] To this end I want to trace the temporal thematics of Rancière's work.

The first thematizing of time occurs in the atmosphere immediately after May '68, right before the launch of the *Révoltes Logiques* journal in 1975. It appears in the pages of *La leçon d'Althusser*, where Althusserian theory is construed as the enacting of so many theoretical ruptures in order that none be put into political practice. Althusserian theory, in other words, becomes in Rancière's work the first example of a temporality proper to "those who know." To those who know is granted the science of the conjuncture, the ability of determining the timing of the revolt, as well as when best to wait it out. What was revealed in the failed meeting between Althusserian theory and the insurrection of 1968 was that the antagonisms and disagreements of empirical politics will never provide philosophy with the right moment to connect with political action: it is never the moment, and it will never be the moment. The temporality proper to those who know is that of waiting, deliberating, persevering, allowing theory to take its time; '68 was not the proper moment. This initial experience and its critique is, I think, at the origin of all of Rancière's subsequent concern with the relation of knowledge and the masses—with theorists who see themselves as advocates of equality but who reconstitute a hierarchy that is in large part a temporality that others are presumed not to share. By positing a relation between temporalities, Rancière's antifunctionalism is already apparent. For in the logic of functionalism, time is encapsulated in a given social system or culture: a singular, flat, unidimensional, linear, or worse, circular time. Each of these cultures can then be studied separately, ethnographically, according to a timeless theory or method. Time within cultures was worth studying, and could be, in any number of taxonomies, but time was virtually eliminated from the study of relations between cultures. It was the relation between different temporalities that, for Rancière, instead merited attention.

Jacotot, the ignorant schoolmaster, develops the theme of a temporal structure of delay, the distance in time that separates pedagogue from student. But before we continue, we need to confront the question raised by the figure of Jacotot himself—and that has to do with the status of the example in Rancière's text. Who are these individuals, these mostly marginal characters who are also historical figures, often drawn forth from the most obscure archives? Jacotot, like Gauny, Blanqui, or the worker poets, arrives like a time traveler as if by accident, neither as spokesperson nor sociological representative, but nevertheless mobilized to do battle or at the very least to serve as a diagnostic of the contemporary situation. Such figures also appear as untimely, remnants or revenants from beyond the reach of standard time, emanating perhaps from the future. Though their ability to straddle great temporal expanses lends them a kind of science fiction–like aura, they do not resemble the characters in Philip K. Dick's *Ubik*, bloodless, or suspended in some half-life. Each retains all of his individual singularity and historical contingency, as befits Rancière's obstinate insistence on staying at the level of the particular case, his insistence—against generalization, system, sometimes even against concept—on the particular, material, interlocutory situation. His concern is, first and foremost, with what specific historical actors have said and written in contingent situations. Yet the particular actions and points of view of marginal individuals, when resuscitated with care and attention, reframed and staged, can be mobilized against the dominant ideology. Provided, of course, that the right transversals are created. Historical figures, framed like literary characters, in order to refute, via philosophy, various political myths or ideologies—Rancière's peculiar and powerful version of transdisciplinarity takes this form. His response—that is, to the institution of fixed disciplinary knowledges—is not to merge or combine different knowledges but rather to use one to undermine and contest the other: to use history against philosophy, or literature against political theory. The way Jacotot is staged has the political effect of denouncing theories that invent the dominated that best suit their theoretical presuppositions. But it also has the advantage of infusing a kind of revitalized energy and potential for the new into history. History, in fact, is given much the same power Rancière grants to fiction: that of reframing, and thus expanding, perception, reconfiguring what is thinkable, scrambling perception management.

So Jacotot is the anti-Bourdieu, whose enterprise of demystification is revealed to be yet another interlocutory situation based on explication, an activity that preserves formally the hierarchies and inherited subject positions it was intent on undermining at the level of content. And Jacotot can also be the anti-Althusser. For Jacotot and the other autodidacts who inhabit Rancière's texts effectively eliminate or short-circuit the very temporality of the pedagogical relation: the principle of infinite regression separating the ignorance of today from the science of the future. At the heart of the pedagogical relation is the representation of inequality as evolutionary epistemology: the people who can never catch up with the enlightened elite, or who can never be completely modern. People who are trapped, without knowing it, at one stage along the trajectory of progressive time, and who are destined to remain there, imprisoned in this other time, that of the child, or that of the primitive. But inequality can't be gradually whittled away, just as equality is not a goal to be one day attained, nor arrived at by dint of a series of concessions made by the state. Short-circuiting the temporality of pedagogy makes equality a point of departure, the point of departure, an axiom anterior to the constitution of a particular staging of politics and which makes such a staging possible. Rather than being the criteria that determines how long it will take for society as it is to become society as it might or should be, equality as an axiom enables thought, experiment, invention.

Jacotot, Rancière tells us, is a man of the previous century, a man of the revolutionary moment, out of sorts or out of sync with the burgeoning century of progress gradually taking shape around him. He is, in this sense, something of an anachronism—the second temporal disjuncture dear to Rancière I want to discuss. Jacotot is a time traveler in his own moment, a figure of noncontemporaneity, and like all such figures, either ahead of or behind his times, residual or emergent—or probably both at the same time. Rancière's 1996 essay on anachronism, perhaps more than the book he devoted to historicity, *The Names of History*, reveals the symptom of the whole naturalizing tendency the *Annales* school put into place, that immobile interlacing of thought, identity, practice, and belief to be encapsulated in the fear of anachronism.[19] Fear of anachronism was another name for the conception Febvre articulated but that others shared as well—the conception that existence means belonging to, coinciding with, or resembling, one's time. Rabelais could not have not believed in God, because disbelieving was inconceivable in Rabelais's era. This is really nothing more than pure Rankian historicism, an extreme version of "cultural respect"—like judging the native by his own standards or judging the period according to its own presuppositions. But Febvre is not alone in seeing the historian's task as being that of establishing what is thinkable in a given era. Foucault's notion of the episteme, which eliminates event or time as agent, does much the same. And the purpose of social history is limited to understanding ideologies and social movements within the particular economic and political contexts these secrete like a mollusk's shell—thus flattening any possibility of event or change. The presuppositions of the more recent cultural history are no different. For the new cultural historians, culture behaves in a way identical to Parsons's social system[20]—as fully formed, with only periodic disfunctions or deviations. Culture and social system, in turn, act like the nation-state—the authority figure behind all these categories, and one that Rancière, to my knowledge, doesn't really address. Social science in general spends its time making the people who don't resemble their moment get back into the harness, making any aberrant speech fit the context—and in so doing affirming not only the noneventfulness, but the unknowingness, even the duped nature, of the objects of history as well—making them at one with the beliefs of their era. For the only way you can belong to your era is without knowing it—which is to say, through belief. The people are people who can't think otherwise.

But in the history of social formations, there is a multiplicity of times, some of which present themselves as repetitions, while others effect tesseracts, wrinkles that join the ancient with the contemporary—different times, as Rancière puts it, "telescoping" into one another.[21] Thus the future appears in the present, the present repeats the past, and what some call anachronisms can inhabit an era. This is all very disturbing for those of us who learned to conceive of "era" as one of those large, homogenous blocs or signifying totalities, as in the books we read as children, books with titles like *The Baroque Period*, where you are made to understand that the baroque period was baroque because back then sculpture was baroque, legal systems were baroque, poetry and even the people who wrote it were baroque. . . .

Perhaps the most audacious and influential attempt to suppress time in the 1970s and 1980s took the tried and true form called "revisionism"— François Furet's influential rewriting of the French Revolution such that it didn't occur. Revisionism, for Rancière, is another name for what happens in the architecture of historical narration when you assemble data in such a way that it remains a pile of data, such that it does not take

on the shape and consistency of a singular event. Extreme contextualization, thick description—these can show that the event really wasn't one.
No new object—or rather, no new subject—appears. Furet showed the
revolution to have transpired to create what was, in fact, already in
place; revolutionary actors acted under "the illusion of defeating a State
that had already ceased to exist."[22] They toppled an enemy that wasn't
even there—the poor fools. They were too late, exerting themselves for
no reason; it wasn't the right moment. The revolution had already
happened without them. But who was to know, until Furet told us two
hundred years later?

Furet's dismantling of the grand narrative of the French Revolution
heralded and enabled the arrival, more recently, of the third temporal
manifestation I want to mention, the particular paralysis of history
Rancière has diagnosed under the name of "endism." This was the attempt made by philosophers, with a gravitas that frequently careened
into hysteria, to create a specifically new and postmodern era based
on announcing the end of art, for example, or the end of ideology, the
end of politics, or, ultimately, the end of meaningful time. All of these
endisms were about ending time, and were in effect a repetition of
Parsons's banishment of time from the social system in the earlier "end
of ideology" of the American 1950s. Much of Rancière's recent work has
had a double focus: that of undercutting the historical pertinence of
the catastrophism that claims to account for the current postmodern
situation, and that of bypassing or dismantling the postmodern paradigm in its pretension to historical newness, its claim to singularity as
a new and distinct era. What appears new in the era of apocalyptic
pronouncements and its "unsatisfactory mise-en-scène of the 'end' and
the 'return,' " is, in fact, just a restaging.[23] Philosophical activity undertaken under the sign of urgency is a new version of an old phenomenon:
the heroicizing of the philosopher's voice, the philosopher as prophet
who can see "the end" that others cannot see. Ambulance philosophy of
this kind first came into being with what Alain Badiou has called the
"Thermidorean subjectivity" of the New Philosophers, who tirelessly
fabricated an end to history and politics out of their own political
disillusionment.[24]

Yet politics, for Rancière, is not a matter of illusion or disillusion, but
of demonstrating or verifying equality. It is an interlocutory event. And
if politics hasn't ended, it is still exceptional or scarce, appearing, as an

event, and then only intermittently. The temporality of politics is not progressive, nor dialectical—a word he uses only rarely—it is not continuous and it's not over. Politics is an event that cannot be predicted any more than its end can be apocalyptically announced. It is always circumstantial, local, and entirely contained in its singular manifestations. Unconcerned with duration or, for the most part, with measuring any social effects or usefulness such events might have—and supremely unconcerned with institutions—Rancière's thought has produced disappointment in readers looking for a prescription or a program for action or, for that matter, a celebration of time spent "in the trenches," so to speak, the temporality of militant organizing.[25] What connects each manifestation to the next seems to be a kind of affirmative repetition; each instance, by departing from and reaffirming equality as a principle, makes possible a new manifestation; each is, as it were, "present" for the next manifestation as it occurs. This repetition is not the transmission of lessons learned or the inheritance of a legacy, nor the fixation—be it melancholy or ecstatic—on some transcendent experience from the past. It has more to do with the attentive embrace of the present situation in all of its contingency. It is worth recalling that such a goal was already apparent in the project statement written by the *Révoltes Logiques* collective in one of the early issues. The "lesson" of history, the collective wrote, is to, at best, "recognize the moment of a choice, of the unforeseeable, to draw from history neither lessons, nor, exactly, explanations, but the principle of a vigilance toward what there is that is singular in each call to order and in each confrontation."[26] In this way, perhaps, Rancière gives a new meaning to "praxis," shifting it away from its emphasis on subjects acting on objects in order to change things along a linear, progressive temporality. Praxis might, then, entail a kind of watchfulness or attention to these intermittent manifestations, to the moments when such demonstrations are produced, the moments when, in fact, something is happening. To happen, events must be perceived and acknowledged as such. Rancière's work contributes to making the moment when such demonstrations are produced more visible.

2.

The Lessons of Jacques Rancière:
Knowledge and Power after the Storm

ALAIN BADIOU

Translated by Tzuchien Tho

Right off the bat, I will announce that I am only going to speak well of Jacques Rancière. In the past, I have spoken critically of him so often that my stock of negative comments has run out. Yes, yes, we are brothers, everyone sees that, and in the end, I do too.

To speak only well of Jacques Rancière is not an easy task, given the positions that the two of us occupy. Perhaps my constant praise might, in fact, be the worst fate that I could have in store for him. Would doing so be precisely the most underhanded way to attack him? If, for example, I were to announce that we are in agreement on a number of important points, how would he take that? Would he rather just as soon change his mind on all those points and leave me behind?

The ethical principle that I am advancing up front is to stay away from all manner of comparisons with myself. I will say nothing about myself, neither in agreement nor in disagreement—nothing of the sort. Rather, we should maintain a pure Rancière, praised in totality. In this, I have chosen to approach his work from a point of departure that is at a real distance from my own, a point of entry that seems to belong to someone else: the relation between knowledge and power. This dialectic of knowledge and power is today a thoroughly academic term in the established systematic reference, one-sidedly, no doubt, to Foucault. Indeed, its vulgar form ("all knowledge is power, down with the authority of knowledge!") has been rather commonplace since the end of the sixties and the beginning of the seventies. Certainly, if someone had been able to succeed in taking this conceptual deployment further than Foucault, it has been none other than Rancière. This was his intention from the beginning, as is clear from the title of his first book, *La leçon d'Althusser*, which meditates on the relationship between the theoreticism of Althusser, his defense of science, and the reactionary political authority of the French Communist Party. Between the knowledge of the intellectual and the power of the party which accompanies it, we find ourselves on a perilous path.

To understand the turning points, we should return to the context of the sixties, and particularly to the crucial sequence between 1964 and 1968, reaching its culminating point in 1966. For the question we are concerned with, this context was absolutely paradoxical: it prepared and organized a balance, from 1968 onwards, between a scientific position that fetishized concepts, and a praxical position that fetishized action and the immediate ideas of its agents. We should not forget that these were Rancière's formative years.

Let's see what happened in those years between 1966 and 1967. The reign of structuralism in those years was also incontestably the reign of science. What was thematically profound, then, was that it did not simply advance an ordinary scientism. It was, rather, a neoscientism which centered on the theme of formalization, ushered in by the success of structuralist linguistics, particularly with respect to phonology. It would find, in the dominant methodologies of the human sciences—those of Marxism and psychoanalysis—veiled theories of form: in the former, the modes of production constituted the forms of history; in the latter, the psychic apparatuses constituted the forms of the subject.

Althusser and Lacan, each in his own way, led the way in these movements and took on the ideal of science, the ideal of formalization: Althusser in radically distinguishing between science and the history of ideology; Lacan by making this formalization, in a canonical text, the ideal of psychoanalysis itself. We then find ourselves in a context where the question of knowledge, in its most rigorous and solid sense, is paradigmatic, in the formalized sciences like logic, mathematics, and the phonological core of linguistics.

However, at the heart of and the end of the sixties there appeared a completely opposed disposition. Such is the initial paradox that one needs to have for a grounded understanding of Rancière's trajectory. This paradox is perhaps the originary example and the subjectively decisive point for something that he would later name (as his primary categories) the relation of a nonrelation, or the nonrelation thought through relation.

We should recall that during the period of intense activity of the Cultural Revolution in China, between 1965 and 1968, the main question was that of the forms of intellectual authority. The student revolt rallied against what the Red Guards labeled "monkish academics," demanding their dismissal and cruel persecution without hesitation. We had, on a large scale, an antiauthoritarian revolt aiming at the reversal of hierarchies founded on the centralization of knowledge. The revolts in the factories established their political form precisely in Shanghai in January '67, where anti-hierarchical revolts challenged the engineers and bosses whose status was founded on the authority of technical and scientific knowledge. The idea was that the direct experimentation of workers should be at the very least just as important as the authority of their leaders. Here we had a sequence which was to be the point of reference for a number of young philosophers, including Rancière, myself, and others, who at the same time were engaging in the apologetics of the scientific concept and its libratory authority. The question of saying whether we were rightly fascinated with the Cultural Revolution is a marginal debate. The fact is that an immense political phenomenon seemed polarized on the question of the denial or radical contestation of the set of authorities based on the centralization of knowledge. That being the case, for the revolutionary scientists that we were aspiring to be, this constituted the most violent of our internal paradoxes.

Now let us return to France. Beginning in 1967, there were a series of factory revolts leading to the month of May 1968. These revolts were qualitatively new because, being often organized by nonunionized young workers, they proposed to overturn the internal hierarchy of the factory, with actions that constituted a particular form. These actions began first as a reticence toward, or even a frank opposition against, union organizational strategy; following this, they developed into a systematic resistance against them. In the months that followed, this would be succeeded by the proliferation of a rather confrontational practice: locking bosses in their offices. I just want to mention a kind of stylistic résumé of all this in a film by Jean-Luc Godard, *Tout va bien* (1972), which we might consider an artistic document of the way in which consciousness was formed by the experience of the upheaval between knowledge and power.

In the end, prepared equally by the many prior dissident movements, notably on the question of sexual and social inequalities, the student revolt of May '68 and the years that followed were explicitly directed against the top-down organization of the transmission of knowledge. The revolts questioned academic authority and the choices concerning one's education and course of study, testing and the possibility of self-led education by students who would organize themselves in the absence of any figure of the professor-scholar.

All of these events organized the paradox: the tension between the prevailing philosophy, which maintained the absoluteness of scientific knowledge, and a series of politico-ideological phenomena which, on the contrary, strengthened the conviction that the connection between knowledge and authority is a politically oppressive construction and should be undone by any means necessary.

Although we each lived with the paradox in our different ways, Rancière, I, and many others were met with the same considerable question: how do we untie or undo the existing configurations of the relation between knowledge and authority, between knowledge and power? This question emerged naturally in the context that I spoke of, from the moment we rallied to one side of the movement in our inaugural gesture as young professors. But I think that the question develops into a more complex form in the following problem: if it is necessary to depose the authority of knowledge, instituted as a reactionary function in the oppressive figures where knowledge is monopolized, how, then, will experience be transmitted? The question of transmission becomes a particularly acute question. If it is not the concept, but rather practical and actual experiences, that form the real sources of emancipation, how does this experience transmit itself? In the first place, to be clear, we are speaking of the revolutionary experience itself. What are the new protocols of this transmission? What emerges once we have undone, untied, and terminated the canonic authority of power and knowledge which has served institutionally as the space of this transmission? What is a transmission that is not an imposition?

We can also ask: what is the new figure of the master that results if one excludes all the validation of institutional authority? Are there masters outside of the institution? Are there masters at all? The importance of the question of masters is certainly clear for Rancière, but it is also absolutely crucial in the work of Lacan. It not only emerges contextually in the abstract or genealogical question of the relation between knowledge and power, but also and above all in the immediate consequences of the engagement in the mass global movement of youth and workers between 1965 and 1975.

Since the start of the Cultural Revolution, this crucial question of transmission outside the institution had been formulated by Mao when he inquired about the successors of the cause of the proletariat. Given that he supported the students and the workers in their revolts, it became clear that this question of transmission could neither pass through the channels of the established authority nor through the channels of the Communist Party in power. The party, as an agent of authority and the supposed concentration of experience, became with each passing day the principal target of these activities. The result was the movement's establishment of Mao as the figure of the absolute master. On the question of whether there are masters outside the institution, the response was: the master uncoupled from the institution is the master of the movement itself. He was a paradoxical master, since he was the master of the movement that aimed to depose the masters. But what, then, was Mao, if not a proper name? What the Red Guards proposed was the subsumption of revolt, infinitely bursting forth through the transcendence of a proper name. The authority of the singular name replaced those of disparate institutions and bureaucracies. To transmit meant to study collectively what is equal to the name. Such was the role of Mao's *Little Red Book*: to give form to what is guarded by the name in the fire of experience. It is difficult today to imagine the enthusiasm around this donation of form, the exaltation that prevailed around the theme of study, which was tied to those previously unseen political trajectories and those unprecedented actions.

In this we find a characteristic example of the problems and particular solutions of the time. Lacan himself personally took on the question of mastery. Not only did he produce a matheme of the discourse of the master, but he meditated on the relation between mastery, transmission, and institution as well. He had, in particular, advanced the remarkable idea of a sort of equivalence between the new schools of psychoanalysis, a space of transmission between foundation and dissolution. If one follows the genesis of real institutions according to Lacan, one will first notice that, outside the instituted forms of mastery, it proceeds nonetheless under the radical guarantee of the proper name of a master (there again, "Lacan," just like "Mao," expresses a condition of transmission). Here, if an institution, in an effort to avoid the "*effet de colle*," attempts to assure the transparency of transmission, we find that it approaches the edge of dissolution with each passing day.[1]

This whole context, this historical and subjective paradox, constitutes our origin, for us, the generation, as one might say, who were struck by lightning in May '68. This origin illuminates Rancière's trajectory of thought, but this illumination extends across the course of his work for the simple reason that, in contrast to so many others, Rancière never repented it. This is the same reason why it illuminates my trajectory as well. It is so much the case that, in renouncing the opening comments of my own essay, I believe it obligatory to engage in some comparisons between Rancière and myself.

I return, obviously, to my initial difficulty: how do I make a comparison to Rancière without immediately implying that Rancière is wrong and that I am right? The Rancière/Badiou comparisons are, little by little, on their way to becoming somewhat canonical in some limited but international and (without appearing too shameless) significant contexts. We do not, neither I nor Rancière, draw any particular pride from this. Full of good sense, Jacques told me one day, "You know, we are advancing only by virtue of seniority." That's true, but we might congratulate ourselves on the passage of a seniority that remains true to the faith and not that of the social advantages found by some colleagues in their trumpeted renunciations ("we were mistaken, oh dear, we believed in Communism, we were totalitarians, yes, yes, yes, long live demo-cracy").

Some words are in order about the methodology concerning this practice of the comparison between Rancière and myself. As a general rule, it has three functions. The comparisons serve, above all, to open a critical apparatus, in demonstrating our differences with respect to certain figures like Mallarmé or Plato or Straub or Godard. Sometimes it serves as a synthetic method for constituting a supposedly unnoticed problem which circulates "between" the two of us. Finally, it serves to shed a positive light on the work of one of the two of us. This third function is one that I shall undertake, trying at each instant, perhaps clumsily, to place myself in the negative role. I will maintain the axiom to "speak only well of Rancière," doing so at the cost of speaking negatively of myself.

On the problem at the heart of the context that I mentioned—that is, on the question concerning not only the relation between power and knowledge but also the singularity of transmission in the undoing of an instituted relation between knowledge and power—I would say that Rancière holds a democratic hypothesis with respect to the possible configuration of a new type of transmission. I call a hypothesis "democratic" insofar as it relates to an eruption, a movement of the masses, a lightninglike rallying together. I also refer here to a "social" separation between those at the bottom and those on the top. The two descriptions establish a correlation between a new regime of transmission, the new mastery, and an always-lingering remainder of old instituted practices. In the background one also finds the correlation of the themes of equality and inequality in their current modes of articulation: that is, in the nonrelation which is, in turn, a relation.

My first remark is that this hypothesis constrains Rancière to mediations of a historical character. In effect, a democratic hypothesis thusly conceived applies itself to observations concerning the dysfunction of certain instituted regimes of distribution, a dysfunction by which a breach is exacted in the possibility of a different distribution of power, of knowledge, of active bodies, and finally of the visible order itself.[2] This different distribution reorganizes a new modality of transmission, a fragile modality, transitory, which no longer passes through the channels of instituted knowledge but rather inscribes itself into the part of that which, in the former distribution, was the no-part. This transmission is truly democratic because it articulates itself directly on the differential of the established regime of distribution. It is articulated at the point where the polis, the virtual city of equal collectivity, separates itself suddenly, while at the same time remaining in contact with the "police." In this, the "police" indicate not only the regime of the established distribution, with its unequally distributed parts, but also the no-part, the necessary figure of all subsequent reconfigurations.

I insist on the fact that Rancière's epochal account unites the consequences of a renewed democratic hypothesis, simply because my own hypothesis is not his. To speak honestly now, this is where I begin to take on a negative role. I believe that my hypothesis is, simply put, aristocratic. In my view, the emergence of a new transmission presupposes the constitution of the effects of a heterogeneous body after the fact. This heterogeneous body is not immediately democratic because its heterogeneity affects the multiplicity, the *dēmos* at the heart of which it constitutes itself in an immanent but separating manner. What makes possible the existence, or at least the propagation, of an egalitarian hypothesis is not itself an immediately equal regime. It is a bit like mathematics: what is more egalitarian than the pure connections in an equation? Thoughts are strictly identical in the face of this formal game where rules are entirely explicit, where everything is inscribed and nothing is hidden. This is why Plato accorded to them the status of an obligatory passage through the dialectic, leading us through the most evident case of equality. Such is his democratic ideal: equal before the idea. However, it is clear that the formation of the body of theorems and the organization of their proper transmission is always the work of a small group of inventive mathematicians. The position from which the mathematicians speak is a particularly aristocratic space, even if their personal disinterestedness and their total dedication to the universal was never in doubt. It is from this case or this paradigm of deep democracy that Plato drew his conclusions about the rarity of guardians. This rarity is maintained while at the same time asserting their position of radical equality, the inclusion of women, and the commitment to absolute personal disinterestedness in the forgoing of private property. It is in this sense that I speak of an aristocracy of transmission, an aristocratic "communism," a form which is today faced with the problem of having to distance itself from the remnants of a political party.

To sidestep the problem, Rancière sticks closely to the collective process in its operation of undoing the established forms of transmission, rather than going further along in the investigation of the very means of the material organization of consequences.

Here, we find the most condensed form of our differences: we have two distinct oxymorons. For Rancière it is the ignorant master, and for me it is the proletarian aristocracy. In certain regards, these two oxymorons—taken as maxims of judgment—are very similar. Viewed from afar, they are the same thing, but focusing more closely now, we find them extremely different. Why? We approach this with a philosophical question that we might say is precise or well formed. Why is this "ignorant master" not substitutable by the "proletarian aristocracy" as an account of the paradox of the sixties and seventies? The oxymoron of the ignorant master activates its place, which is the place of no-place, in contingent collectives. There it undertakes a transmission without any guarantee of what takes place or what it affirms under this title. The ignorant master is an activation disposed in a sort of a potential universality, an activation of what exists and what is becoming. The historical phenomenon of this transmission is at the same time immediate and sequential.

That which I call a proletarian aristocracy is an aristocracy that is contingent as well as prescriptive. It does not democratically testify to the powers of taking place [*l'avoir-lieu*], of becoming placed [*devenir placé*], of the out of place [*hors-place*]. It prescribes what it considers important; it transmits without guarantee. However, its transmission occurs by the incorporation of its own duration, which is a completely different mode of transmission than that practiced by the ignorant master. Here I am simply introducing this term of *proletarian aristocracy* for the sake of clarifying the oxymoron of the ignorant master and also to say that these two new and paired names serve conceptually to name a certain account of the paradoxical context which I spoke of a little earlier.

This duality leads to many shared usages but also to all sorts of differences. We can take Plato as an example. Rancière and I certainly understand—as did Foucault, who would have laughed at seeing all this attributed to him—that the disjunctive dialectic of knowledge and power is, first of all, in philosophy, a Platonic affair. Plato argues, in innumerable pages, for the proposition that there should be a privileged relationship between the protocols of the acquisition of knowledge and the distribution of the positions of power: that is, the hierarchical constitution of the city (the guardians, the warriors, the artisans . . .). For Rancière and me, with respect to this proposition, Plato has been a constant and fundamental interlocutor. Plato is something like a fault line, a shared edge where I believe we walk. In this, we are facing, however, in different directions.

If you observe the construction of *The Republic*, which is thematically paradigmatic, you could say that the text can be treated either from the aspect of the global distribution of occupational positions—the aspect of its social vision, as we might say today—or, alternatively, by concentrating our attention on the education of the guardians. In the first case, we have the conclusion of Rancière, that the essence of Plato is a critique of democracy. Why? Because the principle that governs the distribution of positions is that those who only perform one duty, who are constrained to perform only one duty, cannot really participate in the direction of political affairs. Rancière insists strongly on this point. In the end, that which forms the base of the "social" antidemocracy of Plato is not really the needs of a scholarly idleness or the rigid division between manual and intellectual work. No, what is essential is once again the question of the one and the multiple. The hierarchical distribution of powers, according to Plato, is guided by the conviction that whoever is assigned a productive task cannot properly perform it unless they only perform that task. For the artisan (here the "technique" comprises the poetic technique, art) the principle of the one is rigid: one task, one person. What we have then is a practical univocity. In contrast, the guardians of the city (in other words, the political leaders) are obliged to do many things all at once, even if they are excluded from manual production. For example, they have to do mathematics, gymnastics, martial arts, dialectical philosophy . . .

One can say that in our general approach to Plato, Rancière insists on the reactive dimension of this practical univocity (everyone in his place) while I focus on the theoretical multiplicity (the place of the leaders, always displaced). If, with the abstraction of the social schema, we consider the guardians as a metonymy of a polyvalent humanity, we can read Plato in a communist paradigm. Here we find a coexistence, in the dialogues, of a severe hierarchy that places the productive artisan at the bottom but also affirms a generic communism that hypothesizes—though this is a terrifying but inevitable consideration for Plato—the participation of women in leadership. Plato's distribution is thus a projection of the division between the oxymoron of the ignorant master who organizes thought according to a practical univocity, of a "social" hierarchy, and, on the other hand, the unbearably antidemocratic oxymoron of a proletarian or communist aristocracy, which on the contrary extrapolates the Platonic vision of guardians as the paradigm of a polyvalent multiplicity, of a generic humanity (without class), as the real support of an authentic equality.

Plato concludes this relation between knowledge and power with the suggestion that the key question of politics is education. It is thus interesting to ask oneself how Rancière treats education philosophically. We might remark that, for Foucault, the antidialectic of knowledge and power does not drive toward a theory of education. It seeks, rather, to uncover what we might call the unforeseeable diagonal of practices and, in particular, the pathological and local practices, plebian and excessive, which border on the unnamable and which traverse the schema of the articulations of knowledge and power.

It is time to affirm that Rancière occupies an absolutely original position due to the system of formalization that he has constructed, little by little, from the paradoxical experience that we spoke of. Rancière's work merits particular mention in his interweaving and organization of a wide range of sources. He takes into account the strictly philosophical origins of the question, as well as materials gathered from the experiences of the workers' actions in the nineteenth century. He takes into account the theses of his contemporaries, in particular those of Foucault, as well as examining the positions of sociologists and historians, among them the contentious *Annales* school. Finally, he investigates cinema but also more generally aesthetics. In looking at this broad interweaving, we might see how it makes for a possible formalization of our situation in the sixties and seventies. The heterogeneous material in Rancière's work constitutes, in my view, a convincing formalization of the original paradoxical experience.

What are the stakes of the problem of education? Rancière does not affirm that education occupies a central place in the political process. In this sense, he does not affirm the Platonic position. Yet, neither does he affirm the contrary: that education should not be a privileged superstructure. This is a good example, but perhaps also the source of what I might call his "median" style. By "median," I do not mean centrist, but rather, one that is never immediately conclusive. This median style means that Rancière always looks for a point where inherited solutions encounter problems that obscure them; this obscurity, in turn, proves that the inherited solutions are not as clear as they pretended to be.

The events that I spoke about earlier were foundational for Rancière. He took from them, as I did, the conviction that the struggle is always a struggle on two fronts. It was the principal lesson of Maoism. In politics, the struggle was naturally against those strongholds of bourgeois power, against the capitalist and the imperialist, but this principal struggle could not succeed if we did not also struggle equally against the Communist Party and institutional unions. It certainly was necessary to fight American imperialism, but we could not hope to reach the other side without stigmatizing complicity with Soviet social imperialism. To be brief: a true leftist revolutionary fights the Right as well as the official Left. Such was the very powerful and vast context of the upheaval, enduring right up to the beginning of the eighties, which framed the idea of the struggle on two fronts.

With respect to the theoretical points that remain important today, there is also a struggle on two fronts. There is the struggle against the idea that politics can be dependent on science in institutional transmission, a model according to which politics should be taught to the "ignorant worker" and "common people" by the experts or a party of the working class. However, Rancière struggles equally against the idea that politics is a blind spontaneity, a strange vital conceptual energy totally encapsulated by the gesture of revolt. There is neither a knowing party at the foundation of the movement, nor an immanent vital movement such that the gesture of revolt absorbs or encapsulates the totality of political substance.

With respect to the first front, Rancière exacted a break with Althusser, just as I did in those years, in his writing of *La leçon d'Althusser*. For Althusser, science remained the fixed point from which ideology could be divided. This might be why he remained faithful to the party for such a long time, long after the sequence that we spoke of. It is important to realize that behind Althusser, who was the figure of the knowing master, we found what the Maoists of the time called "ossified Leninism." It was the conviction, apart from any movement, that consciousness comes to the workers from the outside rather than being immanent in workers' knowlege, and that this outside is the positive science of the history of societies: in other words, Marxism.

We should not forget that there is a second front. Rancière detaches politics from all its vitalist identifications, maintains its status as a declaration, its discursive force, its status as a figure of exception. Against the active perpetuation of the forms of life such as they are, his thesis is rather that politics is not transitive to science, on the first front, that it is nonetheless productive of the various forms of knowledge that are necessary to workers engaged in conflicts. Here, on this front, he puts in place a brand new dialectic of knowledge and ignorance.

Finally, these were the dialectics that form the heart of Rancière's work, the part of his work that formalizes those original experiences: the question of the political unbinding of knowledge and power constrained by the necessity of achieving something like a new type of transmission. With respect to the conceptual field itself, this question resulted in Rancière proposing a new dialectic of knowledge and ignorance, and, more generally, on mastery and equality.

This dialectics can be, it seems to me, laid out in two very subtle theses. Their interrelation is subtler still. Formalizing Rancière's formalization, here is how I would write these two theses:

1. Under the condition of a declared equality, ignorance is the point from which a new knowledge can be born.
2. Under the authority of an ignorant master, knowledge can be a space for equality.

To be clear, we retain an essential point, which has become synonymous with the work of Rancière: equality is declared and is never programmatic. This may be obvious for the convinced Rancièrians that we are, but we should also stop to punctuate this major contribution of his enterprise. It was he who first introduced into the contemporary conceptual field the idea that equality is declared rather than programmatic. It was a fundamental reversal, and I pronounced my absolute agreement with this thesis very early on.

Here we pause again for another short comparative sequence. We are in agreement on the declared dimension of equality, but we do not share the same hermeneutics with respect to it. For me, that equality is declared rather than programmatic means that equality is, in reality, the invariant axiom of all real sequences of the politics of emancipation. This axiom is (re)declared each time that an event opens a new sequence of emancipatory politics. It is what I called in 1976, during the period contemporaneous with the initial context, the "communist invariants." A declared equality is the maxim of aristocratic politics grappling with a specific or singular form of inequality. A contingent aristocratic politics is an active body that carries out the maxim in a singular sequence and that has no other task than its deployment, to the extent it is possible in a given situation. This aristocracy is absolutely contingent and uniquely identifiable in the sense that it is articulated in the very effects of the embodiment of the maxim in a given sequence.

All this is quite different for Rancière, who distrusts principles and even more the idea of a prescriptive relationship between principles and sequences. I would say that for him, equality is simultaneously a condition and a productive process. Such is the profound sense of the two theses that I formalized just a moment ago. On the one hand, equality is the condition of a new figure of knowledge and transmission. On the other hand, under the sign of an ignorant master, this new figure, in turn, provides equality in the creation of a space or a new social ordering for equality.

Equality is a condition insofar as its declaration institutes a new relation to knowledge, in the creation of the possibility of knowledge or its distribution in unanticipated spaces. This is why the master of such a sort of knowledge declares ignorance. In this transformation of conditions, the egalitarian prescription institutes a new regime of knowledge and its transmission in the guise of an unexpected undoing of the established relation between knowledge and ignorance.

Equality is a production insofar as the new configuration of knowledge brings about a space of equality that did not previously exist. We had given our blessings on the beautiful formula according to which a part of no-part comes to exist. But I have always felt it just a little too structural to truly summarize Rancière's thought. Everything here is process, occurrence, a lightning bolt of meaning. And in this process it becomes apparent that equality is a double occurrence, one of condition and one of production. It is the knotting of these two functions that makes equality the event par excellence.

This tempts me to once again enter into this forbidden comparison. Yes, one can say that the declaration of equality is, for Rancière, the event itself, the event insofar as it provides a space to an indelible trace. In my vision of political matters, the egalitarian declaration is made possible by the event and is not to be confounded with it. It is that which organizes the body, but in the context of a given eventual condition, and thus is not homogenous with the declaration itself.

To draw out this comparison with even more complexity, we might consider the fact that we took leave of the party in different ways, something that our shared experience made necessary.

Rancière's departure from the party was a decision made outside of the consideration of the question of organization: he left that in suspense. If I decided to change the title of my piece, for the moment I would rename it, "Rancière, or, The Organization of Suspense." The departure from the party and the distance he would maintain from it were worrisome for him. This doesn't mean that he was for the movement and against the party. He left but remained close to its inscription. Yet, a supernumerary point, this inscription was ineffaceable, all this was in the gap, in the nonrelated relation.[3] This we were sure of. This existed. Perhaps it still exists at times. History testifies to it, and we continue to stand by this insight.

Even more than Rancière, I was fraught with concerns and difficulty over my departure from the party. I was concerned, since my conviction was that political continuity is always something necessarily organized. What is it that constitutes a heterogeneous, aristocratic embodiment of equality which is not also an inherited form or an imitation of the wise post-Leninist party, the party of experts? Philosophically, the differences between putting the organizational principle in suspense and its occupation of a central place in political preoccupations has considerable impact in the treatment of the relation between event, participation, body, and consequences. We thus arrive at two philosophical definitions of politics that, while being neighbors, are also sufficiently distinct as to not always be in friendship.

As such, we might have presupposed that the two theses (on the double occurrence of equality) could have helped us complete our understanding of Rancière with a few definitions on politics. However, the difficulty of extracting a few precise definitions from Rancière's texts is not only due to a theoretical problem. Nor do I believe that it is the anti-Platonic slant, a difficulty with the transcendence of ideas, which results in a resistance to definition. On the contrary, his prose is very definitive. There are clearly many surprising formulas that resemble definitions to the point that I might even respond that it seems all too definitional and not the least axiomatic. That perhaps it is too Aristotelian . . . but, for me, that is an accusation so serious that I would immediately strike it from the record.

Rather, we must imagine that the difficulty concerning precision is a formal difficulty connected to Rancière's philosophical style. This style is very singular. It is direct and compact but does not fail to charm us. However, for a Platonist such as I am, charm is always something ambivalent in philosophy. This was, above all, true for Plato. When Rancière charms us, what he looks to do is to cut a path across an equivocation.

Rancière's style has three characteristics. He is assertive; he connects affirmations, but he does so with a singular fluidity that makes it seem as though his assertions are derived only by virtue of his style. It would be very interesting to compare him in detail with the style of Deleuze, who also exerts an equally assertive style, although of a different sort. His is also a style without argumentative discontinuity. One does not find moments where he proposes an isolated demonstration to support a given thesis. It is, in the end, a style that seeks a conceptual unfolding of examples with the goal of creating certain zones of undecidability between actuality and the concept. This is not a question of empiricism. Rather, if Jacques will forgive me, it is a Hegelian inflection: it is a question of showing the presence of a concept, in the real of historic eruptions, in the effects of its rhythmic behavior. Certainly my own style is more axiomatic and formulaic, containing more separations in the various dimensions of arguments. In any case, Rancière's stylistic approach—the fluid affirmation without argumentative discontinuities, the smooth juxtaposition of examples—renders it difficult to extract precise definitions.

I would like to examine this style, taking a famous passage, one that clearly approaches a definition of politics and rearticulates almost all of the themes that we have brushed against in this essay. It is the beginning of the end of *Dis-agreement*, where he states,

> Politics exists wherever the count of parts and parties of society is disturbed by the inscription of a part of those who have no part. It begins when the equality of anyone and everyone is inscribed in the liberty of the people. This liberty of the people is an empty property, an improper property through which those who are nothing purport that their group is identical to the whole of the community. Politics exists as long as singular forms of subjectification repeat the forms of the original inscription of the identity between the whole of the community and the nothing that separates it from itself—in other words, the sole count of its parts. Politics ceases wherever this gap no longer has any place, wherever the whole of the community is reduced to the sum of its parts with nothing left over.[4]

Now, that is the direct and compact style that I spoke of. The intelligibility of the movement is completely guided by the syntax. In saying that Rancière's style is essentially syntactic, with a singular semantic distribution between the concept and the example, it would thus be difficult, in this text, to extract the precise definitions of politics, equality, mastery, or knowledge. . . . But I will attempt to do so all the same.

Let us begin with a very singular definition. What can we call the "end" of politics, or even the end of an existence in this particular conjuncture of a political action? It is a question of sequences where a politics of emancipation exists. Politics ends, Rancière tells us, when the whole of the community is reduced to the sum of its parts, with nothing left over. On this point, I indicate a very suggestive difference between Rancière and myself, a difference more hidden than other differences, since it concerns an ontological question. This question of the sum of the parts presupposes an ontology of the multiple that Rancière does not really provide for us. If we are speaking truly rigorously, a set cannot simply be brought into the sum of its parts. There is always something in the count of the parts that overflows the set itself. This is precisely the excess that I name the state, the state of the multiple, the state of the situation. When a collective is nothing but the management of the sum of its parts, we have what Rancière calls the police and what I call the state. But the similarities end here. For Rancière, the protocol for the cessation of politics is the moment where the collective state, or the policing of the parts, is restored. In my view, there is no cessation of politics in this sense, since the excess of the state is irreducible. There is always some element in the state whose capacity borders on the pure presentation of the collective. There is always some nonpresented in the state. One cannot, then, imagine that politics ceases in the figure of the collective brought to the sum of its parts. I will not continue further on this point but to say that, for me, there is no possible structural description of the cessation of politics. This is the reason why I do not share Rancière's political diagnostic. We do not share the same protocols for diagnosing its cessation. For him, there is a definable structural form for the end of politics; it is the moment where the supernumerary is abolished for a restoration, without remainder, of the totality as the sum of its parts. The affirmation of such a protocol for the cessation of politics allows him to designate its absence, its end. On this point, I do not share this position. Politics, at least structurally, always remains an open question for me. This is perhaps a purely ontological staging of a difference in diagnostics. Can we trace this to an empirical difference? Unlike me, Rancière has not engaged in organized politics for quite some time now.

Now, can we define equality? Equality is a declaration. Although situated in a given regime of inequality, it affirms that there will be a time of the abolition of this regime. It is not the program of this abolition but rather the affirmation of its attainment. I am profoundly in agreement with this essential gesture. We see, then, that this exercise of equality is always registered on the order of its consequences rather than on the order of the pursuit of an end. What is affirmed is causality or consequences, but not finality. This is essential. What we have, and what we need to organize, are the consequences of an egalitarian declaration, not the means by which we pursue equality as an end. On this point, I am absolutely in agreement. In Rancière's conception, what follows is that equality is never an idea. It is not susceptible to being an idea, since it is a regime of a collective existence in a given time in history. The fundamental declaration, in its varying and locally situated forms, is that "we are equal." Although historically supernumerary, it is actualized in the series of consequences that follow from it. Such is the vision of Rancière. For me, equality is fundamentally an idea, but in a very particular sense. It is an idea because it is invariant in the political declarations that are constituted in the various sequences of a politics of emancipation. It is thus eternal in its being, but its local constitution in a determined world is its only possible form of existence. In speaking of eternity and the difference between being and existing, I continue to play the role, you might agree, of the lingering dogmatic. It is without doubt that this point maintains, at the heart of political action, the separation between Platonism and non-Platonism or anti-Platonism: the status of the idea of equality. At the same time, we agree that the exercise of equality is always registered on the order of consequences. However, is this practical agreement sufficient to counterbalance our ontological disagreement? Certainly not, or perhaps only in some local circumstances, but we will eventually find ourselves at odds simply because the eternity of the egalitarian axiom relies on a sort of continuity that Rancière simply cannot maintain.

On the basis of politics and equality, we can enter into a critique of the figure of the master, something like a third definition of Rancière's work. On another occasion, it might be very interesting to do a comparison of the figures of the master in contemporary French philosophy. The well-established critique of mastery has led to a new figure that Rancière has described with much refinement. Through the doublet *ignorant master* and *community of equals*, the figure has the capacity of undoing the relation instituted, since Plato, between the master of knowledge and the leader of the city, between knowledge and power. In Lacan's terms, this means putting an end to the confusion between the discourse of the master and that of the university. I believe that, on this terrain, Rancière demonstrates the fecundity of resources drawn from the inventions and revolutions of the working class in the nineteenth century. We need to salute this extraordinary gesture of the activation of the archives, something that, in my opinion, is more efficient and less melancholic than Foucault's earlier achievements. The workers' archive, unlocked and reactivated by Rancière's magnificent texts, shows its speculative fecundity. Especially on the question of an absolutely original figure of transmission, it constitutes a direct engagement with the original questions we spoke of at the start. In my own terms, I would say that Rancière has found a form for the eternal conceptualization of our naïve paradoxes. He has produced a new idea of transmission outside of the institution.

All this, in the end, turns on the question of what knowledge is. That is to say, what is knowledge when it is thought under the condition of an egalitarian maxim, in a new relationship with ignorance, in the opening of a new space for equality, a situation where knowledge is clearly displaced with respect to the institution? In my own jargon, this would mean that we obtain a form of knowledge equal to the status of truth itself. For Rancière, I believe knowledge, true knowledge, is what a declaration of equality illuminates or accentuates in a regime of inequality. What ignorance, presumed as such in a regime of inequality, produces under the authority of an egalitarian declaration is a new figure in discourse. We might have otherwise said that it is a revolutionary or emancipatory knowledge, a true knowledge, in Nietzsche's sense of a gay science. We might also say that such knowledge is produced by a conscious effect of an encounter with an ignorant master. Here we are rather close to what Rancière considers to be the "good" Plato. Evidently, as with all anti-Platonists, he has his good Plato. It was Plato that encountered, or perhaps invented, the ignorant master. He was the first to have said, "The only thing that I know is that I do not know anything." Socrates was presented as a truly ignorant master. What was produced in the conscience of the youth in this encounter with an ignorant master merits the name of a new knowledge or a true knowledge.

I have not approached anything but the tip of the iceberg, but with all this in mind, we might return to the question of education. I believe that the overturning of the question "who educates whom?" is Rancière's principal reformulation of the question of education. More to the point, the problem is that this question is poorly posed. It poses a false dilemma between the assumption of the figure of the master and that of anarchy, where knowledge and nonknowledge are equivalent in the capacity of life. If everyone educates everyone else, then no one educates anyone. This is a canonic example of the struggle on two fronts. We neither accept the knowing master nor the inconsistent multiple of spontaneous knowledge. The struggle continues against the university and the party, but also against the spontaneous vitalists; the partisans of the pure movement or what Negri refers to as "the multitude." The new conception of the relation between knowledge and politics neither affirms the vision of distinct parties, which is despotic, nor the anarchist vision, which is at the service of opinion; it remains more or less merely the manipulation of the regime of inequality. In both cases, following Rancière's vocabulary, the polis dissolves under the police.

The appropriate formula is the following: the anonymous process of education is the construction of a set of consequences with respect to a situated egalitarian declaration. Here we find a form of emancipatory education. The question "who educates whom?" disappears. All that we can say is "we, we educate ourselves in this process." Here, the "we" is understood as being singular at each point, where each point in the situation reaffirms that the only universal maxim is equality. Conceived in this manner, education is neither a condition of politics, as it is for Plato, nor is it that of ossified Leninism, nor that of Althusser, nor is it indifferent to politics, as it is in the spontaneous vitalisms of the immanent creation of the movement. We are led to a difficult expression that I hesitate to propose: Education is a fragment of politics, a fragment equal to every other fragment.

There is no doubt of my formal agreement on any of this. The difficulty, the space of our contestation, is over the definition or the delimitation of the anonymous "we" in the formula "we educate ourselves in the process." Rancière does not provide us with a prescription on this point; there is no true opening to the cause of democracy. Democracy, in a certain sense, takes as a fundamental precaution not to circumscribe a "we" in its conception. It certainly speaks abundantly to the central motive of a utopian communism, the community of equals. Yet it is as a regulative myth, which is moreover a social result and not an instrument of the political process. We might say that for Rancière, there is no established figure of the militant. On the other hand, in the Platonic reference that I labeled "aristocratic," the "we" is the body of equality, the body of the maxim in a given moment of its process. As a contingent aristocracy, the "we" does not have any function other than the treatment of the relation of the nonrelation, the relation of that which is heterogeneous, in bearing out the consequences of the maxim of equality to the extent of its possibility. It is thus defined by a group of militants, the militants that constitute a body situated in the consequences of truth.

To be a militant means to take on the trajectory, to redefine the limits, to connect improbable connections . . . Within the context with which we began our discussion, this means the very improbable connection between intellectuals and workers. In the end, all this history is simply the history of this connection. We have been discussing, without really touching upon it, the philosophical or speculative history of the connection between intellectuals and workers, as possible or impossible relation, as a relation or a nonrelation, as a gap, and so on. With the Maoist elements of the time, we called for the organization of the masses, but the organization of the masses dialectically implied the power of disorganization. It was this original process of disorganization that unleashed, in an incredible newness, the possibility of this organization. This capacity, however, only constructs its own temporality within a political organization.

In more conceptual terms, we might rephrase our differences as follows: For Rancière, that which has value is always the fleeting inscription of a supernumerary term. For me, that which has value is the focused discipline on an excess. For Rancière, the supernumerary term convincingly describes, in a given regime of inequality, the part of no-part. For me, the result of the discipline of a truth is described as generic multiplicity, underlying all predication. For Rancière, there is no exception other than the epochal or historic. For me, there is no exception other than the eternal.

Ironically, what will allow me to finish without breaking from my ethics of praise is a pointed critical remark. It concerns Richard Wagner and the question of the capacity of undoing, or the generic in art; its production of an embodied multiplicity. In one of his books, Rancière proposes an interpretation of the third act of Wagner's *The Master-singers of Nuremberg* [*Die Meistersinger von Nürnberg*].[5] The subject of *The Mastersingers* concerns the necessity of a reconstitution of the relationship between the people and art. The Mastersingers were an artistic corporation of artisans who maintained and instructed a particular tradition of singing. In Wagner's opera, the key character of this institution was an artisan of the lowest degree. He was a cobbler. We could think of his status as close to that of an "untouchable" in the Indian sense. Yet, as it happens, we find ourselves at a juncture where it becomes necessary to constitute the relation between the people and art as a nonrelation. What is clearly illuminated in this fable is something exemplary for Rancière and me, here, once again, with respect to our original imperatives. In the figure of a young aristocrat, Walther, we find the emergence of a new artist, a new art, a new song. Walther, whose name echoes the name Wagner, competes in a singing contest organized by the masters. The prize of this competition is the hand of a maiden in marriage, the beautiful Eva. The prize of a maiden as the reward for a new art is certainly agreeable to Wagner, and perhaps to other artists as well. This competition is directed by the horrible Beckmesser, whose name echoes the name Meyerbeer and who represents the most entrenched advocates of tradition obviously opposed to the new song. The central character, the cobbler Hans Sachs, was to be the mediator in this reconstruction of the relation where the nonrelational dimension of the new song could be inscribed. He resorts to cunning and intrigue. The details are far too complicated to explain here. All we need to recount is that the young sir is allowed to compete, takes the prize, and through this we find a public construction of a new internal relation interweaving art, tradition, the people, and invention. The "militant" goal of Sachs is to articulate artistic invention to tradition and to do so in such a way so as to reconstitute a new fundamental relation between the people and its historicity in the medium of art.

Rancière and I propose somewhat different interpretations with respect to the section where the knight, surmounting all obstacles, comes to the competition, sings his new melody, and captivates the people. He was told, "Now, you should go and join up with the Mastersingers." But having experienced all the humiliations that were exerted on him, the arrogant and solitary Walther, unrepentant romantic that he is, refuses to join. At this point, the cobbler intervenes. He explains to his young protégé that he needs to accept because it is only in establishing this nonrelation as a relation that a new organon of the collective becomes possible. The people will not be constituted by art unless the nonrelation between the traditional and the new, in one way or another, is exercised as a relation. In Sachs's long tirade he continues in laying out a vision of the destiny of Germany. Here, Hans Sachs supports a very particular thesis, which in my view is quite accurate. The thesis is that the "true," that is, universal, destiny of Germany is none other than German art. Finally, the knight accepts. However, the people do not cry out "long live Walther!" but instead "long live Hans Sachs!" It is a cobbler that is crowned with laurels under the chorus of cheers. All told, the master of the whole process recognized by the people is the miserable cobbler.

Rancière remarks that this is all quite melancholic, since the epoch of the possibility of a true relation between a new art and cobblers has passed. When Wagner composed his opera, he staged a pure nostalgic fiction—the nostalgia of the young Wagner who climbed though the barricades of Dresden in 1848—to imagine the public crowning of a cobbler, a spiritual sovereign of the figure of art. Wagner knew quite well that we were already well along the way toward a complete disjunction between the arts of the avant-garde and the collective of the people.

It is on this point that I note my differences. This scene announces that, in the crossing of a nonrelation, if art is not reconciled with the assent of the public, then it will become insignificant and will be replaced everywhere by consumable "culture," the stereotype that Beckmesser embodies. Hans Sachs renders a theatrical and musical figure to an anticipatory idea, still in suspense today, one that even "socialist realism," which attempted to recapture it, could not replace: the idea of a great art which is neither reserved for the educated bourgeois nor degraded as booming sing-a-longs. The idea is a great art of the masses, something that may sometimes be found today, from Chaplin to Kitano, in cinema. This idea, since the nineteenth century, has been in the torturous process of the becoming of its actual eternity. To crown Sachs the cobbler in this scene for having realized this idea in its course of becoming eternal is certainly justice rendered, even in view of the difficult history of this process in the last century and a half. All this might, perhaps, have been more convincing if in place of a singer singing a new song, Walther had come onto the scene saying: I have a camera, I have invented cinema. In fact, he does not really bring forth an art that, while inheriting the legacy of popular tradition, is the creation of a strong artistic novelty. It is really nothing more than a singer singing a somewhat newer song. Indeed, it is one of the most beautiful of Wagner's arias . . . In the end, the real of the scene is in that which it affirms, rather than in what it does not. Neither Walther's aria nor Sachs's declaration are musically dominated by melancholy. This opera, through its vernal architecture, is artistically the opera of constructive gaiety. It is interesting to see the dimension of Sachs's renouncements (he knows that the new song is for Walther to sing and that he is nothing but a mediator, and thus, even if he is the symbolic father and an admirer of Eva, it is the young man that should marry her). This renouncement, like the lively softness of the theme of the midsummer's night, the sonic invention of the smell of the lime tree, is absorbed in the general energy of a folktale, under a sort of comic hullabaloo in the second act, and, in the third, a blend of patriotic and working-class imagery.

Music creates on its own a generic figure of artistic discipline as an analogy of political discipline, which, for its part, remains in suspense after 1848 and would, after the crushing of the Paris Commune, remain in suspense until Lenin and the revolution of 1917.

This minimal difference is interesting because it concerns the question of history. Rancière incorporates our contemporary standpoint into his evaluation of this allegory. It is true that the hopes of the revolution of 1848 were all but undermined by 1850, but I take my reading in a reverse direction. I argue that the artistic allegory is prospective, anticipatory, and a temporal beacon of the idea's becoming eternal. The circumstantial failures of history should not invoke melancholy but should rather activate the deployment of the idea in the tension of its future, a future to be persevered for a long time. This is what Wagner, through the artistic fanfares, understands by the crowning of Hans Sachs the cobbler. This Wagnerian question, "who is the master of the arts?" has been all the while present in our efforts concerning the work of Rancière, particularly in what has been said about cinema.

Ideas, in their process of becoming within the disparate worlds, should be judged not by what determines the circumstances of their apparent failure in this or that sequence of history, but by the becoming, point by point, through their traversal of unforeseen new worlds, of their universal demand.

3

Sophisticated Continuities and Historical Discontinuities, Or, Why Not Protagoras?

ERIC MÉCHOULAN

As far as Jacques Rancière's works are concerned, I must begin with a confession: I do not find him an easy author to read. Why? Mainly because Rancière offers a very specific way of arguing: he does not analyze authors as such, or even short passages of philosophical works; he makes very few quotations, usually taken out of their immediate argumentative context; he seldom refers to his adversaries' names and claims. What is peculiar is the sense of the discursive continuity of his texts, creating a space, I would even say a "pace," for his readers far from our tendencies to analyze texts or contextualize historically. He seems to tell a completely unusual philosophical story, but without the facilities of narratives, since his arguments are put at their most abstract concentration when he sums up a whole bunch of claims and reasons. It is this movement of a "conceptual tale," so to speak, that may engender misconceptions. His arguments encapsulate reasons offered, brief summaries of plots, and even disagreements (to refer to the possible meanings of the word "argument" according to Webster's dictionary).

Rancière's analytical scrutiny does not prevent him from offering vast syntheses about politics or aesthetics. And this is probably what makes him a difficult author—even if his language is very clear, almost without technical or intellectual gadgetry. This strange intertwining between the fluency of a story and the density of philosophical strings gives both a feeling of prosaic continuity and an impression of poetic condensations.

Nevertheless, such an intertwining presents us with a few difficult problems. Rancière has not only worked on the writing of history; he has practiced and experienced what true archival work implies. We cannot, then, assume that his broad summaries of historical development are the simple result of a pure philosophical mind, detached from the sense of contingencies and situations. On the contrary, he insists on attaching to the notion of politics a sense of interruption and eventuality. At the same time, when he writes about political philosophy, and even if he tries to give another meaning to the very concept of politics, he analyzes the same old philosophers we can find in any traditional history of political philosophy: Plato, Aristotle, Hobbes, Marx. Not only are the authors well known, but Rancière seems to stay in the simple limits of the text. He picks up a few passages—never a whole work—and problematizes them in the course of a general analysis. Nothing about the context of production, the figures of the author, the technical apparatuses, or the institutional devices is taken into account. Texts appear in a kind of perfectly autonomous world where the discontinuity of doctrines plays on the background of a historical linking of ages and societies, as if no real difference between the ancient Greeks and us truely mattered.

It is true that Rancière distinguishes evolutions as well as ruptures, and even puts forward three consecutive conceptions of politics: Plato's archi-politics, Aristotle's and Hobbes' para-politics, and Marx's meta-politics. This division parallels the three regimes in the domain of aesthetics with almost the same actors: Plato's ethical regime, Aristotle's representational regime up to the seventeenth and eighteenth centuries, and Flaubert's and Mallarmé's aesthetic regime up to now. But history does not run through these displacements in a linear way; two or three of them can and do coexist. The discontinuity of productions does not entail a complete substitution of the ancient regime by the new one, but a complex overlapping of the different regimes. Thus we get both a discontinuity of productions and a continuity of produced orders. History is not a matter of succession, but of enduring creations. There are obviously hegemonies and dominances in different ages, but the representational regime keeps certain forms of ethical value of arts, and our supposed modern time still offers mimetical and ethical creations.

Yet, is there not a risk of erasing the complexities of situations, the very contingency of history on which Jacques Rancière insists? These broad and schematic figurations might lose the graininess of history. Let us consider two problematic examples.

When Rancière wants to explain, in one of his latest books, what he means by politics and the "partition of the sensible," he says that

> politics, in fact, is not the exercise of power and the struggle for power. It is the configuration of a specific space, the parceling out of a particular sphere of experience, of objects we take to be shared and stemming from a common decision, of recognized subjects able to designate these objects and to discuss them. Man, Aristotle says, is political because he can speak and thereby share notions of just and unjust, whereas the animal has only the ability to voice pain and pleasure. But the question is, who has the power of speech and who has only a voice. Politics happens when those who "don't have" time take the required time to position themselves as members of a common space and to demonstrate that their mouths can articulate speech that states shared realities and not just a voice that signifies pain. This arrangement and rearrangement of places and identities, the parcelling and reparcelling out of spaces and times, of the visible and the invisible, of noise and speech, constitute what I call the sharing of the sensible.[1]

We see here that we have very crucial definitions of Rancière's way of thinking about politics and experience in general (I would even say that this is probably the core of a brand-new conception of politics which closes a very long age of equating politics with the problem of power and opens for us new possibilities of thought and action). Nevertheless, we must point out that the core of these definitions resides in the reference to Aristotle, and it is perfectly true that Aristotle makes an explicit difference between the voice, which is only "but an indication of pleasure and pain, and is therefore found in other animals," and "the power of speech," which "is intended to set forth the expedient and inexpedient, and therefore likewise the just and the unjust"[2]: good and evil cannot, therefore, be in continuity with pleasure and pain. But if we turn toward someone like Locke, we discover that it is no longer the case: "Amongst the simple ideas which we receive both from sensation and reflection *pain* and *pleasure* are two very considerable ones. . . . [T]o define them by the presence of good or evil is no otherwise to make them known to us than by making us reflect on what we feel in ourselves. . . . Things then are good and evil only in reference to pleasure or pain."[3] Locke is here paradigmatic of the modern interpretation of the relations between pleasure and pain, the determination of good and evil, and the very humanity of human beings. We should even connect this conception of the relation between the sensible and justice, with politics and the idea of human being.

If equality is of paramount importance for the determination of politics in Rancière's eyes (and I think that it is, indeed, one of the great merits of his work to have relocated in the center of the philosophical arena the political question of equality), what do we do with two considerable differences between ancient communities and our modern societies? The first concerns the difference between a society that views slavery as a social necessity and conceives of inequality between free citizens and slaves as perfectly natural, versus a model that views equality as the natural state and inequality as a matter of social construction, a stance imposed by our modern feelings. The second difference contrasts the ancients' idea that freedom begins when need and necessities are outstripped, and that beautiful actions, perfectly well circumscribed, are the lot of political citizens, versus the modern idea that need and necessities form the very structure of modern men, which implies that they are defined as being of desire, an illimitated desire.

What happens, then, to Rancière's broad characterization of politics and the partition of the sensible if his conception obviously occults the displacement induced by Locke's *Essay on Human Understanding* and instead rests on Aristotle's assumptions as if nothing serious has really been touched? Or am I writing now a kind of "Essay on Human Misunderstanding"?

Let us take another example. In *Dis-agreement,* Rancière brilliantly shows how the philosophical "return to politics" is the other face of the sociological description of an "end of politics." He says, "The self-proclaimed 'restorers' of politics and of 'its' philosophy revel in the opposition of the political and social seen to have unduly encroached on its prerogatives. But, in the modern era, the social has been precisely the place where politics has been played out, the very name it has taken on, wherever it has not simply been identified with the science of government and with the means of thinking it over."⁴ We certainly could find contemporary names to put under these restorers of politics against the social (probably beginning with Hannah Arendt), but Rancière himself, when he describes the kind of hermeneutical procedures of historians, seems to criticize their use of the social: "The historian's discourse is a measured discourse that relates the words of history to their truth. This is explicitly what *interpretation* means. But less obviously, it is also what *social* means. *Social* designates at once an object of knowledge and a modality of this knowledge. . . . The social becomes this *base* [ce *dessous*] or background of events and words that must always be wrested from the mendacity of appearances. *Social* designates the gap between words and events and their non-factual and non-verbal truth."⁵

There is, then, a kind of blindness in the science of history, which postulates that immediate events must be given the depth of meaning and have to be deciphered from their very appearances. To express the truth of certain moments of time implies the ability to apprehend what is under the surface of the events, since meaning cannot be elsewhere but in the social depth hidden beneath events. The good historian, like the fine cook, has to take off the scum of contingency in order to eliminate the bad residues and concentrate the flavors of signification.

Rancière's position is nevertheless more complex than a simple opposition or contradiction between these two dimensions of the social. Actually, we can find here a profound force of his philosophical reflexion: the necessity to maintain and describe ambivalence and homonymy:

> This name [the social] is, it is true, similar to the name of its negation. But every politics works on homonyms and the indiscernable. . . . [The social] has been the police name for the distribution of groups and functions. Conversely it has been the name in which mechanisms of political subjectification have come to contest the naturalness of such groups and functions by having the part of those who have no part counted. Finally, it has been the meta-political name of a *true* politics that itself has taken two forms: the positive force of the real movement called upon to take shape as the principle behind a new social body, but also the sheer negativity of the interminable demonstration of the truth of falseness. The social has been the common name for all these logics as well as the name for their interlocking.⁶

It is this kind of intertwining that stimulates Rancière, the kind of intertwining that philosophers try to dismiss or at least clarify. What Rancière wants to do is, rather, to make it visible or readable in all its complexity.

This is where history must play its role. Rancière, far from being blind to historical contexts, explicitly tries to make visible in history what has been muddled and obfuscated by illusory conceptual premises. Concerning, for example, what has been called "modernity," he has tried to "establish some historical and conceptual landmarks, to help with specific problems that are irremediably muddled by notions which make conceptual a prioris out to be historical determinations, and temporal divisions to be conceptual determinations."[7]

What kind of contextualisation is implied? Obviously an institutional and technical context: "The idea of modernity is an equivocal notion which attempts to divide up the complex configuration of the aesthetic domain of the arts, maintaining the forms of rupture, the iconoclastic gestures, etc., by removing them from the context that legitimates them: generalized reproduction, interpretation, museum, patrimony."[8]

It seems, then, that what was complex has been simplified and that the concept of modernity implies a blindness to its own context. What Rancière tries to disentangle in our contemporary debates on politics and aesthetics is precisely this kind of historical confusion. And the way to do so, he advances, is to scrutinize the context which legitimates and permits both the conceptual confusion and the regime of arts which is described: for understanding the aesthetic regime, we must turn our gaze toward technical practices like the modes of reproduction and interpretation, and toward institutional organizations like disciplines (history), established principles even legitimized by the state (patrimony), and a system for the promotion and sacralization of art (museum). This is the kind of investigation which is needed if one wants to avoid oversimplifications and blindnesses.

It is true that Rancière's large historical divisions, a bit like Michel Foucault's *epistemes*, do not have precise limits in time (no real beginning and no true end). The philosophers he analyzes play more a role of developers of history's film than originators of a whole regime. Nevertheless, one can wonder what happens if we step aside and choose other names and other ways of making historical intertwinings visible. Let us try with one brief example.

Plato is supposed to exemplify archi-politics: that is, the supression and replacement of politics (the true mode of interruption of the order of things, the polemical framing of a common world which permits the elaboration of what is audible and visible) by police (the instituted government or the struggle for the control of power). The community is, then, totally placed under the spirit of the law (its *arkhē*), so that every citizen, having internalized the law as a living logos, finds a strict correspondence between his own ethos and his function and role in the city. *Sophrosune* takes the place of the polemical freedom of the *dēmos*. Legislation is therefore a matter of education:

> The order of *politeia* thus presupposes the lack of any vacuum, saturation of the space and time of the community. The rule of law is also the disappearence of what is consubstantial to the law's mode of being wherever politics exists: the exteriority of writing. . . . The good city is one in which the order of the *cosmos*, the geometric order that rules the mouvement of the divine stars, manifests itself as the temperment of the social body. . . . It is a city in which the citizen is won over by a story rather than restrained by a law . . . [I]t is a city in which legislation is entirely resumed in education—education, however, going beyond the simple introduction of the school master and being offered at any moment of the day in the chorus of what is visually and aurally up for grabs.[9]

Rancière's brief summary of Plato's archi-politics is elaborated from *The Republic* book 2, 369c–370c and *Laws* book 7, 823a. What happens if we look at another text, still by Plato, that proposes the anti-Platonist "political philosophy" par excellence: sophism.

In *Protagoras*, the problem is to know whether politics can be a matter of education or not. One answer is to claim that it is indeed a matter of education, and not only education at school, but in everyday life from the very beginning: "As soon as a child can understand what is said to him, his nurse and his mother and his teacher and his father himself strive to make him as good as possible, teaching and showing him by every word and deed that this is right, and that wrong, this good and that bad, this holy and that unholy, 'do this' and 'don't do that.' If he obeys voluntarily so much the better; if not they treat him like a piece of wood which is getting warped and crooked, and straighten him out with threats and beatings."[10] One way to understand it is to listen to stories like the one which is told about the origin (the *arkhē*) of cities, as if *muthos* should especially enhance the persuasive value of reflexion. Here is the story, as I sum it up:

Epimetheus distributes to the various species different capacities and means of protection, but when it comes to man's turn, he has used up all the capacities, leaving man unprotected. Accordingly, Prometheus steals from the gods knowledge of the practical crafts, together with the use of fire, but without the knowledge of how to run a community, since the art of politics is well kept in Zeus's palace. Thus equipped, men begin to develop different techniques: religious rituals, language, agriculture, and the provision of food and shelter. When the fear of wild animals drives men into communities, they are unable, from ignorance of the art of politics (the *technē politikē*), to prevent their mutual antagonisms from driving them asunder, leaving them at the mercy of the animals once again. Zeus then intervenes: Hermes is sent to implant in men *aidos* (respect, reverence, shame) and *dikē* (justice). Hermes asks Zeus if he must distribute these gifts to everyone or to a few men only. Zeus tells him to make sure that everyone receives them, for only on that condition is political life possible.

With this story, we seem to be in a perfect archi-politics: the *arkhē* determines how the law must be incorporated by stories and everyday education, and how politics must become the political technique of government with respect of places and justice of the law in order to live in a harmonious cosmos: "So Zeus . . . sent Hermes bringing respect and justice to mankind, to be the principles of organization of the cities and the bonds of friendship," more literally: "so that there is harmony in cities [*poleôn kosmoi*] and bonds of friendship [*desmoi philias sunagogoi*]."[11] The problem is that it is not Socrates (Plato's usual spokesperson, unless Plato is Socrates's spokesperson, but it does not matter here), so it is not Socrates but Protagoras himself who says what I have just quoted. This archi-politics is actually sophism, that is anti-Platonism.

Of course, one could say that actually it is Plato who writes the dialogue, and he can give to Protagoras whatever position he wants for his purpose. But it is well known that Plato broadly respects the thought and the habits of the persons he stages. Protagoras cannot be a simple puppet in the master's hands.

Another solution would be to claim that we have here excellent proof of the fact that archi-politics is truely a certain regime of the sayable and the visible, since even enemies like Plato and the sophists can share the same references. Such an interpretation would even constitute an explanation of the surprising fact that, at the end of the dialogue, Socrates and Protagoras have exchanged their initial positions: Socrates, who denied that political virtue could be taught, recognizes that it is so, and Protagoras, who claimed that virtue was teachable, ends by assuming that it cannot be. What the dialogue exemplifies would then be a real continuity between philosophers and sophists. They share more elements than they think, or than the philosophical tradition likes to think.

But again, such a solution is not completely satisfactory, since it would stay at the simple level of contents. What about the constant polemical stance between Socrates and Protagoras? The staging of the dialogue is, as usual with Plato, of tacit importance. In a dialogue on education and politics, the very problem of how to speak in order to be heard cannot be skirted round. It is precisely interesting to see how the problem of presentation is itself a crucial matter. When Protagoras is requested to explain how political virtue can be taught, he asks his interlocutors: " 'Would you rather that I showed [*epideixo*] you by telling a story [*muthos*] (as an older man speaking to his juniors) or by going through a systematic exposition [*logos*]?' Several of those who were sitting around asked him to proceed in whichever way he preferred. 'Well,' he said 'I think that it will be more enjoyable [*chariesteron*] to tell you a story.' "[12] We certainly should not think that we find here the usual sophist way of offering something agreeable to the senses instead of presenting something serious to the mind. The Greek *chariesteron* should be better translated by "more gracious," since it comes from *charis*, grace. Moreover, we should not think either that this term is a simple reference to beauty or elegance: *charis* belongs to the political vocabulary, as Christian Meier, a historian of ancient Greece, has demonstrated. For the Greeks, grace is a consequence of liberty: when people are no longer held in the hands of needs and necessities, they can enter into true political relations.

As Aristotle says, "We must then say that it is in order to make beautiful actions [*kalon praxeon*] that a political community exists, and not in order to live together."[13]

Charis is less the exercise of force than it is the authority of seductive presentation and care for others. When Protagoras uses the word in order to explain his choice of the *muthos*, he immediately implies a political issue. And such an immediacy is part of his own gracious presentation: he does not want to look ponderous.

Epideixis ('presentation,' 'proof,' 'public lecture,' even 'parade') puts under the eyes of the interlocutors what is at stake in the issues discussed. The sophistic technique is, above all, a technique of manifestation: how to make visible, how to adopt right perspectives on problems. And this is certainly one aspect of Rancière's work: not acknowledging appearances, but making possible forms of appearing. The very word "manifestation" is an important word, since in French it can mean both demonstration and expression or revelation. In the streets or in a private house, something is suddenly underscored. "Spectacular or otherwise, political activity is always a mode of expression that undoes the perceptible divisions of the police order by implementing a basically heterogenous assumption that, at the end of the day, itself demonstrates the contingency of the order, the equality of any speaking being with any other speaking being."[14]

Now, what exactly is Protagoras's presupposition about the Athenian polis? This is what he reiterates after his myth and after a logical exposition: "It seems to me, Socrates, that I have now adequately shown that your fellow citizens are right to accept the advice of smiths and cobblers on political matters, and also they regard excellence [*aretè*] as something that can be taught and handed on" (324c). Anybody can talk about politics: the sophist confirms the true equality of anyone with anybody.

Does it mean that we could say that Rancière is the sophist of our days? It is not that easy, because such a presupposition of equality was also Socrates's point of departure. Equality is taken, by Protagoras and Socrates, in its institutional implications. It is not a polemical space where the portion of the portionless can be claimed. Both look for a harmonious city, not for a dissensual manifestation. But again, we must look closely at the staging of the text. There are, exemplified in the dialogue itself, expressions of struggle, irony, distance: in a word, dissensus. Even if Protagoras and Socrates seem to have exchanged their initial positions, they remain at opposite ends. We have many figures of misunderstanding, or even disagreement on both sides, that lead at certain moments to roadblocks. Nevertheless, we cannot say that the people (the portionless) are truely taken into account: it is less a political litigation than a rhetorical differend. It is another kind of litigation which appears: the autochtonous against the *xenos*, the stranger. Protagoras explains to Socrates how and why his fellow citizens of Athens are perfectly right to assume equality between anybody, and he explains it from the outside, as a stranger. And Socrates is anxious to see the sophists seducing the young Athenians, because they dare to follow them, far from the city. In the dialogue, there is also this kind of disagreement.

The litigation concerns, then, the immigrant worker: the sophist against the autochtonous. At the very beginning, Socrates's friend asks him who he has seen who has impressed him more'than the beautiful Alcibiades: "*Asto è xéno*," he asks, "a citizen or a foreigner?" (309c). For Athenians, *astos* means the city dweller even if he lives in a faraway village.[15] The portionless who have no time to come to the city and play their political role of citizens are still *astoi*, while the *xenos* does not belong to the space of the city. Even more, what he says cannot be heard, or should we say, *should not* be heard. With the sophist, we seem to have a reverse *mésentente*: it does not concern the impossibility of acknowledging sounds as words, but the impossibility of recognizing sound expressions instead of what looks like a continuous play on words "*logou charin legousin*," says Aristotle in his *Metaphysics* (book gamma, 1011b2) at the end of a long refutation of, precisely, Protagoras. Speaking for the pleasure of speaking, we find here again the word *charis*: "speaking for the grace of speaking." That is what Plato and Aristotle have to reject in order to assure the right use of language for good citizens. When the sophist speaks for the sake of speaking, Plato and Aristotle try to show that he simply does not know what he is doing, just as the people need philosophers or true citizens to tell them what they must do and know. Sophists seem, then, to occupy the other excessive place, symmetric of the one of the *dēmos*: they speak for the (political) grace of speaking as the *dēmos* speaks for the (political) acknowledgment of speaking.

It is not random, then, that what is at stake in Rancière's conception of the political manifestation and interpretation incorporates two of the crucial dimensions of the sophists: dramatization and homonymy. I shall now quote two passages from *La mésentente*. Firstly, in order to make visible litigation cases, "the problem is to construct a visible relationship with the nonrelationship, an effect of a supposedly ineffective power. . . . Politics consists in interpreting this relationship, which means first setting up as theater, inventing the argument, in the double logical and dramatic sense of this form, connecting the unconnected."[16]

Secondly, in order to make audible the power (*la puissance*, not *le pouvoir*) of speech of the speechless, "every politics works on homonyms and the indiscernable."[17]

Sophistic homonymy is precisely the specter Plato tries to conjure up, but he does so by dramatizing the conjuration, and it is, then, far more difficult and complex to evaluate the exact and rigorous Socratic demonstration. Just as the sophist seems to share Plato's archi-politics, Plato seems to be haunted by the sophist specter (Jacques Derrida would have said that Plato's ontology is actually a "hauntology").

I would like to add one last element about homonymy and the indiscernible. In his interpretation of Roberto Rossellini's *Europa 51*, Rancière says that "this practice of egalitarian strangeness imperils everything social and political, everything that represents society, which can only be represented under the sign of inequality, under the minimal presupposition that there are people who don't know what they are doing and whose ignorance imposes on others the task of unveiling. But it is not a question of unveiling, but rather of circumscribing [*cerner*]."[18]

Political interpretation has the task of underscoring and understanding misunderstandings and disagreements. And it is always a difficult task, one which implies a scrutiny and an *attention* (almost in Simone Weil's sense) to precise contingencies.[19] This is why history cannot be put aside. Making litigations visible is a matter of elaborating lines of continuity, drawing circles around people who did not share the same right of expressing themselves, and at the same time showing obvious discontinuities. The political task is ultimately not to present the unpresentable, in the Lyotardian version, but, following Rancière, to dis-cern the indiscernable, *cerner l'indiscernable*.

4.

The Classics and Critical Theory in Postmodern France: The Case of Jacques Rancière

GIUSEPPINA MECCHIA

Starting in the 1960s, a curious phenomenon occurred in French critical theory: regularly, if intermittently, several critics of modernity and even of postmodernity appeared to be going back to the classics when trying to create a ground for their political or aesthetic enterprises.[1] Before talking about the specificity of Jacques Rancière's involvement in this re-curring discursive strategy, it is important to comment, however briefly, on the larger trend. For this purpose a few lexical considerations are absolutely necessary, in order to dispel the numerous equivocations to which references to "the classics" or to "classical" forms of thought lend themselves.

On a first level, we should remark that in French, like in English, the word *classic* can be used either as a noun, in which case it is sometimes capitalized, or as an adjective. In certain contexts, the word *classics* designates, in both languages, either the Greeks or the Romans, which sometimes, more precisely, are also called *les anciens*, the ancients. This second designation is very useful and in fact even necessary in French, because in the French usage the plural noun *Les Classiques* or *les classiques* (the classics) splits itself in two, designating not only the ancient Greeks and Romans but also the playwrights, moralists, and philosophers active during the reign of Louis XIV. Of course, both the ancients and the classic authors of the seventeenth century are a staple of French education, and they were even more so in the 1930s and 1940s, when our modern and postmodern thinkers would have been schooled. While this original engagement certainly played an important role in determining the recurrent appearance of classical authors in late twentieth-century French discourse, it seems to me that this influence belongs to the "necessary but not sufficient" kind of causality, precisely because of the intermittent nature of its effects. Even allowing for ingrained habits and ways of thinking, we are still left with the task of untangling a much more complex web of textual and historical circumstances. The case of Jacques Rancière will, I hope, help us shed at least some light on this issue. A further exploration of the semantic field related to the word *classic* will take us further into this unwieldy complexity and will provide a good introduction to my main argument.

A more casual use of the noun is to be found in sentences like: "What do you mean you haven't read Sartre? It's such a classic!" This somewhat demystified use of the word, common to French and to English, is crucial in the context of our discussion, because it is not tied to any predetermined time frame or even to an explicitly catalogued canon that would be taught in literature and philosophy classes. In fact, its understanding is completely dependent on the singular interlocutor and the specific circumstances of the illocution. This appellation is purely a matter of judgment, and as such—as Rancière has indeed taught us—it is always subject to political "dis-agreement." In this usage of the word, what is a classic for me will not be a classic for someone else, and what was a classic in 1950 will not be considered a classic in 2007.

On the other hand, it is important to note that the adjective *classic* or *classique* functions in a similar way, again in both languages, insofar as it can refer to a quite large array of cultural products, from cars to philosophical arguments, in utterances like "Enjoy the luxury of a classic car: buy a Rolls" or (in a context that will bring us closer to the matter at hand) in a remark such as "This is a classic Marxist argument, I can't believe you are still making it." This is also important, because this kind of sentence alerts us to the incongruities of an appellation which, far from being a guarantee of serious, indisputable value, tends to banalize its objects by putting them in a series of equivalencies where, in truly capitalist fashion, bearded philosophers can, and in fact do, find themselves sharing an attribution with anything at all. In this respect, it is also worth adding that in French there is no one-word distinction between *classic* and *classical*: the adjective *classique* covers some of the semantic terrain of *classical*, which in English we find in sentences designating a certain style, like "this is a classical building," but also when referring to the standard or original form of a certain philosophical doctrine—for example, in a statement like "according to classical Marxist thought, one could say that . . ." In the case of Rancière, we will see that it is precisely Marx's status as a "classic" of political theory that is called into question, from Rancière's early involvement in Louis Althusser's exegetic enterprise to the appearance of Marxist categories in some of his much later works.

In fact, it is this last and final distinction that allows me to articulate the larger thesis that I will try to propose in my argument, which I will state rather crudely saying that the intermittent return to the "classics *qua* ancients" in French postmodern critical theory stems, at least in part, from the gradual and always controversial dismissal of an array of cultural products and doctrines that had been designated adjectivally as classical in different social and political circumstances. I am thinking first and foremost of "classical Marxism," but also, less directly and at a slightly later time, "classical" political economy and political philosophy.

I think that in France, the critical move toward a restaging of "the classics"—which for French theorists would be both the ancients and the seventeenth century's reenactors of antiquity, best exemplified by a Racine or a Molière, but also by moralists such as Pascal or slightly later writers like Fontenelle or (in Rancière's case) Fénelon—seemed to arise precisely at the various junctures within postmodernity when "classical Marxism" and its more-or-less heretic commentators were increasingly questioned by what I will call here very generally the intellectual Left. The necessity, real or perceived, of abandoning a certain set of "classical references" because of political and cultural disaffections periodically forces several leftist thinkers to adopt a safer, less controversial body of reference. The fact that the modalities of this phenomenon are in fact quite distinct in the works of different authors should not prevent us, I think, from recognizing the analogy of the move, and I plan to demonstrate how certain aspects of Jacques Rancière's mode or argumentation might be best understood if seen from this larger perspective.

I will only talk briefly of other figures that could be studied from this point of view: Roland Barthes, for instance, started his career in the late 1940s as a somewhat cautious—and admittedly bland—Marxist theorist of the ideology of everyday life with the essays collected in *Mythologies*, and then—after the various disappointments inflicted by so-called real socialism to French Marxist intellectuals during the 1950s and the 1960s—ended up writing a strange and beautiful book about Racine and using Aristotle more and more as a foundation of literary theory. Jacques Derrida, on the contrary, had always been reluctant to flirt with Marxism until his contrarian and controversial return to Marxist texts with his *Specters of Marx* in the early 1990s, when he was precisely trying to inscribe himself *against* the tendency that I am describing in this essay, a tendency that had already gained immense momentum by the 1980s and reached its zenith after the fall of the Berlin wall in 1989. Derrida had started his career in a modernist fashion, with a critique of Husserl and phenomenology. Soon, though, the need to root his theory of writing and difference in some universally recognized body of work led him to structure his arguments as pointed—some would say pedantic—critiques of Plato and other temporally vague "French classics," such as Descartes, Rousseau, and even . . . Claude Lévi-Strauss! With respect to the ancients, I just want to mention *Plato's Pharmacy*, because this is a text that will be important for Rancière himself, as it is a political critique of speech, writing, and, indeed, of power in and beyond the Greek polis.

Of course, both Barthes and Derrida have repeatedly been accused of anachronism and arbitrariness in their use of the classics: it doesn't seem, so far, that similar attacks have been made against Jacques Rancière. One of the reasons for this difference in reception might simply lie in the nature of Rancière's discourse: after all, political philosophy, as a discipline, has always traced its roots to the classical tradition, and maybe this is why nobody seemed utterly surprised when the classics appeared in *On the Shores of Politics* and *Dis-agreement*. I do think, though, that some of the modalities in which "the classics" function in Rancière are worthy of exploration and indeed of critique, albeit in the most "classical"—that is, nonpolemical—sense of the term.

On a historical level, one of the most interesting aspects of Jacques

Rancière's work, in fact, resides undoubtedly in its position in the larger context of the search for a grounding for political discourse, and maybe even for a new definition of politics that was made necessary by the partial dereliction of classical Marxist theory that occurred among many French intellectuals at different nodal points from the 1960s on. To a certain extent, one could say that Rancière's personal and intellectual itinerary is exemplary in this respect, and I hope that I will not be accused of trying to blindly adopt a petty and outdated, although "classical," approach to criticism, one of the "Life and Works of X" variety, if I recall a few biographical details. It could seem quite pedestrian to point out that Rancière, who was born in 1940 and started his philosophical career as a student and collaborator of Louis Althusser at the École Normale Supérieure, contributing one essay to his "classic" of Marxist scholarship, *Lire le Capital* (1965)—if it is indeed true that each "classic," from the Bible to Aristotle, from Karl Marx to Antonio Gramsci, generates a plethora of commentators or heretics whose heresies later become classics themselves. After breaking with Althusser in the very early 1970s, Rancière was shortly involved with French Maoist circles, but in the mid-1970s he started elaborating a thorough critique of Marxist theories of ideology and cultural hegemony, a process that was already theorized in his *La leçon d'Althusser*, originally published in 1974.

In later years, Rancière was able to give more weight and concreteness to his critique thanks to a very peculiar kind of archival—if not properly historical—work, aimed at investigating the different forms of knowledge and literary production developed by members of the lower classes during the nineteenth century in the context of their larger struggle for social and political emancipation. Among the works that came out of this research, I will only mention *The Nights of Labor* (1981) and *The Ignorant Schoolmaster* (1987). It is only after this plunge into the nineteenth-century archives that Rancière truly defined what, for him, constitutes the essential aspect of politics: the affirmation of the principle of equality in the speech of people who are supposed to be equal but who are not counted as such by the established policing of the democratic community. Their speech, when it occurs, always comes as a surprise, as a dangerous and powerful reminder of precisely what needs to be forgotten—and eventually suppressed—by the hierarchical ordering of the political space.

I think that it is precisely the relationship of the political space to processes of expression and self-representation that later fostered in Rancière a renewal of interest in questions of aesthetics, an interest explored in texts contemporary or slightly posterior to the one I will be mainly discussing in the remainder of this essay: that is *Dis-agreement*, first published in French as *La Mésentente* in 1995. It is in this book, I think, that Rancière, long after his break with classical Marxist thought and his long detour in the French archives, came back and quite literally, as we will see, with a vengeance, to what can only be called "classical political philosophy" and, consequently, to the classics *qua* ancients. It is true that the three essays contained *On the Shores of Politics* already function in a similar way, but it is in *Dis-agreement* that the word "classic" is fully deployed by Rancière, and mainly in its most common usage: that is, as an appellation designating the Greeks and the Romans.[2] There are, though, enough complications in this usage to foster quite a wide array of questions, and it is to this questioning that I will devote the rest of my argument.

The first chapter of *Dis-agreement* is entitled, quite appropriately, "The Beginning of Politics," and it starts with a thorough commentary of the famous passage in Book I of Artistotle's *Politics*, where man is constructed as a political animal because of his faculty to speak. For reasons that will be made clear a little later in my argument, I will transcribe here this first Aristotelian quote as it is present in Rancière's text, with the exception of some minor cuts:

> Nature, as we say, does nothing without some purpose; and she has endowed man alone among the animals with the power of speech. Speech is different from voice, which is possessed by other animals also and used by them to express pain or pleasure. . . . Speech, on the other hand, serves to indicate what is useful and what is harmful, and so also what is just and what is unjust. . . . Humans alone have perception of good and evil, the just and the unjust, etc. It is the sharing of a common view in these matters that makes a household and a state.[3]

When one wants to talk about politics, then, one should "begin at the beginning" (*Dis-agreement*, 1), and for Rancière this can only mean, in this context, that it is in "classical" texts like this one that political philosophy finds its *archē*. Nonetheless, it is quite striking how the different possible meanings of the word, best exemplified by its Latin translation as *principium*, are not developed analytically by Rancière, even though they do surface in their profound ambiguity throughout the book. In the corpus of the text, the *archē* of politics is considered by Rancière mainly as the founding logical principle of the conception of politics and policing as it is articulated by a whole tradition of political philosophy starting with the ancients. But the word *principium/archē* also designates, as we know, two additional things: on the one hand it refers to the temporal beginning of a certain phenomenon, and on the other it can also be an internal, driving force which itself does not always coincide with its logical reconstruction. In this respect, it is very important to remark that, contrary to what happens in the rest of the book, the French title of this first chapter is much closer to the temporal dimension of the *principium*, since Rancière calls it "*Le commencement de la politique*": that is, "the beginning of politics." The inaugural use of Aristotle's text, this early classic of political philosophy, is thus in itself profoundly ambiguous: does Rancière start with this passage because the Greek polis marks *the historical beginning* of the form of government that he's trying to analyze here—even if in its very impossibility—that is, constitutional and representative democracy? Or does he use it because it identifies the shared capacity to speak as the logical foundation of, and maybe even the internal force presiding over, the formation of the "household and the State" *in any* temporal and constitutional frame? This is the kind of ambiguity that can flourish when more systematic— or to use Althusser's formulation, "scientific"—approaches to political philosophy lose their footing and create a void that for the French Left was left gaping by the almost simultaneous demise of Marxism and structuralism. Any reader of Rancière will promptly recognize that this ambiguity remains at the very core of his general methodology and way of argumentation all during the 1990s.

In the case of *Dis-agreement*, when we read further into the text, we quickly realize that if Rancière retains this particular passage from Aristotle's *Politics* as the beginning of his own book, it is mostly because he needs it in his conceptual attempt to untangle the logical issues implied in the difficulties posed from the unmarked shift, in the Greek text, from concepts like "the useful" to heterogeneous notions like "the just" or, even worse, "the good." It is in providing these missing articulations, or in questioning them, that the modern commentators of the ancients inscribe their differences, and also and foremost in their political valuation of the common human function identified by Aristotle: that is, speech, and therefore reason.[4]

In this respect, the noise of all the quarrels dividing modern political philosophers—a category of thinkers that is quite mistreated and finally rejected by Rancière as a model for his own work—in their endless squabbles about how to define the just or the unjust, the useful and the harmful, cannot erase the trace of what Rancière himself had discovered in the archives as the true political *principle* par excellence: the agonistic claim to "equality," as defined, in humans, primarily by the sharing of speech as logos: that is, not mere voice, but reason. For Rancière, this had already been the great discovery of Jacotot, the main protagonist of *The Ignorant Schoolmaster*, when the former revolutionary official had been faced with the fact that his Flemish students—reading a French classical author–had taught themselves French without his help, because their intelligence and their mastery of language were absolutely equal to his own. Politically, this means, for Rancière, that the hierarchical ordering and policing of society is constantly undermined by the absolute equality that characterizes human intellectual faculties and always insures a potential for a truly political intervention. The democratic project, then, is only readable in terms of a radical equality that the lower classes incarnate and keep fighting for in spite of the innumerable forms of economical and political oppression that might plague them at different points in time. This is why the passage of Aristotle on speech as the common grounding for the human social bond is seized upon by Rancière with particular eagerness.

If this were not the case, one would be left to wonder about the meaning of Rancière's decision to privilege that particular passage in Aristotle's *Politics*: after all, when Aristotle himself says in the first book of his treatise that he will start to approach his subject, that is the forming of a *koinonia*, a community, "*ex archē*," he does not start with speech at all, but with the natural necessity of the coming together of the two sexes for the reproduction of the species, and of "natural rulers" and "natural subjects" for reasons of reciprocal support and security. After having stated that the most valuable of partnerships is the one that aims at the good of the larger population, and therefore is the state, Aristotle says:

> In this subject as in others the best method of investigation is to study things in the process of development from the beginning. The first coupling together of persons then to which necessity gives rise is that between those who are unable to exist without one another, namely the union of female and male for the continuance of the species . . . and the union of natural ruler and natural subject for the sake of security. . . . Thus the female and the slave are by nature distinct. . . . From these two partnerships then is first composed the household, and Hesiod was right when he wrote:
>
> First and foremost a house and wife and an ox for the ploughing. For the ox serves instead of a servant for the poor.[5]

Thus, one could easily say that according to the classics, the democratic state is not, in its *archē*, rooted in the equality of speech but, on the very contrary, in the hierarchical ordering of the *oikia* or household, which presupposes a radical inequality in the separation of the sexes and in the dichotomy between free men and slaves. It is true that in Aristotle this natural ordering is initially defined as characteristic more of the *oikia* than of the polis (the democratic state), but the polis does not in any way change the structure of the *oikia*, whose hierarchies determine, in fact, the participation or the exclusion from the political space. It is clear, then, that Rancière's "beginning," in the first chapter of his book about politics, is not necessarily the same as Aristotle's "beginning," and more importantly, it does not serve to promote the same end! To a certain extent, then, we could even say that the Aristotelian principle of politics, which could be construed as stemming from the hierarchies imposed within the *oikia*, would have to be found in *economics*, a proposition that could not be pleasing to a recent refugee from Marxism and political economy such as Rancière.

Not that it should be: if I point this out, it is just to start untangling one of the complications of Rancière's involvement with the classics and the "*exempla*" that they offer him: are they to be understood as historical precedents or as philosophical foundations? In other words: are the classics-qua-ancients relevant to us because they are situated historically at the beginning of Western society, or because they provide us with the logical foundations to understand any political instance at all? This is not irrelevant, because if all that we share with the ancients is the political form of representative democracy, we cannot call on them to support us when we try to establish the ethical and moral values that supposedly found it.

I will come back to this issue at the very end of my argument, as it needs to be introduced by a further level of analysis. For the time being, I will just underscore not only the tension between historical and philosophical argumentation in Rancière, but also the contrast between postmodern notions of equality and democracy and the function that they actually assume in classical antiquity, where slavery and female exclusion from the public scene implied that these two categories of human beings were by definition also granted a much more limited access to the realm of speech and reason.

Interestingly enough, even if Rancière does not confront the issue of slavery in Aristotle, it will be brought up indirectly in *Dis-agreement* in the guise of another "classic," the Greek historian Herodotus, even though we should notice that it is textually confined to the barbarian world of Asian despotism. Rancière comments on Herodotus's account of the revolt of the Scythian's slaves—who in the absence of their masters took their place, claiming equality with them, only to be subdued again when the Scythians came back from war and put them back in their places by their "masterful" use of the whip. This anecdote allows the French philosopher to say, once again, that the issue of equality is at the basis of every major political "dis-agreement." But, significantly, it is ultimately impossible, even for Rancière, to recuperate the tale of the slave revolt into a reflection on the basic principles of democracy, precisely because that principle is not contained in a tale that in fact was clearly intended as an apology of the irreducible difference between masters and slaves and furthermore was also an "Orientalist" sort of commentary on barbarian societies incapable of accessing the truly political ordering achieved by the Greek polis. The use that Rancière makes of Livy, the famous Roman historian, just a few pages later also gives us an opportunity to reflect further on the resistance, put forth not only by history but more importantly by classical authors, to the demand for acceptable general principles articulated by postmodern philosophical approaches to political conflict.

The fact is that in this first chapter of *Dis-agreement* and in those that follow, Rancière is trying to disentangle very complex issues related to the denial or attribution of reason to "the people" by various "political philosophers," both ancient and modern; in this respect, his critique of Plato reminds us very much of the one articulated by Derrida in *Plato's Pharmacy*. According to Plato, the logos cannot belong to everybody; artisans and shopkeepers should keep to their allotted function in society without embarrassing themselves with the burden of thought, speech, or reasoning.

It is important to underscore, nonetheless, that unlike Derrida, Rancière is very keen in differentiating between Plato and Aristotle, and that if he starts with the disciple (Aristotle) rather than with the master (Plato), it is also, I think, for a residual preference for what we might call practice-based models of political theory: Rancière thinks that Aristotle starts with politics as he knows it, that is, from the democratic institutions of Athens, which already presuppose, in their laws, the "equality" of every citizen. Not that Rancière is an Aristotelian; on the contrary, as a realist of sorts, Aristotle is involved in what Rancière will later call, in his fourth chapter, para-politics. Since the *dēmos* is included, by nature, in the polis, the political problem is drastically reduced to assigning "to each his own" through the administration of the conflict between the different parties by a government founded on juridical and technical competencies. Nothing is farther away from Rancière's conviction, stated repeatedly all through the book, that politics is never an assignation of places, or not even the maintenance and modification of the rule of law: this is "policing," pure administration, an activity aimed, according to Rancière, at instituting an order where nobody actually needs to speak anymore because the government is already responding to the nature of man, and therefore all that needs to be done is to put in place what the Americans will later call a system of checks and balances.

Plato was instead engaged in archi-politics: that is, the purely metaphysical construction of a polis as it should be, according to the principles of the just, the good, and the useful, removed from the instability and unpredictability of everyone's view about them. As expressed in *The Republic* and other dialogues, language, for Plato, is not synonymous with logos as reason and therefore cannot found the legitimacy of the democratic state. Those who are not the best will have to be content with the virtue of *sophrosyne*: that is, the wisdom of literally "minding their own business" while the really wise people will take care of the state. For Rancière, the classics-qua-ancients constantly move between these two models of articulating a political philosophy, and even many moderns will always remain within the space framed between these two alternatives, from Hobbes to Rousseau, as ultimately do also very different representatives of postmodern theories of linguistic exchange, from Jürgen Habermas to Jean-François Lyotard.

What Marxism, various Marxist heresies, and later the social sciences add to this "classical" alternative is a third model, which Rancière finds no less faulty than the first two. This is what he calls *meta-politics*: that is, the substitution of another *principle*—mostly economics, but also a modern doctrine like psychoanalysis—for the *principle* of politics. In this sense, the usage of the word *archē* clearly defines the logical foundation or maybe the inner force spurring the existence of politics, and not its historical beginning. What these three tendencies of both ancient classical and French classical political philosophy (in which Rancière does not recognize himself) have in common is that, paradoxically, they seem to desire *the abolition* of politics: in the ideal polis (perfectly functioning in para-politics, corresponding to its principles in archi-politics, and in a classless society in meta-politics), *politics* per se is no longer necessary. So fully realized will the right to speak be, that nobody will ever need to speak anymore, and the political principle par excellence will finally be extinguished. It is quite obvious that Rancière organizes his definitions of political philosophy in such a way that his own discourse cannot possibly be included in it: in fact, the category of "wrong" as the offense against "those who have no allotted part" in the *res publica*, even though they are at work in its units of production and of self-defense, is not found in texts of political philosophy per se, but in *history*, even if this history has been subject to extremely significant modifications. This is remarkable, because the method used by Rancière in his earlier, archival works is presented as a positive strategy precisely when dealing with classical historiography.

In fact, another founding text for the understanding of politics that appears in *Dis-agreement* is Livy's tale of the secession of the plebs on the Aventine, which the Roman historian originally narrated in *Ab urbe condita*. During a long war with the Volscians, tired of being exploited militarily and economically, the plebs enacted what in modern terms could only be defined as a strike: that is, they retreated outside of the city and refused to continue to perform their duties unless their demands be met. Menenius Agrippa is then sent by the Senate, and by telling the plebs the famous tale about the rebellion of the body parts against the belly persuades the plebs to accept a compromise by which it would return to work but also be granted its own representatives in the republic, the famous *tribuni*.[6] In Livy, the plebs is completely silent: the access to politics passes through economic and military blackmail, not through speech. But this is precisely why it is not through Livy, that is, a "classical" author, that Rancière tells the tale. This episode, in fact, can only help Rancière's reconstruction of the political principle—and not of its historical beginning—in the highly imaginative account that Pierre-Simon Ballanche gave of it in 1829, in the context of a much larger opus. The very title of Ballanche's project is indicative of his position in the history of modern thought, and it reminds us keenly of the circumstances in which it was written: "The General Formula of the History of All People as Applied to the History of the Romans." This is clearly a vision of history tied to the progressive-mystical utopias of the nineteenth century, for which the names of Saint-Simon and Fourier will serve as a point of reference. In this account, it is Ballanche, as a modern utopian, who makes of the event—which in Livy was purely a withdrawal of bodies from functions of production and defense—a "matter of speech." Rancière himself comments on the difference between Ballanche's and Livy's account, and he does so in a way that reveals the profound ambiguity of the moderns' appropriation of classical antiquity: "Ballanche reproaches the Latin historian for being unable to think of the event as anything other than a revolt, an uprising caused by poverty and anger and sparking a power play devoid of all meaning. Livy is incapable of supplying the meaning of the conflict because he is incapable of locating Menenius Agrippa's fable in its real context: that of a quarrel over the issue of speech itself."[7]

As in the textual choice that Rancière made when quoting from the first book of Aristotle's *Politics*, the plebeian revolt, although historical in nature, is not understood in an historical sense; all the economical, military, and, indeed, political issues tied to the situation in Rome around 494 B.C. are ultimately deemed meaningless by Ballanche and Rancière alike. Furthermore, by considering that the plebs did indeed score a victory in that occasion, because it was given its own representatives in the republican government, Livy is accused of not having understood what the real issue at stake was. The senators and the patricians do not believe that the plebs can actually speak, and therefore they tell them that they "are not." But in Ballanche the plebs not only listen but also talk back, and therefore it is only in his account that the episode can exemplify what for Rancière constitutes the very essence of politics, which is the "dis-agreement," the dispute over the common space of the polis through the common use of language. The classics, as we have seen for all of the examples given by Rancière, are far from promoting this *principle* themselves, while they might well have lived at the *beginning* of Western forms of democratic government.

I will not comment further on the specificity of Ballanche himself as a modern, even if his quality of traumatized young spectator of the siege of Lyon in 1793 certainly contributed to his profound awareness of the urgency of the question of the people's right not only to speak, but indeed to revolutionize the terrain of politics. Theosophy, Ballanche's own contribution to the diverse landscape of idealist representations of historical development typical of the first half of the nineteenth century, is but another attempt to make sense of the incessantly recurring revolts of the poor, and indeed to find a way to transcend them.

In the context of this essay, I will simply say that it might be clear by now that Rancière's use of the classics is indeed very similar to the one adopted by Ballanche. The classics are the place where the moderns— and in the case of Rancière the postmoderns—inscribe their differences in retracing the "principle," and *not* the historical beginning, of politics. Like the "anachronistic," postmodern lovers of the classics before him— I am referring, of course, to Barthes and Derrida—in *Dis-agreement* Rancière is not truly interested in staging a return to the classics, and more importantly, I will argue, not even to archival research or to historiography, because the "modification" introduced by the search for a general principle is too significant not to determine a qualitative shift in discursive practices. This is why the appearance of Marx at the end of the first chapter of *Dis-agreement* is quite telling from this point of view: before condemning his meta-politics in the fourth chapter, Rancière credits Marx for inventing a notion of the proletariat and of class strug-gle that resembles very much his own notion of a speaking and antag-onizing people: "The setting up of politics is identical to the institution of the class struggle. The class struggle . . . is politics itself, politics such as it is encountered, always in place already, by whoever tries to found the community on its *arkhē*. This is not to say that politics exists because social groups have entered into battle over their divergent interests. The torsion or twist that causes politics to occur is also what establishes each class as being different from itself.[8] Once again, we should notice that Rancière evacuates the economic and social specificity of the concept of class, because, as he will make clear in the fourth chapter of *Dis-agreement*, one cannot reduce politics to a struggle for representation in the political order, thinking that once that process would be completed, the gap between policing and the appearance of the true democratic principle—absolute equality—could be filled. This is the error of meta-politics, and insofar as Marx was engaged in this kind of discourse, Rancière distances himself from him. Nonetheless, in *Dis-agreement* the Marxist text functions precisely like the ones of the ancients, even though, alas, Rancière cannot bring himself to lend him the archetypal function granted to the Greek and Roman classics. Still, while the historical context in which it was written and the economical analysis which funded it is ultimately rendered meaningless by Rancière's analysis, the Marxist concept of class struggle retains a certain value as *exemplum* for the functioning of the concepts that our postmodern philosopher is trying to create.

Let me say very clearly that I don't intend to criticize Rancière for his method of argumentation. On the contrary: the very interest of the use of the classics—ancient and modern, Aristotelians or Marxists—in *Dis-agreement* resides precisely in the fact that the quarrel in which Rancière is engaged is not at all a reenactment of a quarrel of the ancients and the moderns, which, by the way, was even originally a quarrel among the moderns about what Rancière will call "the partition of the sensible": that is, the political and aesthetic regimes of the seventeenth century. Nobody, in Rancière's account, comes out on top, but in the final analysis, nobody is excluded either, except for the people who in the late 1980s considered that the end of real socialism and the discrediting of Marxist ideology should finally have persuaded us to accept the neoliberal dogma as the last word in the current political debate.

If Rancière, in 1990s, went back to Aristotle and Livy, it is mainly to take issue with the advent of an "end of politics" sometimes mourned, sometimes joyously proclaimed, and always delusionally predicted by various postmodern interlocutors. This certainly is to his credit. Be it the clearly mentioned political enemies (the preachers of a post-democratic society of consensus that ends up being quite similar to the Foucauldian society of control insofar as it is intent on killing democracy by proclaiming its triumph); the philosophical adversaries who reduce questions of disagreement to linguistic misunderstanding or to supposed ontological insufficiencies of language (Lyotard, Habermas); or the somewhat elusive possible allies, thinkers of aesthetics, of difference and of multiplicities (Jean-Luc Nancy, Alain Badiou, and Derrida himself), Rancière is surrounded first and foremost by his contemporaries, both in his mode of argumentation and in his concerns.

I can now come back to the question that I raised earlier about the tension—others might say the "contradiction," and which might indeed be unresolved in Rancière—between a historical and a philosophical approach to the understanding of politics. I don't think that it would be too meek to say that this oscillation might just be the very structure of thought, the necessary strategy for the perpetual invention of concepts that Deleuze and Guattari considered to be the true task of philosophy. This structure, by the way, would reenact Marx's own strategy—to remain in a French context, one could think about *The Eighteenth Brumaire*, for instance—so that, as Rancière has shown in *Dis-agreement*, certainly not only as a Derridean specter, but simply as one classic among others, he can and in fact does also find a place in the books of the postmoderns. I do think though, that the presence of the classics, Marx included, in contemporary political philosophy should not be considered a key to the discovery of eternal "political truths," or even of political "principles" whose generality would actually allow us to ignore the economical, social, and cultural specificity of the situation that we are trying to analyze. In this respect, I am indeed "critical" of what I consider to be a possible ambiguity in Rancière's position within the field of political philosophy.

Nonetheless, the construction of concepts, such as equality or politics, is indeed the main task of philosophy, and in his willingness to do so, Rancière has proved his own potential for becoming a new, postmodern reference, who will be in the future just as relevant as Aristotle or Marx. And indeed, engaged as we are in our own struggles and contentions within the antagonistic field of political postmodernity, I am confident that today, when debating questions of democracy, dissent, and equality, many among us are already saying to any apparently still unaware interlocutor: "What do you mean, you haven't read Rancière? He's such a classic!"

Jacques Rancière and Metaphysics

JEAN-LUC NANCY
Translated by John Hulsey

1

Metaphysics is the discipline concerned with the excesses produced by rational civilization. Such excesses are produced insofar as rational civilization, according to its very principle, directs itself toward the automatic production of reason as a division with itself (*avec soi*), or a division in itself (*en soi*). The logos appears as one of two types. It is either a self-instituting and self-governing logic, or else a dialogic or dialectic that divides itself from itself according to the law of incompleteness, for which logical self-sufficiency would be its asymptote—in other words, an impossible possibility.

This division is found in Plato, of course, and is continued in a manner that one is tempted to call undisturbed through multiple variations, from the great avatars of the dialectic (Aristotle, Kant, Hegel) to various versions of excess: that is, specific heterologies such as those known as *faith, other, matter, power, art*. Under these names, and several others, the confrontation between ontology and heterology is regularly made visible, a confrontation that is never exhausted because it proceeds from a division upon which the very possibility of the rational is, in principle, contingent. Under each of the aforementioned names—but also under many others—are held the concept and the force of an "irrational," something irreducible to identification and conciliation according to a regime of reason-giving (Leibniz's *principium reddendae rationis*).

"Under each of these names, but also under many others." Indeed, nothing stops us from extending the list to include *affect, technology, event, history,* and *being,* or, for that matter, *meaning* and *truth.* And the final item on this list would be the *logos,* or reason itself. The regime of division and excess is so deeply lodged within the principle of reason that it separates it and divides it from itself. In the end, the rationality of reason resides in this dissention and intimate discord, while consensus, agreement, and harmony are its fantasies par excellence. In order to justify itself, reason must or should first explain its *principium,* and in order to do this it should go beyond itself to a *principium principii rationis ipsae.*

2

Anyone who has followed me thus far while still wondering how in the world I might end up talking about or addressing Jacques Rancière—this reader has begun to understand. He or she knows, in effect, how determinant the rejection of consensus is in Rancière's analyses. It is not a question, for him, of mere political consensus, nor of consensual politics, which he rightly diagnoses as the political poverty of our time. He is the first, it seems to me, to oppose this model with such lapidary clarity, positing not another model of politics that would aim for a better form of agreement, but another idea of politics in the absolute: politics as the production of the disincorporation of assemblages, regulations, and configurations by which so-called collective bodies imagine themselves to be organized and subsist, and whose natural or supernatural resolution different systems of thought seek to represent with integrity and finality.

It should now be clear where I am going. As much as I share [*partage*] (and the word is carefully chosen, since *share* is a word that, like *com-*

mon, along with a few others, he and I have shared for a long time, and which also takes its share of responsibility for separating us, since it is one of the indices of dissent of which I want to speak)—as much, then, as I share his rejection of consensus, or that which we might call homology in general, I am also surprised by the general distribution of registers and what this implies in his work.

3

Generally speaking, Rancière seeks to do away with all forms of speculation (a term that he often uses to this effect), in which he discerns a fatal attraction for consensus, identity, or harmonic resolution. He wants to be anything but speculative or metaphysical, and one could say that he wants to be anything but a philosopher, if one considers certain texts where the label "philosopher" is identified with an aristocratic, inegalitarian, or aestheticizing posture.

And yet he is indeed a philosopher. First, because it is difficult to see (and he himself does not see) how else one is to speak of him according to the current distribution of roles. But most of all because he preserves, in spite of himself, something of the character of the philosopher, no doubt more than he wants to believe. Which is to say, also, something of the character of the metaphysician.

What he preserves presents itself nonetheless in abstentia. It is this presence through a mode of absence, or this more or less misunderstood persistence, that I would like to point out in speaking of the distribution [*partage*] that both brings us together and distances us. I would like to point this out, simply and schematically, as the opening of a possible discussion and not a closed statement, in terms of the major motifs of politics and art. I seem to observe in Rancière a sort of distancing or silent suspension with regards to both. That which is rendered absent has thus the general character of something "natural"—between quotation marks—as in this sentence: "Man is a political animal because he is a literary animal who lets himself be diverted from his 'natural' purpose by the power of words."[1] One could find other occurrences. In each instance, the use of quotation marks indicates that the author does not take "natural" to be a consistent concept in the most banally metaphysical sense (its most common post-Nietzschean understanding), as in the opposition "nature/culture" or "nature/technology." At the same time, however, he relies on this word in order to designate the idea that allows us to speak of a rerouting or deviation. It is the contradiction between these two logics that intrigues me.

4

Let us resume. The "natural," thus understood, manifestly designates the representation—whether imaginary or ideal—according to which nature in general can be said to exist—and in it or through it a natural destiny of man. Such a representation is "fictional," another term placed in quotation marks, but the word does not here designate an invented story but rather a material assemblage of signs. Indeed, one may wonder why the "fiction" of the "natural" is not one of the possible and acceptable modes of this assemblage (and, ultimately, of the "distribution of the sensible"). Nevertheless, although Rancière does not give any express indication, one must understand from the general context of his work that the designation of a natural destination of man would align itself with a nonpolitical operation, somehow prior to or exterior to "political animality," thus prepolitical or archaic. This operation is elsewhere characterized by the nondivision of *archē*, a nondivision that interrupts the dissent that is proper to politics and democracy.

The difficulty, to my eyes, is the following. If one is required to question all imputations of naturalness, to subscribe to all manners of thinking an originary "denaturing" (I myself have employed this term on occasion, likewise suspended between quotation marks), this cannot be done without fulfilling two conditions:

1. No confusion must be allowed to persist between the imaginary or speculative notion of "nature" and the real system of human affairs that existed prior to or exterior to the appearance of Clisthenian democracy (which is to say, the historical emergence of the West, more generally). Neither before this point nor elsewhere does there exist a "nature," nor do there exist "natural" rights, which is to say the pure authority of a "natural logic of domination."[2] It is not by chance that in this citation, *volens nolens*, the quotation marks that one would expect are absent. Does this mean that Rancière believes, in certain instances and in spite of himself, in some archeo-political "nature"? But how is one to think, in this case, of the democratic irruption and its rerouting of a prior destiny?

2. One must not forget that in philosophy or metaphysics, "nature" never has the natural—without quotation marks—status that an exceedingly summary representation of metaphysics, accredited by the post-Nietzschean and post-Heideggerian vulgate, would like to impose upon it. Metaphysics, according to this vision, is considered a totalizing system of thought in its organicness—whether transcendental, sublime, or ecstatic—of the real and men within it. However, beginning with Aristotle's first reflections on *phusis*, nature is insufficient for arriving at man's ends; these must be pursued through *tekhnē*. It follows that the *zoon politikon* can exist only insofar as political life "denatures" the animal in man.

These two precautions intersect. The "natural" should neither be imputed to that which is outside the West, nor to any naïve belief fostered by speculation in any form. Rancière's remarkable analyses of the birth of politics through the division of *archē*—and the division of the "people" with itself that was produced or enabled by it—leaves one question unanswered: namely, the reason for the irruption or invention of democracy, and the fact that it did not emerge from that which preceded it by a leap from "nature" to logos, but through a series of operations whose effects must be found in a heretofore political assemblage. One cannot simply stop interrogating the requirement to place quotation marks around the word "nature," as around "fiction." In other words, one must continue to question the *remainder* between a supposedly undivided *archē* and the self-division of politics, a remainder that may subsist beneath any projection of "nature," "foundation," or "origin."

What is it that effaces itself with the invention of democracy and philosophy—and whose effacement leaves a mark both on the metaphysical attempt to conceive of an origin and the denunciation of fables of origins (denunciations that, themselves, belong to metaphysics, as witnessed by Rousseau or Kant)? I will not attempt to respond here, but I would like to remind the reader that this question is not "speculative," in Rancière's sense, and may suggest the persistence and resistance, within politics, of yet another division. This would be the division between politics and that from which it detached itself—that which is not and was not politics, religion, or art. Implied here is another distribution of the sensible, certainly, but it is precisely this otherness that must be interrogated. Generally speaking, philosophy—the mode of thought that was born with the polis and the West—has trouble conceiving of that which preceded it as something other than a simple preamble or pure heterogeneity. Thus, Rancière's conception of the nondivided *archē* seems to me to oscillate between something prehistorical moving toward its historical mutation (but how?) and something heterogeneous that exceeds all schemes of political and philosophical thought (but what does this mean?). The philosophical question concerning the "outside" of philosophy persists, then, with an even greater insistence. Indeed, this is a metaphysical question and not a historical or prehistorical one; it is a question concerning an excess of "reason" on this side of reason itself. Perhaps art, if not religion (of which Rancière does not speak), needs to be examined from this angle.

5

One might even be tempted to think that it is precisely because of the problem that I have just pointed out that Rancière joins together so forcefully—and with such a singular manner, in view of all the ways of thinking about politics—the questions of art and politics. His conjunction of the two carefully avoids subsuming one into the other. Art is articulated as the representation of assemblages according to which the sensible is distributed, and politics is the reworking of these assemblages by means of litigation or disagreements that open up, in the (in principle) egalitarian community, the inequality of the community or the "people" within itself. Art and politics are joined and distributed as two orders of "fictions": one is a representation of the distribution, and the other is its reworking. Both form a continuous movement, however, insofar as representations of the distribution introduce lines of "disincorporation" into the received assemblages and thereby open up the possibility for their reworking.

I will not go further into the general logic of this arrangement, whose descriptive and analytic efficacy in treating three great regimes of art, or arts, seems to me very convincing. But this analysis obstinately brings me back to the following question: what is "art," this thing called "art" (in the singular or the plural, under its modern name or before the invention of its name)? Or rather, why is there this specific register of the "representation and reconfiguation" of the distribution (here I am citing the end of *The Politics of Aesthetics*)? I recognize that Rancière's efforts are to dissolve the specificity of art, and furthermore the exception that is attached to it by a considerable spread of contemporary thought. In this effort, I share all that responds to the necessity of arming oneself against aestheticisms, religions of art, or hyperboles in the form of "the end of art" or the surpassing of art. There remains, however—in general, as in Rancière's work—something that persists and resists underneath this name "art," and without which it would be difficult to understand why it is there.

6

Rancière renews, in a highly interesting way, the analysis of the modern emergence of aesthetics and the autonomous and unitary category of "art," which are entirely separated from the registers of *artes* or *tekhnai*, forms of *savoir-faire* or "ways of doing," as he says in a more sensible mode. He thus calls into question the privilege placed upon art by the "paradigm of aesthetic autonomy": the latter is typical of a modernity that wanted to see art as both the sensible manifestation of pure liberty and the valorization of the creativity of labor.

The intention of Rancière's analysis is to attack this privilege as the effect of speculation—a speculation that is blind to the general conditions that govern the configurations by which all social practices make up different regimes of the distribution. I do not have the least intention to make this blindness my own. Yet I cannot avoid bringing up two points. First, the autonomization of art—striking for its belated appearance—is not a random occurrence, but rather the product of a history of transformations and configurations of the distribution. The aesthetic regime is but one of these configurations, whose driving impulses and deep causes merit examination, particularly insofar as the relationship between this form of modernity and democratic, industrial, and atheist modernities is concerned. What interests me here is that Rancière's entire analysis appears to presuppose what it intends to call into question: namely, something of the autonomy and specificity of "art."

It is not enough to prefer the plural expression *artistic practices* to the singular term *art* (a singularity that, in effect, harbors many questions, which several contemporary thinkers have not ignored). The former epithet conserves the concept as such, and the use of the plural (which could be rephrased as "the arts," since the word *practice* is only there to erode the problem of "art" somewhat) simply allows one to better raise the problem of specificity. Why is an irreducible plurality of arts the condition for the existence of "art"? At first glance, and awaiting confirmation, this situation is not homologous to the dyad "science/sciences" or "religion/religions" (whereas "philosophy/philosophies," one might note in passing, is perhaps not as far off). Whether one likes it or not, to speak about arts or artistic practices engages a notion of specificity and thus authorizes one to question the eventual presence of this specificity precisely where it is not named, in regimes other than the aesthetic. This is a question that the problematics surrounding "African art," as well as discussions on Paleolithic or Neolithic pictorial practices, have helped clear up—which is not to say resolve.

7

When Rancière writes "artistic practices are 'ways of doing and making' that intervene in the general distribution of ways of doing and making as well as in the relationships they maintain to modes of being and forms of visibility," one is allowed to wonder how exactly these practices "intervene." This question receives a diffuse but constant response that the end of the same book aptly sums up: "Whatever might be the specific type of economic circuits they lie within, artistic practices are not 'exceptions' to other practices. They represent and reconfigure the distribution of these activities."[3]

Ignoring the fact that the only form of specificity recognized here is that of economic circuits (without failing to note in passing, however, that the relationship between art and wealth, which is as old as figural, musical, architectural, or choreographic practices, certainly merits more attention than the ritual and rather politically correct imprecation against the art market—which is not Rancière's aim, to be sure), I must ask the question: what does "represent and reconfigure" mean?

The answer is not given in Rancière's text, and the pairing of these two concepts seems to go without saying. Yet "represent," whether understood in its imitative or ostensive sense, does not imply the entirely different idea of "reconfiguration." And if the latter indeed designates the establishment of a specific model for the community of existence with "delimitations that define the respective parts and positions within it," the question is opened wide as to why and how the distribution of the commonality [*le commun*] and the commonality of distribution need to be "reconfigured."[4]

The necessity for the commonality to present itself as such, in some way or another, can be at least understood by analogy with the necessity for the subject to have a minimal self-image. (But what status would this image have: imaginary, symbolic, abstract, or felt? Yet art does not seem to be necessarily implicated in this matter, whereas the same might not be said of art's relationship to the "common subject," if we can call it that.) However, the necessity for "that which is common" to (re)present itself in an artistic mode is harder to understand. Why must it be a matter of that which is alternately called "beauty" (even in Plato, who does not think about "art"), "pleasure" (Aristotle or Kant), "liberty" (Schiller or Duchamp), or simply "art" (Hegel, Kierkegaard, Nietzsche, Heidegger, or Adorno)? All of these "speculative" motifs (to which one might add "the sublime," "creation," "nonfinality," and "the ineffable") are nothing other than efforts to modulate what I called an "excess." More precisely, they are excesses of a function of "representation and reconfiguration," when "that which is common" is not subsumed into the regime of "undivided *archē*."

8

One cannot but agree that the emergence of art in the singular is the effect of a general transformation of our commonality, of the conditions for possibility of our being together, and thus of the conditions for the manifestation of this "being together." Indeed, there is much more work to be done to multiply, or ramify, Rancière's analyses on the many stages and forms of art between, say, the eleventh and the twentieth centuries. What comes from another register, however, is the notion that that which emerged brought to existence *for itself* the general condition for all commonalities (at the same time as the question was being raised as to what the commonality is or how it is possible). This condition is, precisely, the condition of representation and reconfiguration: in other words, a specific gesture of monstration and a specific form that is traced by this gesture through diverse artistic practices.

This register is present, even if it is not specified as such, as soon as there is image, song, dance, ornament, monument, or poem. Neither its reabsorption by religious or state powers (as attempted in earlier times) nor its reinscription into the general distribution of practices is able to satisfy this specificity—whatever the legitimacies of these two processes. Rancière's refined discourse and sensibility attests, in every way, to the presence of this specificity, which I dare call quasimanifest in his work. The art that he rigorously reinscribes into the general distribution raises no less vigorously the question of irreducible distinction (which is not to say privilege!): namely, what is the gesture of the Lascaux painter? The question not only persists, but it is renewed through Rancière with a decoupled intensity. What is this gesture insofar as it distinguishes itself from all other practices pertaining to and existing within the distribution?

One could extrapolate from Rancière that art is a means (and perhaps the most common one, considering all the forms of knowledge and power) of understanding our communal existence and the very modes of being-in-common (what brings us together and separates us)—a being-in-common that is, moreover, not exclusive to relationships between humans but is extended, through them, to all things and beings. But the reason for this reason-giving exceeds that which is authorized by rational examination, for it leads back to an examination of reason itself in general and its division with itself. It is at this point that—necessarily, simply, whether through its critics or its deconstructions—metaphysics once again awakens and reconfigures itself.

In Rancière as well? Of course! But distributed in another way, placed in a state of rest or reserve, implicit, yet rising up when one evokes "the great myths of writing, more than simply written but inscribed everywhere in the flesh of things."[5]

POLITICS

6.

What Is Political Philosophy?
Contextual Notes

ÉTIENNE BALIBAR

Translated by Catherine Porter and Philip E. Lewis

Let me begin with some preliminary remarks.[1]

In the first place, all critical reflection on the past and present status of political philosophy puts differing conceptions of temporality into play, along with the alternatives that those conceptions subtend. In a recent paper, Catherine Colliot-Thélène indicated that, openly or not, all political philosophy in the modern era refers back to a philosophy of history that mirrors the articulation between rationality and Western modernity.[2] This remark also holds true for the "returns to political philosophy" that we witness episodically, and most notably right now in the form of what is aptly called neoclassicism. That is why its primary theme is the critique of historicism or evolutionism. But here tradition offers differing models that do not lead to the same conceptions. Rereading Machiavelli while privileging the theme of *la fortuna* is not the same as doing so while inscribing institutions and power relations in a cyclical temporality. Resurrecting Greek thought while aiming at a new doctrine of *prudentia* is not the same as doing so while appealing to the horizon of tragedy. There is nothing really new about such choices. They were already present, via the Nietzschean legacy, in the Weberian critique of forms of domination, and the conflict of ethical systems. They are also evident in Althusser's quest for a critique of historical time, articulating the overdetermination and underdetermination of political action in a trajectory that leads from Montesquieu to Machiavelli by way of Marx (a quite particular Marx, it must be said, since he can be associated tendentiously with either of these models).

In the second place, the debate opposing adherents of social science to adherents of political philosophy takes up antitheses that, in fact, antedate the "birth of sociology," whether we locate it in Comte, Spencer, Durkheim, Tönnies, or Weber. One clear sign of this is Durkheim's designation of Montesquieu and Rousseau as "precursors of sociology." Another is the continuity of a critique of contractual relations: it runs through Montesquieu, Hume, Burke, and Hegel, dividing discourses on the origin of the state from discourses on the foundations of legislation so as to pinpoint a veritable heresy for modernity. But if there is conceptual continuity from the first modernity to the second, over and beyond the revolutionary event (not only French but also American and European) that, as Wallerstein so aptly says, "normalizes change," there is also an effect of suppression.[3] If, in the second, postrevolutionary modernity, political philosophy disappears between philosophies of the subject and theories of social evolution, it is tempting to think that its comeback (with the crisis of modernity, after the world wars and civil wars between and within sociopolitical systems) corresponds to a closing of the revolutionary question (or even to an "end of the [revolutionary] illusion," as François Furet puts it).[4] In reality, it would be just as accurate to note that political philosophy translates a new uncertainty as to the *meaning* of the revolutionary event, and as to its thematic correlates (secularization or disenchantment of the world, individualism and mass society, democratization and the reign of opinion, bureaucratic rationality, and so on), which the discipline of sociology has placed at the core of its descriptive project.

Finally, the unity of neoclassicism is absolutely problematic. If one locates it in the effort to restore meaning to the idea of the polis (or to the idea of the republic), independent of the evolution of social conditions, one sees immediately that the discourse of Leo Strauss is not fully congruent with that of Hannah Arendt.[5] The critique of the subordination of the political to practical and theoretical sociological factors such as work or social class unquestionably brings them close together. But the diagnosis pertaining to the continuity and disruption of tradition (which represents precisely the complement of philosophy that belongs to history) and thus pertaining to the foundation of individual and collective rights, irrevocably opposes them. Here again, as a result, there is no turning back without reproducing a slide into heresy.

These preliminary remarks lead me to sketch out what could be called an anatomy of discursive conflicts in which political philosophy henceforth has its place, and outside of which the very use of that term would be unintelligible. Political philosophy exists, to be sure, only as a multiplicity of tendencies and objects, the stakes of which are identified by the classical categories of community and conflict, rights and power, legislation, sovereignty and justice, authority, representation, responsibility, and so on. The reestablishment of the link between political philosophy and philosophy in general, by means of categories such as action, judgment, rationality, and constitution, appears to have arisen out of debates that took place in the second half of the twentieth century (to which, from this standpoint, thinkers as different as Arendt, Habermas, and Negri contributed). It did not, however, take the metaphysical form of a derivation of the "political sphere" from anthropological or ontological grounds, but rather that of a reciprocal interaction between reflection on political practice and reflection on the meaning of human existence or of "being in the world." This convergence doubtless bears the legacy of a complex history, but it can also be posited axiomatically; to do so is to confer on political philosophy the at least apparent possibility of declaring itself self-sufficient. Conversely, it is precisely this self-sufficiency that is called into question in the *Methodenstreit* that opposes the discourse of political philosophy to critiques of that philosophy. My point is not that these critiques can be seen as extraphilosophical. On the contrary, they will be seen to display the characteristic modality according to which, today, the political object and the difficulty of "thinking" it *divide* philosophy, and thus help constitute it.

The first and most obvious of these critiques, at least on the horizon where we have positioned ourselves, can be called sociohistorical. Whether or not it is intertwined with a viewpoint on the transformation of social relations (or on regulating, or adapting to, their transformation—this is the point of disagreement between Marxists and liberal critics, each claiming to represent the realist viewpoint), the critique tells us that making the political sphere autonomous amounts to inverting the relations between part and whole, or between expression and its condition of possibility. Beyond the political phenomena (the state, institutions, the subjectivity of actors), the real ground of society and of history is what must be found. I shall not develop this well-known perspective further.

But it is indispensable to take into account, in addition, an entirely different critique, for which—following Robert Esposito—I am reserving the name *impolitics*.[6] Instead of opposing reality to representations, facts to values, this critique asks us to pass *beyond* the position of values (and especially legal values, or forms of legitimization of law or the state, but also of civil society or revolutionary action) and to turn toward the genesis or creation of those values and the antinomies involved in that event or process. It is above all a matter of going back genealogically to the moment in the constitution of the community (and of the very notion of community) when violence and love, order and justice, or force and law appear indistinguishable.[7] This move undertakes to deconstruct the autonomization of the political order, not by subjecting it to relativization, to ontological destitution, but by reinscribing at its very center the nonmeaning or aporia that it must—if it is to constitute itself as a positive, normative, or simply analytical discourse—push away to its edges or onto another stage (as Freud does in his writings on the theory of culture).

The term *impolitics*—only recently introduced into French—has diverse origins that have given it differing connotations. On the one hand, there is the *Betrachtungen eines Unpolitischen* that Thomas Mann published in the aftermath of World War I (1918, 1922, and 1925)[8], which represented his personal attempt to elevate himself above the conflict between socialism and liberalism in the name of culture and of an ideal Germany (as he had done allegorically in *The Magic Mountain*); on the other hand, there is Julien Freund's *Politique et impolitique*, which ends up deploring the "distress of the political" in parliamentary societies on explicitly Schmittian grounds. In both cases, the term has an essentially negative connotation. In Esposito's case, this connotation is suspended, or rather, it undergoes a radical change of value. Here, too, the reference to Carl Schmitt plays an essential role, but only inasmuch as it exposes the crisis of political representation (and of any possibility that the political community can be representable) as the end point of the modern movement of secularization and neutralization of the political. More profoundly, then, the term must be referred back to a Nietzschean inspiration, and to its extension in the work of Bataille.[9] The question of impolitics is the question of the negative or the void that comes to inhabit the heart of politics as soon as the substantive absolutes around which the hierarchy of values and the organizational projects (the common good, the divine plan, the will of the people) are suspended or destroyed, even though the transcendent status of the problem of authority or justice or sacrifice cannot be purely and simply abolished in favor of the objective existence of institutions and procedures for achieving consensus. This explains, for example, the privileged role Esposito attributes (in Bataille's wake) to the critique of the category of sovereignty. The problematics sketched out here has an ethical dimension, undeniably, but what sets it apart is that it grounds its formulation of ethical questions neither in anthropological idealities nor in formal imperatives, but solely in the limits or aporias of the political itself—its sacred part or its accursed part. In this sense, it encompasses work that could include all or some of the writings of authors as different as Foucault and Derrida, Negri and Lefort, Nancy and Agamben [. . .]

For want of space to go into all the details here, I shall proceed schematically in two stages. First, I shall summarize a few themes from Esposito's work, focusing in particular on the essays collected in *Nove pensieri sulla politica*. Next, I shall sketch out a confrontation with certain themes found in Jacques Rancière's *Dis-agreement*, in order to try to pin down the conflictual edge of the political philosophy with which we are dealing here.

At various points Esposito uses a characteristic formula: "Place the limits of the political at its center, and thus exit from the presuppositions of political philosophy."[10] From this project two major critical questions seem to emerge. One concerns the freedom that the political community aims to use as its own foundation, to the extent of concentrating it in the sovereign figure of an authentic or absolute decision to be-in-common (let us think of Rousseau: what makes a people a people, in other words, the general will). But freedom as an affirmation of singularities is radically absent from every positive institution of sovereignty, which can only concentrate freedom by turning it into a nature or an ideal. And such is the principle of a headlong rush forward, in which the succession of figures of power carefully avoids recognizing its own intrinsic relation to death. The other critical question concerns the representation—or rather, inversely, the unrepresentability—of the democratic principle, whether in the form of legal equality, procedures for discussion, or delegation of power. At best, this means that democracy is essentially incomplete, that it exists only in the form of an infinite process, without any rules or guarantees. But we have to see—and on this matter, too, Rousseau is situated at the very point where political philosophy turns into its opposite—that that incompletion immediately calls for the complement of myth: the myth of a final or original organic community. On this basis, political philosophy as a whole can be understood to unfold as a rational myth, or a myth of intersubjective communitarian reason.

This compensatory structure is already perfectly expressed in Plato, to whom Esposito refers here: "The relevance of Platonic reflection on politics is unsurpassed: an insoluble antinomy, a schism constitutive of power and the good, of law and justice, of form and value, that is projected into the very heart of politics, according to an inevitable discord that tears it apart forever and that no liberal humanism can ever palliate."[11] Still, there can be no question of reconstituting a Platonism. What the reference to Plato opens up is, rather, the alternative between a *meta-politics* and an *impolitical* line of thought, or, alternatively, between a transcendence and an absence of the One that would underlie any reference to community. The meta-political thread is the one that runs from Plato himself to the Marx of the "withering away of the state" and communism, where "democracy is entirely subsumed, but also annihilated, in the power of its own myth."[12] The One is ultimately represented in the fiber of the social, in the social *practice* that brings individuals into communication, engaging them in a common work, above and beyond their individuality. The impolitical thread, on the contrary, attempts to assume completely what is left unsaid in the ethical self-sacralization of the state—the "terrible concentrate of power and violence that exploded at its origin."[13] In other words, this thread's path takes us through the thematics of the irreducibility of conflict, or division, that Machiavelli, Marx, and Schmitt have bequeathed us, but it prolongs this thematics in a negative politics whose fundamental thesis is that democracy is *always still to come*. Esposito, referring to the work of Nancy, in dialogue with Blanchot, calls this ground a "presence of the unpresentable."[14] The oxymoronic expression serves to reveal at the root of democracy a task or responsibility which is not that of exercising civic or political functions, but rather that of accepting an element of alterity or radical noncommunication, without which there is no communication, and thus of considering the community as the opposite of collective security or "immunity."[15] Community is thereby situated in an insurmountable propinquity of the common good with evil, and political unity with death. The idea of the impolitical is inscribed in a tradition of worldly asceticism, a continual attempt "to belong to one's time against one's time" (Bonhoeffer, Max Weber, Canetti), just as it rejoins some of Derrida's recent propositions (*Specters of Marx, Politics of Friendship, On Cosmopolitanism and Forgiveness*) that establish hospitality to the outsider, "the most unexpected guest," as an "impossible" criterion for democracy.[16]

It is precisely on the basis of this thematics of necessary impossibility, or of democracy as the limit figure of the politics that resists its own institutional camouflage, that it is tempting to make a connection with Rancière's recent work. In *Dis-agreement* in particular, which is subtitled *Politics and Philosophy*, Rancière organizes his entire discourse around a dissociation of two terms that are at once infinitely close and essentially opposed: *politics*, which he relates to the demand for democracy, and *police* (taken in the most general sense, that of French classicism, studied most notably by Foucault), which he relates to the institution of consensus. Their common etymology (*politeia*) is symptomatic of the very problem confronted perpetually by political philosophy, from its Greek origins to the recent developments in globalized politics: for example, the attempt to give a normative content to the idea of international community on the basis of the opposition between ethnic violence and humanitarian intervention.

Policing, in general, is a matter of demands; it seeks to give everyone a fair share in the distribution of the common good, by authoritarian or contractual procedures. Democratic politics, in contrast, has as its unique criterion the "share of the shareless": that is, the requirement of equality set off *against* social identity or personal merit. We may recall here the young Marx's celebrated formula from a manuscript dated March 1843, "democracy is the *essence of all state constitutions*," seeing in this a direct echo of the way the Greeks construed *isonomy*: "the idea that the specific law of politics is a law based on . . . equality."[17] In other words, democracy requires recognition of what, in the facts or in the established order, appears at first impossible, and it takes the incommensurable as its measure: "In this way the bringing into relationship of two unconnected things becomes the measure of what is incommensurable between two orders: between the order of the inegalitarian distribution of social bodies in a partition of the perceptible and the order of the equal capacity of speaking beings in general." It is indeed a question of incommensurables. But these incommensurables are well gauged in regard to each other, and this gauge reconfigures the relationships of parts and parties, of objects likely to give rise to dispute, of subjects able to articulate it. To put it clearly, politics is constituted by the incessant encounter between its own egalitarian logic and the logic of policing, "which is never set up in advance."[18]

What displays this encounter, and simultaneously turns it back into a radical opposition, is of course the uprising of those who, as bearers of the discourse of emancipation, are excluded on principle by and from the distribution of powers and civic rights, those who appear henceforth not as victims of injustice but as the representatives of a wrong done to democracy itself (according to the circumstances and the era: the poor of antiquity, the third estate and the proletarians of bourgeois society, women and foreigners in modern nations). Once again the definition Rancière gives of freedom is essentially negative, even if it engenders a dynamics, a struggle.

> Not only does freedom as what is "proper" to the *dēmos* not allow itself to be determined by any positive property; it is not proper to the *dēmos* at all. The people are nothing more than the undifferentiated mass of those who have no positive qualification—no wealth, no virtue—but who are nonetheless acknowledged to enjoy the same freedom as those who do. The people who make up the people are in fact simply free like the rest. Now it is this simple identity with those who are otherwise superior to them in all things that gives them a specific qualification. The *dēmos* attributes to itself as its proper lot the equality that belongs to all citizens. In so doing, this party that is not one identifies its improper property with the exclusive principle of community and identifies its name—the name of the indistinct mass of men of no position—with the name of the community itself. . . . It is in the name of the

wrong done them by the other parties that the people identify with the whole of the community. Whoever has no part . . . cannot in fact have any part other than all or nothing. On top of this, it is through the existence of this part of those who have no part, of this nothing that is all, that the community exists as a political community—that is, as divided by a fundamental dispute, by a dispute having to do with the counting of the community's parts even more than of their "rights." The people are not one class among others. They are the class of the wrong that harms the community and establishes it as a "community" of the just and the unjust.[19]

From this starting point, we can see how resemblances and oppositions are distributed. There is indeed something *impolitical* in the way Rancière develops his radical critique of consensus and the common good (*common wealth*) or in the way he shatters unitary, identity-based representations of communities: "For politics, the fact that the people are internally divided is not, actually, a scandal to be deplored. It is the primary condition of politics."[20] This also allows us to understand his antipathy for the notion of *citizenship* in the form it takes at the center of a tradition in political philosophy running from Aristotle to Hobbes, Rousseau, and doubtless also to Kant or Arendt. But on the basis of an intricate discussion of the function of sacrifice, Rancière's critique absolutely rejects the theological connotations, even the negative ones, attached to the idea of "community of death" inherited from Bataille. In this sense, the tripartite division of negations, or denegations, from which the originality of the discourse of politics emerges, through difference, is resolutely secular. Rancière labels them, respectively, *archipolitics* (this is, Plato and the project of bringing into being a unified community, a *politeia* in which the order of laws would converge with nature, or the organic life of the polis); *para-politics* (Aristotle and, in his wake, all "the normal, honest regime" of political philosophy, whose telos is to transform "the actors and the forms of action in a political dispute into parties and forms of distribution of the policing apparatus" through the search for the "best regime," the one that contains in itself a principle for regulating or moderating conflicts, an optimal combination of freedom and stability); and finally *meta-politics* (Marx and more generally any theory that localizes the radical wrong in a prepolitical social structure—as it happens, a class structure—of which the egalitarian political language would be only the *ideological* mask, destined to collapse in an "end of politics"). We see that what matters fundamentally is not the unrepresentability of differences, or of singularities, the distinctive features of which make them the objects of a forced "immunization" in the formation of the state, but the unrepresentability of the conflict itself, or of the dispute that takes the status of the "citizen" as its object when the birth of the community occurs.

Philosophically, these are oppositions that cannot be neglected. It is no less evident that, through their very divergence, they disclose a problematic limit of political philosophy—a limit that the return of political philosophy to the foreground, after two centuries during which historicism and sociologism actually or supposedly predominated, only makes more perceptible. Political philosophy, as reflection on the constitution of the public sphere and on the meaning of the kind of life that devolves from it, can no longer give as axioms—neither in a realist nor in a normative or idealist way—the categories of belonging and reciprocity. On the contrary, the uncertainty and, in the extreme case, even the impossibility of conferring a univocal meaning on them have to become the object of reflection about the "common," even when this reflection seeks to establish modalities for conferring citizenship. We would find preoccupations of the same order in Herman van Gunsteren, about whom I have spoken in more detail elsewhere and whom Habermas wrongly believes he can place among the "communitarians."[21] For Van Gunsteren's notion of citizenship as infinite access ("in the making") presupposes that every political community (local or global) is a *community of fate*: not a community of destiny, as Renan and Heidegger would have put it, each in his own way, but a community of chance, whose members are at once radically foreign to one another (or, alternatively, foreign to any common cultural presupposition) and incapable of surviving without one another. This amounts to transposing Hobbes's and Rousseau's problem, that of a fictively natural prehistory, into a "posthistory" that has dissolved frontiers but without instituting humanity as a political subject.[22] This is also what I myself have tried to indicate previously, not only by identifying the question of democracy with that of its frontiers—in all senses of the word—but by characterizing as "emancipation," "transformation," and "civility" the system—a system lacking any a priori principle of unity—consisting of the critical concepts of politics that overdetermine the constitutional question of citizenship.[23]

7.

Rancière in South Carolina

TODD MAY

In late May of 2001, the administrative assistant in the department where I work at Clemson University suggested I attend a meeting taking place in the community. It concerned the accidental death of a twenty-year-old African American named Kashef White. I had not heard of him, although in the coming months I would rarely stop hearing about him.

It seems that Kashef White had been hit and killed by a car, driven by a white student of the university, on or near a street within the university's borders. How this happened remains in dispute. Here's one version of the story. Kashef White had been drinking, had wandered out into the road, and the student hit him. The police arrived and took appropriate measures, including administering a field sobriety test to the driver, who, although he had alcohol on his breath, passed. By that time, there was nothing that could be done for Kashef White. This was the official version, embraced by the police, city officials, and the uncle of the white student, a former sheriff who referred to Kashef White as a "drunk black kid."

Here's another version. Kashef White was standing on the curb, with one foot in the street. The driver swerved, hit him, and drove down the road a little before turning back. The police arrived late, administered the field sobriety test, but never took seriously the possibility that the driver was drunk. This was the story told by the witnesses at the scene, all of whom were African American.

One other detail is worth noting. Although the driver of the car did receive a necessarily subjective field sobriety test, only Kashef White's body was chemically tested for alcohol, and he was found to have been intoxicated. This discrepancy in the testing method did not sit well with Clemson's African American residents.

The meeting I attended was a tense one. The police and several city officials were there. Over two hundred of Clemson's one thousand African American townspeople attended. They cited years of police and city abuse and neglect. In addition to the usual offenses, such as Driving While Black, there was neglect of infrastructure, lack of administrative oversight, and a demeaning attitude toward the city's African Americans. (The latter I was able to see on display that night, and many times after.) It was difficult to distinguish the accurate memories from the faulty ones, the facts from the exaggerations. After all, like most white people in the town of Clemson, I had very little interaction with the African American community and had never spent any time in its neighborhoods. It was clear to me, however, that even if a small percentage of the stories they told were true, this was a city with a racial problem.

The residents demanded that there be changes in the policing practices at Clemson. The police, while denying that there were major issues that needed to be addressed, offered to review those practices. Near the end of the meeting I suggested that the historical record of police self-monitoring was not a promising one, and that perhaps people ought to organize a civilian review board for the police themselves. This suggestion found favor among some of the prominent members of the African American community, and for the next several years I organized with people in that community.

Like a lot of local organizing efforts, this one went well for some months. We had a lot of people and energy at our early meetings. We were able to canvas neighborhoods and leaflet every residence in the African American neighborhoods in Clemson. We created a sense of excitement that, I was told, was uncommon in Clemson's African American community. For its part, the city, while steadfastly refusing to consider a civilian review board, quietly went about building roads and improving parks in African American neighborhoods. They also announced that they would henceforth install video cameras in police cars and use computer programs that could trace patterns of racial discrimination in arrests. And, of course, they created a task force to study the problem of racism in the city they denied exhibited any.

City officialdom's view of the events surrounding Kashef White's death was marked by a vigorous denial that there was anything interesting to be discovered through them. It was unfortunate that someone had been killed, but proper procedure had been followed and proper protocol observed. Even the fact that the victim's blood-alcohol level had been tested, but not that of the driver of the vehicle that killed him, was chalked up to attempts to discover what had occurred that night. After all, the driver did pass a field sobriety test. And, presumably, Kashef White's body did not.

Very few readers of this piece will be tempted to embrace such a view, common though it is among public officials. But that leaves us with the question of how to understand these events. It would be helpful to provide a framework that would not only help make sense of them, but that would allow us to move forward. In other words, it would be helpful to have a way of considering these events that does more than situate them meaningfully in the past, but would also allow us to frame future action, to think about what we might do as well as what we have done.

Here is where the thought of Jacques Rancière assumes its importance.

What I would like to do here is to offer a sketch of several elements of Rancière's political thought that seems to me to capture trenchantly what happened in the couple of years following Kashef White's death. This sketch will suggest not only a way of understanding the past but also of thinking about future political action. Although a discussion of Rancière's entire political approach is too rich to be considered here, I hope at least not to betray the elements of his thought that are implicit here and that influence this essay.

The framework I offer here is one that might be called philosophical, in the sense that it is reflective and broadly conceptual. Rancière himself has offered important criticisms of political philosophy, particularly its project of seeking to suppress politics by offering it a conceptual grounding. A framework for thought, however, is not the same as a ground. What I hope to do here is to offer some philosophy and some politics, without falling into the trap of offering a political philosophy.

Perhaps the best way to start is with the very concept of politics. For Rancière, politics is not a common occurrence. "Politics doesn't always happen," he writes. "It happens very little or rarely."[1] This does not mean, of course, that politics as we understand it in the everyday sense is rare. People vote; they write their elected representatives; sometimes they go to a demonstration. For Rancière, however, these are not matters of politics. Politics concerns something else. It concerns equality. And equality arises only when the traditional mechanisms of what are usually called politics are put into question. "Politics only occurs when these mechanisms are stopped in their tracks by the effect of a presupposition that is totally foreign to them yet without which none of them could ultimately function: the presupposition of the equality of anyone and everyone."[2]

Politics is about the presupposition of equality. Although this might seem the starting place for all political thought, Rancière's approach to it is diametrically opposed to that of traditional theories. And it is in his inversion of the operation of the presupposition of equality that the riches of his thought are to be found. In order to understand this inversion, contrast it with some more familiar concepts of equality.

The economist Amartya Sen argues that "a common characteristic of virtually all the approaches to the ethics of social arrangements that have stood the test of time is to want equality of *something*—something that has an important place in the particular theory."[3] What differentiates these theories is the various things that each argues there should be equality of. Should there be equal liberty, equal opportunity, equality of resources, equality of goods, or some combination of these? Sen himself argues for the equality of the capacity to achieve important functionings.

In appealing to the concept of equality, Sen has provided a common rubric for contemporary theories of justice. He is right to argue that theorists like John Rawls and Robert Nozick can be seen as equality theorists. Moreover, he is right to argue, as he does, that this equality is rooted in their commonly held view that human beings should be treated with equal respect or concern. Their differences lie in the character of the equality they endorse. What is it that equal respect or concern requires? For Rawls, it is equal liberty, equal opportunity, and equal access to the best minimum standard of living the society can provide. For Nozick, the requirement is simply one of equal liberty; anything else would be an infringement upon that fundamental right.

Approaching equality this way may seem clearly correct. Isn't the fundamental question of politics, after all, the question of what people deserve from the society they live in, given that we are all equal? For all of these theorists, and for others writing in this vein—which is to say for the entirety of current mainstream political philosophy—the question of equality is a question of its distribution. What is it that should be equally distributed among society's members? That is the question driving contemporary political philosophy. It has a presupposition that needs to be questioned, and it is not the presupposition of equality.

Where there is distribution there must be a distributor. And indeed, for these theorists there are institutions, usually governmental ones, that are responsible for that distribution. The claim of equality, then, is a claim directed at governing institutions on behalf of the individuals those institutions govern. Put another way, equality is a debt owed to individuals by the governing institutions of a society or a community.

For Rancière, this is not politics; it is policing. "Politics is generally seen as the set of procedures whereby the aggregation and consent of collectivities is achieved, the organization of powers, the distribution of places and roles, and the systems for legitimizing this distribution. I propose to give this system of distribution and legitimization another name. I propose to call it the *police.*"[4] Although Rancière does not, to my knowledge, discuss the distributive theorists of mainstream Anglo-American political philosophy, his definition of policing is an exact depiction of the goals of such philosophy.

To think of politics in terms of policing is a common approach, and not only among political philosophers. Progressives, whether inside or outside of academia, often ask ourselves questions like the following: How should health care or education be distributed? What should the legally enforced minimum wage be? How should we think of affirmative action or reparations for slavery? At the peak of identity politics, many demands were reduced to the question of what was owed to African Americans, or women, or gays and lesbians.

There is nothing wrong with these demands, limited though they often are in scope. But they are not what Rancière means when he speaks of politics. Politics is not a matter of how distributions arise and the principles by which they should be given. It is not what the people who should be the subject of politics do. Distributive approaches to justice imply political passivity. Distributions are what people receive; they are not what they do or create.

Why is this? Distributive theories of and approaches to justice put equality at the end of the process. Equality, in these views, lies in what is given to people, what they are entitled to receive from others. For some philosophers, this may seem an odd way of looking at things. After all, isn't one of the key distinctions in ethical and political theory that between consequentialists and deontologists, where it is the consequentialists that are concerned with the end of the process and the deontologists with the means? For Rancière, however, deontological approaches like that of Nozick or, to a certain extent, Rawls still focus on the end of the process. While they are not concerned with how much happiness or how many goods people wind up with, they are still concerned with what institutions owe to individuals. If goods or happiness do not lie at the end of the process, people still do. Equality is owed to people by governing institutions.

Suppose we were to take things the other way around. Suppose that instead of making equality the outcome of a political process of distribution, we were to make it the presupposition of political action. Suppose that we were to treat equality as something other than a debt— as instead a wellspring, a motivation, a value through which we conceive ourselves and our political interventions. Politics would then be the presupposition of equality, and not its distribution. What would be the significance of this inversion, this reversal?

The first and most important change is that equality would no longer concern, or at least would no longer primarily concern, what governments or institutions do. It would be a matter of what people, those whom Rancière sometimes calls "the people" or "the *dēmos*" (as in democracy), do. The people start from the presupposition of equality, and then act from there.

I would like to look more closely at this presupposition of equality, asking two questions whose answers will lead us back to South Carolina and Kashef White. The first question is one of specification. If we presuppose people to be equal, what is it that we are presupposing people to be equal in? After all, people differ in many ways: height, physical prowess, gender, eye color. Can we say more exactly what the presupposition of equality actually presupposes? The second question is one of the consequences of this presupposition. What follows from it? Where does it lead? Or, to put the question in Rancière's terms, given the presupposition of equality, what is the politics that follows from it?

To answer the first question, we must appeal to Rancière's book *The Ignorant Schoolmaster*. Joseph Jacotot, a partisan from the French Revolution, flees France after the Restoration. His travels lead him to Flanders, where he settles as a schoolteacher. The problem for Jacotot, however, is that he does not speak Flemish, and his students do not speak French. This, of course, is generally considered a stumbling block to effective pedagogy. Jacotot is not dissuaded from teaching, however. He utilizes a copy of Fénelon's *Telemachus* in a dual-language edition, teaching the students from it. Eventually, he assigns them a paper, to be written in French. Their only resource for doing so is the same book. The students turn in papers that are top notch, from which Jacotot draws the conclusion that people are equally intelligent.

What is the basis for this conclusion? The problem of education, Jacotot thinks, is not that people diverge in intellectual abilities. Rather, it is that some attend closely to what they are doing and others do not. There are, therefore, no natural divisions that prevent people from achieving academic success. One only has to get them to engage with the material. Jacotot assumes, among the implications of this view, that one can teach something one doesn't even know. He tests this implication by teaching a course in law, with results similar to his first course.

What does it mean to presuppose that people are equally intelligent? This has nothing to do with standardized tests or with the ability to do advanced math or physics. Instead, it has to do with the ability of people to shape their lives. Everyone, we might say, unless they are damaged in some way, is capable of creating a meaningful life. Not on their own, to be sure, but alongside others. Each of us is capable of meeting the challenges life puts before us, without appeal to an authority that must guide us through our own ignorance. Surely, there are things that others can teach us. But we are capable of cobbling those teachings together into a meaningful whole, and far more capable of teaching ourselves many of those things than the hierarchical order in which we live would lead us to believe.

That is why, in the *Dis-agreement*, Rancière says that the mechanisms of policing cannot occur without the presupposition of equality. He writes, "There is order in society because some people command and others obey, but in order to obey an order at least two things are required: you must understand the order and you must understand that you must obey it. And to do that, you must already be the equal of the person who is ordering you."[5]

Is Rancière *arguing* here that people are equally intelligent? No. He is offering it as a presupposition. Why? In order to see where this presupposition might lead. "Our problem," he writes, "isn't proving that all intelligence is equal. It's seeing what can be done under that presupposition. And for this, it's enough for us that the opinion be possible—that is, that no opposing truth be proved."[6] But who is it, then, who should embrace this presupposition? Those who are seeing what can be done, those who will act under this presupposition: the people, the *dēmos*.

Who are the people, the *dēmos*? They are those who, in every society, are presumed to be unequal to others who are better situated. They are those who, in the police order, have been classified as less equal than others. As Rancière sometimes puts it, they are the part that has no part, the uncounted.

We must be clear here, because it is easy to misread Rancière. There is not a specific group of people who are the uncounted, as though it were those people and no others. In a police order, there are many types of classifications that create many types of inequalities. There are economic classifications, racial and gender classifications, psychological and sociological classifications. The people, the *dēmos*, consists of those who, in a given classification, are unequal to others in that classification. The people are those who have no claim to contribute to the public discussion and debate, those who are, from the perspective of the police order, invisible. Politics, then, is a process of declassification. "The essence of equality," Rancière notes, "is in fact not so much to unify as to declassify, to undo the supposed naturalness of orders and replace it with the controversial figures of division."[7]

This leads us to the second question: that of what follows from the presupposition of equality. What follows is the creation of a situation of what Rancière calls "dissensus." In thinking of politics as dissensus, Rancière goes against much of the grain of political thought, which sees the project of politics as arriving at consensus, at agreement, at a commonly accepted order. Rancière does not deny that there may, at the end of a political process, be some sort of accommodation. We must recognize two things, however. First, the accommodation will not be something offered to *dēmos* by the powers that be; it will be something that the *dēmos* imposes upon those powers. Freedom, as we know, is not given; it is taken.[8]

Second, the accommodation is not where the politics lies. The politics lies in the actions of the *dēmos*, in its acting upon the presupposition of equality. And in doing so, politics is the creation of a dissensus. It is the refusal to recognize the existing order of things, not in the name of another order, but in the name of equality. "Political activity is always a mode of expression that undoes the perceptible divisions of the police order by implementing a basically heterogeneous assumption, that of a part of those who have no part, an assumption that, at the end of the day, itself demonstrates the sheer contingency of the order, the equality of any speaking being with any other speaking being."[9]

We might be tempted to think of the demonstration of equality as one that is made only before or against those who are well situated in the police order. Equality would then be simply the demonstration of dissensus by the part that has no part, to the part that does. That would be a mistake. "This is the demonstration of a struggle for equality which can never be merely a demand upon the other, nor a pressure put upon him, but always simultaneously a proof given to oneself. This is what 'emancipation' means."[10] To act out of the presupposition of equality is a demonstration that runs in two directions: to the other and to oneself.

It is not difficult to see why this must be, both theoretically and politically. If acting out of the presupposition of equality were only a demonstration to the elites, then it would likely undercut the presupposition itself. It would be parasitic on the other to whom the demonstration is made, and thus be more of a Hegelian desire for recognition than a demonstration of equality. Although the motivation for political action must come from the oppression a *dēmos* feels out of being denied equality, this does not mean that its demonstration must be entirely oriented toward those who have engaged in that denial. In fact, to do so risks a becoming parasitical on the other that would subvert the very equality at the heart of political action.

Historically, we can see evidence of this in various political movements, from the black consciousness movement in South Africa under the guidance of Steven Biko, to various indigenous people's movements such as the Zapatistas, to the emergence of feminist and queer studies departments in universities. These are moments of self-demonstration, as well as demonstration to the other. They are at once a proof of equality that the *dēmos* offers to itself and action out of its presupposition.

The history of these moments of self-demonstration, however, is a politically fraught one. They run a risk that is complementary to the one just cited. If political action directed solely toward the other can become parasitical on that other, self-demonstration can, and often has, become self-involved. This is identity politics. The emergence of identity politics, particularly during the 1980s and 1990s, shows the dangers of political self-centeredness. One's own history and oppression become the centerpiece of politics. There is an inability to recognize other oppressions and other political movements. The politics of solidarity gives way to the politics of ghettoization. This not only undercuts political effectiveness (oppressed groups often need solidarity with others in order to succeed); it also reinforces the idea of a police order with given identities and roles.

Rancière's thought, then, provides a barrier against this complementary danger as well. Identity politics is not a form of declassification. Through its rigidity and delegation of identities and roles it is a re-classification. It is a dissensus from a given police order, to be sure, but only in the name of another police order. It is, then, far from a demonstration of equality. Political action, if it is to remain political, does not coalesce into a particular classificatory order; instead, as Rancière insists, it demonstrates the contingency of any classificatory order.

If political action does not yield identities, however, what does it give us? How might we think of the group that engages in political action? What may we say of it? For Rancière, political action does not produce identity; it produces subjects. "By *subjectification* I mean the production through a series of actions of a body and a capacity for enunciation not previously identifiable within a given field of experience, whose identification is thus part of the reconfiguration of experience."[11] What does this production amount to?

A subject is what appears through a political process. We must distinguish this appearance from the more well known subjectification analyzed by Michel Foucault. For Foucault, also, a subject appears through a political process, but in a very different way. The subjectification described by Foucault is an intersection of dispersed practices that create, through relations of knowledge and power, a subject. This subject is a person with particular qualities, behavioral orientations, and understandings of itself.

For Rancière, subjectification is, in one sense, the opposite of this. It is the emergence of a collective subject that is the *subject of action* rather than its object. Where for Foucault subjectification happens to the object of particular political processes, for Rancière it is the active creation of a particular type of political subjectivity by those engaged in it. To become a subject is to refuse one's particular place in a given police order, to reject the hierarchy that has assigned one a certain role. And in doing so, one makes oneself (a oneself that is collective rather than individual) appear, stand out from the background to which one has been assigned. And in that sense, politics is always irreducibly aesthetic; it creates something that did not exist before. A collective subject is produced from the material of a hierarchical social order—one that, like other artistic productions, creates new ways of seeing and being seen.

This is why Rancière writes, "Politics does not happen because the poor oppose the rich. It is the other way around: politics (that is, the interruption of the simple effects of domination by the rich) causes the poor to exist as an entity."[12] This does not mean, of course, that there are no poor people before the creation of a political subject. In fact, it is often poverty that drives politics. Rather, it is that "the poor" come to exist *as an entity*, as a collective subject, only with the emergence of politics. The poor, the proletariat, Palestinians, Native Americans: these are products of political struggle, subjective emergences that arise alongside that struggle, the creation of a people that did not previously exist. Without politics, as Rancière tells us, "there is only the order of domination or the disorder of revolt."[13] If Foucault tells us histories of how people come to be created into certain kinds of subjects, Rancière provides the tools for thinking about how we might *create ourselves* into other kinds.

Politics, then, is always a matter of community. "Democracy is the community of sharing, in both senses of the term: membership in a single world which can only be expressed in adversarial terms, and a coming together which can only occur in conflict."[14] One cannot create politics alone. One finds oneself part of a police order, alongside others. To resist that police order alone requires that one join with them in the formation of a community that is at the same time a political subject. It is not that one cannot speak or act politically on one's own. Our history is filled with examples of this. Rather, it is that that speech and that acting only become political when they result in or foster the creation of a political movement. By themselves, individual speech or action is not politics but rather the invitation to it. It is when a group takes upon itself the refusal of a police order in the name of equality that politics happens. "A community of equals is an insubstantial community of individuals engaged in the ongoing creation of equality. Anything else paraded under this banner is either a trick, a school or a military unit."[15]

To engage in the practice of equality, to become a subject, while it is above all a demonstration to oneself and the formation of a community, is not simply an affair of self-involvement. Rancière's use of terms like *dissensus* and *conflict* indicate this. The practice of equality occurs in the context of a particular hierarchy in a particular police order. Nothing guarantees that politics will create change. The "verification [of equality] becomes 'social,' causes equality to have a real social effect, only when it mobilizes an *obligation* to hear."[16] We must be clear here. Politics is not to be confused with the success or failure of change, even if change is its goal. Politics is a process. It is the emergence of a collective subject acting under the presupposition of its equality, an acting that disrupts a particular police order. This does not mean that the question of political effects or political change is unimportant. It is of the highest importance. Political movements often fail. However, we must distinguish the existence of politics from its effectiveness. Otherwise, we risk missing it in the moment of its happening, and, on the other hand, ascribing it where it does not exist.

Thus armed with this understanding of politics, what are we to make of the events following the death of Kashef White? What understanding does Rancière offer us, and how might it help us think about organizing?

What city officials sought, above all, was to deny that there was a problem of racism in Clemson. In this, the police chief was much more forthright. At the meeting I cited in the beginning of this piece, he admitted that, given what the African American population was telling him, there might indeed be a racial problem in the city. The mayor and the city council, however, would not concede this. (In this, as in other areas surrounding these events, city officials were content to let the police chief hang out to dry.) The strategy of denial took several forms: isolating the event of Kashef White's death from its surrounding context, creating a discursive space for African Americans who agreed with their point of view (none of whom, it should be noted, were residents of Clemson), blaming outside agitators (i.e., me).

These strategies worked for the media, but not in the African American community. They had seen all this before. And the problem the city faced was not simply a problem of media spin. The deeper problem was one of dissensus. There was a group of people whose history of marginalization in this college town placed them at the bottom of the police order. They were keenly aware of this, and they were being encouraged by a group of local organizers to recognize and express their equality. Other measures had to be taken—thus the road building, the park enhancements, the videotape machines, the youth scholarships to the local recreation center, and so on. During the time of our agitation, the African American community was the object of a modicum of city largesse. However, we never did get what we were asking for: a civilian review board. Given Rancière's perspective, it is easy to understand the dynamic at play here. To give what was asked for would be an admission of equality. The city would have had to concede that the African American community was right in what it demanded. Therefore, the equality of intelligence would be vindicated; an obligation to hear would have been motivated. The city government, by offering that which was not asked for but which would be welcomed in any case, remained the source of distribution and the arbitrator of what was needed. There would be gratitude, perhaps, but not equality. The police order would be maintained.

Not that the city told themselves this. The strategy was cynical, but it was not created by folks who had read Rancière. What city officials made clear was that residents could say what they wanted, but, as elected officials, they were in charge of the decisions of who gets what. In addition, they listened, when they did, with an air of palpable condescension. One night in the summer of 2001, the city council agreed to meet with the African American community in a local community center. Residents complained about various inequities that were of long standing in the community. The mayor, in particular, resisted hearing these complaints. He and the city council were there, he announced, only for one purpose: to understand what issues residents had with the police. Of course, conflicts with the police, as every organizer knows, are often merely flashpoints for deeper concerns. The city council was having none of this, however. If there was a problem (which of course it denied), the problem was with the police, not with the mayor or city council. Finally, one resident came to the microphone and shouted in frustration, "Why are we talking to you, since you can't even hear what we're saying?" The residents there hollered in agreement.[17]

Thus the city's response: a project of deflecting and defusing dissensus in an attempt to return to the consensus of the given police order.

What about the other side of the struggle, the one Rancière addresses directly? What happened to the struggle by Clemson's African American community?

We had a good bit of success, at least for a little while. People in the community were very welcoming and eager to present their stories. (I found organizing in the South to be very different from organizing in the North. For one thing, it seems to involve more time sitting on porches drinking sweet tea. I take this to be a good thing.) There were also a good number of people willing to come to meetings and get involved in one way or another. At its peak, our organizing meetings had nearly twenty people. This is particularly impressive, since many of those involved were single parents or worked more than one job.

The success did not last, however. First, the passive support of much of the community did not turn into active involvement. We who organized were embraced but not joined. Second, those who were active diminished in numbers and involvement over time. After the first several months, organizing came down to half a dozen of the most committed residents of the community. Eventually, we tried a different tack, running two residents for city council. They lost, and worse, their campaigns did not increase voter turnout in the African American neighborhoods.

How might we understand this? At the time, it was particularly frustrating for me, since, as I emphasized to the African American community, Clemson, as a college town in the South, did not want to have racial trouble on its hands. We had a lot of leverage; all we had to do was use it. I chalked the failure to sustain a longer term campaign up to a combination of a lack of a civil rights movement and, not unrelated, a history of intimidation. South Carolina in general, and Clemson in particular, did not seem to have a piece of the 1960s civil rights movement. The university quietly integrated when it saw the writing on the wall at other universities, and nobody in the community seemed to have been active during that period. Well, there was one person: the brother of one of the people who organized with us. From the stories I heard, he stood up to the police on a regular basis. One day he was taken into custody and beaten so badly he lost his mind. Nobody was charged in the crime, and the African American community got the message. He still wanders the street aimlessly, as though a warning to those who would dare confront the authorities. I see him every once in a while.

It was not that the movement, modest though it was, was a failure. We earned some concessions, even if they were not the ones we sought. People had the experience of organizing, so they now have skills they didn't have before. This could be important, depending on the future of the community. However, we did not experience what Rancière calls politics. That is the crucial point, and the one that I only began to understand looking back after reading his work. I told myself at the time that people seemed to lack hope. I still think that's right. But there was something else, too. People in Clemson's African American community seemed unable to think of themselves as equal to Clemson's whites. They didn't say this to me, of course, and likely did not say it to themselves. Rather, it emerged through how they acted or didn't act. The intimidation they suffered, their physical isolation and poverty, made it difficult for them to see themselves as actors in their political situation. They were, so it seemed to them, incapable of influencing their social conditions in the way that Clemson's white community was. I think they were mistaken in this. But the important point here is not what I thought but how they thought. They had difficulty acting out of the presupposition of their own equality, because they had difficulty presupposing that equality.

We should not be surprised at this. Rancière counsels us on the rarity of politics, and Clemson's experience is a common example. However, by understanding this we can also understand what else is needed in order to create politics. This can help us in organizing, and in not mistaking politics on those occasions when it does arise. The dissensus that emerged only in germ in Clemson in the summer of 2001 is a possibility that remains, not only in Clemson but everywhere. We must be sober about its difficulty and its fragility. But if we are to retain a sense of politics at all, we must also remain vigilant about its openings. Rancière's political writings provide a significant source of both analytic rigor and, not less important, hope in what can never be less than an ongoing struggle.

8.

Political Agency and the Ambivalence of the Sensible

YVES CITTON

Within a few years, the "partition of the sensible" (*le partage du sensible*) has become something of a household word in France. With this phrase, Jacques Rancière refers to the most basic system of categorization through which we perceive and intuitively classify the data provided to our senses. Literary critics, philosophers, and theorists of aesthetics, but also sociologists and scholars interested in migrations—all seem to find in this catchy phrase what they always wanted to express, but never dared to say. I, of course, count myself among these people seduced by the *partage du sensible*. Its role as a hinge between politics and aesthetics proves extremely useful whenever one attempts to talk just about anything. Far from being weakened by its status of *passepartout*, this phrase allows us to dig tunnels under disciplinary frontiers; it sets up an interface through which various approaches can interact and shed light on each other; it offers a foundational common ground on the basis of which we can better root and articulate our various reflections on some of today's most urgent problems.

Because of its very success and usefulness, I believe that the notion of the *partage du sensible*—and more generally the category of the sensible itself—deserves a closer look, which will be less critical than analytical: as in chemistry, I believe we need to decompose various elements which (usefully) come together under the compound category of the sensible. This analysis will also provide me with the opportunity to discuss the subtle relations of both proximity and allergy which Jacques Rancière seems to entertain with the Spinoza-Deleuze-Negri constellation I am currently associated with, through my implication in the French journal *Multitudes*. I hope to show that what may look like two antagonistic conceptions of politics can in fact, and should indeed, be articulated with each other. Along the way, we will pass by an unlikely gallery of portraits gathering dinosaurs, rhinoceroses, actors, and membranes— through which I will try to map out our current political postures.

TWO SIDES OF THE SENSIBLE

I will start by suggesting that the usefulness of the category of the sensible largely comes from the fact that it neutralizes the traditional opposition between activity and passivity. In an age when political agency appears as more problematic than ever, everybody falls back on issues of sensibility as if it were a protected place where the question of agency can be miraculously (if temporarily) suspended. It does not seem to take much effort, much willpower, much creativity, to sense or feel something. Common sense tells us that objects and events are impressed upon our senses by their own movement, and that it is enough for us simply to *be there*, with our eyes and ears open, in order (passively) to receive such impressions—a fairly reassuring and suitably humble perspective, as it is minimally demanding on our part. We, people of the twenty-first century—aware of all the traps and past failures of political agency, calls to arms, and other glorious revolutionary projects (so the postmodern story goes)—we like it whenever someone suggests that we can be subversive by simply sitting there with our eyes open: our hands are unlikely to find themselves covered with blood in the process; we are unlikely to be hurt or to jeopardize our (after all fairly comfortable) conditions of living.

For, when a philosopher like Rancière writes about the *partage du sensible*, we understand that this passivity is only apparent: our sensitivity results from an activity of partition and of partaking. Things don't just project their images upon the blank screen of the senses: we, humans, actively categorize them. We filter them, we select some and reject others, we classify them according to complex mechanisms of distinction that are both socially constructed over time and individually reconstructed each time we sense anything. The fact that we can develop our sensitivity, our *capacity* to sense, suffices to show that some type of activity, whatever it may be, is involved in the process. We, people of the twenty-first century, are therefore fully entitled to feel good (about ourselves) when we "feel well," that is, when we *do* our best to become sensitive to the existence, sufferings, and rights of all the creatures (women, colonial subjects, gays, and battery hens) that previously fell outside of the *partage du sensible* experienced by our barbarian ancestors.

Seventeenth-century philosophers like Leibniz or Spinoza provide us with a principle that neatly catches these two sides (passive and active) of the notion of sensitivity. They invite us to think that our (active) power to affect and our (passive) power to be affected always tend to develop in direct proportion to each other. I cannot become more powerful without becoming more sensitive; conversely, each time I gain in sensitivity, I also gain in my power to act (effectively). A rock can only be affected by monotonous gravity, centuries of erosion, or extreme temperatures; in return for this insensitivity, it cannot "do" much, except resist winds, fall down a slope if pushed by something else, and so on. A housecat is both more sensitive, i.e., more vulnerable, and more powerful: it is sensitive to smaller variations in temperatures, its perseverance-in-being depends upon the availability of specific forms of food, its happiness relies on the whims of its master; in return, it can, by moving itself, act drastically to shorten the life of a mouse, protect its master from depression, make him cry, and so forth. The same parallel expansion of the power to be affected and of the power to affect is obvious when one turns to us, human beings of the twenty-first century, and when one considers how many things and people our daily lives are sensitive and exposed to, and dependent upon, as well as how many things and people can be affected by our actions (or lack thereof) worldwide. An obvious illustration of all this is provided by U.S. government foreign policies: the "super" power to affect is bound to bite the dust when it launches military expeditions that prove insufficiently sensitive to the metastable realities of the local political field it attempts to reconfigure.

This form of sensitivity, characterizing a solution that espouses (as closely as possible) the specificity of the situation it is faced with, exemplifies the bifacial association of passivity and activity I stressed earlier on. Agents' power to act effectively, their capacity to reach the goal they have intentionally set for themselves, appears to be in direct proportion with their capacity (passively) to record data provided by the situation on which they purport to act. In between the recording phase (where these data can be seen as simply impressed upon the sensory organs) and the moment when a course of action is set and put into motion, a window opens during which "the real action" can take place: not simply the carrying out of a plan, but the very devising of this plan, in light of all the data currently at their disposal. This "real action" takes place at the level that Rancière isolates as the *partage du sensible*: some data are perceived and selected as relevant, others are rejected as irrelevant, others still are simply ignored. Each time this happens, agents inherit a specific social configuration of the *partage du sensible*, which they can retransmit as it has been transmitted to them or which, following the encounter with this singular set of data, can lead them to alter it, at an infinitesimal or sometimes at a more dramatic level. This reconfiguration of the *partage du sensible* appears, within Rancière's system, as the founding moment of political subjectivation: whether I stand in front of a work of art or am involved in a social movement, the possibility of politics rests on such a moment when I am led to reconfigure the *partage du sensible* I have inherited from the majoritarian norm (along with its blind spots, its denial of rights, and its hierarchy of privileges).

FATALISM AND THE RHINOCEROS

The capacity to espouse a given situation has been seen as a major virtue by a number of philosophical traditions, most famously Eastern ones— valuing flexibility, suppleness, adaptability, openness, fluidity, dissolution of the self, all virtues culminating in the Chinese ideal of *wu-wei*, or "action through nonaction." Apart from Roland Barthes's deep interest in *wu-wei*, most notably during his *Cours du Collège de France* on "The Neutral" (1977–1978), which paved the way for a dramatically renewed articulation between aesthetics and politics, one important site of exchanges between Western thinking on agency and Chinese *wu-wei* has been provided by seventeenth-century metaphysicians like Leibniz and Spinoza. While Leibniz was explicitly interested in Eastern philosophy, the "fatalism" of Spinoza was frequently denounced as converging with "Chinese atheism." Here is not the place to study such a convergence between Leibnizianism, Spinozism, fatalism, a certain form of pantheism, and "*l'athéisme des Chinois*," but one can certainly see why such an assimilation may have taken place.[1] If the efficiency of my action is directly determined by my espousing the lines already provided by the reality on which I intend to work, then it is no longer *I* who act on this reality in order to alter it according to *my* choices and desires; I find myself in a situation where reality transforms *itself*, evolves, follows *its* own courses through my intervention. Isn't it what Spinoza suggests when he describes human beings, along with all other natural "things," as mere "modes," determined "modifications" of a substance which is the only reality endowed with the full privilege of agency? Whenever I trick myself into thinking that I (freely) act, it is, in fact, only "the substance" which unfolds itself through this part of nature that I happen to embody.

Apart from being a serious blow to humans—who, during the seventeenth century, were still proud of being God's favorite creatures—such a worldview produces a lasting discomfort that comes from the transparency to which it condemns human (non)agency. Spinoza's "free necessity"—which calls for my understanding of and voluntary adaptation to the laws of nature—suggests an ideal of (non)action in which the data from the situation would impress themselves upon my senses without any waste, would be wholly processed by my intellect, and would be directly translated into a reaction perfectly adapted to all the dimensions of the situation. The fact that Spinoza earned his living by polishing glass becomes an emblem for the ultimate goal (or danger) of his philosophy: to transform us into transparent mediations through which natural necessity expresses and follows its own course.

I know that Rancière has little patience with this type of neo-Spinozist thinking—which, in France, has been filtered through Gilles Deleuze's writings and courses on Leibniz and Spinoza. When asked in 2004 by the journal *Dissonance* to comment upon an excerpt of *Empire*, in which Hardt and Negri claim that "the great masses need a material religion of the senses," he made a series of remarks that I will now quote at length (since this interview seems never to have been published) and that I will later comment upon briefly. After noting that "Negri's philosophy becomes more and more a sort of pantheism, a great pantheism of life" and that, when interpreted through Deleuzian glasses, "the Marxist scheme is turned into a vitalist scheme," Rancière adds, "I believe that [in this neo-vitalist approach] the sphere of politics gets stuck between two things: the sphere of economics, the sphere of productive forces, and the sphere of aesthetics in the sense of a new religion, the romantic idea that the community is a sensitive community [*une communauté sensible*] of people reunited by a faith, by a belief which is shared by [*commune à*] the man of the people and the philosophers."[2]

Let me first raise the question of the relationship that we are to establish (or not) between this Negrian *communauté sensible* and the *partage du sensible*. Doesn't Rancière tell us, through his use of the latter notion, that *any* community is a *communauté sensible*, sharing a certain partition of what is to be felt, seen, noticed, respected, and taken care of (or, conversely, ignored, used, and despised)? Does the main difference between him and Negri come from the fact that the Italian philosopher emphasizes the need to form a community, to construct a platform of reunion, while the French thinker defines politics as a moment of partition, division, secession? I leave such questions open for the moment and move on to a very specific and concrete criticism raised by Rancière against *Empire*, concerning the view that this book proposes on migrations: "In *Empire*, they write about nomadic movements which break the borders within Empire. However, the nomadic movements which break Empire's borders are groups of workers who pay astronomical amounts of money to smugglers in order to get to Europe, workers who are then parked in confinement zones, waiting to be turned back. To transform this reality of displacements into anti-imperialist political movements and energies is something totally extravagant."

I read this (fairly common) criticism of *Empire* as a denunciation of the *rhinocerian danger* that looms over neo-Spinozism. From the ancient Stoics to the Chinese atheists discussed in seventeenth-century Europe to Leibnizian optimism, all forms of fatalism have been suspected of being excessively ready to *accept reality* as it is and to invent hopeful and encouraging forms of coating destined to paint over its various horrors. In the case at hand: destitute migrants following the lines of flight inscribed in the wood of our global economic imbalances *do* point the way that our understanding should, too, *follow*, in order to seize the postnational nature of politics in the global age. Fluxes of bodies crossing national borders indicate profound trends that our analysis must notice, understand by its causes, and finally use positively in our effort to reconfigure the current transformations for the better. A politics of hope finds its foundation in the Spinozian attitude asking us neither to hate (*detestari*) nor to mock (*ridere*), but to understand (*intellegere*) reality as it is. Spinoza suggests in the scholium of *Ethics* V, 10, that, "in arranging our thoughts and conceptions, we should always bear in mind that which is good in every individual thing": in spite of their untold and saddening sufferings—and even if such hardships obviously need to be alleviated, and their exploiters denounced—destitute migrants *do* put national borders under a pressure that tends to erode, in the long run, the very sustainability of the barriers that currently maintain "totally extravagant" levels of inequality among the world's populations.

Of course, as we all know, in the long run we are all dead—and poor migrants unfortunately tend to die much younger than the neo-Spinozist thinkers who try to sense "that which is good" in other people's sufferings. As a matter of fact, this hopeful acceptance of what appears as deep and irresistible trends of reality has been portrayed with remarkable accuracy in Ionesco's *Rhinoceros.* In our post–Cold War era, the play can be disengaged from its anticommunist message and become available for renewed allegorical projections, in particular as a description of our range of attitudes toward globalization, "economic rationalization," and "modernization" at large. Between Bérenger-the-loser, an all-too-human misfit, fragile and mediocre, and his friend Jean-the-achiever, eager to be well adapted, to overcome his weaknesses, and to make something out of his life, the contrast is precipitated by the irruption of rhinoceroses, who unexpectedly and randomly run rampant in the city, trampling and terrorizing people in ever greater numbers. The animals soon no longer appear as intruders but as humans transformed into monsters by a growing epidemic (traditionally read as a metaphor of the spread of Nazism in Germany or of communist conformism in Eastern European countries).

This play could be relevant in a discussion of sensitivity and Spinozism, insofar as it stages a certain form of acceptance of the given based on a certain reference to nature, both of which have long been denounced as inherent dangers looming over this philosophy. The last dialogue between Bérenger-the-loser and Jean-the-achiever, which takes place while the latter is going through his own transformation into a rhinoceros, summarizes this dimension of the play: rejecting traditional morality and asking for its replacement by nature, rejecting any reference to man and calling humanism outdated, Jean claims that he "welcomes change" and has freed himself from all the "prejudices" that portray our species as superior to the other animals. It would be very easy to read between these lines a direct parody of some of the defining theses of the *Ethics*: man in nature is no special "empire within an empire"; traditional morality and transcendental definitions of rights must be replaced by an ontology of power; definitions of the good and the bad are always relative and evolutionary; the relations between individual *conatus* are ruled by the survival of the fittest and the elimination of the misfits.

Jean's trajectory is one of refusing prejudices and accepting reality as it is: he goes with the flow and finds reasons to see this flow as a natural, inescapable, and even desirable reality, a reality in which we can find joy and reasons for hope. Of course, he does not accept it, as Spinozism would like us to do, on the basis of *a rational understanding* of the causal relations at work within this reality; he is mostly carried away by the flow, merely *rationalizing* the changes that affect him (rather than reasoning upon their emancipatory potential). (And this no doubt points to the limit of Ionesco's play: no real event inexplicably comes out of the blue like his rhinoceroses do.) But countless criticisms of *Empire* have presented it as a mere rationalization (and acceptance) of the dissolution of the (national) welfare state, of the erosion of the status of wage earners, of the overlapping of work over leisure time: isn't Negri *condoning* the shuffling around of poor workers by the inhumane laws of capitalism when he "extravagantly" presents destitute migrants as an avant-garde of the anti-imperialist struggle?

Bérenger, on the other hand, is the only character that manages *not* to become a rhinoceros until the end of the play: far from developing a higher understanding of the situation, he does so mostly by clinging to rather ridiculous, narrow-minded, and outmoded prejudices about man, his transcendent duties, and his natural rights. He just *resists* the transformation that affects the world around him, with obstinacy and desperation: he digs his heels into his memory of how things used to be before the arrival of the rhinoceroses. He refuses to adapt to the new reality that surrounds him. Of course, there is an ironical and suggestive chiasm to be read in the fact that, by being sensitive and reactive to the transformations of our world, the likes of Jean are led to become thick-skinned pachyderms, while the short-sighted and thick-spirited Bérenger perceives more clearly the mutilation imposed upon his (old-fashioned) idea of man by an adaptation to the current trends. Similarly, one is led to think that the "extravagance" of those who accept the dissolution of "the people" into mere multitudes results from the fact that their very sensitivity to the logic at work within (cognitive) capitalism tends to make them insensitive and blind to the human reality of constrained migrations.

At this point, we seem to be caught between two equally unappealing figures. On the (traditional) Left hand, we would have the dinosaurs of trade-union leaders, Communist survivors, and populist figures who blame all current social evils on globalization: like Bérenger, they cling onto unsustainable notions (like job security, national sovereignty, or the so-called *idéal républicain*), they invoke mythical entities like "the people" and dig in their heels in an attitude of pure refusal to budge. On the other hand (which we might describe either as "ultra-Left" or "cryptoliberal"), we would have the rhinoceroses of the thinkers of the multitudes: like Jean, they position themselves as sensitive and adaptable to the new reconfigurations of the given, they are ready to revise and amend their partition of the sensible, they are eager to propose new tools to understand, explain, and exploit the new state of things, in which they positively try to discover constitutive potentials for new forms of emancipation—while critics see their work as an extravagant rationalization and acceptance of new forms of alienation.

FROM THE AGENT TO THE ACTOR

Even if Rancière's general definition of politics strikes me as putting a much heavier load on an attitude of resistance, of secession, of refusal, rather than on the positive, inventive, and creative work that Negri pins down under the notion of "constitution," he largely manages to escape from this alternative between the dinosaur and the rhinoceros by opening an original line of flight in the direction of *a theatrical conception of political agency*. I find it highly significant that it is in the same interview with *Dissonance* where he denounced the "extravagance" of *Empire*'s perception of the migrants that he would articulate most clearly (to my knowledge) this theatrical conception as an alternative to the neo-Spinozist tradition emblematized by the Deleuze-Negri couple. Rancière starts by acknowledging the interest of the Deleuzian opposition between the molar and the molecular as a way to escape the limitations of preconstituted individualities and categories: the molecular approach has indeed played a major role in the aesthetic revolution that, for two centuries, has questioned any given *partage du sensible* and denounced such partitions as a mutilating "molarization" of the complexity of the molecular. Rancière rejects, however, the transposition of this "physico-aesthetic" model into the sphere of politics:

> [The authors of *Empire*] try to present [this model] as a solution to the problem of representation. The idea is to oppose to a mass, perceived as fixed in its concept, a circulating energy without subject. This is what multitude means. But the problem is that, in politics, one always creates a stage [*une scène*]. They try to avoid the theatrical model. One could almost say that they try to oppose a novelistic model of dissolved identity to the theatrical model. However, I think that politics always takes, more or less, the shape of the constitution of a theater. It means that politics always needs to constitute small worlds on which units take shape; I would call them "subjects" or "forms of subjectivation"; they stage a conflict, a litigation, an opposition between various worlds. [The thinkers of the multitude] don't want to hear about that. What they want is a world energy that breaks up masses. But this does not constitute politics, that is the problem, at least in my view.

This is how Rancière justifies his clinging onto the "old-fashioned molar concept" of "the people" and his refusal to replace it with "the molecular energy of the multitudes": *the people* "does not constitute a type of group; it is not a mass; it is purely the name of an act of subjectivation."

> For me, politics is never a question of identity; it always stages a gap [*un écart*]. When one says "we are the people," I would say precisely that "we" and "the people" are not the same thing; politics takes place in the gap

between the two. It seems to me that when they oppose the molecular to the molar, they do the contrary: they need some sort of reality for the political subject. For me, politics is the constitution of a theatrical and artificial sphere. Whereas what they really want is a stage of reality [*une scène de réalité*]. That is why they transform any migration into an act of political resistance. . . . This is the consequence of the opposition between the molecular and the molar, which in fact always draws us back to the need for a political subject that would be real, that would be a truly vital energy at work. I do not believe so: a political subject is a type of theatrical being, temporary and localized.

Rancière's escape from the trapped alternative between the dinosaur and the rhinoceros invites us to see ourselves as *actors* and to trade the vocabulary of political acts (with its implications in terms of actions and reactions, activity and passivity, proportionality between power to affect and power to be affected) for a vocabulary of political gestures. The sphere of politics thus appears as a theatrical stage rather than as a battlefield, as a matter of role-playing rather than as a matter of anticipating, espousing, and utilizing flows within an organic body.

Of course, this elegant solution is bound to sound extremely appealing to those of us who have special interests in theater, literature, and the arts. Far from studying marginal and obsolete forms of expression, we suddenly find ourselves at the very core of the essence of political action. The dinosauresque attitude which appeared earlier as one of refusal and secession, vocally denouncing the injustice of the various *mécomptes* at work but falling short of proposing creative ways to adjust our calculation to our pressing needs, this attitude is turned around, now that Rancièrian politics call us to "the constitution of a theatrical and artificial sphere" (the construction of a stage, the design of sets and costumes, the creation of gripping characters, the invention of catchy phrases and slogans).

Such a *fuite en avant* from the register of political action into the register of theatrical performance resonates well, not only with Rancière's current work on aesthetics (cinema, poetry, novel, and so on), but also with the reflection articulated around the notion of spectacle employed by Guy Debord, Jean Baudrillard, and their countless followers. During the second half of the twentieth century, technological and commercial evolutions have turned our mass-communication and mass-consumption societies upside down, inverting the primacy of reality over appearance: no longer a mere (and secondary) expression of reality, the spectacle is seen as that which gives reality its very shape and strength. From Judith Butler's sexual performativity to Peter Sloterdijk's interest in bubbles and foam, a definition of politics as theater is definitely well attuned to a major feature of our Zeitgeist.

The elegance of such theatrical politics also comes from the image of collective agency that it projects: when Rancière evokes political subjects and subjectivation, he tends to describe a world of we's rather than a world of I's. Those who end up climbing on the political stage they have constructed do not speak as individuals but as (problematic and gap-ridden) collectives. This may be a discreet but relevant implication of the opposition between the novelistic model espoused by Deleuzian neo-Spinozists and the theatrical model advanced by Rancière. The multitude tends to present itself as a mere collection of singularities, a chaotic aggregation of the type of personal trajectories described from the inside in modern novels—while the people requires in advance some form of preconstituted group structure, be it strongly organized, as in the case of a theater company, or minimally united, as in the case of a theater audience, which, in spite of its loose nature, falls into what Gabriel Tarde would have labeled a crowd rather than a dislocated public.

More generally, *les sans-parts* are always to be conjugated in the plural within Rancière's grammar: the stage is constituted only after they have managed to speak as a group—even if this group is always constituted by an inner gap, a tension between its "temporary and localized" nature and the universal claims to which it appeals. We can hence see the originality and power of the Rancièrian construct: it provides us with a theory of representation where *the representatives are the represented themselves*, even though there is a distance (a gap) between the two (justifying us in seeing this mechanism as a re-presentation, and not merely as a presence).

Theatrical politics, however, have always been haunted by an anti-model: that of the jester, who represents the voice of the kingdom's lowest subjects in the court of the prince. The fool tends to be looked upon with suspicion, due to his deeply compromised position as the outsiders' voice within the small circle of the insiders: everyone knows that, even if he manages to represent a form of critical reason at the table of the autocrat, he will be tolerated only as long as he does not transgress the threshold of what would be really subversive; his main function is not to give voice to the voiceless, but to entertain the loud laughter of the powerful. In other words, if he is to remain the court's jester, the theatrical gestures through which he may express the grievances of the subjects are bound to betray these very grievances, by the very movement that makes them audible and acceptable to the powerful. Hence the eternal complaints about the traps of representation, and other betrayals of the clerks.

Within Rancièrian theatrical politics, it is no longer a group of (un)representative jesters, but the subjects who invite themselves to play the fools at the king's table. If there is a betrayal, it will come from the ranks of the spectators rather than from those of the actors, since the latter speak for themselves. Rancière thus answers Gayatri Spivak's question: yes, within certain historical junctures, the subaltern *can* speak. These moments are relatively rare: politics, for Rancière, like thought for Deleuze and Guattari, is the exception, not the rule (which is the retransmittal of the existing police or opinion). But it has occurred in the past, and it may be in gestation around us all the time.

Subalterns, however, in Rancière's theatrical politics, never speak *directly* for themselves: it is they who speak, but they do so from under a mask that they have painted upon their face, from under a costume they have collectively designed for themselves, on a carnivalesque stage they are building with each of their interventions. This precision is crucial, because it prevents us from confusing this type of political performance with the form of popular spectacle described by Rousseau in his *Letter to d'Alembert on the Spectacles*. In Rousseau's idealization of his fatherland, the people of Geneva were a predefined collective which comes fully to coincide with itself when a troop of militia men dance in the streets, soon rejoined by joyful young women. Contrary to what happens in the traditional theater that d'Alembert and Voltaire wanted to see allowed in Geneva, the barriers between the stage and the audience, between those who actively play and those who passively watch, between those who speak and those who listen, between the bodies that are present and the characters that are represented—all these barriers vanish, only to leave a community (the people of Geneva) that has become transparent to itself. The fact that they would dance (rather than role-play) emphasizes the immediacy of this presence, which fully collapses the gap between the represented and the representative: even if their steps can be watched by a third party (in this case, Jean-Jacques and his father), their true essence and their goal remain within themselves, they are a self-realization of joy, rather than an evocation of something absent.

Through such dance steps, the militiamen and their female partners assert their identity as "the people of Geneva." Rancière takes great pain to tell us that nothing of the sort is happening in his theatrical politics. What is staged is not an identity, but *a gap* between the "we" that is speaking and "the people" in whose name this "we" purports to speak. This crucial difference takes us from the world of Rousseau's *Letter to d'Alembert* to that of Diderot's *Paradox on the Comedian*. Far from abolishing all barriers and establishing a regime of transparency, this analysis of the comedian's play advocates the erection of a barrier *within* the subjectivity of each agent. A good actor is one who manages fully to distance his person from the persona that he plays. The efficiency of acting is based not on a coincidence, but on an inner distance and a separation between the representative and the represented, even if both are located within one single body. When Diderot attempts to unfold the political implications of his theory, he focuses his attention on the figure of the courtier, which seems to throw us back into the antimodel of the jester. But in fact, he thus subverts in advance—in a very Rancièrian manner—the model of intellectual intervention in the "public sphere" that Kant and Habermas will later theorize. For Diderot, it is insufficient and naïve for the intellectual to conceive of himself as "a scholar writing for other scholars." One always speaks from a certain *position* within complex structures of social dominance and oppression, and, as a result, one always has to *pose* as *this* persona (a serious, disinterested, and rational scholar) or as *that* other persona (the fool, the activist, the despot's adviser). For Diderot also, politics is first and foremost a matter of role-playing. One is never better represented than by oneself; but one has to split oneself in two and maintain a healthy gap between both parts if one wants this self-representation to be fully effective.

The main difference between Diderot and Rancière on this point is that the latter, as we have noted above, describes a collective of actors, while the former only theorizes the behavior of individual agents. This

difference, of course, is very significant. Political agency, within Ran-
cierian theatrical politics, seems to require the constitution not only of a
theater, but also of some sort of collective company. From politics-as-
a-battlefield to politics-as-a-stage, the French language interestingly
uses the same word: *une troupe*. It is by coalescing into a theatrical
"troupe" that individual speaking bodies become a political subject,
"temporary and localized." Here again, the metaphorical field exploited
by Rancière in his theatrical model of political agency proves suggestive:
contrary to a military troop, where organization and order are always
imposed from the top down, a troupe of actors can be more open to
bottom-up forms of self-organization. Given the fact that the play of
politics is never written out in advance, such a troupe has to be conceived as an improvising collective, along the lines of models provided
by the world of modern dance or free jazz. What is at work within the
many "small worlds" of such units is a complex (and dramatically un-
derstudied) dynamics of general responsiveness, temporary guidance,
coordinative framing, opening up of free spaces for individual explora-
tions, exacerbation of singularity through common empowerment and
reciprocal stimulation.[3]

To my (incomplete) knowledge, Rancière has not (yet) attempted to
theorize and map out this dynamics of an improvising troupe, a dynamics which is nevertheless crucial to fleshing out his theatrical model
of politics—although one could of course read *The Ignorant Schoolmaster* or *Nights of Labor* as early attempts to study and understand such
collective dynamics. The question that will lead me into my conclusion
is, however, the following: should Rancière attempt to theorize the dynamics of collective improvisation on which his model of theatrical
politics implicitly relies, wouldn't he be led to fall back on the type
of molecular, vitalist, "physico-aesthetic" models he rejects in neo-
Spinozist thinkers like Deleuze and Negri?

MEMBRANE POLITICS

It would be easy (but possibly pointless) to show that a neo-Spinozist
journal like *Multitudes* spends a good many of its issues trying precisely
to map out this dynamics (for instance, in the work of Maurizio Laz-
zarato and Antonella Corsani with the coordination of the *Intermittents
du spectacle*), or to show that Diderot's theory of politics and justice

as spectacle is intricately linked to its neo-Spinozist vitalism, or even to show how Rancièrian Deleuze was when he stated, on numerous occasions (after Paul Klee), that "the people is what is missing" and that "literature has to invent this missing people."[4] In spite of Rancière's allergy to the vitalist streak of neo-Spinozism, and in spite of the traditional parochial rivalries between churchgoers of various Parisian chapels, I wonder whether Negri's "multitude" and Rancière's "people" are as incompatible as their authors, and some of their readers, seem to think. More precisely, I wonder whether their disagreements do not come from the fact that they each approach the ambivalence of the sensible from a different, but ultimately complementary, perspective.

It is obvious, as Rancière strongly stresses, that the question of representation cannot simply "dissolve" in the molecular flows of a world energy supposedly at work in the given bioeconomic processes that shape globalization. Negri himself often stressed the need to go beyond a naïve reliance on the immediate (re)actions of the multitude and the correlative need to theorize the constitution of collective agents through the actual mechanisms provided by the given "representative democracies." A Rancièrian translation would read: what stage is now to be constituted, on which the theatrical play of mass-media democracies can be best penetrated, in order to redirect its plot toward the empowerment of the people/multitude?

It seems to me equally obvious, however, that one cannot simply disregard the actual pressure of molecular bioeconomic flows in the hope that theatrical politics alone will alter the current relations of power. Migratory pressures (along with the hopes and fears that ride upon them) and productive reconfigurations (whether theorized as cognitive capitalism or under rival models) are at least as likely as theatrical politics to play a role in the reduction (or exacerbation) of our currently extravagant global inequalities. Most migrants are simultaneously displaced, exploited "workers who pay astronomical amounts of money to smugglers in order to get to Europe, workers who are then parked in confinement zones, waiting to be turned back," *and* vectors of movements and energies that *do* carry considerable potentials for "anti-imperialist political resistance." The real question is not to choose between one side of this reality and the other, but to try and see how they can be articulated with each other.

The ambivalence of the sensible discussed throughout this essay may help us make sense of the complementarity between the Rancièrian and the neo-Spinozist approach. There are at least two implicit aspects of theatrical politics that inscribe it within the Deleuzian attempt to "get out of the universe of preconstituted individualities" that Rancière identifies with the aesthetic revolution. From this point of view, the figure of the political agent as an actor tends to dissolve into two contrary directions, toward the collective reality of the troupe and toward the molecular reality of the sensible. If we follow the first direction (toward the collective), we will encounter the Deleuzian notion of *agencement*, through which he characterized his opposition to the psychoanalytical image of the unconscious as (precisely) a theater: one of the main points of the *Anti-Oedipus* was that one should not conceive of desire using the theatrical vocabulary of representation, stage, or masks, but using the constructivist vocabulary of production, fabrication, and machine. In the word *agencement* we obviously recognize *agency*, but an agency that results from *putting things and people together*, an agency that does not result from splitting oneself into two (the representative and the represented) but from connecting oneself in a specific manner to a multiplicity of exterior things. *Agencements* are, by nature, collective. The actor/agent can only act through a certain mode of connection with other actors/agents and with exterior things, as they are determined and conditioned by a specific situation, by a specific state of things. As I suggested above, it seems to me that if we take seriously the implications of the notion of *agencement*, we are likely to meet the type of vitalist questions (about the state of things: their energy, force, production, flows, economics) that Rancière rejects in the neo-Spinozist tradition. This is the "*scène de réalité*" with which the neo-Spinozist thinkers try to articulate their conception of political agency ("*le mouvement réel*," in Laurent Bove's vocabulary): it appears here simply as *the reality of the theatrical stage* of politics.

In the second direction, the figure of the actor tends to dissolve into the molecular complexity of our sensitivity. Theatrical politics draws on the active side of the *partage du sensible*, on our capacity to repartition it along slightly altered lines: we can cross-dress, we can pose as something we are not ("*Juifs allemands*," "*sans papiers*," "*intermittents*," or "*recalculés*") when we demonstrate and yell in the streets, just as we can blur the borders between music and noise when we give a concert. We should not forget, however, that we can only do so from a certain given (inherited) configuration of the *partage du sensible*, a "state of things" that preexists and largely predetermines our possible work of reconfiguration. Before taking place toward *other people* (in our cross-dressing, yelling, and demonstrating), the re-presentation takes place *within us*, within the activity that defines our sensitivity: some of the features of the situation that were present at the level of our sensory inputs are selected as relevant and manage to define the nature and quality of our behavioral output (remaining present at this secondary level), while other features are rejected as irrelevant or simply ignored (and become absent at this secondary level).

Since our initial question is that of agency, I would like to suggest that if anything can be seen as active in us, it is at the precise stage of this selective re-presentation that it should be located. In other words: it is in the process through which certain data perceived by our sensory apparatus get to be considered as relevant, and make it to the point where they become a deciding factor in the determination of our future behaviors (while other comparable data get lost along the way), it is in this process that we can be said to become agents (political or otherwise). This selective re-presentation thus appears as a way to manage a situation of excess: there are too many data in our sensory input for us to give an exhaustive account of all the features. Not everything can count; any given state of things carries an excess, which our perceptual and intellectual faculties do not allow us to absorb and digest in its multifarious wealth, and most aspects of a situation must be discounted.

I find it significant that such issues of accounting (of counts, excesses, miscounts, and discounts) play a pivotal role in the manner Rancière recently articulated political disagreement (*la mésentente politique*) with literary misunderstanding (*le malentendu littéraire*).

> Literature has to do with democracy, not as "the reign of the masses," but as an excess in the relation between bodies and words. Democracy is first and foremost the invention of words through which those who do not count get to be counted, thus blurring the well-ordered partition of speech and silence which constitutes the community as a "harmonious animal," an organic totality. . . . Political disagreement and literary misunderstanding both take to task an aspect of this consensual paradigm which establishes a proportion between words and things. The disagreement invents names, enunciations,

arguments, and demonstrations which institute new collectives, in which anybody can be counted to the account of the discounted. The [*literary*] misunderstanding works on the relation and on the counting from yet another side, suspending the forms of individuality through which the consensual logic attaches meaning to bodies. Politics works on the whole, literature works on the parts.[5]

By its very nature, any *partage du sensible* consists of counting in certain features of a state of things, and of leaving out others. The spectacular gestures of reconfiguration enacted on the political or literary stage merely repeat, on a large scale, the type of minute reconfigurations that are performed at the molecular level when we process sensory data into affective or intellectual perceptions. The "consensual paradigm of a proportion between words and things," as well as the uncovering of an excess from one to the other, find their roots in the gap between the superabundance of features provided by any state of things and our limited capacity (and need) to count some in. Political subjectivation and aesthetic creation both rely on the same mechanism of selective re-presentation.[6]

By locating agency within this moment of selective re-presentation, I may be suspected of falling back on a very un-Spinozist equation between agency and choice—with the implicit metaphysics of free will that usually accompany this notion in our liberal tradition. In order to rule out such interpretations, it should suffice to say that the type of selection and filtering I have described above is best illustrated by the simple workings of a membrane: even if things are, of course, infinitely more complex in the case of human agents than in the case of fuel cells, such mechanisms can generally be described without making any reference to the will (free or not).

In membrane politics, the emphasis is placed less on the moment of expression, as we currently do by seeing the author as the real agent at work in the text, than on the moment of filtering, which would bring to the foreground the active role played by the reader in the actual efficiency of textual communication. For, as we all realize by now, it is the interpreter who selects, from among the superabundant potential meanings conveyed by the text, which ones are to be counted as relevant, which ones are to be discounted, and which ones he will take no account of. As we also know, in this active work of partition of the (textual) sensible, a great deal of the criteria determining these selections are bound to remain beyond the grasp of the reader's intentional will—a fact which should not necessarily undermine the value of the reader's agency. What matters is the quality of the output (the interpretation, the meaning constructed in the text) in its capacity to improve upon the current partition between what counts and what doesn't.

Such reversals could lead to a dramatic reconfiguration of our *partage du sensible*: would it be truly revolutionary, totally extravagant, or merely obvious to locate political agency in the figure of the inventive reader rather than in the politician who yells the same empty slogans meeting after meeting? Doesn't our everyday experience already tell us that the curator matters more than the artists in shaping what modern art really is? That a few popular DJs, even if they never open their mouths or turn up their microphones, have a more decisive impact on a generation's musical tastes than the countless musicians who stomp their feet behind the highly selective doors of commercial radio? That, by filtering which news is fit to broadcast, TV anchor men often have more power than heads of state when it comes to steering national political debates?

Should we say that all such operators of selection work within the register of what Rancière calls "police" and therefore remain outside of the exceptional sphere of politics? Judging by their current submissive behavior, they certainly do. But shouldn't we allow for their position to be at least potentially political, should they one day decide to throw a monkey wrench into "the consensual paradigm which establishes a proportion between words and things" (by venturing outside of their usual playlist)? Another type of political agency takes shape, where the main form of activity does not so much consist in taking on a role or in constituting a theatrical stage as it does in *shifting modalities of selection* without necessarily opening one's mouth, or without even walking onstage. Unglamorous as they may be, unafraid of remaining in the darkness of remote control rooms, such membrane politics may nevertheless deserve to appear on our theoretical radars—as they might be more true to the humble and discreet poses apparently favored by the people of the twenty-first century.

9.

Staging Equality: Rancière's Theatrocracy and the Limits of Anarchic Equality

PETER HALLWARD

Against all those who argue that only the appropriately educated or privileged are authorized to think and speak, Jacques Rancière's most fundamental assumption is that everyone thinks. Everyone shares equal powers of speech and thought, and this "equality is not a goal to be attained but a point of departure, a supposition to be maintained in all circumstances."[1]

In most of the work he undertook during the 1970s and 1980s, Rancière defended this supposition through a painstaking reconstruction of the subversive and elusive world of working-class intellectual production that thrived in the years (the 1830s and 1840s) immediately preceding the Marxist interpretation of class struggle. In much of his subsequent work, he has pondered its implications in fields ranging from historiography to aesthetics (*The Names of History* [1991]; *La Malaise dans l'esthétique* [2004]) and from political to literary theory (*Disagreement* [1995]; *La parole muette* [1998]). The most significant and consistent of these implications is essentially anarchic. As Rancière affirms it, equality is not the result of a fairer distribution of social functions or places so much as the immediate disruption of any such distribution. Equality refers not to place but to the placeless or the out of place, not to class but to the unclassifiable or the out of class. "The essence of equality is not so much to unify as to declassify, to undo the supposed naturalness of orders and replace it with controversial figures of division. Equality is the power of inconsistent, disintegrative and ever-replayed division."[2]

The basic argument that recurs throughout Rancière's work is thus one that pits the presumptions of a disruptive equality against the advocates of an orderly, hierarchical inequality. Rancière's most general effort has always been to explore the various resources of displacement, indistinction, de-differentiation, or de-qualification that are available in any given field. That "everyone thinks" means that they think in the absence of any necessary link between who they are and the roles they perform or the places they occupy; everyone thinks through the freedom of their own self-disassociation. No one is defined by the forms of thoughtless necessity to which they are subjected. On this score, at least, Rancière's point of departure isn't very far from Sartre's familiar account of conscious freedom as indeterminate being for itself: that is, as a way of being that "must be what it is not and not be what it is."[3]

Of the several situations in which Rancière has defended his anarchic conception of equality, perhaps none is more fundamental and illuminating than that of theater—theater in both the literal and metaphorical senses of the term. Rather than a principle of order or distribution, Rancière presents equality precisely as a pure "supposition that must be verified continuously—a verification or an enactment that opens specific *stages* of equality, stages that are built by crossing boundaries and interconnecting forms and levels of discourse and spheres of experience."[4] As Rancière describes it, thinking is more a matter of improvisation than it is one of deduction, decision, or direction. Every thinking has its stage or *scène*, every thinker "plays" or acts in the theatrical sense. Every political subject is first and foremost "a sort of local and provisional theatrical configuration."[5]

The thematics of the stage is certainly omnipresent in Rancière's work. Back in the mid-1970s, *Révoltes Logiques* had already adopted as its point of departure the assumption that, rather than a matter of "popular savagery" or "historical necessity," revolt is first and foremost "a staging of reasons and ways of speaking."⁶ In line with this definition Rancière went on, in *Dis-agreement*, to define politics as a matter of "performing or playing, in the theatrical sense of the word, the gap between a place where the *dēmos* exists and a place where it does not. . . . Politics consists in playing or acting out [*interpréter*] this relationship, which means first setting it up as theater, inventing the argument, in the double logical and dramatic sense of the term, connecting the unconnected."⁷ Before it is a matter of representative institutions, legal procedures, or militant organizations, politics is a matter of building a stage and sustaining a spectacle or show. Politics is the contingent dramatization of a disruptive equality, the unauthorized and impromptu improvisation of a democratic voice. As Rancière puts it in a recent interview, in which he accounts for his critical distance from Negri and Hardt, "Politics is always about creating a stage, . . . politics always takes the form, more or less, of the establishment of a theater. This means that politics always needs to establish those little worlds in which . . . forms of subjectivation can take shape and stage or enact [*mettre en scène*] a conflict, a dispute, an opposition between worlds. For me, politics is about the establishment of a theatrical and artificial sphere. Whereas what they [Negri and Hardt] are after, in the end, is a stage of reality as such.⁸

In what follows, I will try to tease out the several ways in which this theatrical metaphor helps illuminate Rancière's conception of equality and politics before considering, in my conclusion, some of the more obvious difficulties posed by such a conception.

I

The point of departure here, as in so much of Rancière's work, is the inversion of a Platonic position. It isn't difficult to see why Rancière has always been deeply critical of Plato. Plato is the great theorist of an orderly distribution of exclusive functions and roles, the advocate of a world in which each individual says only "one thing at a time." In Plato's *Republic*, to each kind of person there is but one allotted task: labor, war, or thought. Consumed by what they make or do, artisans are defined by identification with their functional place; by the same token they are excluded from those domains of "play, deception, and appearance" that Plato reserves for the exclusive enjoyment of nobility.⁹ Furthermore, as

Rancière has often pointed out, "the exclusion of a public scene of the *dēmos* and the exclusion of the theatrical form are strictly interconnected in Plato's *Republic*." For one and the same reason, Plato excludes both politics and art, "both the idea of a capacity of the artisans to be 'elsewhere' than at their 'own' workplace and the possibility for poets or actors to play another identity than their 'own' identity."[10]

The theater evoked in *The Republic* is a place where people who should know better get swept up in the irrational enthusiasm of the crowd. A gratuitous celebration of pure artifice, theater promotes semblance and appearance over dispassionate truth. It privileges the more "easily imitated . . . passionate and fitful temper" over reason. It allows the "rebellious principle" to prevail over "wise and calm" deliberation.[11] The decadent theatrocracy that Plato criticizes in book 3 of the *Laws* is a regime of unlicensed ignorance and disorder which has its source in a "universal confusion of musical forms" initiated by irresponsible artists. Such confusion "inspired the multitude with contempt of musical law, and a conceit of their own competence as judges," and "once silent audiences . . . found a voice, in the persuasion that they understand what is good and bad in art; the old 'sovereignty of the best' in that sphere has given way to an evil 'sovereignty of the audience,' a theatrocracy [*theatrokratia*]."[12] The Athenian in Plato's dialogue anticipates the probable consequence of this new popular freedom: soon the people will begin to ignore the authority of their elders and betters and then seek "to escape obedience to the law. And when that goal is all but reached, [there will follow] contempt for oaths, for the plighted word, and for all religion. The spectacle of the Titanic nature of which our old legends speak is re-enacted; man returns to the old condition of a hell of unending misery."[13]

The basis for this anarchic catastrophe lies in the threatening duplicity of mimesis per se. As Plato describes them, the mimetic poets "set up in each individual soul a vicious constitution by fashioning phantoms far removed from reality, and by currying favor with the senseless element that cannot distinguish the greater from the less, but calls the same thing now one, now the other."[14] For before it condemns the immoral and decadent effect of fables, as Rancière notes, "the Platonic proscription of the poets is grounded on the impossibility of doing two things at once."[15] By doing two things at once, by refusing to speak in their own name, by acting at a distance from themselves or by imitating the action of another, actors and poets threaten the very foundations of authority itself. Mimesis confounds the order of function and place, and thus opens the door to what Rancière will elsewhere describe as the virtual program of politics as such: "the indetermination of identities, the delegitimation of speaking positions, the deregulation of divisions of space and time."[16] Theater is nothing other than the place in which such vicious indifference to functional place takes on its most seductive shape.[17] As a bulwark to this disorderly improvisation, Plato will oppose the choreographed performance of communal unity and discipline; a similar logic will recur again and again in subsequent theories of orderly political performance, from Jean-Jacques Rousseau to Ngugi wa Thiongo.[18]

On the relatively rare occasions when Rancière addresses the question of theatrical performance directly, his concern is to liberate it from this choreography and all that goes with it. He addresses the relation of performer and spectator in terms illuminated by the theory of equality he adapts, in *The Ignorant Schoolmaster* (1987), from the maverick nineteenth-century pedagogue Joseph Jacotot. Jacotot's simple premise is that "all people are virtually capable of understanding what others have done and understood."[19] Everyone has the same intelligence, and differences in knowledge are simply a matter of opportunity and motivation. On the basis of this assumption, superior knowledge ceases to be a necessary qualification of the teacher, just as the process of explanation (together with metaphors that distinguish students as slow or quick, that conceive of educational time in terms of progress, training, qualification, and so on) ceases to be an integral part of teaching.

Applied to the theater, Jacotot's premise allows Rancière to develop a general account of the "emancipation of the spectator."[20] Classical theorists of the theater, from Plato to Rousseau, considered spectators to be trapped both by their passivity (in contrast with the performer's activity) and their ignorance (in contrast with the performer's knowledge of artistry and illusion). The modern response has most often been to explore the potential of a "theater without spectatorship"—a *drama* purged of passivity and ignorance, either by maximizing the distance between spectacle and spectator (Brecht) or by minimizing it (Artaud). Along the same lines, Debord, after defining spectacle by its externality, was to call for the elimination of all theatrical "separation" or distance. These and comparable responses maintain, however, the basic structure upon which specular inequality depends—the hierarchy of passivity and activity, of "*incapacity* on one side and *capacity* on the other." In contrast, theatrical "emancipation starts from the opposite principle, the principle of equality. It begins when we dismiss the opposition between looking and acting," when we realize that "looking also is an action which confirms or modifies the distribution of the visible, and that 'interpreting the world' is already a means of transforming it, of reconfiguring it. Spectators are active, as are students or scientists: they observe, select, compare, interpret. They relate what they observe with many other things that they have observed, on other stages, in other kind of spaces. They make their own poems with the poem that is performed in front of them."[21]

In theater as much as in politics or art, the distance of the spectacle is essential to its effect. It is because the spectators never wholly identify with what they see, because they draw on their own experiences, because they retain a critical distance, that they are able actively and knowingly to engage with the spectacle. What they see is never simply what the performers present or intend. Spectators "pay attention to the performance to the extent that they are distant." Just as educational emancipation does not involve the transformation of ignorance into knowledge, so too the emancipation of spectators does not involve their conversion into actors so much as a recognition that the boundary between actor and spectator is itself elusive. What we have to acknowledge is that "any spectator already is an actor of his or her own story and that the actor also is the spectator of the same kind of story." By the same token, Rancière's account of social emancipation begins when an actor hitherto condemned to an oppressively definite role (a life defined by exploitation and toil) wrests the privilege of leisure and autonomy typically enjoyed by a spectator (the luxuries of unprofitable time, of "idle" contemplation, of individual or idiosyncratic taste) and thereby changes the general distribution of functions and roles. "This is what emancipation means: the blurring of the opposition between they who look and they who act," between those who are trapped by their function or identity and those who are not.[22]

Rancière's position here bears more than a passing resemblance to the central concern of his contemporary, Philippe Lacoue-Labarthe. For both thinkers, the political is not grounded in a positive human property or way of life, but rather in a more primordial impropriety or lack of foundation.[23] "The subject of mimesis," as Lacoue-Labarthe explains, "is nothing in itself, strictly 'without qualities,' and able for this reason to 'play any role': it has no being of its own." Every "imitation is a depropriation," the dissolution of a "proper" identity, type, or myth.[24] If Plato is especially hostile to theater, it is because those who speak on the stage do not speak in their own name and do not identify with or authenticate what they say: because they behave as what Rancière will describe as *political* actors. Politics, as Rancière defines it, is the process that authorizes the exercise of power by those with no sanctioned authorization or authority. Politics is the process that founds the power to govern other people on nothing other than "the absence of any foundation."[25]

II

In a couple of his contributions to *Révoltes Logiques*, Rancière explores and attacks the logic behind successive plans, in the second half of the nineteenth century, for "a theater of the people." Michelet defends his version of a *théâtre du peuple* in line with Plato's original presumption: "The customs of the theater are what shape the laws of democracy. The essence of democracy is theatrocracy." But Michelet inverts Plato's meaning. Whereas "theatrocracy was for Plato the noise of the mob that applauds itself as it applauds its actors, for Michelet it is a thinking community founded upon the very essence of popular theater." Such a theater operates like a "mirror in which the people observe their own actions," through a "performance without separation in which the engaged citizen writes and enacts his own victories"[26]

We might say that Rancière, no less than Michelet, also agrees with Plato—but rather than invert his interpretation, he revalues it. Rancière's theatrocracy is another untutored expression of the people, but, unlike Michelet's, it is one that proceeds with a maximum of separation, at a maximum distance from the community's sense of itself.

More precisely, Rancière's conception of equality might be considered theatrocratic in at least seven overlapping respects.

1. It is "spectacular." Every verification of equality is part and parcel of what Rancière routinely calls a reconfiguration of the perceptible, a repartition of the sensible and in particular of the visible. Equality is here a matter of a *visible* anonymity (a qualification which suffices, all

by itself, to distinguish Rancière's conception of politics from Alain Badiou's emphasis on the strictly indiscernible status of a generic inconsistency). Rancièrian politics generally begins with a demonstration or *manifestation* of the people. "The essential work of politics is the configuration of its own space. It is to get the world of its subjects and its operations to be seen."[27] Against any *misérabiliste* conception of politics—any account which, like that of Hannah Arendt, assumes that the misfortune of the poor lies is their being unseen, in their exclusion from the political stage—Rancière notes, "all my work on workers' emancipation showed that the most prominent of the claims put forward by the workers and the poor was precisely the claim to visibility, a will to enter the political realm of appearance, the affirmation of a capacity for appearance."[28] There is politics most obviously when people come out to demonstrate in the street. When crowds form in Rancière's work, it generally isn't (as with Sartre) in order to storm the Bastille or its contemporary equivalents; they come together to stage the process of their own disaggregation.

By the same token, the counterpolitical action of what Rancière calls the "police" is antispectacular first and foremost. Against Althusser, Rancière insists that "police intervention in public spaces does not consist primarily in the interpellation of demonstrators but in the breaking up of demonstrations." Rather than solicit a submissive subjective recognition or response, the police dismantle political stages by telling would-be spectators that there is nothing to watch. They point out "the obviousness of what there is, or rather, of what there isn't: 'Move along! There is nothing to see here!'"[29] Whereas political actors turn streets into stages, the police reestablish the smooth circulation of traffic.

2. It is artificial. Like any spectacle, a political sequence flaunts its artificiality. Politics is a masquerade without foundation, the performance of an antinature. A political subject is someone who acts out the principle of equality and in-difference, who plays the role of those who have no role, who takes on the costume of those who have nothing to wear. As a general principle, Rancière believes that "it is in the moments when the real world wavers and seems to reel into mere appearance, more than in the slow accumulation of day-to-day experiences, that it becomes possible to form a judgement about the world."[30] It is in such moments that Rancière's critique of the theoreticism he associates with Althusser, and with the Marxist tradition more generally, acquires its most compelling force. From Kautsky to Althusser, theoretical authority has maintained that "the masses live in a state of illusion," that workers or "producers are incapable of thinking through the conditions of their production" and domination.[31] Rancière's political actors invert both principles: it is because they know exactly what they are doing that the people are likewise the true masters of illusion and appearance.

3. It privileges multiplicity over unity. A theatrocratic democracy is never monological for the simple reason that "there is no voice of the people. There are scattered voices and polemics which in each instance divide the identity that they stage [*qu'elles mettent en scène*]."[32] For the same reason, there is not one form of emancipatory knowledge but several, not one logic of capital but various "different discursive strategies which respond to different problems" in different situations.[33]

4. It is disruptive. Peopled by multiple voices, the theater is likewise the privileged place for a more general displacement. Theater is a place for the out of place. Every theatrical experience undermines the great police project, which is also the ambition of historians and sociologists—the ambition to see people properly "rooted in their place and time."[34] Hence the exemplary importance of those *théâtres du cœur* in mid-nineteenth-century Paris, to which Rancière devoted two substantial articles in *Révoltes Logiques*.[35] A place that suspends conventional relations of obedience or deference, the theater haunts the embattled bourgeoisie of the 1840s as a doubly subversive locale. On the one hand, it is a place in which the "dreams of mutant minorities" can be acted out in fantasmatic form. On the other hand, the material "division of the stalls" turns them into a space of immoral collisions and collusions, a place in which apprentice tailors might pose as "dandies from the world of fashion" and where respectably married men can fall under the ephemeral spell of harlots and actresses. In partial anticipation of those political spectacles which take shape in February and June 1848, these crowded theaters offer a nightly reminder of the fact that only "an uncertain line separates the seated bourgeois audience members from the people standing in their 'little places,' places which aren't proper places." As Rancière presents it, everything about this theatrical experience, from the time wasted in jostling queues through to the impulsive responses of untutored audiences, contributes to its troubling confusion of reality and fiction.[36]

It would not take Napoleon's censors long to devise a defense against this threat, a defense which continues to serve as the guiding principle for cultural counterinsurgency to this day. First and foremost, audience members were fixed in their appropriate place, in a reserved seat, like so many temporary owners of property. At the same time, the theater was safely purged of its working-class spectators, spectators whose time was to be ever more intensively consumed by their economic function alone. Then, in the space thus emptied, new theaters *for* the people could be established on the basis of a dual illusion—that the people, at a folkloric distance from bourgeois culture, are both "spontaneously theatrical" and in need of more deliberate cultivation.[37] The goal is to eliminate any element of spontaneity or improvisation, to reduce every *lieu de spectacle* to spaces in which texts or music are merely performed, in which "nothing happens, in which actors or singers simply execute their roles and their audiences simply consume them."[38] The process will accelerate, of course, with the subsequent invention of the gramophone, of television, and of the attendant management of culture as a commodity for passive and primarily domestic consumption.[39]

5. Its performance is contingent. Every theatrocratic act is of and by, but never "for," the people. Every theatrical or political sequence must invent its own stage. "Politics has no 'proper' place nor does it possess any 'natural' subjects. . . . Political demonstrations are thus always of the moment and their subjects are always precarious and provisional."[40] Democracy is itself nothing other than the power exercised by the unqualified or unauthorized—the power of those who are not *entitled* (by birth, privilege, or expertise) to wield power.[41] This is why Rancièrian politics cannot be accounted for in terms of antagonisms, interest groups, or communication. The model of communicative action "presupposes the partners in communicative exchange to be preconstituted. . . . By contrast, the particular feature of political dissensus is that the partners are no more constituted than is the object or the very stage of discussion."[42]

6. It tends toward improvisation. An art which only won its autonomy through the successive forms of its "impurification—stagings of texts and stagings of props, boxing rings, circus rings, symbolist or biomechanical choreographies," theater is never more theatrical than when it subordinates direction to improvisation, choreography to free play.[43] Such is the enduring lesson of that great manifesto of Rancière's aesthetico-democratic regime, Schiller's *Letters on the Aesthetic Education of Man*. According to Schiller's conception of things, "man is only wholly Man when he plays": in other words when he suspends any effort to impose a direct conceptual or physical mastery on people or things.[44] If in Schiller's famous account the statue of the Juno Ludovisi "has the characteristic of divinity that is nothing less than the characteristic of the human being's full humanity," it is because, notes Rancière, "she does not work, she plays. She neither yields, nor resists. She is free from the links of will and obedience." She is free from the whole regulation of function and place.[45] Though Schiller has other forms of play in mind, there is no better example of this logic than that of playing a role or acting a part. Like the actresses who populate the fictions of Balzac and Nerval, Schiller's goddess attracts through her very inaccessibility: it is the elusive element of play *as such* that evades mastery or confinement.

7. It operates within a liminal configuration. This "excessive" relation of actor to role is one of the clearest instances of perhaps the most characteristic logical configuration in all of Rancière's work, the logic whereby a given term X is precisely that which indiscerns the difference between X and non-X. In the aesthetic regime, for example, postclassical art is that which blurs the difference between art and non-art. At the dawn of the modern democratic age, working-class speech blurs the difference between workers and nonworkers. A genuine teacher seeks to blur the difference between teacher and student, and so on.

Political performance likewise takes place in the gap between two extremes, and it ends when the performers identify with either pole. On the one hand, there are the actors themselves, and action in its direct and unmediated state. A theater in which the actors identify with themselves in an "art without representation," an art that simply expresses or prolongs the working life of its performers, was precisely the dream that inspired most of those who, like Maurice Pottecher, worked at the turn of the century to develop popular theater as a theater of the familiar, the natural, and the sincere.[46] A similar inspiration lies behind the meta-political rejection, which Rancière associates with Marx, of any mimetic gap between reality and representation or appearance, any ideological distance between words and things or between people and roles.[47] On the other hand, there is the role to be played, pure *play* uncontaminated by the grubby complexities of context or personality. Michelet's heroic theater, for example, takes this second pole as its exclusive guide. "What is theater?" he asks. It is "the abdication of the actual person, and his interests, in favor of a more advantageous role."[48] Already at work in the archi-politics that Rancière associates with Plato, variations on this theme will continue to dominate political philosophy from Arendt and Strauss through to the revival, in France, of a "purely political" space in the 1980s, a republican space in which public actors are meant to play exclusively civic roles. A similar pairing of extremes recurs in Rancière's conception of the aesthetic regime of art, itself a fragile liminal state balanced between tendencies either to collapse the difference between art and non-art (as anticipated in post-Hegelian visions of a life lived as art, or as embraced in the more mundane celebrations of a "relational aesthetics") or else to reify the gap between art and life (as affirmed by Greenberg's purified modernism, or by Lyotard's confinement of artistic representation to the domain of the sublime or unrepresentable).[49]

A theatrocratic conception of equality can only proceed, in short, if its actors remain other but not *absolutely* other than themselves. They must adopt the artifice of an "unnatural" role, but not identify with it. The only place they can occupy is the one between themselves and their role—between Rousseau's sincerity and Diderot's technique. Politics is extinguished when the distance between actor and role collapses into a paranoid and definitive immediacy. Precisely this tendency figures as the salient characteristic of what Rancière describes as the pseudopolitics of our present "ethical" or "nihilistic" age. Universal humanity in this postpolitical era can play no role other than that of universal victim or humanitarian object, whose rights are no longer experienced as political capacities. "The predicates 'human' and 'human rights' are simply attributed, without any phrasing, without any mediation, to their eligible party, the subject 'man.' The age of the 'humanitarian' is one of immediate identity between the ordinary example of suffering humanity and the plenitude of the subject of humanity and its rights."[50]

III

Rancière's axiomatic conception of equality rightly affirms the primacy of subjective commitment as the basis of emancipatory politics. Along with the still more axiomatic notion of emancipation affirmed by his erstwhile colleague (and critic) Alain Badiou, in my opinion it is one of the most significant and inspiring contributions to contemporary political philosophy. Its broadly theatrocratic configuration raises, however, a number of immediate concerns.

First and foremost, its effects are unabashedly sporadic and intermittent. Rancière himself is the first to emphasize this point: political sequences by their very nature are rare and ephemeral. Once the stage is struck, little or nothing remains. An improvisational sequence is difficult to sustain as a matter of course.[51] This is a limitation Rancière accepts along with Badiou and the later Sartre. What's missing is an appreciation of political determination or will.[52] What's missing is an equivalent for what Badiou calls "forcing" (that is, the power of a political sequence to impose measurable change upon the configuration of a situation). What's missing is an acknowledgement of the incremental aspect of even so intermittent and disruptive a conception of poor people's movements as the one famously developed by Frances Fox Piven and Richard Cloward.[53] Like Rancière, Piven and Cloward privilege the direct disruption of the status quo over the development of stable if not bureaucratic means of organization (trade unions, political parties, social movements) that are easily accommodated within the prevailing order of things. "A placid poor get nothing, but a turbulent poor sometimes get something."[54] Unlike Rancière, however, Piven and Cloward pay at least some attention to the question of how to hang on to such gains and how to use them to enhance a capacity to make additional gains. They allow for at least some consideration of questions of strategic continuity. Rancière, by contrast, offers little systematic justification for his assumption that the politics of emancipation must or should always proceed by means of disidentification and disassociation.

This leads to a second problem. To what extent is a politics conceived as the suspension of the police a politics based on the primacy of the observer, on what can be *seen* of mass mobilization? Can a so insistently staged conception of politics retain sufficient critical distance from the accommodating logic of a society that has long been organized, as everyone knows, as a society of the spectacle? To what extent does a popular "becoming-spectator" retain a genuine critical edge? To what extent is today's dominant police order, the liberal republican state, genuinely vulnerable to theatrocratic attack? To what extent does Rancière's conception of equality remain a merely transgressive one, and thus condemned to a variant of that same dialectic of dependence, provocation, and exhaustion which he diagnoses so effectively in the logics of modernism and postmodernism? Or to put this objection another way: has Rancière developed an appropriately contemporary response to that deflection of politics he calls "para-politics" and that he traces, historically, to Aristotle?

For rather than Plato, it is really Aristotle who is Rancière's most significant adversary. In both politics and aesthetics, Aristotle is the person who devises a way of containing and disarming the threats first identified by Plato. To the threat of mimetic duplicity, Aristotle responds with what will become the classical or "representative regime of art," the association of mimesis with a particular *tekhnç* and hence with a more sophisticated basis for the purity of art, the hierarchy of genres, and the reign of the *bienséances*.[55] To the threat of democratic disorder, the Aristotelian response (Rancière's modern examples include Tocqueville, Jules Ferry, Strauss, Arendt, and Renaut) is to seek the political incorporation of the people's excess—the part of those who have no part—through the controlled supervision of appropriately managed institutions. The result guarantees the deference, if not absence, of the people themselves in a dispersed, "corrected" democracy.[56] It is no accident that the sort of state which is most tolerant of the sort of theatrocratic disruption that Rancière equates with politics (because it is most secure against it) is precisely that liberal constitutional state whose origins go back to Aristotle's *Politics*. Rancière's rejoinder is to return, in effect, more or less directly to a revalued version of the Platonic diagnosis. Mimesis and democracy regain their subversive force, but in an affirmative rather than derogatory mode.

The question is whether such a move can do much to disrupt today's forms of para-political counterinsurgency. It is worth comparing Rancière's position on this score with that of another more conventional advocate of neoanarchist equality, Noam Chomsky. Like Chomsky, Rancière recognizes that the contemporary context for the question "does democracy mean anything?" began to take shape in the mid-1970s, at the time when the Trilateral Commission solicited its symptomatic report on *The Crisis of Democracy*.[57] And Chomsky would agree with Rancière, that democratic politics always involves the suspension of police power, the disqualification of authority, the equality of "anyone with anyone." But what for Rancière is a sort of conclusion is for Chomsky only a point of departure. The active renewal of democracy proceeds through direct engagement with those developments which have allowed wealthy elites, over the past couple of decades, to weather and then disarm the threat of widespread popular participation in politics: wholesale privatization, the global imposition of structural adjustment, the coordination of transnational finance, rampant consumerism, media compliance, the politics of debt, fear, security, and so on.[58] Rancière, by contrast, came to embrace the rhetoric of mobility and liminality at precisely the time when newly mobile, newly fragmentary post-Taylorist forms of production would deprive them of any clear critical purchase. Rancière developed his account of the interstitial and the out-of-place at a time when, as Marshal McLuhan famously pointed out, there has long been no slogan "further from the spirit of the new technology than 'a place for everything and everything in its place.' "[59]

Now it is a short step from a salutary insistence on our relational liminality to a potentially crippling emphasis on the indeterminate or in-between as such. Rancière defines the democratic or political community as "a community of interruptions, fractures, irregular and local, through which egalitarian logic comes and divides the police community from itself. It is a community of worlds in community that are intervals of subjectification: intervals constructed between identities, between spaces and places. Political being-together is a being-between: between identities, between worlds . . . , between several names, several identities"[60] Rancière overestimates, perhaps, the distance between such positions and the postmodern posture that he appears to oppose. It's far from clear that the resources of the *interval* as such can give effective analytical purchase on the forms of relation (relations of oppression, exploitation, representation, and so on, but also of solidarity, cooperation, empowerment) that shape any particular situation. Rancière is not interested, as a rule, in the domain of theater or anywhere else, in the group dynamics of collective mobilization, determination, or empowerment: the model in each case is provided by the isolated process of intellectual *self*-emancipation.[61] In Rancière's work, as in the work of so many of his contemporaries, relation itself often figures as *essentially* binding, as irredeemably contaminated by mastery and the social weight of domination.[62] Along with his mentor Joseph Jacotot, Rancière conceives of equality as independent of social mediation—in Jacotot's terms, the rational equality of *people* is fundamentally incompatible with the necessary inequality of *citizens* and the unreason of society. In the absence of such mediation, however, Rancière's trenchant egalitarianism seems all too compatible with a certain degree of social resignation.[63] Politics here is less about struggle and fidelity than it is about "sporadic" discussion, improvisation and "infidelity."[64] For Rancière, politics is a matter of acknowledging a generalized disauthorization or delegitimation more than it is a matter of participating in antagonistic processes whereby people come to be newly authorized by a militant affirmation of principle. In short, Rancière's emphasis on division and interruption makes it difficult to account for qualities that are just as fundamental to any sustainable political sequence: organization, simplification, mobilization, decision, polarization, taking sides, and so forth.[65]

In particular (and this is a third problem with the theatrocratic account), Rancière's relative indifference to questions of organization and decision leaves little place for direct engagement with the issues that pose the most obvious challenge to his egalitarian stance—issues bound up with the forms of knowledge, skill, or mastery required for effective political action as much as for artistic innovation or appreciation. No doubt nothing is more theatrical than purely improvised work, but by the same token there is no form of theater (to say nothing of music) that requires more skill or experience. The blurring of art and non-art, the idea that everything could be the subject or material of art, was made possible through unprecedented technical virtuosity—it is precisely Flaubert's conception of "style as an absolute way of seeing" that allows him so radically to democratize the seeing of art. When Rancière reads Flaubert or Mallarmé, he is generally less interested in matters of writing or technique (Flaubert and the *artisanat du style*) than in content or themes (Mallarmé as disenchanted poet of our worldly abode).

Rancière's more general answer to questions about knowledge, science, or skill has long been one of indifference or impatience, as if the only available alternative to the extreme scientism he embraced in his youth is an almost equally extreme antiscientism. Politics, as Rancière understands it, appears to suspend *all* forms of authority or authorization. He assumes as a matter of course—against Plato, Arendt, and other advocates of political privilege—that "the appearance of the *dēmos* shatters any division between those who are deemed able and those who are not."[66] But is the old relation of theory and praxis so easily resolved? Does political action no longer need to be informed by a detailed understanding of how the contemporary world works, how exploitation operates, how transnational corporations go about their business? "We already know all this," Rancière tends to say: everyone has always understood the way they are exploited or oppressed.

As it happens, however, according to Rancière's conception of things there is no clear way of knowing what people may know, since what matters is less the knowledge itself than it is the posture of mastery presumed in any claim to knowledge.[67] At the heart of Rancière's long polemic with Bourdieu is an assumption that knowledge is simply there for the taking, on the model of primary language learning. "As far as human societies are concerned," Rancière/Jacotot maintain, "it's always a matter of learning a language" or using a familiar tool[68]; on this basis, most of the problems of access, empowerment, and validation that Bourdieu explores in his analysis of the configuration of various fields (artistic, scientific, educational) can be more or less dismissed in advance.

The political price to be paid for this indifference to knowledge is prohibitively high. Although Rancière offers a brilliant account of the *enthusiasm* that accompanies and often inspires a political sequence, he neglects many of the more intractable problems of organizing and sustaining such a sequence. This neglect isn't a matter of ignorance. Rancière often draws attention to one of the most insistent features of the emergence, in the nineteenth century, of the modern, postartisanal working class: the confrontation with industrial mechanization and the associated deskilling of work, a process whose implications were already grasped perfectly well by the working-class delegates who attended the Exposition Universelle de 1867 and who are remembered at length by Rancière and Patrick Vauday in a landmark article in *Révoltes Logiques*.[69] It is all the more striking, then, that (again unlike Chomsky) Rancière should have paid comparatively little attention to the more recent development of this process.

In the end, much of what is most compelling and forceful about

Rancière's theoretical position (and this is, again, something he shares with Badiou and Lacoue-Labarthe) seems to rely on an unnecessarily simplistic articulation of all and nothing, of "no one" and "everyone." Rancière's politics, like Badiou's notion of an evental site or Lacoue-Labarthe's notion of theater, depends on the existence of a *part des sans parts*, a "part of those who have no part," a group of people who are literally of "*no* account," an "indistinct mass of people of *no* position" (my emphases). And "whoever has no part—the poor of ancient times, the third estate, the modern proletariat—cannot in fact have any part other than all or nothing."[70] Rancière doesn't consistently recognize the immeasurable difference between "nothing" and "very little," between "no part" and a "minimal part." Rather than no part, there are many who have a very small part, a share that is minimal or marginal but that is nonetheless something rather than nothing. If a universalist project isn't appropriately articulated with this interested, assertive, or defensive aspect, then it will never get off the ground.

The danger, finally, is that Rancière may have fallen victim to a version of his own early critique of Althusser—that he has developed an inconsequential account of democracy.[71] Rancière's theory may encourage us to do little more than "play at" politics or equality. Rancière's egalitarianism, no less than Schiller's notion of play, risks confinement to the "unsubstantial kingdom of the imagination."[72]

Rancière knows as well as anyone that the theater is never more theatrical than when it finds new ways of blurring, without eliminating, the boundaries with the nontheatrical. It may be, however, that any such innovative blurring can only continue, in the domain of both politics and art, if it is illuminated by a decisive commitment that is itself organized, determined, categorical, and combative. In the field of recent critical theory, after all, there are few better illustrations of this point than the consistency and resolve that have characterized, over the last thirty-odd years, the development of Rancière's own project.

10.

Rancière's Leftism, Or, Politics and Its Discontents

BRUNO BOSTEELS

Does Jacques Rancière have a lesson to teach us, or anybody else for that matter? This opening question may seem incongruous for the simple reason that all of Rancière's work is meant to break down the normative claim and hierarchical pretense implicit in the notion that any one person or class of persons would indeed have a lesson to teach to any other person or class. He begins in *La leçon d'Althusser*, where he presents a ferocious indictment of his former teacher and for a long time the very model of the master thinker, and continues in the no less unforgiving rebuttal of Pierre Bourdieu's sociology as seen in particular in the latter's speech upon entering the Collège de France, a speech significantly titled *Leçon sur la leçon*, where Rancière challenges the whole pedagogical hierarchy supporting the very idea of teaching someone a lesson—a *leçon de choses*—and puts into question the distance between the teacher and the taught subjects and objects, between knowledge and nonknowledge, or between the knowing master and the ignorant masses. "The master's secret is to know how to recognize the distance between the taught material and the person being instructed, the distance also between learning and understanding."[1] But through a new and special kind of knowledge that is neither strictly philosophical nor purely historical, insofar as it seeks to do without all figures of mastery still associated with the disciplines of philosophy and history, we also know that this is the distance most stubbornly and systematically meant to be crossed in the writings of Rancière. In fact, in a recent interview, he tries to avoid describing himself as a teacher and instead prefers to compare himself to the well-known image of the eternal student: "I am, in the first instance, a student. I am one of those people who is a perpetual student and whose professional fate, as a consequence, is to teach others."[2] Rancière's professional fate may well have been to turn from student into teacher, but this does not mean that he has a lesson to teach, in the old pedagogical sense of the expression.

And yet, at the center of this body of work we also find the fascinating description of Joseph Jacotot, in *The Ignorant Schoolmaster*, perhaps Rancière's most luminous, and in my eyes certainly his most passionate, book. Subtitled *Cinq leçons sur l'émancipation intellectuelle*, this book also offers an emancipatory reconfiguration of the idea of the lesson itself: a different "lesson on the lesson," in other words—most definitely not one to be confused with that of Bourdieu. "La leçon de l'ignorant" is how Rancière describes this radical alternative in the second chapter of his book, *La leçon de Rancière*, or "Rancière's lesson," I would translate, before asking myself whether there is more to the expression than the mere parallel with *La leçon d'Althusser*.[3] In fact, already in the four chapters of this latter book, as we move from "Leçon d'orthodoxie" to "Leçon de politique" to "Leçon d'autocritique" and finally to "Leçon d'histoire," we can see a subtle and profound shift in the very concept of the lesson and its uses. Thus, the implied author of the final lesson does not quite seem to be the same as the author of the first one. It turns out that Rancière is actually the one who ends up teaching his former teacher a history lesson, so as better to unmask both the profound apoliticism hidden behind Althusser's dogmatic orthodoxy and the revisionism of his botched attempt at a self-critique.

Rancière, however, is no Jacotot. Despite the brilliant use of the free indirect style, his is not exactly the role of the ignorant schoolmaster.

Nor did he ever have to teach French to the Flemish youth of my native Louvain. Rather, he presents himself anachronistically, as it were, as one of Jacotot's imaginary students whose professional fate it is to teach us a few lessons about the lesson of this ignorant master. Jacotot thus serves as a kind of anti-Althusser, following the example of Engels's *Anti-Dühring*.

THE TWOFOLD OPERATION

The difficulty inherent in the notion of Rancière's lesson is intimately tied to a second difficulty, which comes down to deciding whether he is a philosopher or a historian, an antiphilosopher or an archivist of popular struggles. Here too it must be said that Rancière's work introduces an irreparable disturbance in the fixed demarcation of disciplines, with their boundaries between the sayable and the unsayable, the proper and the improper, the legitimate and the illegitimate. Precisely by introducing some play in, or by playing with, the interval between various discourses, the aim is always to derail the regimes of thought that would assign certain ways of doing, speaking, and seeing to a stable set of competences, qualities, or properties.

If it is out of the question to think the singularity of this work in disciplinary terms, perhaps a better approach consists in interrogating Rancière's modus operandi. I am thinking in particular of the following description, which comes toward the end of *La leçon d'Althusser*, when the author, by way of conclusion, seeks to explain the method he has just followed throughout the book, perhaps even with an eye on a future program of studies:

> I have tried to apply a double operation on an exemplary discourse [that of Althusser]: I have made an effort to reinsert it in its history, in the system of practical and discursive constraints that make it enunciable. I have sought to surprise its articulations by forcing it to respond to other questions than those of the partners of complacency that it had chosen for itself, by reinscribing its argumentation in those chains of words in which the necessities of oppression and the hopes of liberation have formulated themselves and continue to formulate themselves. Not a refutation, because it serves no point to refute dogmatisms. Rather a *mise en scène* aiming to deregulate the functioning of one of these wise Marxist discourses that occupy our theoret-

ical space in order to make readable the consecration of the existing order in the discourse of the revolution. By doing so I would like simply to echo that which, in the disparity of the struggles and interrogations of our present, seeks to express itself in terms of a newfound liberty.[4]

For Rancière, the purpose of his thinking no doubt always lies in following this double procedure: to reinsert something (a discourse, a practice, or a regime of doing, seeing, or speaking) in its system of constraints and to derail this system of constraints itself. These two operations, of course, stand in a precarious balance to each other, always on the verge of tilting over in the hypostasis of only one of them, according to their corresponding objects or concepts: the system of constraints, which results from the act of reinscription; and liberty, which is the principle of derangement and which once again constrains the previously established practical and discursive constraints by finding undesirable or at least unexpected bedfellows for them. In a sense rather close to Foucault, liberty thus responds to the structure of constraints with the surprise of an unpredictable reinscription, just as the hopes of liberation make themselves heard as soon as the machine of necessity and oppression is ever so slightly displaced.

This double operation, moreover, may help us appreciate the force or originality of a mode of thinking, including Rancière's own. He himself, thus, writes in the avant-propos to *The Philosopher and His Poor* that one of the presuppositions behind his reading, far from keeping with the habit "not to ask an author any questions except for those that he had asked himself," consisted precisely in understanding that "the power of a mode of thinking has to do above all with its capacity to be displaced, just as the power of a piece of music may derive from its capacity to be played on different instruments."[5]

AESTHETICS AND/OR POLITICS

Actually, with regard to this double operation—which, to this day, seems to me to define the work of Rancière—I want to draw attention to the presence of a profound asymmetry in his treatment of art and politics. Indeed, it seems to me that art and politics are not two domains or two matrices that otherwise would receive one and the same treatment in Rancière's readings. Rather, we should understand how art and politics lead to two approaches or two tendencies that are deeply unequal and asymmetrical. Despite the appearance of a strict homology between them, the two actually appear almost as polar opposites.

Thus, if art is treated according to the vaguely historical order of three regimes of identification (the ethical regime, the representative regime, and the aesthetic regime), without there being any essence proper to art in itself, I want to insist on the fact that the same does not apply to politics. That is to say, especially in *Dis-agreement: Politics and Philosophy*, it seems perfectly possible to define what is specific to politics (*la politique*), and this specificity certainly marks a "proper" which, even if it is constitutively "improper" (whence the commonly assumed homology with art, most notably under the aesthetic regime), is no less universally identifiable or separable as such on this account. Thus, the political triad (archi-politics, para-politics, and meta-politics), though also historical in appearance insofar as it is originally associated with the successive proper names of Plato, Aristotle (or Hobbes), and Marx, does not function in the same way as the three regimes of identification of art. If we are to believe *Dis-agreement*, rather, there exists, after all, an essence or a rational kernel of politics, which subsequently would have been covered up, denied, repressed, or obscurely designated in those three dominant forms of political philosophy.

The result is an insurmountable *plurality* of regimes to identify art, with the pluralization itself being the effect of *one* historical regime among others, whereas politics enables the establishment of a kernel of politicalness, properly speaking, which, while never natural, remains *invariant* throughout history. This is because in the end this is the nonhistorical and apolitical condition of politics itself: that is, what is hidden in the three forms of hitherto existing political philosophy. Besides, as far as I know, these three forms are never called "regimes," and we can easily understand why: this is a last sign, or perhaps one more symptom, of the asymmetry between art and politics: namely, the profuse invocation of the term "regime" for the first and its relative absence in the treatment of the second, for which the term no doubt is too closely tied to the destiny of the form of the political state.

Let me dwell for a moment longer on this asymmetry, both to con-textualize the question of method and to underscore the singularity of politics (or of its treatment) in comparison to art in Rancière's work.

Indeed, following the first half of his double operation, Rancière has always been admirably consistent in stating that there is no such thing as *the* science or *the* people or *the* Marxism but at best a variable series of practical and discursive constraints: to put it in the more recent vocabu-lary, a series of regimes of visibility and intelligibility that allow cer-tain modes of doing, saying, and seeing, all the while excluding others. This is what I would call the principle of a certain nominalism, which could be summed up in the following formula: the universal exists only in the singular—that is, in the plurality of particular modes, places, and operations. Let me recall a few examples of this nominalist tendency in Rancière—a tendency that, though perhaps badly named, he shares with the likes of Althusser and above all Foucault.[6] All these examples are drawn from *La leçon d'Althusser* and from the useful collection *Les scènes du peuple.*

First, with regard to man: "It is not Man who makes history, but men, that is to say, concrete individuals, those who produce their means of existence, those who fight the battle in the class struggle. Marx goes no further in the critique of Feuerbach."[7]

Then, about science: "There is no 'pure' scientific practice; the latter has its forms of existence in a system of social relationships of which propositions, logical chains, and experiments (on the basis of which *the ideal of science* is constituted) are only elements." Or again: "Science does not appear opposite of ideology as its other; it appears in institu-tions and in forms of transmission in which the ideological domination of the bourgeoisie manifests itself."[8]

Further, about the category of time: "Time [*Le temps*] does not exist but only several temporalities [*des temps*], each of which is always itself a way of linking a plurality of lines of time, plural forms of temporality."[9]

And, coming closer to the question of politics that sits at the center of our interrogation of Rancière's work, the famous voice of the people: "History as practiced in *Les Révoltes Logiques* will have repeated this: there is not one voice of the people. There are shattered, polemical voices, dividing at each time the identity they put on stage."[10]

We arrive, in the end, at the question of Marxism itself: "The Marxism of the camp is neither a vain adornment nor a deviation that would not touch upon the pure essence of Marxism. Sure, but this also means that there is no pure essence of Marxism, but Marxisms, determinate montages of theoretical and practical schemes of power, that there is no fatality to Marxism that would globally account for the forms of subservience produced by certain Marxist powers or justified by certain Marxist discourses."[11]

In sum, not only is there *logic to the revolt*, in contrast to the official dogma of Marxism-Leninism, according to which the revolt is merely ephemeral spontaneity when it is not concentrated into revolutionary discipline thanks to the vanguard party; there is also always *a revolt among various logics*. As we read in *La leçon d'Althusser*, there exists always a plurality of conceptualities or—to use an expression from *Disagreement*, referring to politics in the age of militantism—"a multiplicity of modes and places, from the street to the factory to the university."[12] Finally, it is no doubt this taste for the plurality of practices, discourses, and stagings that explains the frequent use of the figure of the banquet as the place of the mixed and the confused for Rancière. In addition to the chapter on Plato in *The Philosopher and His Poor*, where we read, "The order established by the banquet is the order of mixture. If the city began with the clearcut distribution of useful workers, politics begins with the motley crowd of the unuseful who, coming together into a mass of 'workers,' cater to a new range of needs—from painters and musicians to tutors and chambermaids; from actors and rhapsodists to hairdressers and cooks; from the makers of luxury articles to swineherds and butchers," Rancière expresses this festive principle with particular eloquence in his text on André Glucksmann for *Les Révoltes Logiques*: "The discourse of revolutionary intellectuals is always a Harlequin dress, sewn of different logics."[13]

This being said, when it comes to politics, particularly in *Disagreement*, we seem to hit upon the point of exception to this generalized nominalism. Here Rancière all of a sudden seems to exchange his Harlequin coat for the appeal of a dark grey suit. *Dis-agreement*, from this point of view, undoubtedly presents an anomaly in Rancière's work. Here, a thinker who has elevated a certain shyness into a methodological principle suddenly seems to experience no reticence whatsoever before the axiomatic enunciation of "politics" (*la politique*) properly speaking, and, to a lesser extent, of "the political" (*le politique*), as in *On the Shores of Politics*.

These statements are well known. If I quote a large number of them in detail, it is only to enable the reader to appreciate the "special effect" of the repetition as well, as if in a profane litany:

There is politics—and not just domination—because there is a wrong count of the parts of the whole.[14]

There is politics when there is a part of those who have no part, a part or party of the poor.[15]

Politics exists when the natural order of domination is interrupted by the institution of a part of those who have no part.[16]

Now, politics comes about solely through interruption, the initial twist that institutes politics as the deployment of a wrong or of a fundamental dispute.[17]

Politics exists simply because no social order is based on nature, no divine law regulates human society.[18]

Politics occurs because, or when, the natural order of the shepherd kings, the warlords, or property owners is interrupted by a freedom that crops up and makes real the ultimate equality on which any social order rests.[19]

There is politics when the supposedly natural logic of domination is crossed by the effect of this equality. This means that politics doesn't always happen—it actually happens very little or rarely.[20]

Politics occurs when the egalitarian contingency disrupts the natural pecking order as the "freedom" of the people, when this disruption produces a specific mechanism: the dividing of society into parts that are not "true" parts; the setting-up of one part as equal to the whole in the name of a "property" that is not its own, and of a "common" that is the community of a dispute.[21]

Politics exists because those who have no right to be counted as speaking beings make themselves of some account, setting up a community by the fact of placing in common a wrong that is nothing more than this very confrontation, the contradiction of two worlds in a single world: the world where they are and the world where they are not, the world where there is something "between" them and those who do not acknowledge them as speaking beings who count and the world where there is nothing.[22]

Politics occurs by reason of a single universal that takes the specific shape of wrong. Wrong institutes a singular universal, a polemical universal, by tying the presentation of equality, as the part of those who have no part, to the conflict between parts of society.[23]

To recapitulate: politics exists wherever the count of parts and parties of society is disturbed by the inscription of a part of those who have no part.[24]

Or, again, this other recurrent formulation, though less prone to incantatory effects:

Politics begins precisely when one stops balancing profits and losses and worries instead about distributing *common* lots and evening out communal shares and entitlements to these shares, the *axiaï* entitling one to community.[25]

Politics begins with a major wrong: the gap created by the empty freedom of the people between the arithmetical order and the geometric order.[26]

The only city is a political one and politics begins with egalitarian contingency.[27]

The reign of the "humanitarian" begins, on the other hand, wherever human rights are cut off from any capacity for polemical particularization of their universality, where the egalitarian phrase ceases to be phrased, interpreted in the arguing of a wrong that manifests its litigious effectiveness.[28]

Of course, *Dis-agreement*, like almost all books by Rancière according to the author himself, is also a conjunctural intervention, tied in this particular case to the dominant model of consensus from which he seeks to free himself, without for this reason lapsing in the other extreme, which would posit the absolute anteriority of the unrepresentable, or of the sublime. To maintain oneself "equally far removed from the consensual discussion and from absolute wrong"—such is the task of a logic of disagreement according to Rancière. I will come back to this operation, another constant in Rancière's work, which consists in occupying the space in-between, or the non-place between two positions, according to the well-known formula *neither . . . nor . . .* , which at the same time entails a categorical refusal of the false alternative *either . . . or. . . . .* Struggle on two fronts, they used to say not so long ago: neither left-wing opportunism nor right-wing opportunism; neither anarchic adventurism nor orthodox dogmatism. Or again: neither apocalyptic nor integrated. It is within the structure of such a struggle that I would situate the peculiar use of the category of politics in *Dis-agreement.*

In criticizing the use of politics or the political, therefore, my aim is not to chastise the philosopher in the name of some form of antiessentialism. Nor am I taking issue with the axiomatic allure of the formalization per se. I merely wish to interrogate some of the consequences, for politics as a thought-practice, of the style "there is politics when . . ." or "politics begins there where . . ." This last formula, besides, recalls another of Rancière's favorites, the one that precisely opens the first chapter of *Dis-agreement* under the title "Le commencement de la politique": "Commençons donc par le commencement" (Let's begin at the beginning).[29] In the end, my question concerns the exact status of this "there is politics when" or of this "beginning": Is this a theoretical principle or a historical fact? A logical beginning or a chronological start? A transcendental condition of possibility or an eventful occurrence? Or, the last possibility, can we hold on to both interpretations at once in a singular mixture—another banquet, this time methodological—that could very well be constitutive of Rancière's very style of thinking?

SPECULATIVE LEFTISM

I want to tackle this larger question by interrogating just one of the possible effects of Rancière's restricted nominalism: to wit, the risk of falling into what the author himself, in *La leçon d'Althusser,* almost twenty years before the reemergence of this same expression on the part of Alain Badiou, in the meditation "The Intervention," from *L'être et l'événement,* calls "speculative leftism."[30] Indeed, I fear that the definition of politics in *Dis-agreement,* most notably from within the opposition politics/the police, is all too easily assimilated to the leftist scheme that in earlier times opposed, for example, the plebs and the state. This risk is all the more striking, and the objection may seem all the more unfair, insofar as it has been Rancière himself who has given us the necessary tools to dismantle the schematism of this very presentation.

Let us look at a last series of quotations, this time taken from "La bergère au Goulag," which is a long review of Glucksmann's *La cuisinière et le mangeur d'homme.* According to Rancière, this important book by one of the foremost of the "New Philosophers" proposes only a purified version of contradictions, without respecting their dialectical complexity. "The whole book is an organized effect based on a purification of the contradiction: on one hand, power and the discourse of the masters (philosophers, kings, Jacobins, Marxists . . .) organized according to the rules of state constraint; on the other, the class of nonpower, the plebs, pure generosity, whose discourse expresses the sole desire of not being oppressed."[31] It belongs to Lenin, among the first, to have denounced the false dialectic of this kind of dualist oppositions: " 'On the one hand, and on the other,' 'the one and the other.' That is eclecticism. Dialectics requires an all-around consideration of relationships in their concrete development but not a patchwork of bits and pieces."[32] Rancière, for his part, proposes several refutations of this false image of contradiction:

> Everything would be simple for sure if we could move in this purged contradiction: the revolt of the "wretched of the earth" against a state power represented by social-fascism. But reality is not such.[33]
>
> Reality: that there is no principle of subversion drawn from anything other than practices of resistance, that there is nothing beyond the distribution [*partage*] of servitude and of refusal, which is always and for everyone renewed; no movement of history, no ruse of reason that can ever *justify* oppression and servitude. Myth: the incarnation of this division [*partage*] in the pure opposition of power and the plebs.[34]
>
> The plebs: those excluded from power? But who is ever totally excluded from power? . . . Such a division [*partage*] is possible only at the expense of simply identifying the reality of power with the visible face of the state apparatus.[35]
>
> Nowhere does the conflict of power and nonpower play itself out. Everywhere the task of the state stumbles upon not the plebs, but classes, corporations, collectives and their rules, their forms of recognition and democracy, but also of exclusion and even oppression.[36]
>
> The discourses from below are still discourses of power and it is from the point of view of this reality that we can think the position of a discourse such as Marx's.[37]

Here we are back at the heart of the matter. Indeed, once he arrives at the center of his critique of the discourse of the New Philosophers, exemplified by Glucksmann, Rancière himself proposes a lesson, after all, in which we must again and always hear echoes from Marx's thought: "Lesson perhaps of this confrontation: that there is never any pure discourse of proletarian power nor any pure discourse of its nonpower; neither consciousness from below that would suffice for itself nor science that could be imported. The force of Marx's thought—but perhaps also its untenable character—resides no doubt in the effort to hold these contradictions, stripped bare since then in the police fictions of proletarian powers or the pastoral dreams of plebeian nonpower."[38] Instead of purifying the contradiction, the task would thus lie in keeping it open, even if in the end this may turn out to be untenable: to find the knotty point between power and resistance, between power and nonpower, between the state and the plebs. Otherwise, these dualisms would quickly fall into the trap of speculative leftism, according to a Manichaean scheme that is as radical and profound as it is inoperative.

However, I wonder to what extent the author of *Dis-agreement* might have forgotten this lesson. Does not the opposition, no matter how contrarian, between the police as ordered partitioning of the sensible and politics as inscription of a part of those who have no part come dangerously close to the "purification" of the contradiction that would be characteristic of speculative leftism? *Dis-agreement*, whether due to its assertive style or its tactical and strategic goals, remains perhaps caught in the nets of a contradiction stripped down to such *police fictions*, on the one hand, and the *political dreams* of those who have no part, on the other.

But Rancière's essay on Glucksmann is not the only tool at our disposal to reconstruct what I would call a critique of pure leftist reason. Even within the bounds of *Dis-agreement* we can find arguments that run counter to this leftist reading. First of all, the police is never identified without rest with the state apparatus. Second, the police does not represent a night in which all cows are grey: "There is a worse and a better police."[39] Finally, the antagonism between politics and the police, as two heterogeneous logics of being-together, is far from the last word in the book. Rancière insists at least as strongly on the need of a binding, an encounter, or an intertwinement between both logics, without which politics would not have any effect whatsoever on the original situation.

In other words, even if we wanted to keep the two terms, which the author is the first to problematize, there must be an inscription or verification of an effect of politics back upon the police. "We should not forget that if politics implements a logic entirely heterogeneous to that of the police, it is always bound up with the latter," writes Rancière, and further down: "Politics acts on the police. It acts in the places and with the words that are common to both, even if it means reshaping those places and changing the status of those words."[40] In this sense, to posit the radical exteriority and strangeness of these two logics, the egalitarian and the social policing, without letting them ever tie a knot that would not be treacherous, would have been the gravest limitation of the endeavor associated with Jacotot.

And yet, a fundamental ambiguity nonetheless continues to run through the pages of *Dis-agreement*. The book may very well refuse the purely external opposition between politics and the police that would bring it closer to speculative leftism. Thus, for this old Maoist, One continues to divide into Two. There is not two times one. Whence the insistence on the motifs of the originary scission and the torsion; whence, also, the recourse to the double meaning of *partage*, both community *and* separation, sharing *and* dividing. This means that in the final instance, what matters is to hold the untenable, to measure the common between two incommensurables, to think together the rapport and the nonrapport.

Consider, for instance, the way in which Rancière refuses to oppose the pure ideality of doctrine and the impure mixture of reality: "There is not on the one hand the ideal people of the founding texts and, on the other, the real people of the workshops and suburbs. There is a place where the power of the people is inscribed and places where this power is reputedly ineffective."[41] To think politics always entails having to follow this type of return actions and twisted effects—or, as the case may be, their absence. In the final analysis, all this is perfectly compatible with the nominalist principle. Instead of thinking in purified oppositions such as *the* people against *the* power structures, the task would be to study the places where one paradoxically divides and inscribes itself in the other, as well as the historical modalities of this inscription.

But all this also does not exclude the fact that in other fragments of the same book, precisely with regard to the two logics of being-together, it is once again the purification, not to say the Manichaeism, that takes priority over and above the sharing and the intertwining: "On the one hand, there is the logic that simply counts the lots of the parties, that distributes the bodies within the space of their visibility or their invisibility and aligns ways of being, ways of doing, and ways of saying appropriate to each. And there is the other logic, the logic that disrupts this harmony through the mere fact of achieving the contingency of the equality, neither arithmetical nor geometric, of any speaking beings whatsoever."[42] Clearly, we are far from being done with the temptations of a certain speculative leftism and its dual oppositions! Perhaps this is the price to be paid if we wish to maintain a polemical edge in the discussion against the idyll of consensus, whose noisy celebrations, as I mentioned before, *Dis-agreement* seeks to interrupt.

THINKING IN THE PRESENT, OR, THE AGE OF THE SENSIBLE

Given the extent of Rancière's engagement with the history of the Left, from *La leçon d'Althusser* to *Dis-agreement* and beyond, however, it would be an act of bad faith to remain at the level of a mere critique of speculative leftism. Far more important is something along the lines of what Jacques Rancière himself, in an article coauthored with Danielle, calls "the traversing of leftism," historically and genealogically speaking, so as to come to terms, conversely, with the "legend of the philosophers."

Thus, Jacques and Danielle Rancière suggest, in their article for *Les Révoltes Logiques*, that the New Philosophers define the stakes for contemporary thinking only to the extent to which they provoke an "occultation of the militant history" of May '68 and its aftermath. It is this "occultation" or "liquidation" of history that they propose to deactivate by trying to learn a few lessons in the history of politics:

> The stakes for us lie in this occultation of the militant history that the discourse on the Gulag has produced: occultation of the conjunction of student and popular struggles, of the encounter of militant intellectuals and the masses, attempts to throw into doubt the mechanism of representation: instead the figure of a *plebs* appears whom the intellectual represents just as yesterday he represented the proletariat, but in a way that precisely denies representation; the plebs means both and at the same time all the positivity of suffering and popular laughter and the part of refusal, of negativity, that each carries with him, realizing the immediate unity of the intellectual and

the people; liquidation by simple denial of the objectives and aspirations of the struggles as well as of the problems they came across.[43]

Now, for the more recent era, could we not hope for a historical and conceptual analysis similar to the one Danielle and Jacques Rancière present in "La légende des philosophes"? Here I only express my desire that one day we will be able to read the legend, now also in the positive sense of what is truly "to be read," concerning the long and sinuous trajectory that leads from *Nights of Labor* to *Les Révoltes Logiques* all the way to *Dis-agreement*. However, this historical apprenticeship, which remains to be accomplished for the post-leftist age, also poses a problem of a methodological and philosophical nature. As I suggested before, this problem concerns the exact status of the "there is" or the "beginning" and the "end," whether in art or in politics, such as they are captured and sheltered—not without considerable scandal—inside philosophy.

This problem regarding the relation between art or politics and the historicity of their concepts and practices is certainly not unique to Rancière's work, and it seems to me at least an equally burning issue for someone like Badiou. This also means that in their mutual attacks, the one by Badiou in *Abrégé de métapolitique* against Rancière's "apoliticism," and the one by Rancière in *Malaise dans l'esthétique* against Badiou's "aestheticism," what remains hidden or unsaid concerns precisely the other pole—art or the aesthetic regime for Rancière and politics for Badiou—being those conditions of truth, or regimes of thinking, for which each has proven himself capable of setting up a new configuration of historicity, otherwise absent or at least insufficiently elaborated on the opposite side of the polemical chiasm between the two.[44]

By way of conclusion, I would like to give a brief example of this new configuration and of the tasks it imposes on us, using the case of Mallarmé. The principal task consists in coming to an understanding about the double valence of Mallarmé's case, not only as a poet-thinker of the event in and of itself, but at the same time as an innovator within French postromantic poetry.

For Badiou, the first half of this reading seems to take away all interest from the second. "Mallarmé is a thinker of the event-drama," he writes in *Being and Event*, and he continues: "A cast of dice joins the emblem of chance to that of necessity, the erratic multiple of the event to the legible retroaction of the count. The event in question in *A Cast of Dice . . .* is therefore that of the production of an absolute symbol of the event. The stakes of casting dice 'from the bottom of a shipwreck' are those of making an event out of the thought of the event."[45]

However, it is also a matter of understanding the link between this poetry-thought of the eventlike nature of the event, on the one hand, and, on the other, the function of this poetry as an event among others in the history of modern post-Hugolian poetry. Regarding this link, of course, readers will find very little information if they limit their search to *L'être et l'événement.*

By contrast, it is the second half of the question that receives much greater attention in Rancière's short book on Mallarmé. The latter remains without a doubt the great poet of the eventlike nature of the event, emblematized by the sirens: "Mallarmé transforms them into emblems of the poem itself, the power of a song that is capable both of making itself heard and of transforming itself into silence."[46] But we should also add immediately that according to this reading, the eventlike nature of the poem is inseparable from the equally singular relation it establishes with the place and time of its appearance: "The poem escapes the abyss that awaits it because it modifies the very mode of fiction, substituting the song of a vanishing siren for the great epic of Ulysses. What the siren metaphorizes, what the poem renders effective, then, is precisely the event and the calculated risk of the poem in an era and a 'mental environment' that are not yet ready to welcome it."[47] Rancière understands these two aspects—the event and its relation to an era and an environment not yet ready for it—as part of one and the same question.

Based on indications such as these, we can begin to see the consequences of a momentous philosophical decision: The value of affirming the "there is" of Mallarméan poetry, like that of any "there is," is inseparably structural *and* eventual, transcendental *and* historical. Each time there is an event, in politics perhaps no less than in poetry, we witness a breakdown of principle that at the same time allows a reconstruction of its links with history. As in the double game of liberty and constraints, one thing certainly does not exclude but rather presupposes the other. Otherwise, in the absence of such an articulation, which I would gladly call dialectical in a new and unheard-of sense, we would fall back once again on either the liberty or the practical and discursive constraints—which would lead us to a leftist scheme all over again.

On the other hand, when it comes to politics, it is Badiou who in his recent work paradoxically has contributed more elements to reconstitute the link between history and politics, rather than Rancière. I am thinking in particular of the conferences on the Paris Commune and on the Chinese Cultural Revolution, both strongly marked by the category of "historical mode of politics" proposed by Sylvain Lazarus in his book *Anthropologie du nom*.[48] Such a history of different modes of doing politics would evidently be hard to come by if we started from *Dis-agreement*. In this last book, there certainly are "ages" or "eras," such as "the Marxist age" or "the nihilist age," just as the article written with Danielle for *Les Révoltes Logiques* speaks of "the post-leftist age," but in the last instance, history only seems to determine the successive eras of the covering up of an invariant form of politics, to which the book seeks to restitute its "improper property" that is also "the ultimate secret of any social order": namely, "the pure and simple equality of anyone and everyone," which serves as "the basis and original gulf of the community order."[49]

Earlier I mentioned the tactic of situating oneself in the in-between of two previously given extremes. For *La leçon d'Althusser* it was a matter of keeping the sharp edge of his master's discourse while falling neither into pure "theoreticism" nor into "cultural gossip."[50] In *The Philosopher and His Poor*, the impossible goal is to follow a straight line between "the ancient ruses of philosophy and the modern ruses of anti-philosophy."[51] Similarly, with *Dis-agreement*, it is a question of being neither on the side of rational communicability nor on the side of absolute unrepresentability; neither in ready-to-wear sociologism nor in the hyperbole of the pure event. Now, in order for this third way to be tenable, even if the place of this third—as is that of the "third people" between the police and politics—is a non-place, it seems to me that the question of the historicity of thought imposes itself as a question that can no longer be postponed. Thus, we must come to understand what it means to think today under the condition of certain transformations in art or in politics. Not only "What does it mean to think in the present?" but also and above all "What does it mean to think in the present under the condition of certain events from the past, whether in the long or in the short run?"[52]

The risk involved in giving too quick an answer to these questions should be clear enough: the historicity of art or politics would be reduced to mere historicism, the event would be realigned with the system of constraints that made it possible, and the radicalism of the disruption would end up getting diluted in the proverbial water under the bridge. And yet, and yet, it is possible that the price to be paid for not taking into account these questions is even higher: a radicalism pivoting on its own emptiness, a thinking of the pure "there is" of art and politics cut off from any inscription in a place and according to specific historical modes, and finally the falling back into the false appeal of a certain speculative leftism that our age, the nihilist age of the ethical turn and postpolitics, had flattered itself for having been able to do without.

Now, after . . . it is time to return to sender, not the question which knows too much
but the fraternal solitude of the place where it never ceases to resurface.
—JACQUES RANCIÈRE, "Après quoi," 196

But now, after the Holocaust? Then it didn't end? It will never end.
—JEAN-FRANÇOIS LYOTARD, "L'Europe, les Juifs et le livre," 280

11.

Jacques Rancière's Ethical Turn and the Thinking of Discontents

SOLANGE M. GUÉNOUN
Translated by Bambi Billman

"There is no democractic crisis or malaise," Jacques Rancière has continuously argued against all those "doctors of democracy" who, for at
least the last decade, have been making an interminable inventory of
symptoms exhibited by a democratic individual turned consumer, who
represents a new menace to the political order and the social bond.[1]
There are, of course, difficulties inherent in a democracy, conceived by
Rancière not as a form of power or society but as a quasianarchic power
of the "people," a paradoxical power that disrupts the prevailing consensual distribution of function and place. But these permanent tensions of
democracy thus redefined as disagreement and disorder must, according to Rancière, be distinguished from the disastrous evils with which
the so-called therapists brand the people represented as a large "unpredictable and untamable" animal. In fact, in Rancière's view, it would be
these "doctors" themselves who have been struck with one of the oldest
of Western diseases—an endless and perpetually renewed form of "hatred of democracy." This is what Rancière believes to be flushing out of

certain elites who, in his opinion, are more and more enamored with the idea of a "pastoral government" and for whom paternal care of the herd should manifest itself, above all else, in an incessant interpretation of the "malaise of the collective body."[2] But, before returning the compliment to these doctors of imaginary diseases, in his *Malaise dans l'esthétique* (2004) Rancière had already diagnosed and analyzed a new "malaise of civilization" that he called the "ethical turn." Mimicking, among other things, the psychopathological and psychoanalytic knowledge of his colleagues, he brings to light the conceptual confusion that characterizes this malady.[3]

Thus Rancière's recent thinking on discontents—an aesthetic malaise, as well as an ethical malaise of democracy—is embedded in his lifelong struggle against antidemocratic forces and their consensual discourses. Surely, the question of the crisis of art, of anti-aesthetic resentment, had already been addressed, and that of postmodern melancholia discussed many times. As a diagnostician-doctor, Rancière has already made himself well known as the unique specialist of maladies discovered by him and henceforth associated with his name: maladies of consensus as varied and serious as racism and hatred of the Other.[4] And it is in this capacity that he is working here again, to draw up this latest symptomatic tableau, even though the cause (the eclipse of politics as dissensus) and the remedy (the vital and necessary return to dissensus) are, for him in any case, identical. Democracy as disease and cure-all at once.

This expertise which appears restricted is due to a very restrictive definition of politics as dissensus, as permanent conflict of discourses, lives, and worlds linked to a conception of the state as an essentially police state, redefined as a set of practices that use power in order to depoliticize, to exclude that dissension (dissensus) which, for Rancière, constitutes politics.[5] Politics, as the opposite of the police, is a form of dissensus that polemically confirms the axiom of equality—the only political axiom for him.

As we know, Rancière, indignant and indefatigable in his form of dissensual thought, methodically practices what he theoretically preaches. Dissension is at once theory and method, as he reminds us in "Thinking the Dissensus," a paper he presented in September 2003. Furthermore, this "war of lives and of discourses," which he wages implacably against the master-words, means that every one of his discourses is conceived and written as a "machine of war" and that one must know his target in order not to miss the point of his effort.[6] And, since consensus—being the privileged mode of the "symbolic structuration of the community that tears out the heart of politics, namely, dissension (dissensus)"[7]—reconstitutes itself incessantly, this role of "guerilla" is necessarily permanent, and becomes mirrored in Rancière's theoretical and political bellicosity.[8]

"The Ethical Turn of Aesthetics and Politics"—the concluding part of *Malaise dans l'esthétique*—is at once the mapping of a new consensus and the most recent example of this theoretical bellicosity. It was presented first in March 2004 at the "Geographies of Contemporary Thought" forum in Barcelona. In these final 30 pages of a 175-page book, Rancière describes a sort of consensus, a similar symbolic structuring on both sides of the Atlantic, an ethically oriented "dominant interpretive scheme" that has disposed of both politics and aesthetics, in an evolution that was established around 1989.[9] I have chosen to concentrate on this section for a number of reasons but mostly because Rancière's reflection here allows me to reconnect with a question that I have begun to explore: the use of psychoanalysis in his work. Indeed, psychoanalysis—and particularly Lacanian psychoanalysis—is one of the fundamental tools wielded in his analysis of the ethical turn, although in his interview with Peter Hallward in 2003 Rancière acknowledged that he still did not know quite what to do with Lacan's thought.[10]

The term *ethics*, in Rancière, has different meanings. First, it refers to one of the three artistic regimes that he has identified, the other two being the representative regime and the aesthetic regime. In fact, one of the fundamental contributions of *Malaise dans l'esthétique* is the identification of an "ethical regime" conceived since Plato as a form of organic community life without politics, an ethical regime of art that he identifies in philosophical works poles apart from one another, like those of Jean-François Lyotard and Alain Badiou.[11] For Rancière, all conceptions of the aesthetic that suppose an absolute disconnection, a pure radicality of art, by separating it from all promise of political emancipation stray onto paths that lead nowhere, except outside the political.

The other meaning of the word *ethical* presented in "The Ethical Turn" comes from the primary meaning of ethos. This, for Rancière, signifies two things: "ethos is the dwelling and the way of being, the way of life corresponding to this dwelling. Ethics, then, is a kind of thinking which establishes the identity between an environment, a way of being and a principle of action."[12] But it is also (in an aspect that, to my knowledge, has hardly been commented upon until now) a new and specific interpretive schema governed entirely by one event—Auschwitz—emblematic of totalitarian catastrophe and by a single law—"the new law of Moses"—which is a Janus-faced dictum facing, on one side, Moses (a name that has come to symbolize Jewish ethics) and on the other McDonald's (a name which has come to symbolize international capitalism). In fact, in the conclusion of his analysis of Lyotard's "counter-reading of Kant" Rancière writes that the choice is between "either obedience to the Other's law, which subjects us to violence, or subservience to the law of the *self*, which brings us to enslavement to consumer culture."[13] This position he immediately reformulates in a rather shocking manner: "Either the law of Moses or that of McDonald's, such is the last word that the aesthetic of the sublime brings to the meta-political aesthetic." If this were perhaps a mere rephrasing of the aesthetico-ethical thinking of Lyotard, the next sentence leaves absolutely no doubt as to Rancière's position on the subject: "It is not certain that this *new law of Moses* is really opposed to that of McDonald's. Rather, what is certain is that it accomplishes the joint suppression of the aesthetic and the political in order to profit this *single law that now goes by the name of ethics*." This will effectively be the argument of "The Ethical Turn," and it is not one of those "probable assertions" Rancière tries to offer to avoid any dogmatic style.[14]

But how can we explain the effect of affects of this violent formulation on some readers, including myself? Where does the shock of reading come from, a shock not felt at all when reading numerous and current statements on how the global reign of the economy is accompanied by a global reign of morality? Does the shock come only from the identity of opposites—of these two symbolic names? Surely it does not come from the superficial playfulness of assonance between Moses and McDonald's that resonates with the well-known "from Mao to Moses," because, with his icy irony and indignation, Rancière seems in no mood for play here. Far from being a simple wordplay made in passing, this catchy symmetry says as much as possible while taking up as little space as possible. What is outrageous at first in this link between the law of the market economy, of international capital, and the law symbolic of Judaism is its classical association with the rise of anti-Semitism since the nineteenth century. Since this is not inconsequential, something else must be deduced from it, and we should try to understand its deliberate shock value.

Moses is a recurring motif in Rancière's recent work, since his main targets are those French intellectuals who invoke "the law of people instructed by Moses about the word of God."[15] Even if the "destruction of democracy in the name of the Koran" does not escape Rancière, his chosen interlocutors are mostly those democracy-hating Jews with whom he used to share a common philosophical and Marxist language, but who have lately become supporters of American wars.[16] Rancière's relentless attack is also against the "warlike expansion of democracy identified with the *mise en oeuvre* of the Decalogue, hatred of democracy assimilated to the murder of the divine shepherd."[17]

Thus the tone, the violent and somewhat dogmatic style of his discourse on the ethical turn, the staging of a fictitious and theoretical dispute about the word *ethics* and particularly Jewish law and the law of the market (Moses/McDonald's) will be taken here as symptoms of an ongoing, virulent war of discourses, a mirrorlike effect of all the ongoing wars and the hatred that invades everything. "Symptoms" here refers, above all else, to these effects of affects experienced by the reader and the resistance that follows, because, as Lacan demonstrated, the only resistance comes from the analyst. In other words, understanding the theoretical and political stakes of the ethical turn begins with taking into account the effects of affects, the shock given by certain formulations, as well as the feeling of malaise aroused by the apparent relentless animosity toward Lyotard, whom Rancière makes into a sort of significant matrix, omnipresent in all developments of thought, art, and politics over the last twenty years. He goes so far as to retrospectively question Lyotard's "intentions," charging him with the elaboration of a new "grand narrative" whereby the Jewish people would somehow usurp the place of the proletariat, completely contradicting Lyotard's own theorization of the end of the grand narratives. A reading that takes into account these effects of affects is necessarily a reading against oneself, a singular process of subjectivation and disidentification, if one has understood Rancière's emancipatory lesson and his politics of affects. A reading here and now to understand how a strategy of writing, of staging the ethical turn as a war against antidemocratic forces, of the "opinion of equality against the opinion of inequality," can change the current consensual "distribution of the sensible."[18]

Rancière's identification of the ethical turn is made in two stages: it is first organized, in terms of politics, around the figure of George W. Bush, the "war on terror," and humanitarian war. It is then centered, in philosophical and aesthetic terms, on Jean-François Lyotard, the question of human rights serving as a transition between the two foci. If the humanitarian as suppression of the political is a frequent theme in Rancière's work, in "The Ethical Turn" humanitarian war, tied up in the "unending war on terror," is interpreted on the basis of Lacan's notion of the originary distress related to the prematurity of the newborn that Rancière calls "birth trauma."

The second movement of the demonstration revisits themes developed by Rancière since his aesthetic turn of 1996, where he immediately tackled the question of the unrepresentable, linked to the Extermination, before his theorization of the three artistic regimes and the "distribution of the sensible" (2001).[19]

In "The Ethical Turn" ethics is referred to as an "indistinct sphere, where not only the specificity of political and artistic practices dissolved, but also . . . the distinction between fact and the law, between what is and what ought to be. Ethics amounts to the dissolution of the norm into the fact—the identification of all forms of discourse and practice under the same indistinct point of view."[20] We are therefore far from the traditional definition of ethics as a moral judgment brought to bear on either artistic operations or political actions. According to Rancière, in order for this ethical turn to take place, it requires "the specific conjunction of these two phenomena: on the one hand, the instance of evaluating and choosing judgment finds itself humbled before the power of the law that imposes itself and, on the other, the radicality of this law that leaves no other choice is nothing but the simple constraint stemming from the order of things. The growing indistinction between fact and law thus brings about an unprecedented dramaturgy of evil, justice and redemption."[21]

This confusion of law and fact, where all distinctions are abolished in the same indistinct point of view, is condensed in one word, "terror," "one of the master terms of our time," which "designates assuredly a reality of crime and horror" but is also itself a term of indistinction:

Terror designates the attacks on New York on September 11, 2001, or Madrid on March 11, 2004, as well as the strategy in which these attacks have their place. However by gradual extension, this word also comes to designate the shock caused in people's minds by the event, the fear that violent acts that are still unthinkable might occur, the situation characterized by such fears, the management of this situation through State apparatuses, and so on. To talk of a war against terror is to connect the form of these attacks with the intimate angst that can inhabit each one of us in the same chain. War against terror and infinite justice then fall within the indistinction of a preventative justice which attacks all that triggers or could trigger terror, everything that threatens the social bond holding the community together. It is a form of justice whose logic [will] stop only when terror will have ceased, which by definition never stops for us beings who are subjected to the trauma of birth.[22]

To better understand this ethical turn and the new indistinction it promotes, Rancière uses a comparison between the films of Alfred Hitchcock and Fritz Lang, on the one hand, and two films which date from 2003: *Dogville* and *Mystic River*. According to Rancière, we have, in effect, passed from the orthodox Freudian vulgate of the 1950s to a new, Lacanian vulgate in 2003 by virtue of a new conception of trauma. In the 1950s, "the reactivation of a repressed childhood secret" could still save the troubled and the violent, whereas with the new conception of birth trauma, from the "prematurity of *infans*, it is the very condition of an animal born too soon."[23]

The paralyzing effects of indistinction, condensed by the master signifiers *trauma* and *terror*, are furthermore contemporary with the transformations of the rights of man into humanitarianism on the international scene. Having first evolved from the right to intervene into infinite justice against the axis of evil, humanitarianism has become, in Rancière's lexicon, the absolute right of those who have no rights. The humanitarian war becomes "an endless war against terror: a war which is not one but a mechanism of infinite protection, a way of dealing with a trauma elevated to the status of a civilizational phenomenon."[24] Moving, then, from the political to the aesthetic, Rancière centers his analysis on Lyotard's later works.

Rancière's conceptual elaboration is accomplished, among other ways, through a constant interlocution with the thinking of Lyotard, to whom Rancière is "at the same time very close in vocabulary (wrong, *différend*) and in the link between aesthetics and politics, but also absolutely removed from by the promotion of absolute wrong and the unrepresentable."[25] Thus, in *Dis-agreement* (1995) Rancière will first criticize the nihilistic age and denounce melancholia as a postmodern ailment of which Lyotard would be the primary representative, albeit in this apolitical form taken up by the mourning of Marxism and of revolutionary utopias, wrongfully linking modernity and the extermination camps. From *The Politics of Aesthetics* (2004) to *L'inconscient esthétique* (2001) and *The Future of the Image* (2007), the critique of Lyotard's aesthetic of the sublime opens the ethical age. But it seems that Rancière has only recently, since roughly 2002–2004, realized the amplitude of the ethical operation that the sublime represents. Indeed, it is difficult not to remark upon the systematization of Rancière's retroactive demonstration concerning Lyotard's role in the substitution of this new grand narrative —that of the genocide of the Jews—for the revolutionary narrative of the proletariat.[26] To that effect, in September 2003, Rancière wrote the following:

> I disagreed with the idea of a break between a modern epoch where the proletariat would have been the universal victim, subject of a great narrative, and a postmodern time of micro or local narrative. So the argument of a breakaway from the time of the great narrative and the universal victim seemed to me beside the point. *More accurately, it was beside the point unless it was in fact embedded in another narrative of an absolute wrong. My assumption was that this was precisely the point.* What Lyotard was doing was not breaking away from the grand narrative of the victim. It was reframing it, in a retrospective way, in order to make a new use of it.
>
> From this point of view, *Heidegger and the Jews* . . . is a switching point that gives the postmodern argumentation a meaning that perhaps was not there at the beginning. This meaning is that of the substitution of a narrative and a substitution of the victim. In this text, the Jews become the subject of the new narrative of modernity, the new narrative of the western world[27]

If at first glance Rancière's hypothesis seems to agree with that of Elisabeth de Fontenay, for whom "it is not certain that *Heidegger and the 'Jews'* does not signal, in its own way, the invention of a *completely different genre* of '*grand narrative*,' nontotalitarian and nondeadly" in fact, their interpretations are complete opposites because, for Rancière, it is on the contrary, a question of a totalizing and deadly narrative.[28] Fontenay proposes to chronologically analyze the insistence of the Jewish reference in the works of Lyotard since 1969, what she calls his "*causa Judea*" or his "*judaïca*," that which comes "from Judaism, from Levinas, from Israel, from the destruction of European Jews."[29] Rancière, on the other hand, makes it into the matrix of an ambient discourse on ethics, only concerning himself with the negative effect of the Shoah on thought, politics, and art, and the role that Lyotard would have played in this process. For Rancière, as a theoretician of dissensual democracy, the Shoah is, first and foremost, an object of a dominant consensual discourse that blocks the political horizon, a depoliticizing, demobilizing, inhibiting fiction of political inventiveness and an artistic usurper of insurrectional forces.

Rancière has highlighted the decisive importance, in Lyotard, of the notion of original distress, a misery that would join, according to Fontenay, at the same time the "inherent terror of the *infantia*, the onto-genetic angst of gender differences for a language-enabled being incapable of speaking, and the Judeo-genealogic destitution of an interdiction concerning representative and nominative signs."[30] Fontenay has also highlighted the autobiographical element because, in her view, the misery of the child is that of the stranglehold of the familial unit on the child, the confiscation of a child by "a Christian anti-Judaic education: all that he means by misery, childhood, heteronomy, enslavement to the law of alterity" and which refers to his "idea of originary violence."[31]

Let us note that Rancière pays no attention to the sexual, and even less attention to the subjective, aspect of the trauma, both of which cannot be dissociated from psychoanalytic trauma theory. He is concerned only with the ethical recoding it allows in terms of the destiny of civilization. The psychoanalytic notion of birth trauma, divorced from its sexual and singular specificity, is what helps Rancière create the link between humanitarianism and the war on terror, which he accomplishes through his analysis of Lyotard's seminal text of 1993, *The Other's Rights*. This text is an elaboration of Lyotard's reflection on the inhuman over the course of the 1980s. The inhuman is "that which separates the human being from himself," and by which we must understand, according to Rancière, a "positive inhuman": in other words, "that part within us which we do not control, that part which takes on many faces and many names: the dependence of the child, the law of the unconscious, the rapport of obedience towards an absolute Other." Therefore, "the other's rights" become simply "a testimony of the submission to the law of the other."[32] From one shift to the next, any violation of the other's rights is demonstrative of a will to tame the untamable and leads necessarily and inevitably to disaster. This is because, for Lyotard, it is this will to master that "would have been the dream of the Enlightenment and the Revolution, and which led to the genocide of the Jews," the Jews as the people "whose vocation it is to bear witness to the necessary dependence on the law of the Other." All these shifts and passages are condensed into one concept—the theory of the sublime and its central notion of the "unrepresentable." According to Rancière, this is the "fruit" of a double *coup de force*, which successfully threads together the prohibition of representation in the Jewish tradition with the impossibility of the representation of Auschwitz.[33]

When I first presented the paper that would form the basis of the present essay in March 2005, it seems I missed the real target of Rancière's attacks. Having read almost all of his published works to that point, I was a little puzzled by the following statement made in the last pages of "The Ethical Turn," where he talks, for the first time, or so it seemed to me, about a dominant consensus:

> If the Nazi genocide has lodged itself *at the heart of philosophical, aesthetic and political thinking, forty or fifty years after the discovery of the camps*, then the reason for this lies not just in the silence of the first generation of survivors. Around 1989, it took the place of the revolutionary heritage, at the time of the collapse of its last vestiges, which up until then, had linked political and aesthetic radicality to a cut in historical time. It has taken the place of the cut in time that was necessary for that radicality, at the cost of inverting its sense, of transforming it into the already occurred catastrophe from which a god only can save us.[34]

Foreseeing facile objections, Rancière continues: "I do not mean that the politics of art would be completely subject to this vision today. One could easily counterpose some forms of political action or artistic intervention independent from or hostile to that dominant current."

Thus, in my first reading, I asked myself the following questions: if the Jewish genocide has been at the center of a dominant consensus since 1989, or if Rancière really thinks that it has, then Rancière either did not notice it, or he did not critique it. If the Shoah was *not* central to such a dominant consensus, or if Rancière does not really think or care if it was, then he is using the deliberately retroactive construction of such a consensus as a litigious fiction for some present purpose; in this case, too, it is difficult to understand what that purpose might be.

However, my perplexity was short-lived, because in the October 2005 publication of *Chroniques des temps consensuels*, in the selections Rancière presents, we can easily see the elements that retrospectively constitute his ethical turn. "The Ethical Turn" represents, in fact, a synthesis of the themes discussed in *Chroniques des temps consensuels*, but especially after 2001, marking a transition between the theme of the end/return of the political and that of a discourse on exception.

Ethics, then, becomes the name of a new consensus, freed by Rancière's dissensual scalpel and condensed by Lyotard's evolution, thus bearing the weight of "The Decade" and its nightmare.[35] This is the new dominant way of thinking, whose particularity is to have usurped the assets and attires of revolutionary radicality to adorn itself with and to ward off every other promise of emancipation. Because this school of thought "takes its strength from its capacity to recode and invert the forms of thought and the attitudes which yesterday aimed for a radical political or aesthetic change," this discourse is effectively presented as rendering absolute the political and artistic dissensus in the process of being abolished.[36] This is a dominant trend which, after having placed the Extermination of the Jews in the center of thought, politics, and art thirty to forty years after the discovery of the camps, imposed a "theology of time," "of time cut in two by a founding event or an event to come": in this case the traumatic event of the Shoah. This reduced art to "the ethical witnessing of the non-representable catastrophe," where "the moral law becomes the ethical subjection to the Law of the Other."[37] In this ethical configuration, human rights have become "the privilege of revenge," and the world cut in half has become "the war on terror." At least, these are the conclusions drawn by Rancière at the end of his analysis.

It is undeniable that Rancière's thesis, which represents a conceptual contribution to the elaboration of a "geography of contemporary thought," itself participates in the same "distribution of the sensible" that it criticized. But it does so in order to refute the centrality of the Extermination or any political subjectivation on the basis of Jewish ethics (or the Law of Moses).[38] His explicit objective is precisely the political need to step outside of this configuration and to eluding the double-faced concept of terror/trauma that it helped make so commonplace.

Just as *Chroniques* and *Hatred of Democracy* allowed me to note that, in fact, Rancière had brought up all of the elements that would later constitute the theoretical fiction of the ethical turn, in retrospect they also allowed me to better understand certain effects of affects upon reading "The Ethical Turn." On the one hand, I reproached Rancière for his implacable, somewhat unjust critique of Jean-François Lyotard when it seemed to me that his ethical turn had been more targeted toward Heidegger and Levinas. On the other hand, I bristled at certain shocking formulations, notably the definition of ethics as consensus or Janus-faced law—on one side "the new law of Moses" and on the other "the law of McDonald's." But I was not aware that at the same time Rancière was presenting his thesis in Barcelona in March 2004 on "the ethical turn of politics and aesthetics" he was also working on a *Chronique* on "The Criminal Democracy" related to Jean-Claude Milner's book. Behind Lyotard he had Benny Lévy, Jean-Claude Milner, and a "chorus of subcontractors" in his sights.

In this context, the shocking formulation of the new law of Moses/ McDonald's would be symptomatic of a violence linked to a certain editorial actuality in 2002–2003, to "this little bicephalous war machine" that was the publication of Benny Lévy's *L'être Juif* (October 2003) and Jean-Claude Milner's *Les penchants criminels de l'Europe démocratique* (September 2003),[39] preceded by *Le meurtre du Pasteur* (January 2002). It is also symptomatic of a certain state of the world: that is to say, of "manners through which, today, our world gives itself to spectacle and through which the powers-that-be affirm their legitimacy."[40]

Rancière did not wait for Benny Lévy's book to attack "the power of the Voice, of which the shock during the night of fire, was felt by all the Hebrews, while it was given to the human shepherd, Moses, the exclusive task of listening and explaining the words and of organizing the people according to their teaching," as he reads it in *Le meurtre du Pasteur. Critique de la vision politique du monde*.[41] This is what is foundational to his criticism of Lyotard's notion of the sublime, just as it is to his criticism of any plot of exception. But in 2005, Benny Lévy's book would permit him to elucidate the position taken by Milner, who was applauded as one of the "champions of secular Republican education" at the publication of his book on *L'école* (1985), and whose position could be reinterpreted retrospectively in this light. Hidden under republican "transcendence," Rancière identifies the concrete figure of

Moses. And if he reads a similar antidemocratic gesture, from Plato or from the shepherd of the Jewish people, only Plato, of course, can be mobilized for use in his theory of democracy. For the theoretician of dissensual democracy, Moses as guardian of a flock becomes the figure of all guardians of the city; of all those entitled to govern men by their birth, wealth, or science; of every elite, antidemocratic par excellence; and of every law, which essentially implies the subject's enslavement to a single consensual law with two faces, the law of Moses and the law of McDonald's, ethics and economy, Judaism and capitalism.

In the French intellectual context of 2002–2004, Rancière's violent formulations, his relentless and unmerciful critique of Lyotard's aesthetic and ethical thinking, could have been, in the end, dictated by circumstances, the contribution to the "Geographies of Contemporary Thought," and the Lévy-Milner effect, before the real attack targeted toward the haters of democracy, who were finally to be unmasked in *Hatred of Democracy*. Thus Rancière is fully implicated in the ethical configuration, with his ethical turn, and the hypothesis concerning the new grand narrative in which Lyotard substitutes the Jewish people for the proletariat.[42] But he does so in his own way, because he puts Badiou and Lyotard back-to-back and spares neither the Pauline nor the Mosaic universal. He highlights, in both cases, the conception of an "ethical community that dismisses every project of emancipation" and "an idea common to these two visions. Through even the opposition of the power of the incarnation of the word and the Jewish interdiction of representation, from the Eucharistic host and of the Mosaic burning bush."[43] We should note, however, that this ethical reading and its reference to Saint Paul do not appear in the first version of his study of Badiou.[44]

Rancière's war machine—with its triple launch or triple salvo *Malaise dans l'esthétique* (September 2004), *Hatred of Democracy* (September 2005), and *Chroniques pour des temps consensuels* (October 2005) did not wait long to explode and pulverize the intellectual landscape. Even if this impeccably coherent ensemble is founded on his work on aesthetics and politics since the 1990s, it is firmly anchored in the present, as evidenced by the columns composed between 1996 and 2005 for the Brazilian daily *La Folha de São Paulo* or for France Culture on the air. It is an ethical consensus that further provokes his cutting, polemical style and exacerbates his extraordinary capacity to hit his adversary at the most sensitive point.[45]

Even while situating himself outside the debates of the Parisian intelligentsia, Rancière nonetheless shares a good number of the classic positions of the anticapitalist and anti-imperialist radical Left. For example, not recognizing the Shoah as a central event of the twentieth century or as a cut, sharing the universalist rejection of a Jewish exception, the renewed version of the Pauline rejection of a Jewish particularism. And even if he does not go as far as Badiou's injunction to "forget Auschwitz," he does not cease to attack all those who would make it the "object of the century" or purport themselves to be "guardians of the immemorial."[46] But to say that is to say nothing if we do not specify that these positions are, above all else, dictated by his system of thought, his conception of the political and of democracy, and his obsession with political emancipation founded on a single postulate: that of equality. His intolerance of exception, of the event that creates a break, of anything that diminishes or annihilates dissensual capacities stems from it. For Rancière, time, history, and even reality only exist insofar as they are dissensual political and artistic radicalities that create themselves in a constant, mobilizing rewriting of the past, to emancipatory ends.

Rancière's vehement criticism of the "new law of Moses" that cannot avoid being ambiguous in the current context will not concede to any identity blackmail, nor to any "charge of anti-Semitism," because in the current "hunt for anti-Semites" conducted by a few French intellectuals, we must only hear, according to Rancière, all "those who do not think like them."[47] In the same way, his radical, almost allergic rejection to any theologico-political universal brings him to reject any "Jewish conception" of the universal. His thinking of regimes of art and politics is mostly Eurocentric—Greek or German—in a reverse image of those who want "de-Westernization" (following Lyotard's example) or of those who see the intimate intertwinement of Europe, the Bible, and the Greeks, of Jerusalem and Athens, from Proust to Derrida by way of Levinas, for example. This new contemporary philosophy that posits the existence of another "Jewish thought," of an elsewhere that is an "extime," an exterior interior, is fundamentally foreign to him and only arouses his biting rejection—while he himself creates one of the radical breaks he absolutely rejects elsewhere, in this case the irreducible break between philosophy and Jewish ethics. For Rancière, it is the "Greeks who severed the tie with the divine shepherd and inscribed, under the double name of philosophy and politics, the proceedings of this good-bye," relegating to the status of fable the model of social organization founded on the divine shepherd and human shepherds who interpret his voice.[48] Democracy is precisely the rupture with any social organization linked to God the Father and which denies any foundational crime or infinite debt.

That it would unfold in this way, that the political and conceptual debate over democracy happens currently around the law of Moses, the sublime, the unrepresentable, the ethical exception, trauma and terror, apocalyptic discourse, the shock of religions and civilizations, the question of the Jewish name, is not due solely to Rancière: these are the terms of the current public debate and the philosophic debate, of the "distribution of the sensible" that asserts itself within a small group of intellectuals but also in the ambient discourse relayed by the media. Rancière's original contribution was to reframe the stakes, to displace them to his own philosophical and political terrain, without leaving them totally immune to the politics of affects that hold sway around the "simple" or "difficult" universal, be it Pauline or Mosaic.[49]

Rancière's polemical and theoretical device of fictitious dispute makes the often violent war of discourses and completely irreconcilable positions "treatable" in verbal, epistolary, or written exchanges, without falling into insults or anathema. Thus, we see Rancière thanking Milner "for responses made" to the remarks he had addressed to him concerning the theses of his book, still reserving for his ideas a polemical and theoretical treatment that is ruthless and unrelenting.[50] By the same token, Milner, on the air, the Internet, or in writing, refutes the theoretical positions and denounces the weaknesses of Rancière's argument without ever severing the discussion. For Milner, there is a "misunderstanding" on the part of Rancière, which takes as "central the question of filiation," which should instead be only a derived notion. This is a misunderstanding that goes along with "the promotion of democracy at the expense of the republic," that goes hand in hand with Rancière putting aside the question of names—about which Milner, a former linguist, has something to say.[51] The polemical and theoretical stakes thus clarified free the irreconcilable concepts of democracy, for the one, and "republic," for the other.

The argument of the ethical turn does not have the pettiness of the settling of scores currently in progress among the old friends of May '68—ex-Maoists, ex-Trotskyites, irreparably divided, as Slavoj Žižek writes rather summarily, between "Zionists and anti-Zionists"—for the simple reason that Rancière invented a dissensual philosophic style that keeps him above the fray.[52] One of the paradoxical traits of Rancière's philosophical writing is to adapt the style and tone of the subject under discussion to the "places" or circumstances at hand, without ever abandoning an equal conceptual "haughtiness" to use his terms, a philosophical writing that combines the two regimes—representation and aesthetic—in a clashing mix. He does not hesitate, on the one hand, to judge all the antidemocratic criminals on the basis of the single postulate that he has posited—that of equality—and, on the other hand, to treat texts and discourses equally and indifferently, on their own merits and not on the basis of the declared intentions of their authors or their notoriety. This is the source of the thinly veiled contemptuous irony toward the "chorus of subcontractors," of which Alain Finkielkraut—one of his whipping boys—is the representative; but it also gives rise to the ruthless treatment of thinkers more worthy of being discussed, as soon as he catches them lacking in "democracy."

The original conception of ethics according to Rancière allows us to grasp the bellicose ideology currently at work in political practices, governmental or not (Bush's war on terror, humanitarian war). Terror and trauma are theorized on the basis of the birth trauma, a concept that allows Rancière to link (Bush's) politics and the aesthetic of the sublime. This litigious fiction functions, then, to delegitimize the ethical consensus constructed as an antidemocratic trend, linking Jewish ethics and wars, the law of Moses and the law of McDonald's. It also reveals the invisible strings that tie together a host of inherent difficulties of dissensual democracy and the mourning of Marxism, a knot that Rancière wants to untie. He does so in order to give to Lyotard's aesthetic and political thinking a resistance in the face of the ambient catechism of the ethics of the Other.[53]

But, at the same time, it is a symptom, a trace, of the conflictual history of the leftist Parisian intelligentsia, elevated to the status of global discontents, thanks to the weaving together of two master-words, *trauma* and *terror*. From this point of view, Bush, Lyotard, and Milner share the same ethical ideology—religious or materialist—in the precise sense that Rancière has outlined. Their common Lacanian parlance of trauma and terror in Rancière's theoretical fiction should not surprise us. As to the effectiveness of the violent formulation of the ethical two-sided law—the law of Moses and the law of McDonald's—and of the salutary shock that it represented, we could perhaps measure it against the effort of thought it aroused here, to get out of the community confusion of sentiments along with the consensual confusion of concepts, under the seduction of Rancière's passion for dissensual democracy.

In theorizing the current malaise as inherent in the "aesthetic regime," in denouncing the conceptual confusion that makes the democratic individual's malaise into an "ethical turn," Rancière effectively denounces the malaise of the powerful elites. He launches his theoretical fiction at past and present enemies of the *dēmos*, of democracy as a dissensual practice. Democracy requires forgetting the shepherd and denying his murder, separating the political community from any link to the Father and the law, and endlessly denouncing the criminal penchants of democracy haters. But this unfinished and endless war, is it the promise of a future of the past, of a hatred of democracy which we will never be able to overcome? Is not Rancière's idea of malaise always itself dependent upon the imaginary doctors of democratic man and society, of the antidemocratic criminals? Is it not an interminable form of fratricide, murder in absentia, of all enemy brothers of democracy? In that case, there is hardly anything to rejoice about when the shadow of the Father does nothing but hover over democracy. In the meantime, the show—the staging of psychoanalysis, and the fable of the disappearance of the Father—must go on.

AESTHETICS

12

The Politics of Aesthetics: Political History and the Hermeneutics of Art

GABRIEL ROCKHILL

In the recent history of politicized art, two forms are readily identifiable. The first form, which might be referred to as *content-based commitment*, is founded on the representation of politicized subject matter. The second form, which might be called *formal commitment*, locates the political dimension of works of art in their mode of representation or expression, rather than in the subject matter represented. In the postwar era in France, content-based commitment is often identified with the work of Jean-Paul Sartre. Roland Barthes's *The Degree Zero of Writing* (1953), a critical reappropriation of Sartre's *What Is Literature?* (1948), can be seen as one of the pivotal publications in the turn toward more formal concerns, which eventually led to the work of the French structuralists and "poststructuralists," the Tel Quel group, the *nouveau roman* circles, and certain members of the French New Wave.

There is, however, a notable difference between these two socially recognized positions on the question of artistic commitment and the specific arguments formulated by the authors and artists who purportedly defended them. It is worth recalling, for instance, the following features of Sartre's position in *What Is Literature?* and other publications from the same time period: he generally restricted the notion of commitment to prose, he affirmed that the very act of writing leads to an inevitable form of commitment independent of the author's intentions, he insisted on the importance of the literary and stylistic dimension of committed prose, he formulated a distinct conception of poetic *engagement*, he made explicit reference to a type of reader's commitment based on the social nature of writing, and he considered that *engagement* was always bound to a specific situation.[1] Concerning the work of Roland Barthes, it should be remembered that the history of *l'écriture* he proposes in *The Degree Zero of Writing* is not a history of style or language (*la langue*) but a history of the formal signs used by an author to situate his or her writing in relationship to society. In other words, when he claims that Form remains "the first and last instance of [literary] responsibility," he is not referring to an author's style, or to language in general, but to a third formal reality, writing, that links literary production to the larger social order.[2] Writing is what he calls an act of historical solidarity by which an author, through a general choice of tone and of an ethos, commits himself or herself to a particular conception of language and its relationship to various sectors of society. Barthes's work in *Mythologies* (1957) extended this reflection on the social function of signs—irreducible to the standard form-content distinction—outside the domain of literature to include the entire field of cultural production.

It is partially in response to these two positions on commitment and the intellectual communities within which they emerged that Jacques Rancière has formulated an alternative conception of the relationship between art and politics. Instead of searching for the definitive solution to the long-standing problem of the connection between these two realms, he attacks the guiding assumption upon which this problem is based: that art and politics are separate domains in need of being linked together.[3] The notion of the "distribution of the sensible" (*partage du sensible*) succinctly sums up Rancière's unique position: art and politics are consubstantial insofar as they both organize a common world of self-evident facts of sensory perception.[4] In fact, the very delimitation and definition of what are called *art* and *politics* are themselves dependent upon a distribution of the sensible or a regime of thought and perception that identifies them as such.[5] Rancière has thus far outlined three principle regimes of identification for the arts (the ethical regime of images, the representative regime of the arts, and the aesthetic regime of art), which very loosely correspond to three regimes of politics (archi-politics, para-politics, and meta-politics). In other words, not only does he reject the idea that there is an a priori separation between art and politics, but he also argues that these are "contingent notions:" "The fact that there are always forms of power does not mean that there is always such a thing as politics, and the fact that there is music or sculpture in a society does not mean that art is constituted as an independent category."[6]

Rancière's criticisms of his contemporaries never compel him to simply discard their theories as incorrect. On the contrary, he goes to great lengths to show that their mistaken assumptions are the result of certain systemic conditions produced by a regime of thought. In other words, his polemics are always *explanatory* or *synthetic polemics* insofar as he insists on providing a genealogical account of the theories he attempts to refute. In this way, he not only purports to disprove the theories he is arguing against but he simultaneously co-opts them as elements in his own system of explanation. For example, he calls into question Sartre's distinction between the transitivity of prose writing and the intransitivity of poetry by highlighting the difficulty he had explaining why prose writers such as Flaubert used language intransitively like poets. He then relates Sartre's assessment of Flaubert's "petrification of language" to similar critiques that had been formulated in the nineteenth century (most notably by Charles de Rémusat, Barbey d'Aurevilly, and Léon Bloy) and claims that Sartre's work participates in the same interpretive regime.[7] This means that Sartre's mistaken position is, in fact, the result of a new set of interpretive possibilities introduced by the aesthetic regime of art, which reconfigured the function of meaning ("a relationship between signs and other signs" rather than a "relation of address from one will to another"), the interpretation of writing (which was no longer considered to be the imposition of one will on another but rather an act of presenting and deciphering symptoms), and the role of politics in interpretation (which became centered on the investigation of the underbelly of society through the symptoms of history instead of on the conflict of wills and interests sharing a common stage of struggle).[8] Rancière refers to this new interpretive model, which attempts

to tell the truth about literary discourse by deciphering its hidden political message, as the "'political' or 'scientific' explanation of literature."[9] Although Sartre criticized Flaubert's "aristocratic assault against
the democratic nature of prose language," he shared the same interpretive framework as the nineteenth-century critics who condemned Flaubert's disregard for the distinction between high and low subject matter
as a symptom of democracy.[10] In both cases, it is a matter of interpreting
literary discourse as the symptom of a latent political meaning. This
symptomatological approach to literature is, in fact, part of a long-
standing tradition that emerged within the aesthetic regime and has
spanned at least the last 150 years, from Marx and Freud to Benjamin
and Bourdieu.[11] In rejecting its account of the relationship between art
and politics, Rancière simultaneously integrates it into his own system
of historical explanation.

Roland Barthes's early work, most notably *Mythologies* (1957), was
heavily indebted to the tradition that held meaning to be latent in works
themselves and in need of interpretation. According to the terms he
would later use in *Camera Lucida* (1980), he concentrated on the *studium* at the expense of the *punctum*. Whereas the former is a set of
decipherable meanings and significations, the latter is an affective force
that resists all forms of explanation. The evolution of Barthes's corpus, for Rancière, attests to an attempt to atone for his early sins as a
mythologist who purported to have transformed the spectacle of the
sensible into a system of symptoms. He did this by privileging the
punctum that escapes all mythological interpretation and remains an insurmountable obstacle to the exchange of meaning. This decision is not
unrelated to a conception of art that Rancière has identified most notably with the work of Adorno and Lyotard. Art, in this tradition, is no
longer the symptom of a political meaning; rather, it is political precisely insofar as it resists the communicational flow of meaning and the
exchange economy of signs. Art, it might be said, is political because it is
an obstacle to interpretation rather than a symptom of latent meanings.

In rejecting this second conception of the relationship between art
and politics, Rancière once again integrates it into his own system of
explanation. Barthes's primary mistake consisted in failing to recognize that both of these approaches—the symptomatological and the
asymptomatological—are based on "a reversible principle of equivalence between the muteness of images and their speech."[12] In other

words, these two conceptions of the political potential of art correspond to the two sides of what Rancière has theorized under the heading of "silent speech" (*la parole muette*). This expression refers to the contradictory dialectic of signification in the aesthetic regime of art. On the one hand, meaning is a hieroglyph in need of interpretation, a mute sign requiring an interpreter who speaks in its place and reveals its inner truth. On the other hand, meaning is immanent in the things themselves and resists all external voices to the point of sinking into an irretrievable silence. Barthes's attempt to maintain a strict opposition between *studium* and *punctum* not only tries—unsuccessfully—to resolve this contradiction, but it also has the unfortunate consequence of foreclosing the genealogy of this very opposition.[13]

It would be a grave mistake to confuse Rancière's position on the consubstantiality of art and politics with either the notion of committed art or—a slightly more understandable confusion—with the conception of art that affirms its innate political force as a form of resistance to the status quo. In order to further elucidate his position, it is first necessary to dissipate a dangerous and perhaps unnecessary ambiguity. Rancière has recourse to at least two different definitions of politics.[14] More often than not, he refers to politics as the "dissensual reconfiguration of the distribution of the sensible" by intermittent acts of subjectivization that disturb the police order.[15] In his most recent work, however, he has increasingly referred to politics as itself a distribution of the sensible: "What really deserves the name of politics is the cluster of perceptions and practices that shape this common world. Politics is first of all a way of framing, among sensory data, a specific sphere of experience. It is a partition of the sensible, of the visible and the sayable, which allows (or does not allow) some specific data to appear; which allows or does not allow some specific subjects to designate them and speak about them. It is a specific intertwining of ways of being, ways of doing and ways of speaking."[16] The readers of *Dis-agreement* and *On the Shores of Politics* will have little difficulty understanding this definition of politics because it is strictly equivalent to what Rancière had earlier called the "police": "the police is [thus] first an order of bodies that defines the allocation of ways of doing, ways of being, and ways of saying, and sees that those bodies are assigned by name to a particular place and task; it is an order of the visible and the sayable that sees that a particular activity is visible and another is not, that this speech is understood as discourse and another as noise."[17] As is well known, Rancière maintained, in principle, a rather rigorous distinction between politics and the police: "Political activity is always a mode of expression that undoes the perceptible divisions of the police order [*les partages sensibles de l'ordre policier*] by implementing a basically heterogenous assumption, that of a part of those who have no part."[18] Has Rancière abandoned or reformulated this earlier distinction in his most recent work? Is the separation between politics and the police order not as strict as he once claimed it to be?

Eliminating these apparent ambiguities is essential to understanding Rancière's most recent work. To begin with, the primary link between art and politics is clearly the fact that they are both distributions of the sensible: "art and politics are not two permanent and separate realities about which it might be asked if they *must* be put in relationship to one another. They are two forms of distribution of the sensible tied to a specific regime of identification."[19] On numerous occasions he reminds his reader that art is not, in and of itself, an act of political subjectivization. On the contrary, art as a distribution of the sensible often acts as a police order that inhibits political subjectivization, as is the case with the meta-political art of the aesthetic regime. This being said, it is equally clear that Rancière does not simply want to identify art as a police distribution of the sensible that excludes political dissensus. It seems that art is inherently political for him insofar as it acts as a potential meeting ground between a configuration of the sensible world and possible reconfigurations thereof. In other words, the epithet "political" would be better understood neither in terms of what Rancière earlier defined as politics qua subjectivization (*la politique*) or the police order (*la police*), but according to what he sometimes calls "the political" (*le politique*), that is, the meeting ground between *la politique* and *la police*. However, this solution does not eliminate all of the difficulties highlighted above.

In an attempt to clear up the remaining ambiguities, it is important to remind ourselves that Rancière's earlier work on politics (*Dis-agreement* and *On the Shores of Politics*) often maintains a rather strict opposition between a consensual order and acts of political dissensus. In spite of his criticisms of his former colleagues, Deleuze and Lyotard, and his welcome critique of "irreducible difference," his work from this period nonetheless bears the mark of the logic of identity and difference, which continues to dominate one sector of contemporary political theory.[20]

The limitations inherent in this logic are numerous, but there are at least four that should be highlighted: (i) it reduces the dynamism of the social world and the complexity of history to monolithic conceptual constructs that purport to explain the totality of events; (ii) it is anchored in an implicit value system that is never fully justified or questioned, which consists in everywhere privileging the concept of difference over the notion of identity, as if difference was an innate ethical and political good[21]; (iii) since identity and difference are purely relational terms, it freely—if not arbitrarily—fixes the threshold between what is "the same" and what is "different" based on the needs of the situation; and (iv) anything *truly different* from the logic of identity and difference remains unthinkable, and this logic becomes a universal lens for interpreting the world.

Although Rancière is clearly indebted to the logic of identity and difference, it is arguable that some of his most recent work has led to a slightly more nuanced position, perhaps by foregrounding elements that remained somewhat peripheral in his earlier work.[22] Instead of simply juxtaposing a consensual distribution of the sensible and dissensual acts of political subjectivization, Rancière increasingly uses the terms "politics" and "art" to refer to both distributions *and* redistributions of the sensible order. In other words, in providing a more detailed account of the conjunction of art and politics, Rancière has been led—at times—to break down the rather strict opposition between an established order and intermittent moments of destabilization. In *Malaise dans l'esthétique* (2004), the distribution of the sensible clearly refers to both of these elements: "This distribution and redistribution of places and identities, this delimitation and redelimitation of spaces and times, of the visible and the invisible, of noise and speech constitutes what I call the distribution of the sensible."[23] The note at the end of this sentence refers the reader to *Le partage du sensible* (2000). However, the primary definition Rancière gives to the distribution of the sensible in this work focuses on only one of the two features highlighted in *Malaise dans l'esthétique*: "I call the distribution of the sensible the system of self-evident facts of sense perception that simultaneously discloses the existence of something in common and the delimitations that define the respective parts and positions within it."[24] A similar change in vocabulary is visible in his use of the term "politics," which he defines in *Malaise dans l'esthétique* as "the configuration of a specific space, the delimitation of a particular sphere of experience, of objects established in common and coming from a common decision, of subjects recognized as capable of designating these objects and arguing about them."[25] As mentioned above, this definition differs considerably from the description of politics he provided in *Dis-agreement* (1995) and *On the Shores of Politics* (1992/1998), and seems much closer to what he had earlier called "the police."[26] In emphasizing—at least implicitly—the police process in politics and the dissensual elements in the distribution of the sensible, Rancière breaks down the rigid opposition between stable structures and intermittent acts of reconfiguration. Politics, in *Malaise dans l'esthétique*, is a distribution of the sensible insofar as every distribution presupposes at least the potential for a redistribution. If art is consubstantial with politics, it is not simply because it is a meeting ground between a police distribution of the sensible and political subjectivization. It is primarily because it is, like politics (*la politique*), at once a distribution and a potential redistribution of the sensible.

POLITICAL HISTORY

I have thus far made a concerted effort to remain within Rancière's conceptual framework in order to emphasize significant recent developments in his work, point to a specific set of problems, suggest solutions to these problems that appear feasible within this framework, and urge him in a certain direction (namely away from the logic of identity and difference). In the remainder of this essay, I will jettison this heuristically constructed internal perspective in favor of a critical evaluation of his project from the outside. In doing so, I will concentrate primarily—but not exclusively—on the more schematic account of the relationship between politics and aesthetics that I have been edging him away from with the help of certain passages in his most recent work.

I would first like to call into question the near absolute lack of any historical approach to politics. Rancière argues that his decision to avoid the historicization of politics is based on a strategic choice complicit with his historical analysis of art. In both cases, he claims, it is a matter of showing that "*art* and *politics* are contingent notions."[27] This is done through a historical dismantling of the idea of an eternal essence of art, on the one hand, and through a decoupling of the link between specific historical developments and the notion of politics on the other. The latter move requires a "dehistoricization" of politics and a transhistorical definition thereof: "Politics exists when the figure of a specific subject is constituted, a supernumerary subject in relation to the calculated number of groups, places, and functions in a society. This is summed up in the concept of the *dēmos*."[28] It is interesting to note that, in the same passage, he is quick to add: "of course, this does not prevent there from being historical forms of politics, and it does not exclude the fact that the forms of political subjectivization that make up modern democracy are of an entirely different complexity than the people in Greek democratic cities." Implicit in these statements is something akin to the philosophic distinction between *empirical history* and *conceptual history*, or what we might call, following Heidegger, *Historie* and *Geschichte*. While there can be differences in the banal factual configuration of politics through the course of empirical time, the conceptual nature of politics nonetheless remains a historical constant for Rancière. Showing that politics is a contingent notion therefore amounts to severing the proper nature of politics from any specific historical conjuncture. Strictly speaking, however, this does not make the notion of politics "contingent." It simply makes all historically specific definitions of politics contingent if and when they do not live up to the transhistorical concept of politics proper. Since it is this concept that Rancière himself purports to have access to, this amounts to saying that every definition of politics is contingent *if and when it is not identical with Rancière's definition.*[29]

This transhistorical approach to politics has reached its zenith in one of Rancière's most recent works: *La haine de la démocratie* (2005). His bête noire throughout the entire book is *democratophobia*: the perennial fear and hatred of democracy—understood as politics proper—insofar as it disturbs the established police order. Although this hatred has changed through the course of history, as he illustrates with his analysis of a handful of contemporary books criticizing recent forms of cultural democracy, he clearly takes *democratophobia* to be a historical constant: "The hatred of democracy is certainly not something new. It is as old as democracy for one simple reason: the word itself is an expression of hatred."[30]

Rancière's account of democracy suffers from what I call *transitive history*: the object of historical analysis (democracy, in this case) is assumed to be a historical invariant that simply takes on different external forms through the course of time. Historical transitivity of this sort loses sight of the fact that there is no "democracy in general," but only specific sociohistorical practices like "democracy in ancient Greece," "democracy in modern Europe," and so on. It succumbs to a form of *teleological archeology* by which the final historical phase of an idea or a practice is retroactively projected back onto its entire history as a unifying agent. It is only by overcoming such historical myopia that it is possible to bring to light the fundamental structural differences, for example, between *dēmokratia* in ancient Greece and modern democracy, be it at the level of representation, citizenship, the separation of powers, rights, elections, political expertise, or the relationship between the individual and the community.[31] It is important to recall, in this regard, the general disappearance of the term *democracy* from popular vocabulary between antiquity and the eighteenth century (a period during which the term was primarily used by specialists and the practice itself more or less vanished).[32] When the word reappeared during the eighteenth century, it was still very distant from its contemporary meaning and was mainly used as a pejorative synonym for *Jacobin*.[33] It is only very recently that the concept of democracy has met with near universal acclaim, at least within Western polities.[34]

Rancière's own book is, in fact, a direct product of this historically specific *democratophilia*. It is a perfect illustration of the way in which democracy has become, especially over the last twenty years, a value-concept whose analytic content has been siphoned out and replaced by an inchoate mass of positive moral connotations.[35] *Democracy* has largely become a signal—to use Barthes's term—used to indicate what is morally condoned by the author using the word.[36] In Rancière's own case this is quite obvious, because he actually has no need for the term *democracy* in his conceptual arsenal. In fact, if this word does anything, it introduces unnecessary confusion. Since it is more or less an exact synonym for politics (*la politique*) understood as subjectivization (*la subjectivation*), it is questionable whether it plays any analytic role whatsoever.[37] One might assume, following common sense, that Rancière uses it to pinpoint the specificity of democratic developments, particularly within the modern world. However, such commonsense assumptions would be misguided because Rancière goes to great lengths to show that his own personal definition of democracy is extremely far from—and often incompatible with—the common understanding of democracy.[38] Why, then, does he insist on using a term that has little or no analytic purchase and which, on the contrary, only seems to introduce confusion? The answer is to be found in the widespread valorization of democracy in the contemporary world: he wants to imbue his own stance on politics with the positive and progressive connotations attached to the term *democracy*. In other words, he uses the word less as a *denotative signifier* to indicate a distinct signified (he already has *politics* and *subjectivization* at his disposal) than as a *connotative signifier* that indirectly signals the positive, progressive value of his own political discourse.

This detour into the question of democracy shows to what extent it is necessary to resist Rancière's political ahistoricism in the name of a sociohistorical analysis of political cultures. Contrary to what Rancière affirms, there is no "politics" in general, and certainly no "politics proper" (even if the *properness* of politics is to *be improper*); there are only political cultures—understood as practical modes of intelligibility of politics—that change through the course of history and are variably distributed through social space. As we have seen in the case of his faulty universalist claims regarding democracy, Rancière's own discourse is dependent upon a socially and historically specific political culture.

THE HERMENEUTICS OF ART

Now let us turn to Rancière's work on aesthetics. I have had the opportunity elsewhere to discuss some of the shortcomings of his project, including his negative dialectic of modern history, the lack of a genetic explanation that accounts for *why* the aesthetic regime has emerged, his restricted focus on the modern European world, his unqualified disdain for the social sciences, his tautological definition of art and politics, and his underlying aesthetic ontology.[39] In what follows, I will therefore restrict myself to one central problem in his work: the relationship between art and politics.

The first thing to note is that Rancière jettisons the notion of committed art as being vacuous and undetermined. Since there is "no criterion for establishing a correspondence between aesthetic virtue and political virtue," artists will use different means at various points in time to try and politicize their work.[40] The art that results from their choices can, however, be interpreted as being politically progressive just as well as it can be judged politically reactionary or nihilistic. Citing the example of American films on the Vietnam War from the 1970s and 1980s, such as *The Deer Hunter*, Rancière writes, "It can be said that the message is the derisory nature of the war. It can just as well be said that the message is the derisory nature of the struggle against the war."[41] Since there are no criteria for properly politicizing art, it is generally the "state of politics" that decides if a work of art is interpreted as harboring a political critique or encouraging an apolitical outlook.[42] Given this lack of absolute reference points, Rancière wants to step back from the social battle over the political meaning of works of art in order to elucidate their inherent *politicité*. It is thereby presumed that each work of art, in spite of whatever motivations might be behind its creation or how it may be received by a public, has an objective political being.[43] This is what I propose to call Rancière's *hermeneutic epochē*: by bracketing the realm of the political "experience" of art, he purports to isolate its pure political being. It might be said that he is fundamentally interested in the *politics of art* (understood as the politics ontologically inscribed in works of art), and that he therefore excludes the *politicization of art* (the social struggle over the political dimension of art, be it at the level of production, distribution or reception).

I would argue that Rancière here suffers from the *ontological illusion*. What he perceives as the politics of art is, in fact, only the sedimentation of the politicization of art, much like what Sartre calls the practico-inert is a sedimentation of praxis. Works of art have no political being; there are only sociohistorical struggles over the political dimension of art-work, some of which have led to recognizable formulas of politicized art. Rancière's own claims regarding the objective political being of art are, in fact, only one more contribution to the ongoing battle over art and politics. By overstating his case and acting as if his own *politicization of art* is coextensive with the true *politics of art*, he of course wants to convince his readership that he has provided the definitive account of the politics of aesthetics.[44] However, he has actually only made one more contribution to an ongoing debate. In resisting these claims, it is important not only to remind ourselves of Rancière's rhetorical strategies but also to provide an alternative account of the politicization of art.

Let us therefore take a specific example. The film *Lili Marleen* (1981) demonstrates at more than one level the way in which works of art are always *social works in progress*. The focal point of the film is the unique history of the famous song *Lili Marleen*. After being exposed to the complex motives and circumstances behind the song's production, the spectator is led through the story of its singular distribution and reception. The first time it is sung, by Willie, the main character, it is in a music hall where a group of Brits get in a fight with a band of German soldiers because they won't keep quiet. The image of Willie singing as the brawl breaks out and envelopes the entire music hall visually sums up the future of the song: it gave birth to a battlefield with shifting allegiances. Through the course of the film, the song is listened to approvingly by Robert Mendelsson, a classical-music aficionado and Willie's lover across the border; judged macabre by Goebbels; admired by Hitler; used by the Nazis to torture Robert, discovered to be a Jewish resistance fighter; blacklisted by the German government; sung by a mass of German soldiers when they see Willie, in spite of the fact that "*Das Lied ist verboten!*"; sung by Willie during a major Nazi spectacle organized after her attempted suicide, where her shadow—as in the song *Lili Marleen*—bears the trace of Robert's fedora and trench coat; and heard at the front by Willie's former pianist, who assumes he has stumbled upon allies, only to get shot by the Russians, who were apparently admirers of *Lili Marleen*!

It is commonly assumed that there is an ontological opposition between the work of art *in and of itself* and the appropriation of the work for certain interpretive ends (hence the idea that the song was simply co-opted by various listeners). However, this opposition is founded on a fundamental misapprehension, which is undoubtedly rooted in the practical habituation to individual objects through physical experience and language use. In spite of what its delimited physical nature and title might suggest, a work of art is by its very nature a *social object*; it is a site of collective meaning production. The creator of a work of art is not an isolated, subjective will that arbitrarily organizes the world according to his or her personal whims. An artist is a participant in socially recognized rituals and institutions that sculpt what is artistically possible.[45] This is one of the reasons why the controversy about authors' intentions is a false debate. Contrary to what the "anti-intentionalists" claim, it *is* possible to tap into the production logic of a particular work of art by understanding the historical time period, the social setting, the institutional framework, the poetic norms of the time, the artist's *habitus*, the operative modes of distribution and circulation, the spectators' or readers' "horizon of expectation" (the system of objectifiable references), and so on.[46] However, this does not amount to reducing a work of art to its "context," as if there were some external monolithic construct determining the totality of artistic production.

The fundamental problem with Rancière's approach is that he wants to be able to judge the constituent political forms of a work of art outside of the social struggle over such forms. Like Robert Mendelssohn in *Lili Marleen*, who says to Willie, "I must know what side you are on," Rancière wants to know once and for all where things stand. Willie's response to Robert can here be taken as a hint for how we should reply to Rancière: "on your side, as long as I live. . . . But one cannot always choose how to live when one wants to survive." Fassbinder's psychopolitics, here as elsewhere, reveal to what extent decisions are always made within a conjuncture of circumstances that preclude simple binary value judgments from the outside. The title of the film can be taken as a synecdoche summing up this gray-zone politics of survival. Just as the song—which is named after two women—has many different social lives, Willie has at least two different sides to her: she is at once Willie, Robert's lover, and Lili Marleen, the singer of a famous song under the Third Reich. As the film shows, it would be shortsighted to wholeheartedly condemn her for being Lili Marleen, since it is as *Willie* that she makes the majority of her choices.[47]

Rather than having a single, fixed political valence that can be determined once and for all by ontological deduction, works of art are sites of contestation and negotiation in which meaning is dynamically produced and reproduced. To use the vocabulary I've just introduced, we can be more or less successful in tapping into a work of art's production logic. This means that we can, without appealing to the "political being" of an artwork, provide better or worse arguments for understanding the political issues at stake.[48] With this in mind, I'd like to turn to Rancière's interpretation of three films released in 2003: *Dogville*, *Mystic River*, and *Elephant*.[49] According to his argument, by presenting average Americans as evildoers equivalent to America's "enemies" throughout the world, these films reflect the flip side of the global American crusade against the "axis of evil." In both cases, there is the same basic logic at work: finite evil can only be overcome—domestically or internationally—by recourse to an irreducible, infinite evil. The political dimension of these films is thus to be found in the ways in which they reflect a new era of evil, replete with a novel understanding of good deeds as deeds to be punished (*Dogville*), a new definition of humanism as the acceptance of the impossibility of justice (*Mystic River*), and a unique brand of neo-hippie nihilism where the naïve solution "make love, not war" is replaced by the utterly inane proposition "make films, not war" (*Elephant*).[50]

Although Rancière is a careful interpreter who always sheds interesting light on the works of art he analyzes, there are grounds for believing that his particular account of the supposedly objective political being of these films masks as much as it reveals. In the case of *Mystic River*, for instance, he has obscured the absolutely essential role of religion, community, and family values. As the very title of the film suggests, there is a mystic river linking the cycles of crime and punishment. The entire story takes its root in an event that would forever bind together three childhood friends: Jimmy Markum (Sean Penn), Sean Devine (Kevin Bacon), and Dave Boyle (Tim Robbins). Upon Jimmy's instigation, the boys decide to write their names in a patch of freshly poured concrete in their neighborhood. When they are apprehended by two men claiming to be undercover policemen, the one boy who doesn't live in the immediate vicinity, Dave, is escorted back to his home. However, he never arrives at home and is instead sequestered in an isolated location and sexually abused by the two men. Although he finally escapes from "the wolves" and makes it home, he would never be the same again, as symbolized by his unfinished name forever etched in the neighborhood concrete ("DA") and his inability to ever really be at home again with himself, his family, or the rest of the community.[51]

Years later, Sean Devine, who had since become the "good cop," is called in on a murder case in "the old neighborhood." When he recognizes the victim to be the cherished daughter of his old friend Jimmy Markum, he murmurs, half aloud, "What the fuck am I gonna tell him? 'Hey Jimmy, God said you owed another marker. He came to collect.'"[52] And when Jimmy does learn the news, a sea of policemen hold him in a position of near-crucifixion as he screams "Oh, God, no!" beneath a vertical crane shot retracting into the heavens, followed by a second crane shot of his dead daughter in the old bear cage that swoops up to an image of the beyond. The message should be unequivocal: the mystic river linking sin to retribution has caught up with Jimmy. In case it wasn't clear, Jimmy later mutters to himself in a moment of private rumination on his porch, and prior to yet another helicopter shot of the

Mystic, "I know in my soul I contributed to your death. But I don't know how." And when he eventually becomes convinced that it was Dave who murdered his daughter and decides to finish him off, he declares, prior to hurling his bloody knife into the waters of the Mystic, "We bury our sins here, Dave. We wash them clean."

The only catch is that Jimmy apparently kills the wrong man. It wasn't Dave who murdered his daughter but Ray Harris, the mute brother of the boy who was dating Jimmy's daughter. However, this is not a simple remake of Fritz Lang's *You Only Live Once* (1937) or Alfred Hitchcock's *The Wrong Man* (1956), nor is it, as Rancière claims, a script based on the promised victim in which Eastwood and his collaborators are calling for us to accept the slipshod—and unjust—work of justice in much the same way as the discourse on the axis of evil.[53] On the contrary, the message is that the Mystic River is doing its work of higher justice above and beyond the free will of the individuals involved (hence all of the helicopter shots of the river and neighborhood). Even though Ray Harris—along with his friend—apparently killed Katie to prevent her from taking his brother away from him, he was unknowingly paying Jimmy back not only for having contributed to Dave's demise, but also for having killed Ray's father, "Just Ray" Harris, whose body Jimmy had thrown into the Mystic years ago: "Just Ray" was the *just* man who had sent Jimmy away to prison and then looked after his family.[54] Jimmy half recognizes this higher truth when he explains how he felt when he killed "Just Ray" Harris, who had himself admitted that Jimmy was "a good man": "I could feel God watching me, shaking his head, not angry, but like you do if a puppy shat on a rug." And even though Jimmy apparently killed an innocent man, Dave deserved to die—according to the mysterious logic of the Mystic River—for at least three reasons: (i) he was guilty of the murder of a pedophile (described, but not portrayed, as a violent "wolf"); (ii) his wife had sinned by turning him in for a crime he did not commit, and she thereby deserved to lose her husband and be exiled from the community; and (iii) Dave had, in fact, died years ago and was, according to his own description, a vampire, a werewolf in the neighborhood. These are the reasons why Dave's sacrifice, as the final shots of the movie illustrate, is for the "good" of the neighborhood.[55]

The moral of the film is that a mystic river holds us in its sway in spite of our intentions, and that it is only through the—voluntary or involuntary—sacrifice for past crimes that a community survives. At the end of the movie, this is made clear at three different levels: (i) "the old neighborhood" where the boys grew up has been "cleansed" of its past crimes; (ii) the solidity of the family unit is reaffirmed in the juxtaposition between Jimmy's "royal" family reunion and Celeste's bewildered wanderings; and (iii) the *Devine* couple is reunited since Sean, after recognizing and implicitly condoning Jimmy's act of higher justice, apologizes to his wife for past sins, an act undoubtedly provoked by his growing awareness of the "mystic river."

Dogville also has a deeply religious dimension. Grace, the main character, wanders into a small town of "good, honest folks" while trying to escape from her past life as a gangster. After she is apprehended stealing a bone from the dog, Moses, she decides to follow the advice of the town luminary, Thomas Edison Junior, and tries to be accepted into the town as a refuge from her past life (thereby serving, for Edison, as the perfect moral illustration of the acceptance of a gift). In offering her services to the townspeople in order to be integrated and atone for her past sins, she at first meets with resistance because they did not need her help. However, she soon gets her foot in the door, and the vacuum from the lack of need is filled by a growing desire. After a springtime filled with a relative balance between the gift—Grace—and its acceptance, things slowly turn sour. As the police search for Grace intensifies, the town democratically decides that from a "business perspective" it is more and more expensive to keep Grace. Therefore, they ask her to work more to fulfill their nonexistent needs. Through a long series of events, including several acts of rape and a failed escape, she is eventually transformed into a modern-day masochistic Christ who becomes the benevolent pincushion for the community's deep-seated psychological problems. She is turned into the unseen dog from which the town takes its name, replete with Moses's collar around her neck and unbridled bestial abuse of her person.[56] Given the paradigmatic nature of this democratic town of "good, honest folks" (which is intensified by the film's theatrical minimalism and its debt to Brecht), the larger commentary on the twisted and corrupt nature of American democracy in the early twenty-first century is not difficult to discern: the gift of *grace*, the manifestation of *God*, is "accepted" as a *dog* to be sadistically abused—partially from a business perspective—in order to cathartically alleviate the "suffering" of a community that has no dire needs.[57]

However, in a kabalistic deus ex machina, the *dog* of the community is given the powers of *God* with the return of the Father.[58] Following a change in the light, Grace's masochistic phase comes to a close, and the vengeful power of the God of the Old Testament is released through firepower onto the town.[59] The *dog*-become-*god*, seated at the right hand of the Father, gives the town what it deserves for how it treated the arrival of *grace*: it merits the same rigorous moral judgment that Grace had inflicted on herself. The moral of the story is not simply, as Rancière claims, that it is impossible to be good in an evil world. It is also not—as Luis Buñuel suggests in *Viridiana* (1961)—that a soft but constant perversion undergirds and withers away the supposed good of religious devotion and social facades. On the contrary, it is that those who don't recognize grace for what she is, and particularly those who mistake the gift of God for a pitiful dog to be democratically abused from a "business perspective," those who, in short, act like this good little American town, will be mercilessly punished on judgment day.[60]

Rancière's interpretation of *Elephant* is the most egregious. He claims, to begin with, that it situates itself "outside of all considerations of justice and all causal perspectives."[61] It portrays the world of adolescents as being innocently devoid of reasons, law, and authority, to such an extent that normalcy and monstrosity become equivalent.[62] The final shot reminds us, according to his interpretation, that this is all only a film, and the underlying message in this naïve and nihilistic movie is "make films, not massacres."[63]

As an explicit reaction to the Columbine shootings and an implicit response to Michael Moore's *Bowling for Columbine* (2002), Gus Van Sant's entire film is constructed on the logic of false leads in order to resist the monocausal determinism that runs rampant in documentaries like Moore's.[64] The problem with such films is not only that they tend to drastically reduce the complexity of the sociopolitical world by attempting to single out a unique cause behind an entire series of events, but also that they aim primarily at edifying the viewer: by identifying the source of evil and locating it in the external world, spectators are bequeathed with an all-too-welcome dose of self-righteous moral superiority.[65] As Van Sant himself says, "It's in our interest to identify the reason why so that we can feel safe, . . . so that we can feel that we're not part of it, . . . it's demonized and . . . it's identified and controlled."[66] It is precisely this moralistic approach to political films that he wants to avoid. This does not, however, mean that he simply takes a headlong plunge into the abysmal pool of nihilism.

It is worth reminding ourselves, to begin with, how carefully and systematically Van Sant has constructed a network of false leads, set as so many traps for those viewers craving the cathartic identification of evil outside of themselves: (i) the opening shots with John's father drunk-driving him to school and then talking about going hunting with the gun "grandpa" brought back from the South Pacific after WWII; (ii) Nathan's lifeguard sweatshirt, suggesting that he is going to save someone; (iii) John crying alone, only to be discovered by an apathetic Acadia; (iv) Alex grabbing and shaking his head, as if one could simply say, "he is crazy"; (v) the kitchen help smoking pot; (vi) the elephant drawing in Alex's room; (vii) Alex's frustration at not being able to master Beethoven's "Moonlight" sonata; (viii) the rapid weather changes and the storm coming in, as if one could say "maybe it's the weather"; (ix) the Nazis on television; (x) the "homosexual" relationship between the boys in the shower; (xi) Alex's recitation of Macbeth's first lines in the eponymous play: "So foul and fair a day I have not seen." Some of these false leads are clearly revealed as such: John is very thoughtful and protective, the "lifeguard's" cross becomes the crosshairs for Alex's gun as Nathan is apparently unsuccessful in saving his girlfriend or himself, Alex and Eric are uninformed and dismissive of the Nazis, and Eric has never kissed anyone before and doesn't really know what his sexual orientation might be. Others are left more or less hanging, like the passing reference to insanity, the elephant drawing, Alex's piano playing, the kitchen help, the weather, and the reference to *Macbeth*. Finally, this long chain of false leads allows Van Sant to introduce what might be *false* false leads: (i) the discussion of electrons at "Watt High School" and the statement that the electrons farthest from the nucleus—like Alex in the back of the classroom—are "high energy" and can be kicked out of the atom when energy is added; (ii) the spit wads thrown at Alex; (iii) the *Gerry*-style video game in Alex's room; (iv) the website "Guns usa"; (v) the general lack of parental presence at Alex's house. In any case, a single cause is never identified, and the aim of the film is to show that multiple determinants participate in the production of any event. This logic of false leads is combined with a *huis clos* aesthetic: there is generally one plane of focus with slow, semisubjective tracking shots in which characters are stalked as if from a zero point of visibility, a technique borrowed from scenes in Stanley Kubrick's *The Shining* (1980), as well as Alan Clarke's *Elephant* (1989). Moreover, there are no establishment shots by which the viewer can grasp all of the spatial relations in the school (there is only Alex's map, which is part of his "plan"; his exit strategy from the labyrinth of adolescent life), and time doubles back on itself through multiple perspectives on the same event, making film time longer than real time just prior to the moment the shooting begins.[67]

This does not add up to nihilistic relativism. It amounts to replacing the determinist monocausality of self-edifying, moralistic political films by a set of overdetermined concatenations and chance relations that don't allow us to identify a single cause behind each event. Instead of being placed on a moral throne, viewers are thrust into the *huis clos* existence of the labyrinthine and prisonlike hallways of American high schools, where cliques and personas trap everyone in a complex network of social forces beyond their control. In refusing to isolate a single identifiable cause of high school violence, the film forces us to think for ourselves in trying to grapple with the ways in which an overdetermined sequence of events can produce the most extreme forms of violence.[68]

This radical change in perspective, which is not—as Rancière claims—a turn toward nihilism, is clearly illustrated in the Buddhist tale that is one of the sources of the film's title.[69] According to the tale, three blind men examine different parts of an elephant, and each one of them thinks he knows its true nature. The one who touches a leg thinks it's a tree trunk. The one who touches an ear thinks it's a fan. And the one who touches its trunk thinks it's a snake. However, none of them realize, from their limited point of view, that it is an elephant. The problem Van Sant is pointing to in a popular brand of political films is the tendency to mistake elephants for trees, fans, or snakes. Instead of trying to reduce the complexity of events to a single edifying cause, he urges his viewers to let the enormity of events stand on their own, even if it's at the price of our own rational and moral mastery of these events.

In the beginning of this essay I situated Rancière's account of the politics of aesthetics in relation to his immediate predecessors and emphasized significant developments in his most recent work. In an attempt to clear up certain ambiguities in his project, I presented what I take to be the most feasible—and textually justified—way of shoring up his account, which is largely based on distancing his work from the *franco-française* logic of identity and difference. I then went on to examine and evaluate Rancière's project from an external perspective, and I indicated two central points where our paths diverge. First of all, I questioned his ahistorical approach to politics and his ever-present political ontology.[70] In emphasizing the limitations inherent in Rancière's schematic account of democracy and his fondness for "transitive history" in the realm of politics, I advocated a truly historical analysis of political cultures. Secondly, I called into question his *hermeneutic epochē* in the realm of aesthetics and his attempt to philosophically bracket the sociohistorical struggle over the politics of art. In light of this critique, I argued that works of art are never fixed objects that can be judged once and for all from the privileged position of the philosopher of art. Artistic production is a dynamic process that is part of a sociohistorical world. This means that there is no permanent politics of art; there are only various modes of politicization. And these take place in different dimensions: not only at the level of historical regimes (Rancière) but also at the level of production, circulation, and reception. To provide concrete examples of my divergence with Rancière on the politics of aesthetics, I concluded my analysis with a critical evaluation of his interpretation of three recent films. This critique was not simply based on an appeal to the "facts"; it was fundamentally methodological in nature insofar as it broke with the reference to the political being of works of art in the name of an interpretive intervention founded on the production logic of these films and aimed at directly participating in the ongoing battle of the politicization of art.

13.

Cinema and Its Discontents

TOM CONLEY

Jacques Rancière is too practical a writer and too much a historian to figure in a canon of French film theory or its theorists of the past three decades. He is not the occasional philosopher, as he once described André Bazin, who brings ontology to the seventh art in order to ponder what cinema might be. He shares with Bazin an imperious need to ask what cinema *is*, and like the founder of *Cahiers du Cinéma* and father of the New Wave, he relegates theory to the operative principles of close attention to details that betray the governing traits of the medium. He does not share with Christian Metz the linguist's or the psychoanalyst's affinity for cinema that would define the spectator as a voyeur. Nor does he share with the late Serge Daney a taste for a critical chronicle of cinema when it loses its national character in the global market. He does make extensive reference to Gilles Deleuze, whose neo-Bergsonian philosophy of cinema has been a beacon of theory for over twenty years, yet he does so less to uphold a system of cinema than to bring into the analytical field study of unrestricted sensation and microperceptions that inform both the aesthetics of cinema and the aesthetic age to which he says it belongs. Without the slightest deference to Freud or Lacan, Rancière would prefer to refer to Hegel and Schiller to discern how the unconscious informs the seventh art in general.[1] No sooner does he philosophize to learn how to appreciate cinema than he turns about and away, in the direction of literature and its practicing theorists—Mallarmé, Maeterlinck, but Flaubert above all—who embody the qualities of the medium prior to its advent. In a word, to pigeonhole Rancière somewhere in forms of cinematic theory or its philosophies would do injustice to the ways he studies the conflicted and conflicting character of the medium.

To sift through *La fable cinématographique* and his publications in *Cahiers du Cinéma* and *Trafic* in search of the concepts that drive his analyses of history and philosophy would risk attenuating the contingent force and enduring results of his engagement with specific films and directors. To say that film redistributes sensation inherited from other aesthetic media, or to observe how it divides sensation—say, as plotted and shuffled among producers, distributors, strategists, and consumers—would reduce film criticism to a sociology or a rhetoric of the very kind that pitches and markets the medium. To look for dissensus within a film, in the contradiction between its objectives and the style that calls it into question, would ultimately thematize much of what Rancière studies in the broader currents of contemporary culture.[2] It might also be misleading to let what he calls the modern or aesthetic age serve as the containing category for cinema, inasmuch as, for starters, Rancière tends to make that observation repeatedly and to mold it as an intellectual matrix for his studies in other areas.

For the purpose of this short essay, a study of what he "does with" specific films and how he regroups his observations seems appropriate: as a practical viewer of cinema, like two of his model critics, Michel de Certeau and his late and deeply missed colleague Marie-Claire Ropars-Wuilleumier, Rancière works inventively, in view of immediate and contingent ethical issues, and with a sharp edge that cuts through the fabric of everyday life. Certeau studies history, it can be recalled, as the displacement of a chosen topic—from what the historian thinks is *there*, another point in time, to the present, unnamed, and even unnamable moment, *here*—by which a place is opened by means of evacuation and substitution. What was subtracted from the present in respect to the reconstructed past becomes what the historian must not avow. A masked law legitimizes the presence of motives that for institutional purposes must remain unsaid and unspoken. He or she "does with" or "makes of" the topic a moving relation that betrays the stabilizing effects of claims of disinterest and truth. In a similar way, his cinematic take on the past is that of a paleographer who looks at a film as a virtual landscape of images, letters, and words in continual flow and fusion, replete with relief, its hills and valleys adjacent to pools and fissures that turn the site into a hieroglyph.[3] What he "does with" a film (and his analyses are given to mystical cinema, in which absences or empty spaces figure in the center of the designs[4]) is tantamount to drawing an itinerary along which the reader moves in and across a text and image so as to create a space by way of the ways the "places" are exchanged, redistributed, and practiced.[5] This mode lifts an ostensibly stable object into a space of practice.

Rancière's studies of cinema are similar. They displace films into a context where they would not belong by treating them not as moments or documents of time past but as symptoms of times present, by partial virtue of the "dissensual" status they gain when they are lifted out of their original time and place. Thus in *La fable cinématographique* he chooses to study not one or several authors but a panoply of silent, early sound, classical, and somewhat contemporary films. Although the book is crafted from earlier articles, its spatial art of juxtaposition attests to a pragmatics of analysis: indeed, what he will later call a politics embedded in the unlikely—but vital—*art of interpretation.* The gist or the setting, landscape, and tenor of the readings in all of the chapters of *La fable* all attest to what elsewhere, when he considers the politics of literature since Madame de Staël's coining of the term (in 1802), bear witness to a "blurring of the opposition between interpretation of the world and transformation of the world."[6] Through close and differential reading, the world is changed in small but crucial ways and on a scale often imperceptible to strategists of ideology. The careful student of cinema is a tactician; he or she attends to its politics of form in order to discern what both constitutes and mobilizes its transformative virtue.

Thus the *muthos* or implicit narrative on which the chapters of *La fable* are based begins with the place of cinema in the arts, a place on which it depends and from which its own signal traits are defined. A first section on the "fables of the visible" begins with Eisenstein, takes up Murnau's silent *Tartuffe* (in which the evil protagonist is obliged to utter "*couvrez ce sein que je ne saurais voir*" in cinematographic and not in spoken language), and studies Fritz Lang between the "classical" age in *M* (1931) and what would be, given the presence of television in postwar America, a hypermodern aesthetic in *While the City Sleeps* (1955) and, to a different degree, *Moonfleet* (1954). The first one of the next two sections, on·"classical" narration (Anthony Mann's western phase) and "romantic" variations (Nicolas Ray), abuts the second, on aesthetic or "modern" cinema as embodied in Deleuze's theory, Rossellini's neoreal and postwar cinema, and Jean-Luc Godard. The last unit studies Chris Marker and Godard as historians who use inverse means to redeem film in its relation to memory and trauma. Eisenstein, however, is the first theoretical touchstone in the overall project.

Eisenstein's didactic treatment of dialectics in *Film Form* is shown to be effective where it does *not* reach or impart the director-theorist's wisdom. Montage, what Eisenstein called "cinematography, first and foremost," as opposed to cinema, "so many corporations, such and such turnovers of capital, so and so many stars, such and such dramas," is clearly endowed with *graphic* power: it is an art of drawing and writing.[7] The figural aspect of film becomes the writing that undoes or redirects, often in aberrant directions, much of its meaning. And writing, because it is displaced into a visual field, bears spatial and figural tensions that confirm and interrogate intended meaning. What is at once foreign and integral to cinema is taken to be what fabulates and what betrays fabulation.

At this early juncture, the reader might think that Rancière wishes to rehearse the contradictions that Marie-Claire Ropars-Wuilleumier had put forward in her close reading of the same material: that film writing neither transmits absent or present speech nor broadcasts themes at the crux of the narrative design. Film writing, what Alexandre Astruc associated with the "*caméra-stylo*" and Agnès Varda with "*cinéécriture*" is, rather, an art of tracing and of spacing; its moving images alter the nature of speech. The autonomous tracks of the medium introduce what can often become a contrariety between things viewed and things stated or uttered. When understood in its complex graphic design, cinema can lead the spectator into unforeseen areas. Montage is a hieroglyphics that, like Freud's *Zusammensetzungen*, articulates in the same expression conscious and unconscious effects.[8] But Rancière does not hold to the implied semiotic or psychoanalytical project that would define cinematic language as a combination of ideated and sensorial elements, by which the former would belong to diegesis and the latter to the image or areas to which the eye is sensually attracted. For him the apparatus, the camera itself, is stripped [*délestée*] of its mimetic function because, as adepts of Eisensteinian montage would wish, the ends of ideology reside in its dialectical form. Yet the stripping, close study reveals, does not always serve the purpose of ideology—what Rancière's teacher, Louis Althusser, called our imaginary relation to real modes of production. Ideation is lost when the image, bearing unpredictable sensorial latency, touches the nervous system directly, without the mediation of a plot set in motion by characters expressing their feelings and drives. Using what Deleuze called a logic of sensation to alter the inherited meanings of montage, he shows how the affective charge that the spectator experiences of the image (or a concatenation of images) causes cinema to become "more soberly the art that guarantees the decomposition and non-mimetic recomposition of the elements of mimetic effects."[9]

The stakes of the reading are multiple when Rancière wishes to bring a common calculus to the communication of ideas and the "ecstatic release of sensory affects."[10] He historicizes Soviet montage by relating it to the success that Nietzsche's *Birth of Tragedy* held among theorists of symbolist poetry in Russia, where the "Apollonian" language of images confers plastic form upon discourse, and the "Dionysian" counterpart, in brief, sensations. The mathematical element in the Apollonian aspect of the cinema, he argues, is no less Dionysian than its apparent contrary. Sensation is redistributed into the Cartesian realm, and as a result—and here the flow of Rancière's words shows further how his film theory is congruent with writings on politics and aesthetics—this "new idiom [*langue*] of an immediate union of intelligence with sensation is *opposed to the earlier forms* of mimetic mediation."[11] Cinema belongs, then, to the aesthetic age that has dissolved the hierarchies of form and made obsolete the Aristotelian principle of representation on which, nevertheless, it must be based. Eisenstein, it is well known, appealed to the masters of mimesis—Dickens and Griffith—to fashion his practice of montage. The seventh art, no sooner than it affiliates with a modern aesthetic sensibility, is obliged to work against or despite itself. In doing so, it makes clear the interaction of the active and passive aesthetic agencies it brings forward as had no other medium: mimesis, the guarantor of classical art that went with the form of an Apollonian creator (or, in standard auteur theory, the director) applies to matter, finds its antithesis and complement in ubiquitous *aisthēsis*. The latter is harnessed to the unconscious, which comes forward both in the mechanism of the technology of cinema and on the part of the spectator. The camera records more than what the director would wish because whatever is adjacent to the field of the image bears names or language that belong to other registers of cognition.

The order of Rancière's sentences translates well the observation. Glossing "Film Form: New Problems," a lecture from 1935 in which Eisenstein linked cinema to preconceptual or "primitive" logic, he notes how the theorist sees the "formal operations of cinema assur[ing] an adequation between the pure *conscious calculus* of the communist project and the *unconscious logic* that governs the deepest layers of sensorial thinking and the practices of non-traditional people."[12] Things at once new and old, modern and primitive, rational and sensual, are in concord and conflict in the aesthetic theory that Rancière locates in the German romantics who, at the dawn of the nineteenth century, felt that art had to serve the advent of the "new community."[13] When, he adds, we find ourselves ill at ease with *The General Line* because we would prefer not to be rid of its beauty in the same breath when we denounce its propaganda, Rancière writes of what unsettles and causes discomfort, what is indeed a *malaise . . . esthétique*, the very condition that will soon become the topic and title of a broader reflection on contemporary culture. Viewers of Eisenstein's films are dazzled when the beauty of the shots supersedes the political aims of their composition. Eisenstein becomes a film fabulist when he causes one register of the film to work against another and where, in turn, he deprives the viewer of the certitude of its message. The aesthetic discontent that results from countereffects becomes a critical ground for interpretation. And it can be added that interpretation quickly moves from ideology in its general meaning to a field where cinematic images carry the contradictions that specify the "imaginary relation" it holds with societal machinery.

The end of the essay refines its theoretical stakes. Contrary to Brecht, who propagated a "certain aesthetic modernity, with an art that stages the denunciation of the age-old ideals of art" that has since become the banal and predictable alliance between artistic novelty and the critique of dominant ideologies, Eisenstein today prompts "discomfort," in other words, *malaise*, less in respect to communism than to its aesthetization.[14] The linkage of aesthetics to politics is put to the test of cinema, and not the other way around, at least as propaganda would have it. The ecstasy, the unconscious drive turning "connections of ideas into concatenations of images" inaugurates "a new regime of sensitivity" that, he implies, works because it is tied to the older model of mimesis that it cannot sublate.[15] When one regime is perceived to be at odds with another, a feeling of unease inspires a labor of interpretation in which politics and aesthetics are inextricably mixed.

Now, in what seems to be an outrageous flourish at the end of the chapter, Rancière begs us to wonder in what century we are living when we react as we do to the sensuous excess of *The General Line* (that is, to the heroine Marta's robust body seen beneath her torn shirt). When we take pleasure, he says, "with a copy of Deleuze in our pockets," adjacent to Marta and her tractor, in seeing the love of a young woman of the first class and a man of the third class on the deck of a sinking ocean liner, Rancière asks us to wonder in what century we are living, and why. Are we staunchly in the postromantic age, when Schiller, the Schlegels, and Hegel opened the path to the aesthetic era of Flaubert and company, along with the postrevolutionary redistribution of sensation? Are we in the postcommunist era, in which allusion to rampant cinematic capitalism is made by way of allusion to *Titanic*, James Cameron's megablockbuster of the same year? Or are we somewhere between 1929, the date of the *General Line*, synchronous with the Great Depression in the West, and the years in which Gilles Deleuze's philosophy of cinema (published in 1983 and 1985) was taking hold? The answer to all these questions would be affirmative. Rancière displaces Eisenstein into the context of the spectacle of *Titanic* in order to temper its enthusiastic reception in France (some editors of the *Cahiers du Cinéma* had reclaimed Cameron as a new auteur) but also to inquire into the so-called sensuousness of its computer-generated cinematography. Rancière juxtaposes the image of the amorous couple (Leonardo DiCaprio and Kate Winslet) implied to "transcend" class conflict to that of Marta, by her tractor and cream separator, whose erotic machinery would drive the revolution to its destiny. Reference to Deleuze suggests that the "affect-image" of the close-ups of the hero and heroine of the feature fashioned for a global market are effective only when they are seen in an interfilmic way: the controlled *aisthēsis* shows that, unlike Eisenstein, Cameron and his cohort do not let cinema call into question the signs and shapes of flexible capital. The creamy images of *Titanic* are at odds with what Rancière draws from the contradictions that generate the mixed pleasures of *The General Line*.

The reflections on Eisenstein take a turn toward history in the middle section of *La fable* that touches on the question of cinema and modernity. What is the modern age of the medium, if not that of the last two centuries? And if the modernity of cinema must begin in its own history, when would it be? At this juncture, Deleuze becomes one of Rancière's crucial interlocutors or "intercessors." In the prologue that anticipates the broader treatment, the philosopher is scripted to play a keystone role in *La fable*, especially where *Cinéma 1* and *Cinéma 2* are called an encyclopedia that, with their analogue, Jean-Luc Godard's *Histoire(s) du cinéma*, are said to attempt to "sum up the power of cinema."[16] Each begs the question of the ontology of the medium. Deleuze takes a cue from Bazin, for whom images are the things they represent. As events, understood in the strong philosophical sense, they collapse mimesis into *aisthēsis*.[17] They are part of a process of open-ended *devenir*, becoming, and take part in an "ontological restitution" by which the qualities of the medium exceed what is shown to be the "old art" of their narratives.[18] In the modern regime, cinema becomes what it "is" when its fable tells of itself and its own way of advancing and of screening its narrative. In his appreciation of modern (post-1945) cinema, Deleuze sees and reads images in terms of sensation and duration. He advocates a tactile reading of film that draws attention to its "haecceity" or quiddity.[19] Rancière clearly mobilizes Deleuze's reflections on the affective nature of images.

But he also puts to the test of close reading the categories, taxonomy, and analyses that drive Deleuze's philosophy of cinema. The hinge on which the two volumes are joined and swing, as might the panels of a sacred diptych, he notes, reveals a typology that aims at redeeming the essence of medium after its fall into contemporary history. Deleuze had stated unequivocally that his was a taxonomy and not a history of cinema, and that film can be classified according to the quality of its images. Those which are classified as movement belong to three orders: perception, action, and affection. Each distinguishes itself in montage by intervals that the viewer distinguishes through sensori-motor means. The perception-image tends to rehearse the birth of visibility or even the "prehension" of the world and thus tends to be a long shot in deep focus, and more often than not is a take of a landscape or a broad view. The action-image drives narrative. Figuring in shot-and-countershot constructions, and generally of a medium depth (that is, a *plan améri-cain* that frames figures around mid-thigh), it espouses the movement in which it is an active part. The affect-image embodies emotion and is usually in close-up and given to the face or forms that elicit affective response. By contrast, the time-image cues on duration and not so much on perception, action, or affect. It isolates its subject in its field of view so that autonomous sounds and visible forms exceed the narrative designs in which they figure. The time-image makes duration—a sense of time without beginning or end—become a critical feature in cinema, much as it had been in its early and experimental era. Time-images are not distinguished by intervals but by interstices, and as a result they are less grasped by emotive means—association and attraction—than by a sense of spacing. Each image is such that it "tears itself from a void and falls in again."[20]

Rancière notes that the symmetry of the project is bespoken when Deleuze builds his distinction not over a formal design, as he had announced at the beginning of *L'image-mouvement*, but over thematic and historical bases. What Deleuze calls the cinema of "modernity"—of the time-image—breaks the cadre of mimesis in order to break free of the chains of plot and narrative. Yet the distinction itself is based on a historical typology in which the one species of image can only be in and of the other, either as reminiscence or prefiguration. Even though it claims to be a "natural history," "Deleuze's division [*partage*] of the movement-image and the time-image does not escape the general circle of modernist theory."[21] Faithful to the modernity of Bergson's theses on matter and movement, Deleuze shows that images are not transfers or doubles of things seen, but rather, they are things themselves, "an order of pure events."[22] They belong to a project that restores and redeems the image, much like what Godard undertakes in his *Histoire(s) du cinéma*, but now a "history of art that through its labors abstracts the pure poten-tialities of sensitive matter."[23] It renders images, by means of the spirit of classification, to the world whence they had been detached. Yet two "ages" of film, one of movement and the other of time, are separated by a *crisis* that happens—just happens—to be the Second World War.

The moment that Rossellini describes in his war trilogy becomes the line of divide. A category foreign to the "natural" history betrays the design of the project. The war and its trauma intervene: events that organize the narrative begin to disperse, the camera acquires a character of its own when it begins to stroll and wander about as do the characters, and the sensori-motor or emotive attractions on which cinema had been based lose their linkages. Rancière locates the beginnings of the end, or of the "exhaustion" of the movement-image, where Deleuze writes of postwar paralysis in the *thematic* register of Hitchcock's American cinema. In *Rear Window*, Jeff (James Stewart), his leg broken, is confined to a wheelchair and can only be a voyeur where he had formerly been a photographer. Scottie (James Stewart), in *Vertigo*, is so plagued by vertigo that he cannot reach the scene of a crime—simulated as a suicide—on the rooftop of a tower in northern California. And the wife (Vera Miles) of the musician (Henry Fonda) in *The Wrong Man* falls prey to psychosis. Deleuze uses narrative causes, not the cinematic lexicon on which the study is based, to argue for the weakening of the movement-image. Its end is found in its own attributes. The "movement image is in a state of crisis because the philosopher needs it to be in crisis."[24] By the means of what seems to be an effect of Freudian transference, Deleuze borrows narratives of castration and paralysis to paralyze cinema for the sake of its future redemption with the coming of the time-image. But where he has recourse to thematic segments to buttress his analysis, Deleuze nonetheless isolates image-units from their narrative schemes. He does what Godard undertakes in his *Histoire(s)*. The filmmaker extracts and recombines fragments from a panoply of films (including his own) to compose what seems to be a universal history, an avatar of Malraux's *Musée imaginaire*, of cinema that has passed through its own shattering and dismemberment.

The order of the gloss reveals as much about Rancière as it does about Deleuze. The shift between active and passive regimes, the former attributed to classical and the latter to modern cinema, is drawn over the distinction of the movement-image and the time-image, and so too once again is the memory of Flaubert, the classical-and-modern author who wished to conflate the distance between the artist and the machine. Yet, as Rancière made clear through allusions to Jean Epstein and Elie Faure, "classical" cinema had already caused the camera to be active in its passivity and thus to undermine the distinction between two eras or two ages. The effort to have the advent of the time-image, born of the

Holocaust, a time when its documentary images made clear how sterile or inert images were in light of the horror of the events they were attempting to register. The *image,* a word that in *Histoire(s)* Godard quotes through shots of the title page and first paragraph of Beckett's opuscule of the same name, bears redemptive power all the same. The end of the image and of art that comes with the liberation of the death camps can only be provisional. For Deleuze it is the time-image that succeeds in its acknowledged failure to represent what it records, and for Godard the image must be broken into pieces, reconverted and altered from its former character.

It is worth lingering on how history affects philosophy at a point where Rancière identifies Deleuze and Godard as fashioning two versions of the same redemptive typology. In a close analysis of a sequence from the *Histoire(s)*, Rancière asks why the director seems so prurient, excessive, and even outrageous in citing color footage, shot with a 16 mm handheld camera, that George Stevens took of the liberation of Auschwitz and Ravensbrück when he served in the U.S. Army Signal Corps. An iris-dissolve gives way to a scene from *A Place in the Sun* (1953) where, first, Montgomery Clift reposes on Elizabeth Taylor's ample lap, before she emerges, Venus Anadyomene, from a swimming pool and is about to be rescued, it appears, by the outstretched arms of Giotto's Mary Magdalene. The Christian saint uncharacteristically looks *down* on the scene from above. In composing the sequence, Godard has taken a detail from Giotto's fresco of the Crucifixion, turned it at a right angle, and transformed the sacred figure into an angel. The irony of Godard's voice-over says much about what is at stake: "Et si George Stevens n'avait utilisé le premier le premier film en seize en couleur à Auschwitz et Ravensbrück . . . jamais sans doute le bonheur d'Elizabeth Taylor n'aurait trouvé une place au soleil [And had Georges Stevens not been the first to utilize 16mm color film at Auschwitz and at Ravenbrück . . . Elizabeth Taylor's happiness would never have found a place in the sun]." We witness a montage of the conscious and unconscious motives at once of George Stevens as auteur and, more generally, of postwar Hollywood cinema. Repressed images taken from the camps give way to their unlikely redemption in the false aura of Hollywood realism. According to George Stevens Jr, who narrated his father's biography *Georges Stevens: A Filmmaker's Journey* (1984), the elder Stevens had confined the traumatic footage to the basement of his home, and only upon his death was it exhumed (before figuring in *D-Day to Berlin* [1988], directed by George Stevens Jr.). Godard threads a snippet of what are now familiarly traumatizing images into a sequence from George Stevens Sr.'s *A Place in the Sun* (1951), an adaptation of Theodore Dreiser's *An American Tragedy*, a film which is now seen in view of what the director perhaps would have preferred to forget. The viewer is left to wonder if the repression of war in *A Place in the Sun* (which Leonard Maltin blithely called a "depiction of the idle rich, and American morals, [that] seems outdated") is shown to be a signal trait either of Hollywood's repression of history or the traumatic latency of cinema that becomes palpable when the regime of the time-image begins. In all events, the impact of the combination of citations, here as in much of Godard's epic film, is devastating.

Rancière's slant on the sequence cues on the unlikely power of Giotto's saint, who is turned about, he notes, to attest to the new freedom of invention in video editing. Her strange placement in the image bears witness to the "reign of mechanical artifice and simulation" that, to the contrary, "a new spiritualism bring about, a new sacralization of the image and of presence."[25] Godard rescues and resurrects the image after it had been shown in mimetic deficit in and following the documentary footage of the Holocaust. Despite the efforts Claude Lanzmann and (especially) Steven Spielberg, after Auschwitz neither poetry nor images could, it had been said, ever redeem reality. But Rancière's Godard redeems the image *after* the death warrant the filmmaker had imposed upon it. He "complexifies" the image, and he redirects "the endless tension between the two poetics, both solitary and antagonistic, of the *aesthetic age*."[26] Godard, congruent with Deleuze, fits into Rancière's own historical diagram. It is not by chance that he sees Hitchcock's "wrong man," the figure from Hitchcock's eponymous film, who opened the field of contradiction in Deleuze's paradigm, as the perfect double of Godard. He is the one who demonstrates the "innocence of this art that ought to be guilty in order, *a contrario*, to prove its sacred mission."[27]

To conclude abruptly: along with those on Lang, Mann, Murnau, Ray, and Rossellini, the chapters in *La fable cinématographique* on Eisenstein, Deleuze, and Godard arch back to the beginnings of what Rancière calls the aesthetic age. His is a way of studying the deeper and longer heritage of cinema and its inherent structure of contradiction and contrariety. The medium is defined by concurrently active and passive forces—indeed, of conscious and unconscious drives—that inform its words and images. The "fable" that cinema always tells against itself is grounded in a postrevolutionary tradition in which aesthetic hierarchies are leveled and where the arts, which are by nature composite because of their coextensive plastic and verbal elements, are at once autonomous and mixed. Cinema that would be "old" or "primitive" in its early years is no less "modern" than its avatars in the digital age. Even though it can be categorized and historicized according to typologies of redemption, it unequivocally owes its power to an ability to be at once what it never was—pure narrative, pure mimesis—and what it is said to be—a screen of moving images on which singular and collective fantasies are fashioned and plotted. Its capacity to share and to allocate or redistribute these fantasies pertains to its active and strong ideological charge, while its ability to let or make perception and events happen unbeknownst to its conscious designs turns it into an arena of vital conflict and constant interpretation. The latter can well be its discontent, that is, the space where dialogue and dissonance or dissensus can help its viewers or "users" not only to sort through "the opposition between interpretation and transformation of the world" but also, no less, to cope with the ambiguities, unease, and discontent both about the medium and the worlds, in full contrariety, it both represents and invents.

14

Politicizing Art in Rancière and Deleuze: The Case of Postcolonial Literature

RAJI VALLURY

In two recent critical texts, Jacques Rancière offers a highly original perspective on Deleuzian thought by exploring it through his own
understanding of the relationship between aesthetics and politics.[1] Aesthetics, for Rancière, is not a discipline or a theory of art, or even a
division of philosophy. Rather, it is a specific mode of thought that is
also a mode of perception of thought, an idea of thought that is imbri-
cated within a field of the sensible. It refers to the manner in which a
space given as common is divided or distributed among the entities
identified as forming part of it. Aesthetics defines and delimits a field of
the perceptible by determining what is visible or invisible within it. It is
thus a configuration of ways of being, doing, and speaking that operate
as forms of exclusion and inclusion within a common sphere. Politics
occurs when a given field of the sensible is redistributed, when ways of
being, saying, and doing are reconfigured to make room for the emergence of new modes of subjectivization and inscription within a common world. Politics disrupts determined allocations of parts, roles, and

functions through an act of democratic dissensus, whereby previously unheard and unseen subjects open up a space and time in which they affirm their capacity to participate equally in a given sphere of experience.[2] Politics is aesthetic in principle, while aesthetics is implicitly political. Aesthetics and politics are tightly bound up with each other, but they are not synonymous or even equivalent. Their intertwining does not suggest an interchangeability or a mutual reciprocity. There is no correlation between the politics of aesthetics and the aesthetics of politics, no convenient correspondence between aesthetic virtue and political virtue.[3] As we will see at some length in what follows, Rancière attributes the lack of an expedient congruence between aesthetics and politics to the nature of the sensible within which they each operate. Aesthetics produces two modalities of the sensible, suspending itself within a sensorium that is distinct from the perceptible field where Rancière locates politics.

Rancière situates the fundamental inequivalence he sees between the politics of aesthetics and the aesthetics of politics within the gap that aesthetics introduces between two regimes of the sensible: the representative and the aesthetic. According to him, art and aesthetics have only existed as such for the past two centuries, emerging from a rupture with the norms of Aristotlean poetics, or what he terms the *poetic* or *representative regime of art*. Founded on the principle of *mimēsis*, or the imitation of an action, the representative regime of art lays down normative forms (*formes de normativité*) that determine which subjects are worthy of representation, codify different genres, establish a hierarchy between them according to the subjects that are represented, and define manners of expression that are most suited to the subjects represented. The representative regime of art is thus driven by a principle of adequation between action and signification, by a will to render the links between ways of being, doing, and speaking causally rational and intelligible. It seeks to ensure that the logic that underlies the order of poetic fiction is in keeping with the logic of the world in and upon which men act. The verification of the consistency between the logic of fiction and the logic of the world is to be sought in the effect that the poetic work produces on its audience, in the power of words to move, affect, and act upon their listeners. With the *aesthetic regime of art*, however, *aisthēsis* (the capacity to feel or sense) undergoes a shift from the position assigned to it within the representational regime of art: it is dislocated from the place of the receiver to that of the work itself, becoming at one and the same time "the work's material and its principle."[4] *Aisthēsis* is no longer a question of a speech act addressed to a receiver; it is henceforth a relation of the work to its origin. To this displacement corresponds a new mode of thinking of art, one that is concerned with the power of thought that inhabits the work of art, and which is identical to the idea of thought itself.[5]

The aesthetic regime of art produces a split within thought and the sensible by separating the sensible from an insensible, and thought from nonthought. It thus introduces a difference in the sensible from itself and a difference in thought from itself. However, this disjunction also constitutes a conjunction or meeting point where the sensible confronts the insensible, the visible contends with the invisible, and thought grapples with nonthought. The shift from the poetic or representative regime of art to the aesthetic regime marks a parallel change in the relation of words to the visible. While in the representative regime speech makes thought visible and words make things appear, in the aesthetic regime words must render visible the invisible power that brings forth speech, make sensible the insensible that gives rise to the sensible, and present the nonthought from which thought emerges. The work of art is no longer a mode of adequation between speech acts and subjects, nor is it determined by a relation of address to its audience. Rather than the effect of an action exerted by one will upon another, it is the expression of impersonal forces that escape the intentionality of a subject: "The place of art is the place of the adequation between a sensible different from itself and a thought different from itself, a thought identical to non-thought. . . . [It is] the place where thought comes to the sensible and where the sensible comes to thought."[6] Aesthetics thus founds itself on the idea of a heterogeneous (or at the very least, a dual) sensible, an insensible that it separates from the perceptible field of ordinary experience, or the sphere of representation. In other words, aesthetics operates at the disjunction it sets up between the sensible and itself, with all of the tensions and contradictions that such a split entails. For at the very moment that the aesthetic regime suspends the sensible into a difference from itself, it also establishes *aisthēsis* as a point of equivalence or identity of the sensible and the insensible, thought and nonthought.

For Rancière, Deleuzian thought, or what essentially amounts to the same thing, Deleuzian aesthetics, displays all the conflicts and paradoxes of the aesthetic regime of art. A radical departure from Aristotelian poetics, the aesthetic regime of art breaks with the hierarchies that subtend the former's partition of the perceptible and instead grounds itself in a metaphysics that affirms the immanence of thought within the sensible. To take the example of literature, the literary work of art declares its autonomy by identifying itself with a particular kind of heteronomy, with a specific mode of being in which matter and thought are co-present to one another. In this shift to a different ontological ground, an entire metaphysics of representation and signification comes to be abandoned, along with its modes of individuation and the relations of causality and inference between them: "The unique power of literature finds its source in that zone of indeterminacy where former individuations are undone, where the eternal dance of atoms composes new figures and intensities every moment. [. . .] The new power of literature takes hold [. . .] just where the mind becomes disorganized, where its world splits, where thought bursts into atoms that are in unity with atoms of matter."[7] But this metaphysics that grounds literature, the groundless ground of undifferentiated, nonindividual life, also suspends it in an interminable movement between autonomy and heteronomy, logos and pathos, between the immanence of thought within that which does not think and the immanence of that which does not think within thought. Deleuze's readings of literary texts, notes Rancière, are caught within the contradictions of such a metaphysics, wherein he is constantly led to betray the aesthetic ground that also constitutes the ground for his thought: the world of a-signifying atoms and molecules freed from the organizational hierarchies and divisions of representation, or in other words, the world of impersonal, nonrepresentative, and imperceptible becomings. This is an indeterminate universe constituted by the free dance of atoms and molecules that are undifferentiated and indifferent, where no one atom has an ontological priority over another; it is a world of pure ontological equality, regulated by the principle of nonpreference, in which the identity of difference is an indifference. However, such an aesthetics of indifference proves to be untenable in Deleuze's reading of literature, where he inevitably returns to that from which he seeks a rupture: the mimetic world of representation and signification:

Deleuze's analysis thus inscribes itself within the destiny of aesthetics as a mode of thought, within the destiny of the modern work (*of art*) that is tied to this pure sensible, in excess with respect to the schemas of the *doxa* of representation. It establishes itself in the zones where pity—that is to say, the sympathy with in-individual life borders on madness, with the loss of all worlds. Deleuze has to contend with the modern work as a contradictory work in which the pathic element, the thought-tree or the thought-pebble, undoes the order of the *doxa*, but where this pathic element is itself included, redeemed within an organicity and a logos of a new kind.[8]

For Rancière, Deleuze's readings tear the work of art from the world of representation only to transport it into the symbolic and the allegorical:

> To challenge all reintegration of molecular revolution into the schemes of representation . . . he [Deleuze] asserts a performative conception of literature, but by so doing, he returns it to the logic Hegel designated as symbolism. . . . Deleuze chooses an exemplary literature and an exemplary discourse on literature: a discourse in which literature shows its power, at the risk of showing only fable or allegory, a discourse where one can show it in the process of performing its work. But showing that operation most often signifies, in Deleuze, focusing the analysis on the figure of an operator. . . . He descants on the virtue of molecular multiplicities and haecceities, of non-personal forms of individuation. He goes on about the individuality of an hour that dreams, or a landscape that sees. But his analyses always come to center on the "hero" of the story.[9]

Thus, what Deleuze's readings ultimately favor is not the undifferentiated emergence of affects, haecceities, and becomings, but an exemplary character who emblematizes becoming. In other words, he returns to the terms of classic Aristotlean poetics: those of the story and its hero, of the choice between character and action.

At stake in this seeming inconsistency that characterizes Deleuze's reading of literary texts is the very nature of the politics that literature entrusts to itself. Deleuze's incessant return to the exemplary character or the figure, and his inevitable tendency to allegorize the work performed by the work of art, are symptomatic of the political combat peculiar to the aesthetic regime of art, the struggle over the kind of political community that can emerge from the conflictual equivalence between the two regimes of the sensible, the sensible world of ordinary experience or representation, and the insensible, a-signifying ground from which it comes forth. As Deleuze's analyses of painting illustrate, the rendering visible of invisible forces—in other words, the making sensible of the insensible—can only end in the madness of the a-signifying desert, in the absence of the work of art. The artistic composition must be preserved from "the power of dissociation exerted by pure sensation, the schizophrenia that plunges every figure into chaos," and from "the will to return to original groundlessness and reasonlessness."[10] Deleuze's literary equivalent of the pictorial figure, the eccentric or the Original, is caught in the throes of a similar battle: the creation and preservation of a political community "where human multiplicities are ordered according to their deserts" from and against the indifferent, a-pathetic and nonpreferential equality of the insensible desert.[11]

According to Rancière, Deleuze's choice of the exemplary hero must first be understood in Schopenhauerian terms: the Original expresses the power of the real that subsists under the world of masquerade and representation, that is to say, the power of the a-signifying, undifferentiated world of atoms and molecules. The eccentric symbolizes the encounter between two worlds: the world of representation on the one hand, and the world of nonrepresentative atoms, molecules, and becomings on the other. This encounter is also the confrontation between two natures: a secondary nature governed by the Law and the Father, and a primal nature that knows no such Law. Deleuze's mythical figure is charged with a specific political program for which he is endowed with a certain power: the power of fabulation, or that of inventing a people to come, of creating a fraternal community against the paternal one. The community of the Father and the justice of Law must be replaced by the community and justice of the fatherless sons or the brothers. However, the creation of the political community of brothers comes at a price, which is the betrayal of the truest, deepest equality there is: the equality of the molecular that derives from the principle of nonpreference. This is an ontological equality that challenges the fraternal community which must be created in lieu of the paternal one, because the principle of indifference that characterizes it deprives the fraternal community of any ontological priority it may have over the community of the Father. *Ontological equality is indifferent to the difference between the injustice of the Father and the justice of the fatherless sons or brothers.* A fraternal political people cannot be invented from a

Deleuzian ontology: "Nothing [...] is formed except the identity of the infinite power of difference and the indifference of the Infinite."[12] Summoning the image that Deleuze assigns to the fraternal community he asks his exemplary figures to create, that of an "archipelago," "a wall of loose, uncemented stones," Rancière explains why Deleuze is led to betray the metaphysics of literature and why Deleuzianism hurtles itself into the wall: both stem from the impossibility of actualizing impersonal, imperceptible, and indiscernable modes of being into a political community grounded on the equality of every subject that forms part of it. Deleuze, who seeks to chart out a passage from ontology to politics, stops short before the wall of uncemented stones, wherein the undifferentiated dance of atoms, molecules, and becomings cannot translate into the creation and operation of a fraternal community. Ontological equality or indifference is unable to make a difference with respect to political equality. "We do not go on, from the multitudinous incantation of Being toward any political justice. Literature," concludes Rancière, "opens no passage to a Deleuzian politics."[13]

One way of understanding Rancière's intellectual engagement with Deleuze is to view it as a philosophical disagreement between a thinker of equality and a thinker of difference, or an expression of polite skepticism as to whether a thought of difference can allow for the demonstration of political equality, that is to say, the appearance of a subject that claims its part within a common perceptible, thereby undoing a given distribution of the sensible. But what is at the heart of this confrontation is the possibility that each of these philosophers accords to the politics of literature and to the value of the political community it invokes. For as we saw earlier, Rancière refuses an easy equivalence between aesthetic and political equality. The democracy of the written word cannot equal democracy as a political form. In the interview he gave for the English edition of *The Politics of Aesthetics*, he states categorically, "Literary equality is not simply the equality of the written word; it is a certain way in which equality can function that can tend to distance it from any form of political equality."[14] To the extent that it breaks symbolically with a determined order of hierarchical relations that subtend the representative regime of art, literature sets into play the free circulation of words that are indifferent to their subject matter, their location in an origin, or their destination in an addressee. But this dissociation of all order results in a radically egalitarian impropriety that threatens to abolish the very difference between literature and life, between art and non-art. The very democracy that makes literature possible threatens to suppress it.

To combat the risk of its disappearance into the condition of its literariness [*littérarité*], literature transforms its politics into a meta-politics that denounces the disorderly noise of orators and the false democracy of the political scene, to which it then opposes the truth of its molecular equality. In other words, seeking to differentiate itself from the sensible of ordinary and everyday experience that deprives the community and its people of an authentic politics, literature invents a sensorium, people, and community that are (im)proper to it: "What literature opposes to the usurpations of democratic literariness is another power of the signification and action of language, another relation of words to the things that they designate and the subjects that utter them. It is, in short, another sensorium, another manner of linking a power of sensible affect and a power of signification. Now, another community of meaning and the sensible, another relationship of words to things, is also another common world and another people."[15] As we saw earlier, in the aesthetic regime of art, art evacuates its audience or the people who receive it, for which it substitutes a people of its own invention.[16]

It is at the point of withdrawal of aesthetics into a sensorium that is unique to it (a sensible that then doubles itself into the insensible) that Rancière situates the node of equivalence and nonequivalence between literary and political equality, or the difference that he sees between literary misunderstanding and political dissensus. The equality established by literature is a passive immanence, in contrast to the equality of political subjectivization. Both political dissensus and literary misunderstanding proceed from a democratic miscounting that disrupts the well-ordered divisions that unify the political community into an organic totality. However, political dissensus works on the level of the collective, in a process of subjectivization that links a group of anonymities constituted as a "we" with the reconfiguration of a field of political subjects and agents. Literature, on the other hand, seeks to undo and unmake the perceptible field organized around a subject of enunciation toward anonymous percepts and affects. Political dissensus is the construction of a sensible, while literary misunderstanding is a deconstruction or even an invalidation of its coordinates. If there is a whole that is still operative in literature, it is one that cannot be consubstantial with the individualities that compose it—whence the limits of its politics. Literary equality lays out a scene that is opposed to the scene constituted by democratic equality, "the scene of mute things that are without reason and meaning, and which drag the conscience into their aphasia and their apathy, the world of subhuman micro-individualities which impose another scale of grandeur than that of political subjects."[17] For Rancière, the politics of literature tends toward an indifferent muteness, an apathy that cannot constitute a sufficient ground for the testing out of democratic equality in an act of political subjectivization.

And yet, a Deleuzian will no doubt recognize, in this difference established between political disagreement and literary misunderstanding, the persistence of a very familiar ontological field, a plane of consistency that moves between the two poles of the molar and the molecular. In an interview published in the journal *Angelaki* in 2003, Rancière describes the process of political subjectivization in terms that are strangely reminiscent of Deleuze and Guattari's distinction between macropolitical and micropolitical assemblages: "I wanted to show that [. . .] forms of subjectivation or disidentification were always at a risk of falling into an identitarian positivation [. . . and that] the figure of subjectivation itself was constantly unstable, constantly caught between the work of symbolic disincorporation and the constitution of new bodies."[18] Furthermore, in the interview for *The Politics of Aesthetics* to which I alluded earlier, Rancière proposes a way of conceptualizing the knot between the aesthetics of politics and the politics of aesthetics in a more permeable, rather than a dichotomous, manner, by allowing for the entry of aesthetic modes of individuation into the field of the aesthetic possibilities of politics: "There is a limit at which the forms of novelistic micrology establish a mode of individuation that comes to challenge political subjectivization. There is also, however, an entire field of play where their modes of individuation and their means of linking sequences contribute to liberating political possibilities by undoing the formatting of reality produced by state-controlled media, by undoing the relations between the visible, the sayable, and the thinkable."[19]

My point here is not to indulge in a facile enumeration of moments when Rancière's thought reveals a Deleuzian "contamination" that undermines any difference in the manner in which they conceptualize the politics of aesthetics. We have noted that Rancière marks his distance from Deleuze in the nature of the sensoria that demarcate aesthetics and politics. For Rancière, Deleuzian ontology (or the aesthetic sensible) is neither consubstantial with nor commutative to the field of the political perceptible. My purpose in identifying some points of intersection between Deleuze and Rancière is, rather, to question the sensorial divide between aesthetics and politics by asking whether the Deleuzian (or aesthetic) sensible is as incapable of giving rise to forms of political subjectivization as Rancière suggests. In order to explore this issue, I would now like to consider the case of a postcolonial literary text.

If Rancière's formulations of the node constituted by aesthetics and politics are concerned primarily with the artistic practices of the western European tradition, they nonetheless offer an extremely rich vantage point from which to explore the politics of colonial and postcolonial literature.[20] Inversely, the postcolonial novel provides an interesting margin from which Rancière's theses can be tested and challenged. For instance, does the aesthetic evacuation of the audience and the community of the political scene continue to hold true for a vast body of work that is still concerned with the category of a nation and the people who constitute it? To take the specific example of Tahar Djaout, an Algerian journalist and writer who was assassinated for the disruptive power of both his literary and political writings (speech acts undertaken in full consciousness of their indifference, but also of their capacity to affect and be affected), can one sustain the argument for a meta-politics of literature that oscillates between a condemnation of the vain proliferation of empty words and the indifferent ontological apathy of atoms and molecules?[21] Or, on the contrary, does literature reveal a capacity for politics in the Rancièrian understanding of the term, as the demonstration of equality through an act of subjectivization?

It is in order to examine some of the above questions that I would like to turn my attention to Tahar Djaout's novel *The Watchers*. Proceeding from the unsuspected convergence between Deleuze and Rancière that I mentioned earlier, as well as the more porous enmeshing of aesthetics and politics that Rancière later advances, I will contest the latter's heterology of the perceptible, partitioned into the sensible of everyday experience with its accompanying politics on the one hand, and the sensible of aesthetics (which is split further between the pure sensible of art and the insensible that constitutes its ground) and its meta-politics on the other. By reading *The Watchers* with Deleuze and Rancière, I will argue that it is the plane of imperceptible and invisible haecceities and becomings that gives rise to a new partitioning of the perceptible, allowing for the emergence of a political territory where none existed before and for a new visibility of those who are of no account. I will show how allegory functions as an operator in the creation of a community of brothers opposed to the unjust hierarchies of a despotic state machine. Dream, metaphor, and symbol function as agents of deterritorialization that undo and rework the unequal distributions of the police state to configure a political space where the most invisible and "weakest of God's creatures" has a part. The allegory of the machine then functions at both its most metaphoric and most literal level: as a symbol of the nation, as well as a machine (a machinic assemblage or becoming) capable of counteracting that of the state in order to ensure the survival of the community. In other words, it is the novel's impersonal and molecular politics (its literary misunderstandings) that make for the appearance of political dissensus and subjectivization.

Published in 1991, two years before his assassination in 1993, Tahar Djaout's last novel is a savagely ironic denunciation of the Algerian police state and a warning against the dangers of totalitarianism, despotic nationalism, and religious extremism. *The Watchers* interweaves the trials and tribulations of two Algerians: Menouar Ziada, an ex-combatant in the Algerian war of independence, and Mahfoudh Lemdjad, a young professor of mathematics who invents a weaving machine that he first seeks to patent before entering it in a competition at an international fair in Heidelberg, Germany. The narrative painstakingly details Mahfoudh's battles with state bureaucracy in a Kafkaesque fashion, from his initial attempts to get his machine patented and then obtain a passport to travel to Germany, to his efforts to clear its way through customs and immigration in order to make it back to Algerian soil. Lemdjad works on his invention at night in a little house in the municipality of Sidi-Mebrouk, on the outskirts of Algiers. This arouses the suspicion of a group of vigilantes, former members of the Algerian Resistance who now enjoy the state's protection and consecrate their time and efforts to safeguarding the latter. Menouar Ziada, who forms part of this group and first notices Lemdjad's nocturnal activity, unwittingly sets off a series of persecutory acts against Lemdjad. But when Lemdjad returns to Algeria after having obtained the first prize at the international fair for his invention, he is fêted as a national hero. To avoid any future embarrassment or punishment for their persecution of Lemdjad, the group of vigilantes decides that Menouar Ziada has to be sacrificed. Their leader, Skander Brik, convinces Menouar that he needs to "disappear" in order to preserve the nation from shame and dishonor. The novel closes with Menouar's suicide.

The Watchers is not just a Kafkaesque exposition of the nightmarish nature of a state apparatus. It is also a novel charged with a political project: that of wresting the space of the nation from the despotic territorializations of the state in order to chart out space that allows for the expression of creative flows and desires. It lays out the topography of a political community freed from the Law of the Father-State and opposed to the police logic of the latter. Allegory, metaphor, and symbol function as the operators in the emergence of such a community or communities.

From the outset, *The Watchers* maps two cartographies of the nation. In the first of these, state, nation, and community are identical to one another and form a cohesive and uninterrupted whole, an immense body composed of one all-encompassing organ, the stomach. The other is constituted by the lines of flight that elude capture within the all-devouring gut of the nation-state to escape toward the head and hands, or the productive flows of dream, imagination, invention, and assemblage. Concerned solely with self-preservation and self-conservation, the "esophageal universe" of the state is characterized by two codings of desire that are the inverse of each other: an excessive rapacity and consumption on the one hand, and on the other, a stasis and immobility that do not allow for alternative expressions of desire. Its body politic oscillates between a polyphagian gluttony and an apathetic inertia: in this "country shaped like a voracious mouth and an interminable gut, without any horizon or illusions," Mahfoudh is led to wonder "at times whether the people in this city know any other forms of hunger besides that of the stomach."[22]

The energy and dynamism liberated by the birth of the nation are immediately territorialized into an "insatiable desire for cement" within a stagnant and diseased urban landscape incessantly hammered by the raucous din of machinery. Intelligence and speech collapse into the stomach; ideas and theories are swallowed within collective acts of mastication and ingurgitation. Mahfoudh flounders in the formless magma of words and sounds at a café, engulfed by the violence of a noisy and indistinct clamor of speech that can only result in a voiding or emptying of all thought: "The discussion is delving more and more deeply into metaphysical abysses. [. . .] Ideas are being wielded like insults" (65). Things are no different with the state, a "devious and labyrinthine machine of the police and the bureaucracy. [. . . in] which absurdity, indifference and contempt prevailed in an immutable system" (49).

To this labyrinthine space that comes from a proliferation of walls and order, Djaout opposes other spaces that do not immure or block, but which instead permit movement and escape toward an open horizon. The maze of streets and stairways of old Algiers that meander every which way to map out the shortest route to the sea, and the network of alleyways that give rise to dreams of a multitude of mysteries and marvels, evoke the city that was once open to the sea and the adventures of the unknown, but which has now forgotten its lines of flight to reterritorialize upon itself: "The city is a lazy homebody, turning its back on the sea again, breaking every connection with the open water, and finding refuge among its rocks" (126). But an Algiers that is removed from the claustrophobic confines and barriers of the urban is not completely lost for Mahfoudh; there exist lines of flight toward imagination and energy, refuges from the ingestive space of the nation-state: "For him it [Algiers] is the cozy shelter of childhood, the domain of dreams, effort, and painful and true passions all at the same time" (127).

La maison de l'aventure, or the enchanted world of childhood, books, invention, and creation, is one such nomadic space. Here, Mahfoudh understands how books work: not to please and instruct, but to open passageways onto alternative worlds, as planes of composition or machines for the exploration and construction of new territories:

> [Mahfoudh] was traveling deep inside the book among the underbrush of letters and the fluid outlines of objects. He was in an uncertain world covered by a tenacious fog that would lift from time to time to reveal a defined square in the landscape [. . .] the piercing eyes of a wolf. [. . .] Mahfoudh dug in deeply, sometimes stumbling or feeling his way in the half-light. [. . .]

He was handling objects randomly (only in his head, or with his hands? the borderline wasn't very clear) whose purposes were undefined. [. . .] Many times a landscape or a fantastic exploit put together with difficulty, word by word or letter by letter, would remain rudimentary, fleeting, or crumble in a stampede of frenzied letters. This crude decomposition of objects and places caused Mahfoudh a great deal of discomfort. Sometimes he would start the construction work over again; other times he would skip the obscure section and continue his exploration. (79–80)

In the above passage, any distinction between the image and the object, between fiction and reality, is undone in favor of the real, understood in the Deleuzian sense of assemblages and becomings, or creative productions of desire. Writing, reading, building, and inventing constitute such planes of composition: "Since he had discovered books and especially since he had seen Aliouate and Khaled handle traps, slingshots, and other devices (he also had been watching his grandmother weave enchanting patterns and decorate ceramics), the fever to make things had been gnawing at his head and hands" (83).

During one of their expeditions into the country fields, Lemdjad and his childhood friends chance upon a garbage dump (to which they refer as a "construction site") and decide to use some of its contents, such as broken tools, bits and pieces of building material, and the remains of what was once a scooter, to build a boat. It is not difficult to see the boat that the children recreate from a number of disparate, discarded objects and fragments as a metaphor for an alternative conception of the Algerian nation, an Algeria that is once more capable of reaching out to wider horizons, an Algeria that can and must be (re)constructed with patience and determination: "The wind of the open sea, laden with the unknown, pulled at him like a magnet. Still, something chained him to the land. What was it? Oh yes, he had to work at the construction site if he wanted the boat to take to the open sea one day" (84).

Similarly, Lemdjad's loom is at one and the same time a literal object and a highly charged symbol. It is a machine that must literally find its way out of a convoluted administrative machinery, one that opposes its elegance and efficacy to a system that is singularly devoid of these qualities: "The essential thing is to find the most aesthetic, the least cluttered, and the most functional model" (26). And at its most aesthetic and metaphoric, the machine performs the operation that Rancière assigns to politics: an apparatus that disrupts the distributions of the police order and reconfigures the field of the perceptible to inscribe a fragile and fleeting equality.

To the police logic that assigns forms, functions, and tasks to those who form part of the community, which decides what one can do, and when, where, and how, Lemdjad's weaving machine, created in the dark of night, opposes the free expression of a productive desire. At the ceremony honoring Lemdjad, the mayor presses his work and labor into the service of the nation's prestige and political program. Lemdjad's loom is yet another courageous weapon in the war against ignorance, one that continues the war of Algerian liberation. It is a machine for the preservation of the state: "As for Mr. Mahfoudh Lemjad, through him we salute the sober and useful young who spend their time not by minding other people's business, by criticizing this or that government decision or action, as has become the fashion these days, but by trying to enrich their fellow men with the fruits of their genius" (179). The state tries to establish a seamless continuity and perfect equivalence between the revolution, the nation, the state, the soldiers of the Algerian war, the popular masses, workers, and football players (144–45). Within this perfectly ordered distribution of bodies, and their places and roles, Lemdjad's speech allows for the inscription of those who are conspicuously absent from the stage, the women who are of no account in the community: "As for my modest machine that is receiving somewhat excessive homage this evening, I will only mention all that it owes to others, especially to the women who are absent from our celebration here tonight, but who for centuries have labored to weave together, thread by thread, our well-being, our memory, and our everlasting symbols. By means of a tool with which they ruined their eyes and hands and that, now that it has almost disappeared, I have reinvented, I express my wholehearted gratitude to them and return to them an infinitesimal part of the many things they have bestowed on us" (181–82). And by so doing, he effectuates a disidentification from the place of the nation-state, opening up a disjunctive space of visibility for those relegated to the invisible.

Like the loom, the books and the boat created by Lemdjad and his comrades are spatial configurations, planes of compositions, or modes of existences that escape attributions of parts, forms, and functions. They are, as Rancière notes in *Dis-agreement*, the emergence of a perceptible that is distinct from any judgment about the use to which it is put. They define "a world of virtual community—of community demanded—superimposed on the world of commands and lots that gives everything a use."[23] They reveal modes of existences that have eluded the allocation of parts and lots, virtual worlds or communities that are also worlds in dissension with those defined by the state, metaphors that are litigious aesthetic and political worlds.

What is worth noting here is that at its most literal and at its most symbolic, the metaphor is not a sign (understood in the Saussurian sense of a unit composed of a signifier and a signified within a structure of signification), nor a unit within the hierarchical divisions of a system of representation.[24] Let us recall how Deleuze understands the symbol (via D. H. Lawrence): it is a combative power, a harnessing of forces, "each of which receives a new meaning by entering into relations with others," in other words, a power of becoming opposed to the judgment of God.[25] "Judgment," he writes, "prevents the emergence of any new mode of existence. For the latter creates itself through its own forces, that is, through the forces it is able to harness, and is valid in and of itself inasmuch as it brings the new combination into existence. Herein perhaps lies the secret: to bring into existence and not to judge."[26] A symbol is an expression of the creative power of becoming. The books Lemdjad reads, the boat he builds with his friends, the loom he reinvents are, at one and the same time, machinic assemblages or haecceities, and the bringing into existence of political worlds and communities: a becoming-machine, a becoming-woman, a becoming-Algeria. They are modes of being that also constitute a mode of politics; they are an ontology that is also the bringing into existence of a political community.

It is in order to further explore this passageway between a Deleuzian ontology and politics that I would like to now turn my attention to the other principal character in the novel, Menouar Ziada. Even more than Mahfoudh, Menouar finds himself trapped within a nightmarish circle from which he desperately tries to escape: "Having a space to flee is vital" (8). Having left his native village to enlist in the Resistance more out of a fear of the enemy than any patriotic conviction, and incapable of putting down roots in the capital that has blocked every desire ("Desire is a word that has become foreign to him," we are told [190]), Menouar is suspended in a limbo between the two. Orphaned, childless, and displaced, Menouar is the man without a territory, with no place either on the inside or the outside of the nation-state, exempt from the community of the Father and the Law, as well as the society of brothers in which he is assured of having a place. "You know our strength comes from our solidarity," Skander Brik tells him, "from our concern to share equally both pleasures and disappointments, to act as one under all circumstances. Our relationships should be absolutely transparent. What will become of us if one brother begins to unnerve the other?" (101). But Menouar is ultimately betrayed by all those who form the camp of the just, the Father and the brothers. Suspected of treason by the maquis leader, Menouar finds himself abandoned to the elements by a God-Father turned indifferent, "a terrible and glorious father, with a devastating love. [. . .] He believed in his love, in his magnanimity, and in his omniscient fairness" (106). And if the tyrannical father spares him from death in this instance, it is in the name of his impenetrable and divine justice that Skander Brik will later demand the ultimate sacrifice (suicide) from Menouar. "The State is like God. Both demand our respect and our submission. Moreover, the designs of both are inscrutable and just" (158).

But the novel does not end with Menouar's disappearance. Suspended in a dream, Menouar escapes into a subterranean world which awakens him to the marvelous dangers of this one: "Menouar, the time has come for you to meet the splendid and perilous earth" (186). It extends the protection of its night over Menouar, a night that is also the rebirth of life and desire, and reaffirms his affinity with the creatures who share it: "God's weakest creatures, the insects [. . .] can now enforce their presence. They'll begin to make noise, sing, coo, and get carried away for the parade of love" (203). It is a world far removed from the laws of men and exempt from the wrath of God, a world of absolution, not condemnation and judgment. It marks its difference from the community ruled by the indifferent justice of the Father and the betrayal of the brothers. To this community that measures the value of lives according to their use, Tahar Djaout opposes a community of true brotherhood and equality, where the most fragile of beings has a place. This is a dream that is different from all those that have preceded it, those "always-unrealizable dreams" that "run parallel to the stunted course of his life" (197). The dream into which Menouar reawakens reconfigures the distance between the community of judgment and the community of equality.

Menouar is finally able to construct a single plane of consistency that brings together two inconsistent worlds, a world that had no place for his dreams and desires, and one that bears the promise of their existence: "Menouar knows a village. A tangle of alleyways runs through it. They link the things of this world and the things of worlds foretold—the silted river, the stars that guide lost souls [. . .] the cemetery on the edge of the village connected to it by an underground passage. . . . In this underground passage Menouar . . . (205–6). Maintained in the three points of suspension that end the novel, Menouar is the "*être de fuite* [the being of flight]" or the "*existence suspensive* [the suspended existence]" that Rancière describes in *On the Shores of Politics*, who flees along the line of an existence that is also a nonexistence, in a joining of community with noncommunity. The final line of suspension is what continues and sustains his vigil on the community to come, or to use Rancière's words, "a community that occurs without taking place [*une communauté qui a lieu sans avoir place*]."[27]

To conclude, what I have tried to show in the course of this essay is not that the vocabulary and theses of Rancière can be happily grafted onto a Deleuzian reading of literature. Rather, what I have attempted to demonstrate is how certain convergences between Rancière's articulation of politics and Deleuze's ontology can make visible the imperceptible passage that Deleuze lays out in "Bartleby; or, the Formula": the literary characters, the Originals who bear the fruit of the fraternal community and the people to come, do so by dint of belonging to primal nature (and not, I believe, as Rancière's reading of Deleuze implies, despite of it), whose principle of equality must be reconciled with the laws of secondary nature. In other words, it is the ontological equality of the molecular world of becomings that can and must found the fraternal community. In its mapping of modes of individuation that distend narrow forms of subjectivity toward a profoundly democratic and egalitarian union characterized by *a nonpreferential sympathy with multiple modes of being*, Djaout's novel shows us that it is becomings and haecceities constructed in a relation of unity and sympathy (rather than the a-pathetic, passive, and indifferent equality of all things molecular or atomic) that can allow a new form of political subjectivization to emerge from obscurity. And if it is a task fraught with much peril and danger ("so much caution is needed to prevent the plane of consistency from becoming a pure plane of abolition [. . .] from turning into a regression into the undifferentiated," Deleuze and Guattari warn in *A Thousand Plateaus*), the community to come or the virtual community always tries to break through the wall, to appear on the most invisible line of flight to the horizon. This, I believe, is what Tahar Djaout accomplishes in *The Watchers*, as a writer who is also the "bearer of a collective enunciation [that] preserves the rights of the people to come, or of a human becoming."[28]

In a sense, the temporal deferral of the community into the future, into the people to come, lends total credence to Rancière's contention that aesthetics evacuates its audience to invent a people that it propels outside of the here and now through one of two forms of a counter-teleology: the (Hegelian) nostalgia for the lost communion of the past, or the (Deleuzian) projection into the future, which is construed as a logical step within the "history of the fulfillment of the aesthetic will."[29] This is the price paid by the work of art in order to separate itself from non-art and mere life. And the people invented by aesthetics bear the marks of its constitutive divide between the sensible of everyday life and the doubled aesthetic sensible, split between its actualization in the future and its desire for dissolution within an originary chaos or groundlessness. The Deleuzian capture of the figure (or the aesthetic suspension of the people) within the future attests to the aesthetic will to preserve the work of art and its people from disappearing into either of the two sensibles, the sensible of ordinary experience and the *doxa*, or the in-sensible of *aisthēsis*. And this fundamental gap is what bars the easy passage from an ontology to a politics. But the Deleuzian (or aesthetic) deployment of the people within the future can also be regarded as a virtual unfolding of the community that is not unlike the virtual community which, for Rancière, ensures the appearance of politics: "And this equality defines, designs a community, on the sole understanding that this community has no consistency. It is, on each occasion, borne by someone for some other, a virtual infinity of others."[30] Deleuze's "virtual," in this sense would correspond to the disjunctive temporality of Rancière's scene of politics. As we have already noted, for Rancière, politics introduces a gap within a space-time sensorium, an incommensurability between two worlds within the sensible, imposing a community that only exists in and through the demonstration of "the pure, empty quality of equality" over the one given as common.[31] The appearance of politics is thus equally contingent upon an initial projection outside of the here and now of the community. Viewed in this light, Deleuze's virtual/temporal suspension of the people and community would appear to be not so much the (tortured) fulfillment of an aesthetic destiny of the will to self-preservation which preempts the possibility of politics for aesthetics as it is a move whereby politics is preserved for aesthetics.

tu cognosce tuam salvanda in plebe figuram
—BISHOP AVITUS OF VIENNE, in Erich Auerbach,
Scenes from the Drama of European Literature, 46–47

15.

Impossible Speech Acts:
Jacques Rancière's Erich Auerbach

ANDREW PARKER

It seems unlikely today that an Anglo-American reader will encounter Erich Auerbach's magnum opus *Mimesis: The Representation of Reality in Western Literature* except through the mediation of Edward W. Said. Indeed, the fiftieth-anniversary edition of the book's English translation is framed by the introduction Said wrote for the occasion, one of the last essays he completed before his death in 2003. Said's interest in *Mimesis* spanned the length of his career, with discussions of varying length appearing in nearly all his critical works, from *Beginnings* (1975), *Orientalism* (1979), *The World, the Text, the Critic* (1983), and *Culture and Imperialism* (1993) to his final (and fullest) reflections in the introduction to *Mimesis*.[1] For Said, Auerbach was, together with Leo Spitzer and Ernst Robert Curtius, one of the last of the great German comparativists for whom world literature could still be an object of study. Marked inherently but undiminished by its Occidentalism, *Mimesis* remained, for Said, "one of the most admired and influential books of literary criticism ever written."[2] Strikingly, what Said valued most about the book—what he singled out time and again, and in terms that hardly varied across four decades—was not its celebrated philological method, each chapter of *Mimesis* beginning with a literary fragment from which Auerbach adduced nothing less than the entire culture that produced it.[3] Instead, Said turned repeatedly to the penultimate paragraph of the epilogue to recall, as exemplary for modern-day "critical consciousness," the particular circumstances of the book's production:

> I may also mention that the book was written during the war and at Istanbul, where the libraries were not equipped for European studies. International communications were impeded; I had to dispense with almost all periodicals, with almost all the more recent investigations, and in some cases with reliable critical editions of my texts. Hence it is possible and even probable that I overlooked things which I ought to have considered and that I occasionally assert something which modern research has disproved or modified. . . . On the other hand, it is quite possible that the book owes its existence to just this lack of a rich and specialized library. If it had been possible for me to acquaint myself with all the work that has been done on so many subjects, I might never have reached the point of writing.[4]

While we've since come to appreciate that Auerbach's isolation as a German Jewish exile was rather more legend than fact,[5] Said took this passage to suggest that "it was precisely his distance from home—in all senses of that word—that made possible the superb undertaking of *Mimesis*": "In other words, the book owed its existence to the very fact of Oriental, non-Occidental exile and homelessness. And if this is so, then *Mimesis* itself is not, as it has so frequently been taken to be, only a massive reaffirmation of the Western cultural tradition, but also a work built upon a critically important alienation from it, a work whose conditions and circumstances of existence are not immediately derived from the culture it describes with such extraordinary insight and brilliance but built rather on an agonizing distance from it."[6]

Transforming this distance into a requisite condition for critical consciousness *tout court*—a consciousness for which, in the memorable phrase by Hugh of St. Victor's quoted by Auerbach and repeated frequently by Said, "the entire world is as a foreign place"—Auerbach became for Said an image of the consummate cosmopolitan, "equally wary of an imperial universalism and the beleaguered solace of tribal identities."[7] A figure, in short, very much like Said himself.

If this is the Auerbach with whom Anglo-American readers are familiar today, they may well decide that the Auerbach discussed by Jacques Rancière is someone else entirely. And they would largely be correct. Though Said and Rancière each wrote about the Gospel tale of Peter's denial of Christ from which Auerbach developed his important account of *figura*, this is where their common interests seem to end.[8] What drew Said to *Mimesis*, as Aamir Mufti put it, "is not so much the Auerbachian text, the text whose author-function bears the name of Auerbach, but rather Auerbach *as* text," the writer "himself" in his existential situation.[9] Rancière, on the other hand, is much less interested in Auerbach's biography than in his writing—specifically, in the history *Mimesis* recounts of the rise and fall of the classical doctrine of decorum, the hierarchical alignment of literary genres with the class identities of their represented subjects: "There were high genres, devoted to the imitation of noble actions and characters, and low genres devoted to common people and base subject matters. The hierarchy of genres also submitted style to a principle of hierarchical convenience: kings had to act and speak as kings do, and common people as common people do. The convention was not simply an academic constraint. There was a homology between the rationality of poetic fiction and the intelligibility of human actions, conceived of as an adequation between ways of being, ways of doing and ways of speaking."[10]

Just as, to my knowledge, Rancière has never remarked upon Auerbach's exile in Istanbul (let alone construed it as the condition of his achievement as a critic), Said showed scant interest in the question of decorum in *Mimesis* until his late introduction. I want to follow Rancière here as he reads a long passage from Tacitus's *Annals* that occurs in the middle of the second chapter of *Mimesis*. This fragment merits close attention not only because it tends to be overlooked, preceding as it does the story of Peter's denial that forms the highpoint of that chapter and, indeed, of the entire book. The passage will also help to illuminate some of the political issues at stake in Said's and Rancière's respective approaches to Auerbach. Here, first, is the passage from Tacitus:

> Thus stood affairs at Rome, when a sedition made its appearance in the legions in Pannonia, without any fresh grounds [*nullis novis causis*], save that the accession of a new prince promised impunity to tumult, and held out the hope of advantages to be derived from a civil war. Three legions

occupied a summer camp together, commanded by Junius Blaesus, who, upon notice of the death of Augustus and accession of Tiberius, had granted the soldiers a recess from their wonted duties for some days, as a time either of public mourning or festivity. From this beginning they waxed wanton and quarrelsome, lent their ears to the discourses of every profligate, and at last they longed for a life of dissipation and idleness, and spurned all military discipline and labor. In the camp was one Percennius, formerly a busy leader of theatrical factions [*dux olim theatralium operarum*], after that a common soldier, of a petulant tongue, and from his experience in theatrical party zeal [*miscere coetus histrionali studio doctus*], well qualified to stir up the bad passions of a crowd. Upon minds uninformed, and agitated with doubts as to what might be the condition of military service now that Augustus was dead, he wrought gradually by confabulations by night, or when day verged towards its close; and when all the better-disposed had retired to their respective quarters, he would congregate all the most depraved about him.

Lastly, when now also other ministers of sedition were at hand to second his designs, in imitation of a general solemnly haranguing his men, he asked them—"Why did they obey, like slaves, a few centurions and fewer tribunes? When would they be bold enough to demand redress, unless they approached the prince, yet a novice, and tottering on his throne, either with entreaties or arms? Enough had they erred in remaining passive through so many years, since decrepit with age and maimed with wounds, after a course of service of thirty or forty years, they were still doomed to carry arms; nor even to those who were discharged was there any end of service, but they were still kept to the colors, and under another name endured the same hardships. And if any of them survived so many dangers, still were they dragged into countries far remote, where, under the name of lands, they are presented with swampy fens, or mountain wastes. But surely, burdensome and ungainful of itself was the occupation of war;—ten asses a day the poor price of their persons and lives; out of this they must buy clothes, and tents, and arms,—out of this the cruelty of centurions must be redeemed, and occasional exemptions from duty; but, by Hercules, stripes, wounds, hard winters and laborious summers, bloody wars and barren peace, were miseries eternally to be endured; nor remained there other remedy than to enter the service upon certain conditions, as that their pay should be a denarius a day, sixteen years be the utmost term of serving; beyond that period to be no longer obliged to follow the colors, but have their reward in money, paid them in the camp where they earned it. Did the praetorian guards, who had double pay,—they who after sixteen years' service were sent home, undergo more dangers? This was not said in disparagement of the city guards; their own lot, however, was, serving among uncivilized nations, to have the enemy in view from their tents."

The general body received this harangue with shouts of applause, but stimulated by various motives,—some showing, in all the bitterness of reproach, the marks of stripes, others their hoary heads, many their tattered vestments and naked bodies.[11]

As you may recall, Auerbach argues throughout this second chapter of *Mimesis* that the New Testament succeeded in providing a complex and serious rendering of the lives of common people where the Romans writers failed to do so, bound as they were by rules of decorum that mandated for the depiction of the lower classes the low language of comedy. As a result, Roman writing could not be realistic since it lacked, in its adherence to unchanging ethical categories, all capacity for historical consciousness. There could be in it, for Auerbach, "no serious literary treatment of everyday occupations and social classes—merchants, artisans, peasants, slaves—of everyday scenes and places—home, shop, field, store—of everyday customs and institutions—marriage, children, work, earning a living—in short, of the people and its life."[12]

The Tacitus passage may seem initially to fulfill these criteria for realism in the highly particularized details included in the soldiers' complaints. Auerbach notes, indeed, that "the grievances of the soldiers discussed in Percennius's speech—excessive length of service, hardships, insufficient pay, inadequate old-age provision, corruption, envy of the easier life of the metropolitan troops—are presented vividly and graphically in a manner not frequently encountered even in modern historians."[13] But the fact that these grievances are presented not in Tacitus's voice, but as "utterances of the ringleader Percennius," makes them something other than historically typical or realistic: "The factual information [Tacitus] gives on the causes of the revolt—information presented in the form of a ringleader's speech and not discussed further—he invalidates in advance by stating at the outset his own view of the real causes of the revolt in purely ethical terms: *nullis novis causis*."[14] That Percennius is further portrayed as a master of imitation—trained in the theater, he mimics "a general solemnly haranguing his men"—disqualifies him still further; in place of the "silence of military discipline," we are given only the negative values associated with what Rancière terms, in *The Names of History*, "the roar of urban theatrocracy."[15] Why, then, put Percennius on stage at all if Tacitus was hardly "interested in the soldiers' demands and never intended to discuss them objectively"? The reason, Auerbach explains, is "purely aesthetic":

> The grand style of historiography requires grandiloquent speeches, which as a rule are fictitious. Their function is graphic dramatization (*illustratio*) of a given occurrence, or at times the presentation of great political or moral ideas; in either case they are intended as the rhetorical bravura pieces of the presentation. The writer is permitted a certain sympathetic entering into the thoughts of the supposed speaker, and even a certain realism. Essentially, however, such speeches are products of a specific stylistic tradition cultivated in the schools for rhetors. The composition of speeches which one person or another might have delivered on one or another great historical occasion was a favorite exercise. Tacitus is a master of his craft, and his speeches are not sheer display; they are really imbued with the character and the situation of the persons supposed to have delivered them; but they too are primarily rhetorical. Percennius does not speak in his own language; he speaks Tacitean, that is, he speaks with extreme terseness, as a matter of disposition, and highly rhetorically. Undoubtedly his words—though given as indirect discourse—vibrate with the actual excitement of mutinous soldiers and their leader. Yet even if we assume that Percennius was a gifted demagogue, such brevity, incisiveness, and order are not possible in a rebellious propaganda speech, and of soldiers' slang there is not the slightest trace.[16]

What Auerbach seems to be pondering here is nothing less than a question we have learned to pose in a rather different context: "Can the plebeian speak?" To which, for Rancière, the answer would be "no": "Percennius doesn't speak; rather, Tacitus lends him his tongue."[17] If we were expecting him to declaim in *propria persona*, we soon realize that "Percennius had no place to speak," since, as a represented member of the poor, he has only "an essential relation with nontruth."[18] The justifications for the revolt that are credited to Percennius are not refuted by or even commented on by Tacitus; the historian has no need to do either, since the argument Percennius provides can *be* neither true nor false:

They have, fundamentally, no relation to the truth. Their illegitimacy is not due to their content but to the simple fact that Percennius is not in the position of legitimate speaker. A man of his rank has no business thinking and expressing his thought. And his speech is ordinarily reproduced only in the "base" genres of satire and comedy. It is ruled out that an essential conflict would be expressed through his mouth, ruled out that we would see in him, in a modern sense, the symptomatic representative of a historical movement that operates in the depths of a society. The speech of the man of the common people is by definition without depth.[19]

Thus Tacitus, as Rancière reads Auerbach, explains the revolt twice, doubly dispossessing Percennius by stripping him both of his justifications and his voice.[20] According to Rancière, Auerbach here would be marking, "in his own way, the relation between a politics of knowledge and a poetics of narrative around the question of the politics of the other."[21] But this other is not simply excluded by Tacitus, whose discourse nonetheless manages, precisely, to give a place "to what it declares to have no place."[22] While Auerbach left underemphasized the question of "the modality of the poem's enunciation," Rancière suggests that what makes Percennius's speech not only fascinating but politically efficacious is its "indirect style," the narrator's "they" replacing the expected "you" in Percennius's address to his audience. What results from this substitution is much less a new synthesis than a torsion between two distinct pronominal points of view—both of which nonetheless inhere at once: "The indirect style, in practice disjoining meaning and truth, in effect cancels the opposition between legitimate and illegitimate speakers. The latter are just as much validated as suspected. The homogeneity of the narrative-discourse thereby constituted comes to contradict the heterogeneity of the subjects it represents, the unequal quality of the speakers to guarantee, by their status, the reference of their speech. Although Percennius may well be the radical other, the one excluded from legitimate speech, his discourse is included, in a specific suspension of the relations between meaning and truth."[23] For Rancière, then, Tacitus records in his discourse a speech event impossible to imagine phenomenally as a historical utterance. Rancière stresses that this very impossibility is what opens a political future: "By invalidating the voice of Percennius, substituting his own speech for the soldier's, Tacitus does more than give him a historical identity. He also creates a model of subversive eloquence for the orators and simple soldiers of the future. The latter henceforth will not repeat Percennius, whose voice has been lost, but Tacitus, who states the reasons of all those like Percennius better than they do."[24]

Rancière's discussion of this passage runs over five dense pages in *The Names of History*. By way of contrast, Edward Said says of this same material only that "Tacitus, for example, was simply not interested in talking about or representing the everyday, excellent historian though he was."[25] Notwithstanding his deep antipathy to identity politics, Said clearly identified with Auerbach, who "often seems to function as a stand-in or alter ego for Said himself."[26] Of course, Said's identification with an exiled German Jew is especially poignant, given his lifelong exertions on behalf of Palestine. But projecting oneself into an other always risks an effacement of difference: "In order to be able to under-stand a humanistic text," Said wrote of *Mimesis*, "one must try to do so as if one is the author of that text, living the author's reality, undergoing the kind of life experiences intrinsic to his or her life, and so forth, all by that combination of erudition and sympathy that is the hallmark of philological hermeneutics."[27] Said performed this surrogation strikingly when, in the absence of direct quotation, he, rather than Auerbach, seems to be narrating the epilogue to *Mimesis*: "[Auerbach] explains in the concluding chapter of *Mimesis* that, even had he wanted to, he could not have made use of the available scholarly resources, first of all be-cause he was in wartime Istanbul when the book was written and no Western research libraries were accessible for him to consult, second because had he been able to use references from the extremely volu-minous secondary literature, the material would have swamped him and he would never have written the book."[28] Whose story *is Mimesis*? Taking Auerbach's place as the narrator, Said sought here to "live the author's reality" even at the level of voice.

In "Politics, Identification, and Subjectivization," Rancière pursues a different confusion of tongues, a politics of "impossible identification, an identification that cannot be embodied by he or she who utters it." Rather than erase the difference between one subject and another, im-possible identifications take "the difference between voice and body" to generate otherwise unimaginable political effects:

"We are the wretched of the earth" is the kind of sentence that no wretched of the earth would ever utter. Or, to take a personal example, for my generation politics in France relied on an impossible identification—an identification with the bodies of the Algerians beaten to death and thrown into the Seine by the French police, in the name of the French people, in October 1961. We could not identify with those Algerians, but we *could* question our identification with the "French people" in whose name they were murdered. That is to say, we could act as political subjects in the interval or the gap between two identities, neither of which we could assume. That process of subjectivization had no proper name, but it found its name, its cross name, in the 1968 assumption "We are all German Jews"—a "wrong" identification, an identification in terms of the denial of an absolute wrong.[29]

To say "we are all German Jews" is quite different from identifying with one particular German Jew. If that latter act constitutes, for Said, the essence of "critical consciousness," Rancière may have learned a different lesson from Auerbach—namely, how a politics can be predicated on an impossible phenomenality of voice.

The fact remains that any mode of thinking that is the least bit singular reveals itself in always saying basically the same thing, which it cannot but hazard every time in the colorful prism of circumstances. Contrary to what interested parties may say, only imbeciles ever truly change, since they alone are free enough regarding all thought to feel at home in any particular mode of thinking. I personally have always tried to follow a simple rule of morality: not to take for imbeciles those about whom I was talking, whether they happen to be floor layers or university professors. —JACQUES RANCIÈRE, *The Philosopher and His Poor,* xviii

16.

Style indirect libre

JAMES SWENSON

Jacques Rancière is a philosopher whose works rarely appear in a recognizably philosophical form. In the first instance this can be described as an effect of the diversity of subjects about which he has written: from nineteenth-century labor history to film studies, with detours into romantic poetry, modern historiography, and ancient politics. In its constitutive diversity, however, Rancière's work has always been driven by the development of a single thesis that is located at the intersection of the domains of "aesthetics" and "politics," namely the intellectual equality of university professors and floor layers. Intellectual equality implies that people generally know perfectly well what they do and say, that the world is not—must not be—divided between those who think and those who need someone to think for them or to explain what they really think. The progressive elaboration of this thesis has traversed a variety of fields, but it has been articulated through a set of fairly consistent stylistic choices, which this essay will attempt to explicate. Rancière's style allows him to speak about floor layers and university professors in a single discourse. There is no clear formal distinction in his writing corresponding to generic or disciplinary divisions between descriptive social history, literary criticism, and political philosophy. This highly personal style is attained primarily by a refusal to set forth philosophical positions or theses in a singular voice.

It is well known that Rancière began his academic career in the early 1960s as a student of Louis Althusser and a contributor to the seminar that resulted in *Reading "Capital."* Beginning with a 1969 essay, "On the Theory of Ideology," whose theses would be developed in *La leçon d'Althusser*, Rancière broke publicly and violently with the master.[1] Our sense of the continuity of his work must begin from this point. In later years, Rancière refers to Althusser fairly infrequently. When he does, however, he tends to cite a single text which appears as a point of fidelity, a way of marking why he might have been an "Althusserian" in the first place and might in some sense continue to be one. This reference opens the essay on Althusser entitled "La scène du texte," where it manifests "the flash of lightning or the singular seduction of the Althusserian project, which set our generation its task."[2] It also occurs, with a similar pathos, in the sudden autobiographical turn toward the end of the discussion of Rossellini's *Europa '51* in *Short Voyages to the Land of the People.* The citation comes from Althusser's preface, "From *Capital* to Marx's Philosophy": "Our age threatens to appear in the history of human culture as marked by the most dramatic and difficult trial of all, the discovery of and training in the meaning of the 'simplest' acts of existence: seeing, listening, speaking, reading—the acts which relate men to their works [*œuvres*], and to those works thrown in their faces [*retournées en leur propre gorge*], their 'absences of works.'"[3] In the context of *Short Voyages*, the emphasis tends to fall on the notion of gesture, the gesture of appeasement that Irena learns to make and that we must learn to interpret—or more properly not to interpret but to receive and perhaps repeat. The reading in *The Flesh of Words* underlines the play in the meaning of *œuvres*—the relation between the rational works of Marxist philosophy and the irrational works of communist history—and the dramaturgy of Althusser's use of quotation marks, here divided between the citation of Foucault and the scare quotes, as we often call them, putting into question the simplicity of simple gestures. I would further emphasize the seemingly gratuitous importance of the throat, the figure of the (here threatened) unity of voice and body.

If these gestures are less simple than they seem, it is because there is more than one way to establish a relation. There is the relation between the manifest and the hidden, the image or discourse and what lies behind it. Rancière cites, in Italian, the words of the communist journalist Andrea in *Europa '51*, "*mettere in relazione.*" Andrea is the man of consciousness, the go-between who organizes visits to the people and knows that truth lies behind appearances. He represents the great historical figure of reading as "critique." Rancière has consistently and forcefully rejected this hermeneutics of suspicion as bound to a radically inegalitarian division of intellectual and manual labor, a separation of the roles and capacities of philosophy professors or journalists like Andrea and floor layers. Rancière's criticism of the notion of ideology in Althusser, for example, focuses on the way the opposition between the illusions of consciousness (whether bourgeois, petty bourgeois, or proletarian) and Marx's science is linked to the sociological model of reproduction and social cohesion. Ideology, in this sense, is the idea that the agents of social practice are necessarily deceived as a function—even as a condition of possibility—of their action. In *The Philosopher and His Poor*, Bourdieu's sociology of culture and education appears as a perfected version of the theory of ideology: a theory of the *necessary* misrecognition of social relations as the very mechanism of their reproduction. In his essays on literary topics, Rancière will similarly reject notions of depth and obscurity. This is why he insists that Mallarmé is a difficult author, rather than a hermetic one, and that what is difficult about his work is not understanding what it means, but rather accomplishing the task it proposes.[4]

There is another figure of relation in Rossellini's film: Irena herself. Irena learns to have confidence (Socratic *pistis*) in people and in herself, in her own steps. She learns to look to the side, out of the frame. This lesson represents reading or relation as a journey and a possible encounter. Irena's confidence is that of the poet Wordsworth at the opening of the *Prelude*:

> The earth is all before me: with a heart
> Joyous, nor scared at its own liberty,
> I look about, and should the guide I chuse
> Be nothing better than a wandering cloud,
> I cannot miss my way.[5]

This properly romantic confidence appears frequently in Rancière's analyses. The most extreme form of such a confidence is no doubt that of Jacotot's method of intellectual emancipation, whose postulate is fundamentally that anyone can free him or herself if they only enact the confidence in their capacities that they have by right. A particularly eloquent figuration is given to it by Michelet in both *The Names of History* and *Short Voyages to the Land of the People*. Rancière describes Michelet as seeking to restore "to every child its mother, to every grief its voice, to every voice its body."[6] In the historical poetics that Michelet founded and the *Annales* school continued this guarantee of meaningfulness is not necessarily easy—it requires the constancy of a mother's care and attention—but it is always possible. In a far more fragile way, Althusser will continue to bear witness to this romantic conception of meaning in his effort to assure the community of Marxist philosophers and communist proletarians, of rational and irrational works. For romantic reading, there is no *absence d'œuvre*. The stones themselves speak.[7]

But our words do get stuck in our throats, and not every voice finds its body. Nothing assures that the voyage will be a happy one in the sense that an encounter will actually happen: Wordsworth famously missed the crossing of the Alps. Like the urchins listening to the fable of the overturned flowerpot in *Woyzeck*, the children Büchner sees at the Christchild fair are shivering, stupefied, and motherless. No weeping Magdalena sings folksongs for them; no hooting owls call them across the still water. *Short Voyages* presents something of a catalog of such figures of motherless children and missed encounters. It is the tale of the heretical writing of the children of the Book, rolling this way and that without knowing whom it is for. They must tread a path whose arrival at a destination cannot be assured and assume the risk of wandering and crying in the desert as "a motherless child, a voice separated from the body, a body separated from the place."[8] In order to read these errant voices—such is my hypothesis—it is necessary to invent, to reinvent, a style, a poetics in the sense Rancière himself gives this term in *The Names of History*.

Whenever Rancière speaks of the trajectory of his own career, in occasional texts such as interviews, prefaces, or afterwords, he always begins with the stylistic problem that *The Nights of Labor* posed.[9] The project began, he tells us, as a quest for the authentic voice of working-class experience, oriented by notions of popular culture, sociability, and working-class ethos derived from the history of mentalities. This orientation, however, turned out to be incompatible with the material uncovered in the course of research. This incompatibility can be stated as a series of propositions: the working-class militants of the 1830s and 1840s who invented the discourse of class identity were, in fact, marginal figures who were not representative of anything and did not found their militancy upon immersion in any workers' culture. They came from despised and weakly organized trades where pride in skill played little or no role. Their militancy, in fact, expressed a conscious rejection of an identity as "worker" and stemmed in no small part from a tenacious desire and effort to appropriate the leisure and culture of the bourgeoisie. But this made them neither fish nor fowl; in many ways they were either pseudobourgeois or lumpen proletarians. Their voices, as they have survived until today, may be true, but they are not "authentic" expressions of a workers' culture or ethos.

What is most interesting for us in this account is the way in which Rancière describes the nonrepresentative character of these figures as having posed a problem of style. One would search the text of *The Nights of Labor* in vain for the sort of propositions listed above; they are to be found instead in the postpublication interviews or in a conference presentation such as "The Myth of the Artisan." Rancière clearly felt that the story he had encountered in the archives required a different sort of telling, one that recognized, in the later terms of *The Names of History* and *Short Voyages*, that it was about motherless children. A 1994 interview published in *Communications* puts it this way:

> But I realized that this kind of explanation did not account for the reality in question, that, by enclosing these expressions in a sort of collective worker's body, I was in fact negating the kind of truth that was in question there. The question of writing was thus posed in the following way: I could not adopt a kind of story, a kind of narration, based on a realist or naturalizing function. I could not adopt the kind of story that in some sense derives a body from a place and a voice from this body. This kind of story, which we can call *realist*, "authorizes" the position of the speakers it stages by camping them in "their" world. But what was at stake here was to account for the constitution of a web of illegitimate discourses, discourses that broke a certain identity, a

certain relation between bodies and words. . . . What was at stake was the construction of a story in which we could see not the production of voices by a body but the gradual sketching out of a sort of collective space by voices.[10]

There is one work that Rancière pretty much invariably mentions as a model for this sort of stylistic procedure: Virginia Woolf's *The Waves*.[11] With its interlacing of the voices of an immense cast of characters, prismatically shifting focus, and complete lack of thetic statements, *The Nights of Labor* indeed resembles a modernist novel far more closely than anything else in the historiographical tradition.

We generally take the term *style* to refer primarily to the organization of the sentence, including syntax, subordination and coordination, tropes ("figures of style"), and diction (vocabulary). I certainly think that these are important—the discussion of Lucien Febvre in *The Names of History* carries much of its persuasiveness at this level—but what I mean by style equally concerns the overall construction of the argument, particularly the art of transitions. As *La parole muette* reminds us with respect to Flaubert, "style is entirely contained within the 'conception of the subject.'"[12] When Rancière is discussing the style of an author or period, he most fundamentally emphasizes the relation between this "conception of the subject," which always poses a question of hierarchy, and what Plato calls *lexis*, the "mode of enunciation" or "the way in which the poet as subject relates to the subject of the poem, identifies with it, differentiates himself from it or hides himself behind it."[13] My opening epigraph serves to recall that one of the most consistent aspects of Rancière's project is the refusal of any hierarchy of dignity in subject matter. I think that his style is fundamentally the same whether he is discussing Plato or Mallarmé, Gauny or Flaubert. What is important, then, is to try to describe a consistent mode of enunciation.

As my title indicates, I've chosen to use the traditional term *style indirect libre* to characterize this mode. Direct, indirect, and free indirect discourse all designate a relation between two discourses, one which cites, reports, or recounts the other. Free indirect discourse is thus a third-person narration of reported speech or thought, capable of a smooth melding with exterior narration of actions and description of scenes, distinguished by the erasure of certain marking effects (quotation or other diacritical marks, "he said that . . ." and so on). Because it often blurs any line separating the narrator's discourse from that of the "character," it inevitably raises questions of distance under the sign of irony (does Flaubert take Emma and Felicity "for imbeciles"?).[14]

Now, Rancière does use plenty of direct discourse, in other words, he cites his sources abundantly (and even writes accurate footnotes, something I'm particularly sensitive to as a translator). But on the whole, I think that his dominant mode is paraphrase or narration of argument in a free indirect manner. What is particularly notable here, in a discursive rather than fictional context, is the extent to which he reduces logical marks of differentiation between his own discourse and that of the author he is discussing. As we shall see, he almost never says that such-and-such a statement is wrong, and that the truth is something else. He never says that if so-and-so says one thing, what he really means is something else. He even avoids the use of the conditional that, in French, allows for a hypothesis to be stated without being espoused.

Let's begin with an example from *The Ignorant Schoolmaster*, which I've chosen more or less at random (it's neither a particularly important nor a particularly beautiful passage).

> Let's learn, then, near those poets who have been adorned with the title genius. It is they who will betray to us the secret of that imposing word. The secret of genius is that of universal teaching: learning, repeating, imitating, translating, taking apart, putting back together. In the nineteenth century [*Au siècle dix-neuvième*], it is true certain geniuses began to boast of super-human inspiration. But the classics, those geniuses, didn't drink out of the same cup [*Mais les classiques, eux, ne mangent pas du pain de ce génie-là*]. Racine wasn't ashamed of being what he was: a worker [*un besogneux*]. He learned Euripides and Vergil by heart, *like a parrot*. He tried translating them, broke down their expressions, recomposed them in another way. He knew that being a poet meant translating two times over: translating into French verse a mother's sadness, a queen's wrath, or a lover's rage [*la douleur d'une mère, le courroux d'une reine ou la fureur d'une amante*] was also translating how Euripides or Vergil translated them. From Euripides' *Hippolytus*, one had to translate not only Phèdre—that's understood—but also Athalie and Josabeth. For Racine had no illusions about what he was doing. He didn't think he had a better understanding of human sentiments than his listeners [*Il ne croit pas qu'il ait des sentiments humains une meilleure connaissance que ses auditeurs*].[15]

At this point there follows a citation from Jacotot's *Langue maternelle*, confirming the final point: "If Racine knew a mother's heart better than I, he would be wasting his time in telling me what he read in it; I would not recognize his observations in my memories, and I would not be moved."

The first thing we should note is simply that this is indeed a case of what I am calling, for lack of a better term, free indirect discourse, combined with the direct discourse of the citation. There are none of the markers of standard indirect discourse (Jacotot argues that, and so on); indeed, the citation itself is identified only by the quotation marks and the footnote. Throughout the original version of this book (and I think this is true of all the French editions other than *La nuit des prolétaires*), the citations are integrated into the body of the text rather than set off by indentation and smaller typefaces (American editors tend to insist on this practice for the translations). It is furthermore made clear by the citation that Rancière has taken the example of Racine from Jacotot's own text, that he has not invented an example of his own to illustrate the point. Rancière's goal here is precisely, as the passage puts it, to recompose Jacotot's argument in another way. I insist on the point that what is being recomposed is the argument, rather than the meaning, in order to differentiate Rancière's procedure here from the one he ascribes to Michelet in *The Names of History*: Michelet "tells us what they [that is, the love letters of the Festival of the Federation] say: not their content but the power that causes them to be written, that is expressed in them."[16] There is no question here of a difference in levels, of looking behind Jacotot's words to discover their secret motivation, of explaining why he said them. There is no critique, only rewriting in order to understand. The one moment when Rancière can be seen to step slightly away from Jacotot's argument, typically, takes the form of a concession, a recognition of the "knowledge" that the reader may think he or she already has: "*Il est vrai que . . .*" These moments occur frequently in Rancière's writing; most often, they are introduced by "*bien sûr.*" What is conceded can generally be attributed to what Rancière at one point calls "the good sense of demystification," which is not so much contested as rendered slightly irrelevant by the sentence beginning "*Mais . . .*" that invariably follows.

At a more detailed level, we might next notice the simplicity that characterizes Rancière's syntax here, the relative lack of complex subordination. There are a significant number of strings of appositives, whether of verbs, nominal phrases, or clauses, and when clauses are joined by something other than commas or colons there is a high frequency of the minimal predication "*c'est*." This syntactical simplicity or informality is combined with a notable use of inversions of a sort that are always possible in French but that tend to be associated with a certain poetic diction (for example, "*siècle dix-neuvième*" or "*Il ne croit pas qu'il ait des sentiments humains une meilleure connaissance que ses auditeurs*"). At some moments an elevated diction is taken over, more from Racine than Jacotot, particularly in the series "*la douleur d'une mère, le courroux d'une reine ou la fureur d'une amante*." These examples of classical *style soutenu* coexist with choices in diction that move in the opposite direction and produce an effect of contrast: "*ne mangent pas du pain de ce génie-là*," where the "*là*" strongly reinforces the idiom, "*besogneux*," which I would be tempted to translate as "grind," and the parrot analogy. I have not been able to check these against Jacotot's text, but I would strongly wager that they are not to be found there. If commenting a text whose own diction was low, Rancière would be likely to introduce more "elevated" philosophical or poetic turns of phrase in order to produce a similar effect of contrast or mixing of genres.

I've chosen to begin with *The Ignorant Schoolmaster* because it presents an extreme, purified version of this style, which in some senses is as atypical as it is typical. Rancière fully adopts Jacotot's vocabulary: the key terms *émancipation, explication, abrutissement*, and so on are all his. He gives the responses Jacotot gave to the objections he encountered. He rigorously avoids any anachronism in his references. Primary citations are largely drawn from the circle of Jacotot himself, his detractors, and his defenders. The small number of other authors referred to—notably Tracy, Bonald, Ballanche, and Bentham—are all strict contemporaries whom Jacotot likely read. There is no moment at which we leave this circle. *The Ignorant Schoolmaster* re-presents Jacotot's theses, that is, presents them a second time. This is most notable in that it includes a point on which we know from later essays that Rancière is unwilling to follow Jacotot, that of the question of whether intellectual equality can in some way be incorporated into a social order. This avoidance of anachronism and even the shadow of critique corresponds to the radical anachronism of the book's intervention—its simple re-presentation of Jacotot's theses—in a different political and institutional context.

Perhaps the simplest way to characterize the exceptional character of *The Ignorant Schoolmaster* is to note that, other than the *Mallarmé*, it is the only monograph Rancière has written. All of the other books—and indeed, most of the chapters of those books—stage confrontations between a plurality of voices, each of which is treated in turn (in the case of *The Nights of Labor*, the turns can be very brief and the succession rapid) in what we have described as the free indirect manner. Most of the points we have derived from looking at our previous example can be carried directly over to this context. In particular, the free indirect manner implies that each of the voices on stage is treated with equal consideration, that none is taken for an imbecile. There is never a moment at which Rancière tells us that Plato, for example, is right and Aristotle wrong, or vice versa. There are, to be sure, moments of polemical harshness where this style begins to break down. Such moments invariably concern the demystifiers: *La leçon d'Althusser* as a whole, for example, the treatment of Furet and Cobban in *The Names of History*, or the final chapter on Bourdieu in *The Philosopher and His Poor*, which Rancière clearly felt got out of his control. But it is typical for Rancière to note his disagreement with a position by describing it as "*un peu court.*" We might note that the discussion of Plato in *The Philosopher and His Poor*, whatever reservations Rancière may have about his treatment of cobblers, remains entirely within the free indirect mode. Likewise, the analysis of Febvre in the opening pages of *The Names of History* is a model of this style. And the reading of Michelet in that book is so sympathetic—and so wonderfully exciting—that I still remember my surprise when, in my first reading, I discovered that Rancière was arguing, at the end, that his historical poetics had become exhausted. There are also (further concession), particularly in works such as *Dis-agreement* and the stylistically very similar *La parole muette*, plenty of historical and philosophical theses stated in what is unambiguously Rancière's own voice. But the limits we placed on the effect of polemics apply here as well. It is emphatically not the thesis of *La parole muette* that expressive poetics is better than representative poetics, or that the difference between them can in any way be conceived of in terms of truth or value.

In order to analyze the way in which the free indirect mode links different voices, we will take an example from the opening pages of the essay "The Uses of Democracy" in *On the Shores of Politics*.[17] This passage presents sequential readings of Thucydides, Plato, and Aristotle to argue that democracy, ancient as well as modern, is characterized by a division of the social or political body from itself that frequently appears as a loss of unity but that must be understood, Rancière proposes, as foundational. Since this is not exactly the argument of any one of the authors discussed, much less all three of them, the handling of their texts in the free indirect mode becomes accordingly more complicated. Rancière's argument begins with the relation between what our contemporary vocabulary would call civil society and the public sphere in Pericles's funeral oration:

> Let us simply recall one of the founding texts of democracy's reflection on itself: the funeral oration delivered by Pericles in Book II of Thucydides's *History of the Peloponnesian War*. This speech begins by proposing a concept of *freedom* which treats it as the unity of a particular idea of what is common to all and a particular idea of what is proper to each [*une certaine idée du commun et une certaine idée du propre*]. In the words that Thucydides puts into his mouth, Pericles says something like this: we conduct the affairs of the city together [*en commun*]; but we let everyone conduct his own business, what is proper to him, as he pleases.
>
> The concept of freedom unites the private and the public, but it unites them in their very separateness [*distance*]. Our political regime, says Pericles in essence, is not that of mobilization. We do not prepare for war as the Spartans do. Our military preparation is our life itself, a life without constraints and without secrets. The democratic political subject has a shared domain in the very separateness of a way of life characterized by two great features: the absence of constraints and the absence of suspicion. *Suspicion*, in Thucydides's Greek, is *hypopsia*, looking beneath. What characterizes democracy is the refusal of the *look beneath things* that the modern social sciences will raise to the level of a theoretical virtue, necessary to grasp, beneath common appearances, the truth that belies them.

From a technical point of view, the most notable feature of this passage is the use of *paraphrase* rather than free indirect discourse as such. The expressions "*dit à peu près ceci*" and "*dit en substance*" indicate that the words that follow are not the precise words used by the speaker (even setting aside the question of the relation between Pericles and Thucydides), but another way of saying the same thing, and in particular a shorter way of saying the same thing. The sentences that immediately follow these markers are in both cases in the first-person plural and could indeed be enclosed in quotation marks (which are, in fact, what define the difference between direct and free indirect discourse) without creating any grammatical anomalies.[18] These sentences share with the examples we analyzed from *The Ignorant Schoolmaster* a tendency toward simple, indeed informal, syntax and vocabulary. The formal rhetorical style required by the funeral oration disappears in favor of a more conversational tone. The paraphrase is, indeed, extremely economical; major elements of Pericles's argument, such as the passages on recreation, beauty, and friendship—all of which could be used to support Rancière's reading—are left unmentioned. The key elements of Thucydides's vocabulary, however, are carefully retained (noting in particular the use of "common" and "proper" where almost all translations use "public" and "private"). The sentences surrounding the paraphrase, then, are distinguished by their explicit reference to the terms used within the paraphrase *as concepts*. They therefore create a distance that is both historical and linguistic.

There follows one of the moments of concession that we have already identified. "Of course nothing forces us to take Pericles or Thucydides at their word . . .": let us say, in short, that both war mobilization and practices of suspicion were, in fact, common in ancient Athens. Then comes the overturning of the concession: "But there remains an idea consistent enough for the adversaries of democracy to share it with its supporters: from the outset, democracy links together a certain way of practicing the political community with a style of life characterized by intermittence. The man of the democratic city is not a permanent soldier of democracy."[19] The key word here is "intermittence." As far as I can tell (and I am not a Hellenist), this does not translate any particular expression in Thucydides's text. But it is, in any case, this term that allows the transition between the funeral oration and Plato's *Republic*. It is precisely by summarizing Pericles's characterization of democratic civic life as "intermittent" that it can be identified, beyond the reversal of values, with that of Plato.

The treatment of Plato that begins here contains similar markers of paraphrase but stays significantly closer to its source text, book VIII of *The Republic*. The slight difference between Rancière's paraphrase and a direct translation would seem to lie in a touch of generalization that, without changing any of Plato's examples, opens them to a contemporary context.[20] This movement prepares a more direct comparison:

> We could easily give a modern translation of this portrait: this democratic man, moving between politics and diets or between exercise and philosophy looks a lot like what has been described as the postmodern individual. Plato has already drawn a picture of the schizophrenic individual of consumer society, who is so frequently described as the ruin or decline of democracy but who, in Plato's caricature, appears as its very incarnation. Democracy, in its essence, for Plato, is this system of variety, which also concerns the political choices offered for sale [*l'offre politique*]: democracy, he says, is not a constitution but a bazaar for constitutions that includes them all and where everyone can choose whichever he wishes.

This is once again a near-citation, and in particular the key term "bazaar of constitutions [*pantopolion politeion*]" is taken directly from the text.[21] The term *bazaar* allows for a precise transposition of the egalitarian confusion Plato is mocking into the distracted consumer of postmodernism.

The turn to Aristotle is initially made in terms of appearances, of democracy as a "regime that everyone can see differently." This characterization is important for what Rancière will go on to say about Aristotle, but it involves a slight distortion of Plato's text, where someone who is seeking to establish a government can find whatever constitution he wants on sale. But the distortion is slight, and we could argue over whether it is, in the end, a distortion at all. Once again, there is a moment of a concession: *sans doute*, Aristotle's *politeia* is not really a democracy, and Aristotle finds it no easier than Plato to conceive of a specifically democratic virtue. Rancière pursues:

> But, on the other hand, the good regime is precisely characterized by the fact that it is always a mixture [*mélange*] of constitutions, a bazaar for constitutions. A regime without mixture, a regime that wants to make all its laws and all its institutions the same as its principle [*semblables à son principe*] condemns itself to civil war on account of the unilateral character of that principle. In order to approach perfection, each regime has to correct itself, try to take in the opposite principle and become unlike itself [*se rendre dissemblable à lui-même*]. Indeed, there is no good regime, only deviant regimes caught in a perpetual effort of self-correction or, we might even say, self-

dissimulation. We thus could counter Plato's jokes about the market [*foire*] for regimes with the text from book IV of the *Politics* where Aristotle explains: we should be able to see both regimes, democracy and oligarchy, at once—and yet neither of them. The wise politician is he who makes the oligarch see oligarchy and the democrat democracy.

The paragraph ends with a footnote that refers to (but does not cite) the following passage: "In a well-tempered polity there should appear to be both elements and yet neither."[22] Now, it is incontestably the case that Aristotle's doctrine in book IV of the *Politics* is that all good regimes are mixed regimes, and the *politeia* itself is a mixture of regimes: "Polity or constitutional government [*politeia*] may be described generally as a fusion [*mixis*] of oligarchy and democracy."[23] Rancière's summary of Aristotle's reasons for thinking this seems to me perfectly accurate. But "bazaar" is not his term; it is Plato's. The terms Aristotle uses for mixture of regimes—*memeichthai*, *mignumi*, and *mixis*—are forms derived from a root that refers primarily to the mixing of liquids. None of them have the metaphorical values of a bazaar. Nor do the connotations of blending lead in any direct way to the principle of self-dissemblance. My point here is that I think that the power of the passage—its force of conviction—derives fundamentally from the displacement of Plato's notably different vocabulary into that of his former student. This procedure is, I think, always at the heart of Rancière's "conception of the subject." It is the function of shoemakers in *The Philosopher and His Poor*, of stones in *La parole muette*, or of abandoned children in *Short Voyages*. These are all figures that are fundamentally not self-identical. It is through them that the free indirect mode speaks.

I began with a citation from the opening pages of *The Philosopher and His Poor*, the second of two "presuppositions of reading [*partis pris de lecture*]." By way of conclusion, I will end with the first: "I have never been able to subscribe fully to the golden rule that prevailed during the era of my schooling, which is not to ask an author any questions except for those he had asked himself. I have always suspected a little presumption in that modesty. And experience seemed to teach me that the power of a mode of thinking has to do above all with its capacity to be displaced, just as the power of a piece of music may derive from its capacity to be played on different instruments."[24]

I have perhaps insufficiently displaced Jacques Rancière's thought here, although I hope to have verified the way in which it displaces. While my citations have no doubt been more often linked by the platitudes of standard academic indirect discourse than by the elegance of the free indirect style, I do not think I have said anything that is not stated fairly explicitly in Rancière's own texts. I have simply tried, regarding one particular aspect, to decompose and recompose.

Afterword

The Method of Equality:
An Answer to Some Questions

JACQUES RANCIÈRE

Among the questions that have been raised about my work, it is possible to single out three main issues. First, how should we understand equality and its "lessons"? Second, why did I set up the relationship between politics and aesthetics through the concept of a "distribution of the sensible"? Third, how should my way of writing and arguing be characterized? I think that it is possible to epitomize at once the object, the stake, and the method of my research by focusing on an example. I shall borrow it from one of the little narratives which played a strategic role in my book *The Nights of Labor*. Those little narratives and my way of dealing with them can allow us to understand how "aesthetics" is involved in matters of equality and what a method of equality means, as regards the practice of writing.

The text on which I shall focus was written by a nineteenth-century joiner, Gabriel Gauny, who left us the archives of his intellectual life. From the 1830s to the 1880s he wrote an impressive number of texts which remained unpublished. But this essay, which relates the workday of a floor layer who works as a jobber, is an exception. It was published in one of the numerous and ephemeral newspapers that blossomed during the French revolution of 1848. It came out in that newspaper as a contribution to a collective political affirmation. But before taking on this collective meaning in a revolutionary context, it was the product of both the joiner's individual experience and his personal appropriation of the power of writing. Therefore, the close reading of this extract can help us understand the way in which I set out to tie up matters of writing and matters of equality.

> This man is made tranquil by the ownership of his arms, which he appreciates better than the day-laborer because no look of a master precipitates their movements. He believes that his powers are his own when no will but his own activates them. He also knows that the entrepreneur is hardly upset by the time he spends at his work, provided that the execution is irreproachable. He is less aware of exploitation than the day-laborer. He believes he is obeying only the necessity of things, so much does his emancipation delude him. But the old society is there to treacherously sink its horrible scorpion claws into his being and ruin him before his time, deluding him about the excitement of the courage that he uses for the benefit of his enemy.
>
> But this worker draws secret pleasure from the very uncertainty of his occupation.[1]

Why focus on such descriptions of a worker's experience and give them a role in the elaboration of a philosophical question? Because what is at stake in the "description" is the whole idea of the way in which the facts of equality and inequality are involved in matters of perception and belief. What is at stake is a new understanding of what Marxist theory had put under the concept of ideology. I assumed that those narratives were much more than descriptions of everyday experience. They reinvented the everyday. This text proposes, in fact, a reframing of one's individual experience. In our text, this operation of reframing can be evinced by the relation between two conjunctions, two *buts*. The joiner believes that he is free, that he is only obeying the necessity of the work he is doing, *but* the old society is there and makes him pay for his illusion. The old society makes him pay for his illusion, *but* he draws secret pleasure out of the freedom that this illusion gives to him. The text tells us about the efficacy of a "delusion," an efficacy that is mediated through two feelings: belief and pleasure. I contended that the description of that "delusion" encapsulated both a tiny shift and a decisive upheaval in the understanding of the relationship between exploitation and delusion. According to the traditional view of "ideology," people are exploited and oppressed because they don't know the law of their exploitation or oppression. They have wrong representations of what they are and why they are so. And they have those wrong representations of their place because the place where they are confined hinders them from seeing the structure that allots them that place. In short, the argument on the mechanism of ideology reads: they are where they are because they don't know why they are where they are. And they don't know why they are where they are because they are where they are. The positive conclusion had it that they could step out of that place only if they were given a true scientific knowledge and right artistic representations of the reasons for their being there.

The tiny shift that I perceived in the little narrative of the joiner, and that I decided to develop as a large theoretical and political shift, consists in stripping the argument, in order to set forth its core. The schema of knowledge and ignorance, reality and illusion, actually covers up a mere tautology: people are where they are *because* they are where they are, because they are incapable of being elsewhere. This matter of *incapacity* must be stripped of its "scientific" disguise. People are not *unable* because they ignore the reason for their being there. They are *unable* because being *unable* means the same as being *there*. The point is that those who have the *occupation* of workers are supposed to be equipped for that occupation and for the activities that are related to it. They are supposed to be equipped for working, not for peripheral activities such as looking around and investigating how society at large works.

This is what a distribution of the sensible means: a relation between occupations and equipment, between being in a specific space and time, performing specific activities, and being endowed with capacities of seeing, saying, and doing that "fit" those activities. A distribution of the sensible is a matrix that defines a set of relations between sense and sense: that is, between a form of sensory experience and an interpretation which makes sense of it. It ties an occupation to a presupposition. As Plato put it once and for all, in a way that made every future theory of ideology an academic joke, there are two reasons why workers must stay in their place. The first reason is that they have no time to go elsewhere, because work does not wait, which is an empirical fact. The second is that God mixed iron in their makeup while he mixed gold in the makeup of those who are destined to deal with the common good. This second reason is not an empirical fact. It gives the reason or the logos which sustains the empirical state of things by identifying the place where work does not wait with the place where universal thinking is not expected to stay, the place of the particular. In order that social functioning be identified with the working out of inequality, it has to rest on an inequality in terms of nature. This is what the logos provides. But it provides it in the guise of a *muthos*, a myth or a lie about what "fitting" means: the story of the deity who mixes gold, silver, or iron in the souls.

This is the dialectic of the distribution of the sensible, which is more tricky than the dialectic of ideology. One splits up into two. The empirical given—the lack of time—is doubled by its logos. The logos is a *muthos*. The argument is a story, and the story an argument. The social distribution rests on that circle of the empirical and the prescriptive. This means that it rests on a form of legitimization which delegitimizes it at the same time. The reason for inequality has to be given in the guise of a story. But the story is the most egalitarian form of discourse. It makes of the philosopher the brother of the children who enjoy stories and of the old women or the old slaves who tell them stories.

The logos must be presented as a story. And the story, Plato says, has to be believed. In order to understand what is at the stake in the "belief" of our joiner, we have to define what it means to believe. Obviously, Plato does not demand that the workers have the inner conviction that a deity truly mixed iron in their soul and gold in the soul of the rulers. It is enough that they *sense* it: that is, that they use their arms, their eyes, and their minds *as if* it were true. And they do so even more so as this lie about "fitting" actually fits the reality of their condition. The ordering of social "occupations" works out in the mode of this *as if,* which ties it to a "belief." Inequality works out to the extent that one "believes" it. But that "belief" can be conveyed only in the egalitarian mode of the story. Inequality has to be performed by those who endure it as their life, as what they feel, what they are aware of.

We can now understand what is at stake in my little narrative and in my way of reading it: it is the subversion of that performance of inequality. In the construction and the writing of his sensory experience, the joiner implements a different *as if* that overturns the whole logic which allotted him his place. But this overturning is far from the canonical idea of the freeing power of awareness. The jobber frees himself by becoming *less aware* of exploitation and pushing aside, thereby, its sensory grip. He frees himself by nurturing a power of self-delusion. That power makes him work still more for the benefit of his enemy, against his own employment and the conservation of his health. But this counter effect, which results from his way of reframing the space and the time of exercise of his force of labor, is the source of a new pleasure, the pleasure of a new freedom.

Such is the performance of equality that is meant by the word "emancipation." It is a subversion of a given distribution of the sensible. What is overturned is the relationship between what is done by one's arms, what is looked at by one's eyes, what is felt as a sensory pleasure, and what is thought of as an intellectual concern. It is the relationship between an occupation, the space-time where it is fulfilled, and the sensory equipment for doing it. This subversion implies the reframing of a common sense. A common sense does not mean a consensus but, on the contrary, a polemical place, a confrontation between opposite common senses or opposite ways of framing what is common.

In a first approach, this is what the relationship between aesthetics and politics means. Politics is a polemical form of reframing of common sense. In that sense, it is an aesthetic affair. Now, this reframing does not come out of the blue. The political "workers' voice" implemented by this newspaper of 1848 stems from a multiplicity of microexperiences of repartitioning the sensible, a multiplicity of operations that have reframed the place of the worker, the time of his work and his life, the exercise of his gaze, the way he speaks, and so on. It is not a question of knowing what was ignored. Knowledge is always the other side of ignorance. The emancipated worker's new "awareness" of his situation means the "ignorance" of the logic of inequality. The balance of knowledge and ignorance is what our joiner calls a passion. This is how he demonstrates to one of his fellow companions the necessity of new passions: "Plunge into terrible readings. That will awaken passions in your wretched existence, and the labourer needs them to stand tall in the face of that which is ready to devour him. So, from the *Imitation* to *Lelia*, explore the enigma of the mysterious and formidable chagrin at work in those with sublime conceptions."[2]

As is well known since Plato, a passion is a certain balance of pleasure and pain, which results from a certain balance of ignorance and knowledge. When our joiner says that the proletarian needs passions, he means that he has to tip over from a given balance to another, that he needs an imbalance or an excess with respect to an empirical balance of time and work, resting on a symbolic distribution of iron and gold. He needs to steal a certain sort of gold, a sort of gold which is at once more and less precious than the gold which is supposed to be mixed in the soul of the rulers, which is both sublime and up for grabs. The joiner teaches his fellow the way to steal it, which is *reading*. Reading is not only an activity bringing about knowledge or pleasure. It is the achievement of a redistribution of the sensible that is involved in writing. Plato has also taught that writing is not merely a means of transcribing the signs of language. It is also a status of language that defines an excess, an imbalance in the relationship between signs, things, and bodies. As he conceived it, writing meant the wrong circuit on which words are launched as orphans, available to anybody, without being guided by the voice of the master who knows how they have to be related to things and also who is entitled or not entitled to make an appropriate use of them. In my terms, writing—and its other side, reading—is a redistribution of the sensible. Writing frees words from a given relation between signs and bodies. By so doing it blurs the distinction between gold and iron and it makes this mix-up available to anybody.

What are made available by writing and reading are not messages or representations, but *passions*. What the proletarian has to steal from literature is the secret of a "mysterious and formidable chagrin." It is the sort of pain that he lacks, the misfortune that he ignores by definition: the misfortune of having no occupation, of not being fit or equipped for any specific place in society, which was embodied at the time of romanticism by literary characters such as Werther, René, or Oberman. What literature endows the workers with is not the awareness of their condition. It is the passion that can make them break their condition, because it is the passion that their condition forbade.

Literature does not "do" politics by providing messages or framing representations. It "does" it by triggering passions, which means new forms of balance (or imbalance) between an occupation and the sensory "equipment" fitting it. This politics is not the politics of the writers. Goethe, Chateaubriand, or Senancour, who invented those characters, were certainly not concerned with the aim of arousing such "passions" among the laborers. It is the politics of literature—that is, the politics of that art of writing—which has broken the rules that made definite forms of feeling and expression fit definite characters or subject matters. It is through this upheaval of the poetic hierarchy that literature contributed to the constitution of a new form of sensory experience, the *aesthetic* experience, where the emblems of power, the decorations of the palaces, and the icons of faith lost their function and destination and were relocated in new locations—new material and symbolical forms of distribution of the sensible—called museums or art histories. In these new locations, they became available for the free pleasure of visitors who would know less and less what those emblems or icons were fit for, whom they represented, and what story they told. This new form of experience opened a new field of verification of equality, interacting with the field of verification of equality opened by the modern constitutions and declarations of rights. For sure, it was not the same equality. It was a strange new form of equality which had among its properties that of disconnecting looking and working. The aesthetic appreciation of the form of a palace has nothing to do with any consideration of the finalities for which it has been designed and built, nor with the labor of the builders, as Kant explained in the *Critique of Judgment*. This is the disjunction between the work of the hands and the pleasure of the eyes that our joiner emphasizes as he relates his workday: "Believing himself at home, he loves the arrangement of a room, so long as he has not finished laying the floor. If the window opens out on a garden or commands a view of a picturesque horizon, he stops his arms and glides in imagination toward the spacious view to enjoy it better than the possessors of the neighboring residences."[3]

It is possible to move from the spectacle opened by that window— that *written* window—to another spectacle, the spectacle proposed by the face of the *Juno Ludovisi* which, fifty years earlier, in his *On the Aesthetic Education of Man in a Series of Letters*, Schiller had read the promise of a new form of equality, a true sensory equality instead of a mere legal one. The deity promised that equality because she was idle. She did nothing; she did not work. She did not command anything, nor did she obey anybody. But we can reach back still earlier in the history of the aesthetic disjunction. Let us remember the description of the *Torso* of the Belvedere made by Winckelmann thirty years before Schiller's *Letters*. He supposed that the *Torso* represented Hercules, the hero of the Twelve Labors. But it represented an idle Hercules, a Hercules having finished his labors and sitting among the idle gods. He decided that that headless statue, deprived of arms and legs, was the masterwork of Greek art and therefore the full implementation of Greek liberty. This beheaded statue stood up as the emblem of an aesthetic revolution that would both parallel and oppose the revolution emblematized by the beheading of the French king. Between that crippled emblem of Beauty and Liberty and the inhibited arms and the emancipated look of our joiner we can draw a line, even if it is not a straight line.

I am aware that my assumptions rouse a strong suspicion. The objection has it that, whatever our joiner may believe as he looks through the window, the room remains the possession of its owner and his force of labor the possession of his boss. The equal and disinterested pleasure of the gaze is just as delusive as the promises of equality written in the Declaration of Rights. Both are expressions of false equality that delude him and block the way that leads to true equality.

I answer that the claim of "true" equality dismisses the reality of the operations of the verification of equality. It dismisses it at the same time that it grasps the struggle over the *as if* in the pincers of appearance and reality. Appearance and reality are not opposed. A reality always goes along with an appearance. For sure, the joiner remains in the world of domination and exploitation. But he is able to split up the tautology of the being-there. He is able to locate his ownership in the ownership of the master and the owner. He actually builds up a new sensible world in the given one. A verification of equality is an operation which grabs hold of the knot that ties equality to inequality. It handles the knot so as to tip the balance, to enforce the presupposition of equality tied up with the presupposition of inequality and increase its power. For instance, the perspective gaze, that has been long associated with mastery and majesty, can be assumed and verified as a power of equality. That verification contributes, thus, to the framing of a new fabric of common experience or a new common sense, upon which new forms of political subjectivization can be implemented.

This is a lesson of equality. Such lessons can be found everywhere. It is possible to find everywhere new examples of the disjunctive junction between a *being-there* and the reason for that being-there. It is possible to disentangle in every case the *as if* which is involved in the "that's the way it is." From this point on, it is also possible to imagine a method of equality specifically aimed at detecting and highlighting the operations of equality that may occur everywhere at every time. This method can be given various names. Joseph Jacotot, the thinker of intellectual emancipation, called it "panecastic philosophy," because it was a method for finding in every (*ekaston*) peculiar manifestation of intelligence the whole (*pan*) of its power: that is, of the power of equality.[4] I once called it a "poetics of knowledge": a poetics that extricates the fictional construction of the *as if* and its political enactment from the descriptions of objects and the declarations of method that are at work in the human and social sciences. This is how I extracted my little narratives from the fabric of social history, where they had the status of expressions of a certain "workers' culture" in order to make them appear as statements on and shifts in the distribution of the sensible. I showed that those descriptions were *muthoi*, enacting the disjunctive junction of story and argument, legitimization and delegitimization, equality and inequality. Those who wrote them were writers—no matter whether good or bad. They used the same kind of poetical inventions as Michelet did when he described the revolutionary festivals, the same kind as Plato when he said in *Phaedrus* that he would speak truly about Truth. In order to tell the truth about the Truth, Plato used a story, the story of the journey and the fall of the souls.

By doing so, he shattered in advance the pious discourse which presents Philosophy as the discipline that gives its epistemological ground or its ontological foundations to the methods of positive sciences. He suggested a quite different view of what Philosophy does. Instead of giving foundations or legitimacy to the social and human sciences, Philosophy would be the discourse that sends them back to their nature as stories about the being-there and the reason for the being-there. History, sociology, political science, literary theory, art history, and so on contend that they have their objects and the methods fitting them. Philosophy instead would say: your objects belong to everybody; your methods belong to anybody. They are stories that anybody can understand and tell in turn. I tell stories; you tell stories. And the reason we have to tell stories is that we are at war. The so-called division of labor between disciplines is, in reality, a war. It is a war over fixing boundaries. No positive boundary severs the field of sociology from the field of philosophy, or the field of history from the field of literature. No positive boundary separates the texts that make up the discourse of science from those which are merely the objects of science. Ultimately, no positive boundary separates those who are fit for thinking from those who are not fit for thinking. This is why boundaries are continuously traced and retraced. The human and social sciences always try to force the fundamental aporia of the equivalence of logos and *muthos*, legitimization and delegitimization. The method of equality—or the politics of knowledge—returns descriptions and methods to their status as weapons in a war between discourses.

The warriors may be knowledgeable and well-minded. They may go to war for the sake of the common good and equality. For instance, history and sociology have their democracy, and they fight for it. Philosophy has its equality and fights for it. This is the point: democracy is the struggle about democracy, equality is the dissensus about equality. Equality never goes alone. Nor does inequality. This is why there are lessons of equality—lessons of the dissensus about equality, of the conflictual knot of equality and inequality—everywhere. This is also why the method of equality is a method of untimeliness. Kristin Ross has opposed my practice of historicization to the spatializing trend which characterized sociology and history in the 1980s.[5] It is not merely a matter of stressing time over space. Disciplinary thinking uses time itself as a principle of spatialization. It makes time a place that encloses and defines those who are in it. It replays, as a methodological principle, the Platonic assertion that "work does not wait," which amounts to locking up workers in the space of their absence of time. And the experience of emancipation consists in locating another time in that time, another space in that space.

This is why the method of equality must implement, at the same time, a principle of historicization and a principle of untimeliness, a principle of contextualization and a principle of de-contextualization. You must make words resound in their concrete place and time of enunciation, instead of the generalizations of historical discourse. But you must also draw the line of escape, the line of universalization on which the poor romantic floor-layer meets the aristocratic philosopher of antiquity and verifies that they have something in common, that they speak about the same thing: the capacities or incapacities involved in the fact of *having* or *not having* time. The untimely method of equality implies another way of thinking the Universal. The Universal is not the law ruling over the multiple and the particular. It is the principle at work in the operation which calls into question the distribution of the sensible separating universal matters from particular matters. Accordingly, untimeliness is a way of thinking the event in terms of multitemporality, in terms of intertwining plots. This way of thinking the event is opposed to the conception of the transcendence of the Event or the stroke of the Real or the Thing that has been shared by many contemporary thinkers, from Derrida and Lyotard to Badiou and Žižek.

There are lessons of equality that occur anywhere in various forms. This is why those lessons cannot be easily encapsulated within programmatic schemas or drill orders such as "politicized" art for instance. Gabriel Rockhill pointed out a possible contradiction between my concept of the distribution of the sensible, which ties together art and politics, and my desire to maintain a separation between them, which sustains my denunciation of ethical confusion and my suspicion regarding the notion of a committed or politicized art.[6] In addressing this issue, there are different levels that need to be distinguished. Indeed, politics is an "aesthetic" affair, since it is about what is seen and what can be said about it, about what is felt as common or private, and about experiences of time and space. And Art—as it shapes common spaces or singular times, as it changes the coordinates of the visible or the ways of making sense of it, as it changes the relationships of the part and the whole or the singular and the anonymous—produces a politics of its own. But this means that there cannot be a plain relationship between art and politics as two realities existing per se. Politics and art exist only through definite regimes of identification. It is not "art" that frames, on its own, the "disinterested" look that is borrowed by the floor-layer. The politics that endows him with a new gaze is not the outcome of the commitments of artists and writers. It is the aesthetic regime of art that defines a new distribution of the spaces of experience and of the sensory equipment that fits the topography of those spaces. If the joiner can borrow this gaze, it is not due to revolutionary painting, whether it be revolutionary in the sense of David or in the sense of Delacroix. What enables him to appropriate this aesthetic look is not so much a revolution in the subjects or procedures of painting as it is the new kind of equality—or indifference—which makes them available to anybody and offers to the same look and the same pleasure the Roman heroes of liberty, the dishes of Dutch kitchens, or the characters of the Old Testament. And if he can rephrase his experience with phrases borrowed from Hugo or Chateaubriand, it is because those phrases belong to the open circulation of literature, notwithstanding the peculiar aims pursued by those writers and the versatility of their political stances.

In short, the idea of "politicized art" covers the complexity of the relationship between the politics of aesthetics and the aesthetics of politics. The aesthetics of politics is fostered by the shifts in individual and collective perceptions, by the reconfigurations of the visible and the symbolic, and the redistributions of pleasure and pain that I described earlier.[7] Nonetheless, politics has its own aesthetics, which implies specific concerns and specific procedures. It not only shapes specific forms of community; it also shapes the general forms in which the common of the community is empowered and emblematized. Politics is about the very existence of a common sphere, the rules of functioning of that sphere, the count of the objects that belong to it and of the subjects who are able to deal with it. Politics is about the configuration of the space of politics, the redistribution of matters into private or public matters, the redistribution of places between private and public spaces. It implements a specific activity consisting in recounting the parts of the community. A process of political subjectivization creates forms of enunciation and manifestation of the supplementary part which comes in addition to any consensual calculation of the parts of the population: the part of those who have no part. This miscount is staged in a specific way: the construction of a *we*. There is political agency when there is the construction of a *we* that splits up the community and the invention of names for that *we*. I said that the *dēmos*—or the people—was the generic name of those invented subjects which divide the community as they supplement it. This means that politics builds the stage of a conflict between alternative figures of the people.

Literature is not concerned with the setting up of a *we*. For sure, it is concerned with matters of counting and miscounting. It works on the whole and the parts in its own way. But it is not concerned with singling out the part of those who have no part in the form of a *we*. In other terms, its population is not a *dēmos*. It is much more concerned with dismissing the difference between the first and the third person and overcoming it by the invention of new forms of individuation. Literature works, as politics does, in order to undo the consensual forms of gathering and counting. But it does it in a different way. It invents its own democracy and its own equality. The democratic uprising that Zola relates as an epic *is not* the Paris Commune. It is the rush of the women pouncing on clothes in *Au bonheur des dames*. It is the insurrection of consumption that turns fashionable Parisian women into modern Bacchantes. Zola implements a politics of literature that sees the action of the political subjects constructing such and such case of equality as a superficial agitation. From that point of view, the politics of the political subjects is an old rhetorical performance through which one must break in order to reach true equality, or rather, to dismiss equality in favor of the sympathy or fraternity of the subterranean drives or impersonal rhythms and intensities of collective life. True equality or true fraternity, thus, is supposed to exist only at the molecular level of preindividual states of things or haecceities—as Deleuze says—where nobody holds democratic flags or shouts out egalitarian mottos.

In short, aesthetics has its own politics, just as politics has its own aesthetics.[8] But this politics cannot be enclosed in a simple cause/effect relation. I said that we can draw a line from the paradigm of the crippled hero and the idle deity to the disjunction between the arms of the worker and his eyes. But you can draw from that disjunction very different interpretations of what the politics of aesthetics is. You can contend that the disjunction must lead to a new conjunction. The idle deity and the pause in the activity of the worker open on the future of a new world where labor and art will no longer be separated from each other, where they will merge into one and the same activity. In this view, art and politics have to suppress themselves as separate activities in order to construct a new sensory community, where art and labor, production and public life, will be one single process of shaping forms of life. But you can also draw an opposite conclusion, contending that the promise of equality is enclosed in the idleness, which means in the self-containment, of the statue. If this is so, it means that it is the suspension of the will of the statue, the suspension of the activity of Hercules and of the worker, which holds the power of emancipation. Art must not merge into life. On the contrary, it must stay in its solitude as both the visibility of the separation between art and labor and the promise of reconcilement.

In several essays I tentatively spelled out the logic of those two emplotments of the aesthetic promise.[9] I also emphasized that they intertwined in various ways. The Deleuzian interpretation of art and literature is a telling case of intertwinement, an attempt to identify the power of subversion of the artwork as both a break with the mainstream economy of sensation and the constitution of a new sensory fabric of individual and collective life. From that point of view, the disjunction between the arms and the eyes of the worker can hold as a break with the sensori-motor schema. The window through which his look glides makes the outside inside. It dismisses the grammatical fabric of subjects and predicates and the physical fabric of subjects and objects in favor of a linguistic world of verbs and adverbs and a physical world of becoming and haecceities. In this world, the productions of art are no longer works standing in front of us. Nor must art suppress itself in the framing of new forms of collective life. The productions of art are blocks of percepts and affects torn away from the sensori-motor schema. They are manifestations of the productivity of Life, of the relentless process of disruption which is the ontological constitution of the multiplicity. As such, they are already political, they are already a "people to come." One could say that the tension between the opposite politics of aesthetics is settled in this "people to come." But the tension soon reappears. The politics of literature, which was supposed to consist in blocks of collective enunciation, is embodied for Deleuze by heroic characters such as Bartleby. Bartleby, the character who "prefers not to," is identified by him as a new Christ or "a brother to us all." His nonpreference is the "idleness" of the *Juno Ludovisi* turned into the passion of a new Christ, releasing Humanity from the chains of activism. This activism of non-activism bears witness to the inner contradiction of the politicization of ontology—or ontologization of politics—which is at the heart of Deleuze's aesthetic thinking. But this contradiction keeps in line with the whole politics—or meta-politics—of aesthetics. Before being a brother to us all, Bartleby, the activist of nonactivism, is the brother of the Marxist revolutionary leader who at the same time lets the productive forces break, by their own dynamism, the chains of the old world and decides the right moment when the sleight of hand of an uprising minority performs the task of the break with the new world. This brotherhood comes as no surprise, since the political performance of the literary character, as Deleuze conceives of it, and the revolutionary performance in Marxist theory spring from the same source. The Marxist idea of Revolution and the Deleuzian view of Art are both rooted in the meta-politics of the aesthetic revolution. This is why Deleuzian thought could recently foster a revival of Marxism. This is also what makes the enormous amount of Marxist political interpretation of art and literature so often futile. It most often forgets that the contradictions that it ferrets out so vividly in its objects are, first of all, the contradictions of the meta-politics on which it is itself predicated.

The development of this point, which I cannot carry out here, could bring out some elements for answering one of the questions raised by my work. I have insisted on the historicity of the regimes of art, while my discussion of politics often tended to skip over centuries and societies, from Plato to the last social movements or the last statements on the return or the end of politics. This does not mean that I take politics to be a kind of ahistorical essence. I tried to challenge mainstream views that linked emancipation or democracy to a certain historical sequence, by making democracy the outcome of a "murder of the king" amounting to a murder of the father, or by linking emancipation to a messianic faith in History. But this does not mean that I dismiss the existence of historical forms of politics, as Bruno Bosteels suspects.[10] Politics is always emplotted in historical configurations. There is a history of the political, which is a history of the forms of confrontation—and also the forms of confusion—between politics and the police. Politics does not come out of the blue. It is articulated with a certain form of the police order, which means a certain balance of the possibilities and impossibilities that this order defines. Nor does politics ever go alone. A historical form of politics is always more or less entangled with forms of archi-politics, para-politics, or meta-politics, as I defined them in *Disagreement*. The modern politics of emancipation has been entangled from the beginning with the meta-politics of the aesthetic revolution. But this does not mean that it has to be identified with that meta-politics.

The matter of confusion regarding these distinctions will serve as my conclusion. The categories by means of which I tried to think politics, art, and their relationships are not ontological determinations. If I thought it necessary to establish distinctions and oppositions by distinguishing several regimes of identification of art, opposing the police and politics, or separating politics from meta-politics, it is precisely in order to allow for an intelligibility of their entanglements. If a distinction of regimes of identification of art can be useful, it is because we are confronted with mixed forms that are intelligible to the extent that we identify the different logics that they bring together. If the distinction between politics and the police can be useful, it is not to allow us to say:

politics is on this side, police is on the opposite side. It is to allow us to understand the form of their intertwinement. We rarely, if ever, face a situation where we can say: this is politics in its purity. But we ceaselessly face situations where we have to discern how politics encroaches on matters of the police and the police on matters of politics. As I conceive of them, concepts are neither Platonic ideas nor mere empirical designations. They are tools with which we can draw a new topography in order to account for what happens to us and with which we can try to weave a mode of investigation and action equally distant from the consent to things as they are and from the hyperboles of imaginary radicalism.

Notes

INTRODUCTION

1. In a curious bit of intellectual history, it is remarkable that the image
    of Rancière-the-Althusserian persists in the English-speaking world, in
    spite of the fact that his contribution to *Lire le Capital* did not make it
    into the English translation in 1970, or into later editions of *Reading
    Capital*. The first translation of the entire article into English appears
    to date from 1989 and is not widely available. The same is true of his
    major critical engagement with Althusser, *La leçon d'Althusser*. The book
    has not yet been translated in its entirety, and only the original critical es-
    say, "Pour mémoire: Sur la théorie de l'idéologie," is available to the
    Anglophone public (see the bibliography in Rancière, *The Politics of
    Aesthetics*).

2. Some of the authors in this collection have used other terms to translate
    Rancière's concept of *partage*, including "partition," "division," and
    "sharing." Rather than systematizing these references to one of Rancière's

key notions, we have decided to let them stand so that the authors can highlight various features of Rancière's use of the terms *partage, partager, la part des sans-parts*, etc.

3. *La leçon d'Althusser,* 26–27.
4. Rancière, *On the Shores of Politics,* 54.
5. Ibid., 93.
6. *Dis-agreement,* 37.

1. HISTORICIZING UNTIMELINESS

A shorter version of "Historicizing Untimeliness" was published in the collection of papers from the Cérisy colloquium on Rancière's work under the title "Rancière à contretemps" in Cornu and Vermeren, *La philosophie déplacée.*

1. Rancière, "On War as the Ultimate Form of Advanced Plutocratic Consensus," 256–57.
2. For a discussion of "Perception Management" and its relation to contemporary U.S. policy, see chapter 4 of Grandin, *Empire's Workshop.*
3. In France this offensive, which I discuss in chapter 3 of *May '68 and Its Afterlives,* was part of an effort to sever the leftist activism of the May '68 from its real content and to unlink that event from an immanent politics of equality.
4. Ross, "Introduction."
5. Halimi, "Un mot de trop" and "Les 'philo-américains' saisis par la rage."
6. Rancière, *The Philosopher and His Poor,* 76.
7. De Certeau, *The Practice of Everyday Life.* See especially the chapter entitled "Walking in the City."
8. Ibid., 93.
9. Ibid., 26.
10. De Certeau writes, "I would simply like to present to you some work in progress on 'ways of doing' and 'everyday practices' to which I would like to give the name of 'ordinary culture' in order to avoid the accepted expression 'popular culture,' in which the word 'popular' carries too many ideological connotations." "Pratiques quotidiennes," 23. For an elaboration of this critique of de Certeau and Bourdieu, see my "The Sociologist and the Priest."
11. De Certeau, "La beauté du mort."
12. See Foucault, "Pouvoirs et stratégies."

13. See Collectif "Révoltes Logiques," *L'empire du sociologue*, especially Cingolani, "*Eppur si muove!*" and Rancière, "L'éthique de la sociologie."

14. Rancière, *The Names of History*, 98.

15. See Farge, "L'histoire comme avènement," 461–66.

16. Benveniste, *Problems in General Linguistics*, 1:226. Monique Wittig, *The Lesbian Body*, trans. David Le Vay (New York: Avon, 1976).

17. Rifkin, "Il y a des mots qu'on ne souhaiterait plus lire," 105. For Rifkin, the intellectual adventure implied by the title *Révoltes Logiques* (a title borrowed from Rimbaud) relocated revolt in this "setting aside," this *écartement* from and of the doctrinal concerns of disciplinary formations —even at the moment of their most radical self-consciousness. He makes the point that it would be an error to confuse this effect with that of Derridean *différance*, since the process of *écartement* that characterizes Rancière's most compelling work is highly specific and emerges in his working through of a particular set of arguments regarding a painting, a film, or a social formation. It is not, in other words, a theoretical procedure that can be generalized as with Derrida.

18. Rancière, *The Names of History*, 98.

19. See Rancière, "Le concept de l'anachronisme et le vérité de l'historien."

20. Talcott Parsons, *The Social System* (Glencoe, Ill.: Free Press, 1951).

21. Rancière, "Histoire des mots, mots de l'histoire," 93.

22. Furet, *Interpreting the French Revolution*, cited in Rancière, *The Names of History*, 38.

23. Rancière, *The Aesthetics of Politics*, 11.

24. See Badiou, *Metapolitics*, 128.

25. See, for example, Daniel Bensaïd's critique of what he takes to be Rancière's sophisticated avoidance of politics, which in his view risks, through its emphasis on politics' rarity or intermittent temporality, an esthetic or philosophical posture in flight from contradiction. Bensaïd, *Eloge de la résistance à l'air du temps*, 45–46.

26. Editorial, *Révoltes Logiques* 5 (spring–summer 1977): 6.

2. THE LESSONS OF JACQUES RANCIÈRE

This essay was published in French as "Les leçons de Jacques Rancière, savoir et pouvoir après la tempête," in *La philosophie déplacée: Autour de Jacques Rancière*, ed. Laurence Cornu and Patrice Vermeren (Paris: Horlieu Editions, 2006).

1. "*L'effet de colle*" literally means the "sticking effect" which also has reso-
   nances with *l'effet d'école*, or the "effect of school" and *faire école*, which
   means "to acquire a following." The term itself was used by Lacan in
   the development of independent study groups in L'École Freudienne de
   Paris, called "cartels." The main point was that cartels are only truly
   productive if they do not continue beyond a certain period of existence.
   Members in different groups should split up and form other groups with
   other people. In this way there is no individual constantly in the "leadership position" or "the most diligent worker." This form is discussed in his
   founding text of the school, "L'acte de foundation de L'École freudienne
   de Paris," of June 21, 1964, as well as the more theoretical discussion
   in "D'écolage," of March 11, 1980. These texts can be found on the Web
   site of L'École de la cause freudienne at http://www.causefreudienne.net/
   orientation-lacanienne/cartels/.
2. Rancière's notorious use of the word *partage*, which means distribution
   or sharing, has many other idiomatic senses. I follow Gabriel Rockhill's
   precedent in translating it as distribution. This follows in the path of
   establishing a technical sense of the word in English which can help avoid
   potential confusion. Rancière, *The Politics of Aesthetics*.
3. Badiou's term "*surnuméraire*" is translated as "supernumerary" following Norman Madaraz's early translation of Alain Badiou's *Manifesto for
   Philosophy*.
4. Rancière, *Dis-agreement*, 123.
5. Rancière includes a long discussion of *Die Meistersinger von Nürnberg* in
   the second section of *The Philosopher and His Poor*, 57–124.

3. SOPHISTICATED CONTINUITIES AND HISTORICAL DISCONTINUITIES

1. "La politique, en effet, ce n'est pas l'exercice du pouvoir et la lutte pour
   le pouvoir. C'est la configuration d'un espace spécifique, le découpage
   d'une sphère particulière d'expérience, d'objets posés comme communs
   et relevant d'une décision commune, de sujets reconnus capables de
   désigner ces objets et d'argumenter à leur sujet. . . . L'homme, dit Aristote,
   est politique parce qu'il possède la parole qui met en commun le juste et
   l'injuste alors que l'animal a seulement la voix qui signale plaisir et peine.
   Mais toute la question alors est de savoir qui possède la parole et qui
   possède seulement la voix. . . . La politique advient lorsque ceux qui 'n'ont

pas' le temps prennent ce temps nécessaire pour se poser en habitants d'un espace commun et pour démontrer que leur bouche émet bien une parole qui énonce du commun et non seulement une voix qui signale la douleur. Cette distribution et cette redistribution des places et des identités, ce découpage et ce redécoupage des espaces et des temps, du visible et de l'invisible, du bruit et de la parole constituent ce que j'appelle le partage du sensible." Rancière, *Malaise dans l'esthétique*, 37–38, my translation.

2. Aristotle *Politics* I 1253a9–18.

3. John Locke, *An Essay Concerning Human Understanding*, II, XX, 159–60.

4. Rancière, *Dis-agreement*, 91.

5. Ibid., 123. "Le discours de l'historien est un discours mesure qui rapporte les mots de l'histoire à leur vérité. C'est ce que veut dire explicitement *interprétation*. Mais c'est aussi, d'une manière moins évidente, ce que veut dire *social*. *Social*, en effet, désigne à la fois un objet de savoir et une modalité de ce savoir. . . . le social devient ce *dessous* ou cet arrière-fond des événements et des mots qu'il faut toujours arracher au mensonge de leur apparence. *Social* désigne l'écart des mots et des événements à leur vérité non événementielle et non verbale." Rancière, *Les mots de l'histoire*, 69.

6. Rancière, *Dis-agreement*, 91–92.

7. " . . . marquer quelques repères, historiques et conceptuels, propres à reposer certains problèmes que brouillent irrémédiablement des notions qui font passer pour déterminations historiques des *a priori* conceptuels et pour déterminations conceptuelles des découpages temporels." Rancière, *Le partage du sensible*, 10.

8. "L'idée de modernité est une notion équivoque qui voudrait trancher dans la configuration complexe du régime esthétique des arts, retenir les formes de rupture, les gestes iconoclastes, etc., en les séparant du contexte qui les autorise: la reproduction généralisée, l'interprétation, l'histoire, le musée, le patrimoine . . ." Ibid., 37.

9. Rancière, *Dis-agreement*, 68.

10. Plato *Protagoras* 325c–d.

11. Plato *Protagoras* 322c2–3.

12. Plato *Protagoras* 320c.

13. Aristote *Politics* III 9.1280b42–1281a3.

14. Rancière, *Dis-agreement*, 30.

15. See Gernet, *Droit et institutions en Grèce antique*, 268.

16. Rancière, *Dis-agreement*, 88.

17. Ibid., 91.

18. Rancière, *Courts voyages au pays du peuple*, 158–59.

19. "Reflections on the Right Use of School Studies," in *Waiting for God* (New York: Putnam's Sons, 1951).

4. THE CLASSICS AND CRITICAL THEORY IN POSTMODERN FRANCE

1. My use of the terms *postmodernity* and *postmodern* in this essay is historical in nature, and it tries to unify the definition of the "postindustrial" and "postdemocratic" stage of consensus democracies described by Rancière himself in the chapter 5 of *Dis-agreement*. Rancière generally ties the term *postmodern* to the philosophical interpretation given to it by J. F. Lyotard, and as such he avoids it quite carefully, but this is not the definition of postmodernity that I invoke.

2. The famous comic playwright Molière (1622–1673) nonetheless makes a witty and significant intrusion in the text, where he's welcomed simply as a representative of "our theater" (*notre théâtre*). This "our" is so profoundly French that I think logically it must be subsumed under the category of the "French Classics." Fénelon had infiltrated the argument of *The Ignorant Schoolmaster* in a somewhat similar manner, where it is his *Télémaque*, a classic of seventeenth-century French literature, that is at the center of the pedagogical experiment leading to the discovery of absolute equality.

3. Rancière, *Dis-agreement*, 1.

4. The term *difference* here has to be understood precisely in its multiple meanings, which are temporal, textual, and argumentative.

5. Aristotle *Politics* I, 1, pp. 2–6.

6. As Christopher Mackay says, "During the first secession, the plebs swore an oath that they would kill anyone who harmed their elected representatives, the tribunes. This marked the beginning of the corporate organization of the plebs as a kind of a 'state within the state.' Eventually, the organs of the corporate plebs were absorbed into the state, and to some extent the state assimilated itself to the organization of the plebs." *Ancient Rome*, 35.

7. *Dis-agreement*, 23.

8. Ibid., 18.

Nancy's essay was published in French as "Rancière et la métaphysique" in the same collection as Badiou's essay (*La philosophie déplacée*). We would like to express our gratitude to Badiou, Nancy, and the editors of this collection for allowing us to publish the English translations of these essays.

1. Rancière, *The Politics of Aesthetics*, 39.
2. Rancière, "La division de l'arkhe," 87.
3. Rancière, *Politics of Aesthetics*, 13, 45.
4. Ibid., 12.
5. Rancière, *La parole muette*, 176. Translator's translation.

This essay was originally published under the title "Qu'est-ce que la philosophie politique? Notes pour une topique," *Actuel Marx* 28 (2000): 11–22. We thank Étienne Balibar for allowing us to print the English translation of the essay in this volume.

1. The notes that follow come from a talk given in 1998 at the École Normale Supérieure of Fontenay-Saint-Cloud in a doctoral seminar on the question "Political Philosophy or Science of Society?" The opening talk was given by Catherine Colliot-Thélène.
2. Catherine Colliot-Thélène writes, "What holds true for the opposition between universalism and cultural relativism also holds true for the opposition between order and conflict, or between individualism and 'holism,' and many others as well: they traverse the field of what passes for political philosophy as well as the field of the social sciences. If one sets aside the difference in 'trade' (interpretation of texts on the one hand, methodical analysis of collected empirical data on the other), the lines dividing philosophy from the science of society are often fluctuating, all the more so in that the 'science of society' is at least as heterogeneous as political philosophy. But to the extent that philosophy finds itself obliged to specify the differential nature of its discourse, it constantly falls back upon the question of the link between rationality and Western modernity. It is in this sense that it is always engaged with the philosophy of history, whether it acknowledges this or not. In its classic form, the philosophy of history had the noteworthy merit of directly confronting

the question of the historicity of reason: how can one reconcile the fact that reason has a history with the claim of universality that it encompasses? If certain contemporary political philosophers believe they can finesse this question, they nevertheless attest to astonishing complicities between the criteria they propose for rational freedom and the political forms ('Western democracy,' or, in Popper's terms, 'open society') that are characteristic of the modern West." "Philosophie politique ou science de la société," paper read at the École Normale Supérieure of Fontenay-Saint-Cloud, October 21, 1998; text not revised by the author.

3. Wallerstein, *Unthinking Social Science.*

4. François Furet, *The Passing of an Illusion.*

5. See Amiel, *Hannah Arendt.*

6. Esposito's *Communitas, origine e destino della communità*, has been published in French translation as *Communitas, origine et destin de la communauté.* See also, among other works, *Categorie dell'impolitico, Nove pensieri sulla politica*, and *Oltre la politica.*

7. Derrida, *Force de loi.*

8. In English as *Reflections of a Nonpolitical Man.*

9. See especially Esposito's commentary on Bataille's unfinished work on sovereignty in *Nove pensieri sulla politica*, 87–111, where Esposito stresses the constitutive contradiction of the category of "subject," a correlative of the representation of sovereign power.

10. Ibid., 13, 25.

11. Ibid., 42.

12. Ibid., 47.

13. Ibid., 37.

14. Nancy, *La communauté désoeuvrée.*

15. The original divergence of these two notions, *community* and *immunity*, starting from their common etymology (*munus*), along with their reciprocal contamination, is the guiding thread of Esposito's most recent book, *Communitas, origine e destino della communità*, following an itinerary that leads from Hobbes to Bataille.

16. Ibid., 58.

17. Marx, "Contribution to the Critique of Hegel's Philosophy of Law," 30; Rancière, *Dis-agreement*, 95.

18. Rancière, *Dis-agreement*, 32.

19. Ibid., 8–9.

20. Ibid., 87.

21. Balibar, "Vers la citoyenneté imparfaite."

22. Van Gunsteren, *A Theory of Citizenship*.

23. Balibar, *Les frontières de la démocratie*; *Masses, Classes, Ideas*; and *Droit de cité*.

7. RANCIÈRE IN SOUTH CAROLINA

1. Rancière, *Dis-agreement*, 17.

2. Ibid.

3. Sen, *Inequality Reexamined*, ix.

4. Rancière, *Dis-agreement*, 28.

5. Ibid., 16.

6. Rancière, *The Ignorant Schoolmaster*, 46.

7. Rancière, *On the Shores of Politics*, 32–33.

8. Rancière denies that the accommodation politics leads to will lead to a consensus. "The political wrong . . . can be addressed. But addressed does not mean redressed. . . . The political wrong does not get righted. It is addressed as something irreconcilable within a community that is always unstable and heterogeneous." Ibid., 103.

9. Rancière, *Dis-agreement*, 30.

10. Rancière, *On the Shores of Politics*, 48.

11. Rancière, *Dis-agreement*, 35.

12. Ibid., 11.

13. Ibid., 12.

14. Rancière, *On the Shores of Politics*, 49. On this issue, see also Rancière's discussion of subjectification in his essay, "Politics, Identification, and Subjectivization," where he writes that subjectification (translated in that essay as subjectivization) "is the formation of a one that is not a self but is the relation of a self to an other" (66).

15. Rancière, *On the Shores of Politics*, 84.

16. Ibid., 86.

17. At the outset of *Dis-agreement*, Rancière recounts Aristotle's view of human beings as capable of speech, in contrast to slaves and others who can make grunts and take orders, but cannot really engage in meaningful conversation. When I read this passage, it recalled the events of that evening vividly.

1. On these issues, see my articles "L'ordre économique de la mondialisation libérale," and "ConcateNations."

2. Interview with Jacques Rancière, destined to appear in the French journal *Dissonance* in 2005, but apparently never published. My translations.

3. On such issues, see the dossier devoted to the "Power of Collective Improvisation" in *Multitudes* 16 (2004): 131–78, http://multitudes.samizdat .net/rubrique444.html. See also the various issues of the online journal *Critical Studies in Improvisation* at http://www.criticalimprov.com.

4. See Deleuze, "Les Intercesseurs," in *Pourparlers*, 172; and Deleuze, "La littérature et la vie," in *Critique et clinique*, 14.

5. Rancière, "Le malentendu littéraire," 128–29. Translation mine.

6. For more on these issues, see the chapter 4 of my book *Lire, interpréter, actualiser*.

Earlier versions of this essay were presented at two conferences on Jacques Rancière's work, one organized by Phil Watts at the University of Pittsburgh, March 2005, and one organized by and Laurence Cornu and Patrice Vermeren at Cerisy, May 2005; a slightly different version was published in *New Left Review* 37 (January 2006) 109–29.

1. Rancière, *The Ignorant Schoolmaster*, 138.

2. Rancière, *On the Shores of Politics*, 32–33. For a more general survey of the anarchic orientation of Rancière's work, see my "Jacques Rancière and the Subversion of Mastery."

3. Sartre, *Being and Nothingness*, 67.

4. Rancière, "The Thinking of Dissensus: Politics as Aesthetics," my emphasis.

5. "Entretien avec Jacques Rancière." *Dissonance* 1 (2004). Pierre Campion notes the prominence of theatrical analogies in his detailed review of Rancière's *Le partage du sensible*, in *Acta Fabula*.

6. Rancière, *Les scènes du peuple*, 10.

7. Rancière, *Dis-agreement*, 88. Translation has been modified by author.

8. Rancière, "Entretien avec Jacques Rancière."

9. Rancière, *Le philosophe et ses pauvres*, 36, 84.

10. Rancière, "The Thinking of Dissensus"; see also *La haine de la démocratie*, 41–47.

11. Plato, *The Republic* in particular 392d–398b and 595a–608b.

12. Plato, *Laws* 701a. As Samuel Weber notes, even by comparison with unruly democracy, what Plato finds "so frightening and fearful about the *theatrocracy* is that it appears to respect no such confines. And how, after all, can there be a *polis*, or anything *political*, without confinement? The previous divisions and organization of music into fixed genres and types is progressively dissolved by a practice that mixes genres and finally leaves no delimitation untouched or unquestioned." "Displacing the Body: The Question of Digital Democracy," 1996, http://www.hydra.umn.edu/weber/displace.html. Accessed December 13, 2007.

13. Plato, *Laws* 701b–c.

14. Plato, *The Republic* 605b–c.

15. Rancière, *Partage du sensible*, 14; see also 67–68.

16. Ibid., 15.

17. Plato, *The Republic* 604e.

18. See, in particular, Thiongo, "The Language of African Theatre."

19. Rancière, *The Ignorant Schoolmaster*, 2.

20. Rancière, "The Emancipated Spectator."

21. Ibid.

22. Ibid.

23. See, in particular, Rancière, "Biopolitique ou politique?"

24. Lacoue-Labarthe, *L'imitation des modernes*, 276, 100; see also Lacoue-Labarthe, "Stagings of Mimesis," 59.

25. Rancière, *La haine de la démocratie*, 56.

26. Rancière, *Les scènes du peuple*, 174–75.

27. Rancière, "Eleven Theses on Politics."

28. Rancière, "Politics and Aesthetics," 202.

29. Rancière, *Aux bords du politique*, 242.

30. Rancière, *Nights of Labor*, 19.

31. Rancière, *La lécon d'Althusser*, 144, 96, 121.

32. Rancière, *Les scènes du peuple*, 11.

33. Rancière, *La lécon d'Althusser*, 154.

34. Rancière, *Les scènes du people*, 8; see also Rancière, *The Names of History*, 65, 73.

35. Jacques Rancière, "Le bon temps ou la barrière des plaisirs" and "Le théâtre du peuple," both reprinted in *Les scènes du peuple*.
36. Ibid., 12.
37. Ibid., 236–39.
38. Ibid., 214.
39. Ibid., 243; see also Balandier, *Le pouvoir sur scènes*.
40. Rancière, *Aux bords du politique*, 245.
41. See, in particular, Rancière, *La haine de la démocratie*, 54; and *Aux bords du politique*, 229–31.
42. Rancière, *Aux bords du politique*, 224.
43. Rancière, "Aesthetics, Inaesthetics, Anti-Aesthetics," 230.
44. Schiller, *Letters on the Aesthetic Education of Man*, 80; see also *Malaise dans l'esthétique*, 42–45.
45. Rancière, *Malaise dans l'esthétique*, 132; see also Schiller, *Letters*, letter 15.
46. Rancière, *Les scènes du peuple*, 169, 181–85.
47. Rancière, *Dis-agreement*, 85–87.
48. Jules Michelet, *L'etudiant*, quoted in Rancière, *Les scènes du peuple*, 175.
49. Rancière, *Malaise dans l'esthétique*, 31–32, 162; see also Rancière, "The Aesthetic Revolution and Its Outcomes," 148.
50. Rancière, *Dis-agreement*, 125–26; see also Rancière, *Malaise dans l'esthétique*, 172.
51. See also Rancière, "Politics and Aesthetics," 196–97.
52. See also Hallward, "What's the Point: First Notes Towards a Philosophy of Determination," 148–58; Hallward, "Dialectical Voluntarism."
53. Fox Piven and Cloward, *Poor People's Movements*.
54. Piven and Cloward, *Regulating the Poor*, 338.
55. Rancière, *Partage du sensible*, 23, 68–69; see also Rancière, *Malaise dans l'esthétique*, 16.
56. Rancière, *Dis-agreement*, 72–76.
57. Crozier, Huntington, and Watanuki, *The Crisis of Democracy*; see also Rancière, *Le haine de la démocratie*, 12–14.
58. See, for example, Chomsky, "Deterring Democracy in Italy."
59. McLuhan and Fiore, *The Medium Is the Massage*, 16.
60. Rancière, *Dis-agreement*, 137–38; see also Rancière, *The Names of History*, 93, 98.
61. Rancière, *Les scènes du peuple*, 44–45; Rancière, *The Ignorant Schoolmaster*, 105–6, 133–34.
62. See, for instance, Rancière, *The Ignorant Schoolmaster*, 77. As Alain Ba-

diou notes, Rancière's presumption is that "every social tie implies a master." Badiou, *Abrégé de métapolitique*, 123.

63. See, for instance, Rancière, *The Ignorant Schoolmaster*, 134.

64. Rancière, *On the Shores of Politics*, 41; Rancière, *La chair des mots*, 11.

65. I develop this point in more detail in "The Politics of Prescription."

66. Rancière, "Politics and Aesthetics," 202.

67. See, for example, Rancière, *Les scènes du peuple* 275, 279–80.

68. Rancière, *The Ignorant Schoolmaster*, 65; see also 5–6.

69. Rancière, *Les scènes du peuple*, 63–84; see also ibid., 100–1; Rancière, *La lécon d'Althusser*, 162–63.

70. Rancière, *Dis-agreement*, 9.

71. Rancière, *La lécon d'Althusser*, 207–8.

72. Schiller, *Letters*, 128.

10. RANCIÈRE'S LEFTISM

1. Rancière, *The Ignorant Schoolmaster*, 5.

2. Rancière, "Politics and Aesthetics," 194. With thanks to my friend Peter Hallward for giving me a copy of the original transcription of this interview, conducted in Paris, August 29, 2002.

3. Rancière, *The Ignorant Schoolmaster*, 19–43.

4. Rancière, *La leçon d'Althusser*, 226. Unless otherwise indicated, all translations from this text are my own.

5. Rancière, *The Philosopher and His Poor*, xxviii.

6. I am thinking not only of Althusser's famous statement according to which Marx would have taught him that "nominalism is the royal road to materialism, in truth it is a road that leads only to itself, and I do not know of any more profound *form* of materialism than nominalism," but also of the captivating analysis of Foucault's nominalism by Étienne Balibar, "Foucault et Marx: L'enjeu du nominalisme." For Althusser's affirmation, see *L'avenir dure longtemps*, 243; and compare with Warren Montag's analysis, "Althusser's Nominalism."

7. Rancière, *La leçon d'Althusser*, 26–27.

8. Ibid., 254n, 250.

9. Rancière, *Les scènes du peuple*, 7.

10. Ibid., 11.

11. Rancière, *Les scènes du peuple*, 314. With regard to this recurrent gesture of nominalistic pluralization, I am tempted to quote the expression of

doubt coming from Rancière himself: "One doesn't change the nature of a concept by putting it in the plural. At best one masks it" (*La leçon d'Althusser*, 261).

12.   Rancière, *La leçon d'Althusser*, 154.

13.   Rancière, *The Philosopher and His Poor*, 9–10; *Les scènes du peuple*, 317.

14.   Rancière, *Dis-agreement*, 10.

15.   Ibid., 11.

16.   Ibid., 11.

17.   Ibid., 13. Rancière plays with the echoes between *torsion*, here translated as "twist," and *tort*, "wrong."

18.   Ibid., 16.

19.   Ibid., 16

20.   Rancière, *Mésentente*, 37; see also *Dis-agreement*, 17 (the English translation skips the first sentence in this quotation).

21.   Rancière, *Dis-agreement*, 18.

22.   Ibid., 27.

23.   Ibid., 39.

24.   Ibid., 123.

25.   Rancière, *Mésentente*, 24; *Dis-agreement*, 5 (translation modified to keep "politics" for *la politique*).

26.   Rancière, *Dis-agreement*, 19

27.   Ibid., 71.

28.   Ibid., 125–26.

29.   Ibid., 1. The expression is actually quite common. See also "L'éthique de la sociologie," in *Les scènes du peuple*: "Commençons par le commencement: la dissimulation de la politique que Durkheim aurait opérée pour faire accepter la sociologie à l'Université" (355). Or the beginning of *Le philosophe et ses pauvres*: "Au commencement il y aurait quatre personnes" (17) (In the beginning there would be four persons.) *The Philosopher and His Poor*, 3. Or, again, in *Le destin des images*: "Partons donc du commencement" (9).

30.   Rancière writes: "The double Althusserian truth after May '68 is shattered into two poles: the speculative leftism of the all-powerful ideological apparatuses and the speculative zdanovism of the class struggle in theory which interrogates each word to confess to its class" (*La leçon d'Althusser*, 146). The definition of the concept according to Badiou is as follows: "We can term *speculative leftism* any thought of being which bases itself upon the theme of an absolute commencement. Speculative leftism imagines

that intervention authorizes itself on the basis of itself alone; that it breaks with the situation without any other support than its own negative will. This imaginary wager upon an absolute novelty—'to break in two the history of the world'—fails to recognize that the real of the conditions of possibility of intervention is always the circulation of an already-decided event. In other words, it is the presupposition, implicit or not, that there has already been an intervention. Speculative leftism is fascinated by the eventual ultra-one and it believes that in the latter's name it can reject any immanence to the structured regime of the count-as-one. Given that the structure of the ultra-one is the Two, the imaginary of a radical beginning leads ineluctably, in all orders of thought, to a Manichean hypostasis. The violence of this false thought is anchored in its representation of an imaginary Two whose temporal manifestation is signed, via the excess of one, by the ultra-one of the event, Revolution or Apocalypse." See Badiou, *L'être et l'événement*, 232; *Being and Event*, 210. For a more detailed commentary, see Bosteels, "The Speculative Left."

31. Rancière, *Les scènes du peuple*, 317–18.

32. Lenin, "Dialectics and Eclecticism," 93.

33. Rancière, *Les scènes du peuple*, 322.

34. Ibid., 329.

35. Ibid., 318.

36. Ibid., 319.

37. Ibid.

38. Ibid.

39. Rancière, *Dis-agreement*, 30–31.

40. Ibid., 32–33.

41. Ibid., 88.

42. Ibid., 28.

43. Rancière, (with Danielle Rancière), "La légende des philosophes," in *Les scènes du peuple*, 307–8.

44. See Badiou, "Rancière et la communauté des égaux" and "Rancière et l'apolitique"; in Badiou, *Metapolitics*, 107–23; Rancière, "L'inesthétique d'Alain Badiou.," in *Malaise dans l'esthetique*.

45. Badiou, *Being and Event*, 191 and 193.

46. Rancière, *Mallarmé*, 24.

47. Ibid., 25.

48. Badiou, *La révolution culturelle*; and Badiou, *La Commune de Paris*. Both conferences have now been translated as part 3, "Historicity of Politics:

Lessons of Two Revolutions," in Badiou, *Polemics*. The second of these conferences is also thoroughly reworked and reprinted in *Logiques des mondes* (Paris: Le Seuil, 2006), 383–402. For my own translation of the first conference, as well as a wider bibliography on Badiou's Maoist inflection of the relation between politics and history, see the special dossier which I helped put together on entitled for the special issue of *positions*, edited by Tani Barlow, entitled "Badiou and Cultural Revolution," including my contribution, "Post-Maoism: Badiou and Politics" (576–634). See also Lazarus, "Singularité et modes historiques de la politique." For a discussion of the thorny issue of the relation between historical modes of politics and the eternal nature of all truths as established in Badiou's philosophy, see the long note at the end of *Logiques des mondes*, 544–47.

49.   Rancière, *Dis-agreement*, 79.

50.   Rancière, *La leçon d'Althusser*, 205.

51.   Rancière, *The Philosopher and His Poor*, xxvii. Rancière quickly adds, however: "I forgot that I had never known how to draw a straight line" (ibid., xxvii).

52.   The figure who best sums up the stakes of this question, of course, is Michel Foucault. For a long time the very model of work for Rancière, Foucault is also mentioned in "La légende des philosophes" as one of the intellectuals responsible, perhaps unwittingly, for the "liquidation" of militant history in France. "If, among the thinkers of my generation, there was one I was quite close to at one point, it was Foucault. Something of Foucault's archaeological project—the will to think the conditions of possibility of such and such a form of statement or such and such an object's constitution—has stuck with me," Rancière says in his interview with Peter Hallward (Rancière, "Politics and Aesthetics," 209), but after the "New Philosophers," this influence may seem suspicious: "Now, it is first of all Foucault's discourse and intervention that serve as support today for the new magisterial and prophetic figures of the intellectual: it is as application of a general theory of knowledge/power that the analysis of the Soviet concentrationary system as accomplishment of the knowledge of master-thinkers presents itself. And it is similarly based on Foucault's analyses that others prophetize the coming of the Angel, the cultural revolution freed by the vanishing of the old knowledge of Man or the barbarism of a power coextensive with the social order" ("La légende des philosophes," 300–1).

1. Jacques Rancière, "Élection et raison démocratique," *Le Monde*, March 22, 2007. Alain Finkielkraut's and Marcel Gauchet's interview "Malaise dans la démocratie," in *Le Débat* (September–November 1988), could appear here as one of the first moments of identification of this "new" malaise. As to "La démocratie et ses médecins," see Rancière, *Chroniques des temps consensuels*, 205–9.

2. Rancière, *Chroniques des temps consensuels*, 181, 192–93.

3. The ironic wink reference to Freud's *Malaise dans la Civilisation* (*Civilization and its Discontents*) was not lost on anyone, but it comes with a single difference: even if the aesthetic malaise were as impossible to eliminate as Freud's civilizational malaise, in Rancière there is no sexual enigma to resolve or symptom to interpret, just an inherent contradiction in the aesthetic regime and a conceptual confusion to elucidate.

4. Racism is "*the* malady of consensus" because "except for the religious person, alterity can only be political, that is to say founded on an irreconcilable *and* treatable wrong." Without this argumentative devise, the pseudo "appeasement of the people's political passions" leaves room for "its necessary underside: the return of political animality, the pure rejection of the other." See Rancière, "La démocratie corrigée."

5. Rancière, "On War as the Ultimate Form of Advanced Plutocratic Consensus," 253–58.

6. Rancière, "La philosophie en déplacement," 31.

7. Rancière, *Malaise dans l'esthétique*, 152.

8. Rancière, "La méthode de l'égalité," 519.

9. In the citations that follow, the page number is given for "The Ethical Turn of Aesthetics and Politics"; the original French edition of the chapter was entitled "Le tournant éthique de la politique et de l'esthétique."

10. "Politics and Aesthetics." See also my "Jacques Rancière's Freudian Cause"; Rancière, "Politics and Aesthetics," 207.

11. Rancière, *Malaise dans l'esthétique*, 47.

12. Rancière, "The Ethical Turn of Aesthetics and Politics," 2.

13. Rancière, *Malaise dans l'esthétique*, 141.

14. Hallward, "Politics and Aesthetics," 208.

15. Rancière, *La haine de la démocratie*, 104.

16. Ibid., 8.

17. Ibid., 104.

18. Rancière, "La méthode de l'égalité," 519.

19. See Rancière, "Sens et figure de l'histoire," where he already denounced the "retrospective link between unrepresentable horror of the camps and the anti-representative rigor of modern art" (21) and reminds us that "the age of antirepresentation is not the age of the unrepresentable" (23).

20. Rancière, "The Ethical Turn of Aesthetics and Politics," 2

21. Ibid., 2

22. Ibid., 5.

23. Ibid., 2. This restrictive conception of "trauma" is nevertheless part of a larger contemporary discussion. See, among others, Fassin and Rechtman, *La fin du soupcon*; and Fassin and Rechtman, *L'empire du traumatisme*, which show the rapid development since the 1980s of humanitarian psychology, victim psychiatry, and the psychotraumatology of exile in France and elsewhere.

24. Rancière, "The Ethical Turn of Aesthetics and Politics," 8.

25. According to Duroux, "Jacques Rancière et ses contemporains,"23.

26. One can trace Rancière's retroactive critique of Lyotard's theory of the sublime in his rewriting of the first version of "S'il y a de l'irreprésentable," first published in *L'art et la Mémoire des Camps: Le Genre Humain*, for its republication in *Le destin des images*, as well as the rewriting between these texts and *Malaise dans l'esthétique*, with its "Ethical Turn," in 2004. The new post-9/11 master-words *trauma* and *terror*, the idea of an ethical turn, the link between the American wars and the aesthetic of the sublime, Bush and Lyotard, the law of Moses/law of McDonald's—all are new historical and discursive symptoms of his thinking of discontents, or the Lévy-Milner effect on the "malaise of aesthetics."

27. Rancière, "The Thinking of Dissensus," my emphasis.

28. Fontenay, *Une tout autre histoire*, 190.

29. Ibid., 15.

30. Ibid., 185. See also "Exister 'avant' d'exister," a program aired on *France Culture, Les Cheims de la connaissance*, May 1, 2007.

31. Fontenay, *Une tout autre histoire*, 231, 232.

32. Rancière, "The Ethical Turn of Aesthetics and Politics," 7.

33. Ibid., 15.

34. Rancière, "The Ethical Turn of Aesthetics and Politics," 18. Emphasis added.

35. To my knowledge, no history of ideas gives such a role to Lyotard, includ-

ing that of François Cusset on *La décennie: Le grand cauchemar des années 1980*, which shows him resisting the "thought police" and only envisioning his "aesthetic of the sublime" as a retreat from the political and critical scene of the 1970s. Even if they agree on the principle actors of conservative ideology, Cusset establishes no link between this reactionary turn and the later work of Lyotard, nor between the new moralists and the dominant paradigm of the Shoah, as Rancière proposes.

36. Rancière, "The Ethical Turn of Aesthetics and Politics," 18.

37. Ibid., 171, 18, 19.

38. Martine Lebovici agrees, in "A plusieurs voix autour de Jacques Rancière," in criticizing the excesses of Jean-Claude Milner's theses, notably the direct link he establishes between modernity, democracy, and the genocide of the Jews. But, for her, that impedes neither recognizing the extermination of the Jews as a central event nor saying that the name "Jew" cannot give way to a political subjectivation.

39. According to François Noudelmann, in "La question du nom juif," 189.

40. Rancière, *Malaise dans l'esthétique*, 26.

41. Rancière, *La haine de la démocratie*, 38; Lévy, *Le meurtre du Pasteur*.

42. See "S'il y de l'irreprésentable," in *Le destin des images*.

43. Rancière, *Malaise dans l'esthétique*, 33.

44. Rancière, "Esthétique, inesthétique, anti-esthétique."

45. On the subject of this polemic violence, see Campion, "Jacques Rancière et la démocratie.

46. See Badiou, *Circonstances*, vol. 3, *Portées du mot "juif."*

47. Rancière, *La haine de la démocratie*, 98.

48. Ibid., 40–41.

49. See Milner, *Le juif de savoir*, written in response to Badiou, *Circonstances*, vol. 3.

50. Rancière, *Le haine de la démocratie*, 36.

51. Milner, "Théorie du nom juif."

52. See Marty, *Une querelle avec Alain Badiou, philosophe.*

53. Badiou, *L'éthique*, is one of the explicit intertexts of Rancière's book, but Badiou takes care to distinguish ethics as a "new name of thought" for Levinas from the contemporary ideology and catechism to which it gave birth, that of the "right of difference" (36–37). Rancière, who never names Levinas, treats only the transformation of Lyotard's "ethical" thought into an antipolitical consensus or "new law of Moses."

1. Sartre's stance on commitment evolved very quickly through the course of the late 1940s and into the 1950s, as evidenced perhaps most notably by his discussion of the functional and committed aspects of "black poetry" in "*Orphée noir*," originally published in 1948 and reprinted in *Situations III*.

2. Barthes, *Le degré zéro de l'écriture*, in *œuvres completes*, 1:183 (also see 147). Unless otherwise noted, all translations are my own.

3. See Rancière, *Malaise dans l'esthétique*, 40.

4. See most notably Rancière, *The Politics of Aesthetics*, 12–19.

5. Rancière provides at least three different definitions of politics: (i) the act of political subjectivization that breaks with the police order; (ii) the meeting ground between police procedures and the process of equality; and (iii) the overall distribution of the sensible. It is primarily this last meaning that is being discussed here.

6. Rancière, *The Politics of Aesthetics*, 51.

7. See Rancière, *La parole muette*, 17–18, and Rancère, "Politics of Literature." The essay "Politics of Literature" was reworked and published in French as the opening chapter in *Politique de la littérature*.

8. Rancière, "Politics of Literature," 16, 17, 18, 19.

9. Ibid., 20.

10. Ibid., 11. Rancière writes on page 20 of the same article: "Sartre's flawed argument about Flaubert is not a personal and casual mistake."

11. According to Rancière, "The patterns of their critical explanation of 'what literature says' relied on the same system of meaning that underpinned the practice of literature itself. Not surprisingly, they very often came upon the same problem as Sartre. In the same way, they endorsed as new critical insights on literature the 'social' and 'political' interpretations of nineteenth-century conservatives. Further, the patterns they had to use to reveal the truth on literature are the patterns framed by literature itself. Explaining close-to-hand realities as phantasmagorias bearing witness to the hidden truth of a society, this pattern of intelligibility was the invention of literature itself. Telling the truth on the surface by travelling in the underground, spelling out the unconscious social text lying underneath—that also was a plot invented by literature itself" (ibid., 20).

12. Rancière, *Le destin des images*, 19.

13. Rancière has provided this genealogy most notably in *La parole muette* and, more recently, in *Le destin des images*.

14. As mentioned in footnote 5, there is an additional sense in which he uses the term.

15. Rancière, *Aux bords du politique*, 13. The 1998 French edition of *Aux bords du politique* includes a number of articles that are not available in the 1995 English translation (*On the Shores of Politics*) or the original French edition that appeared in 1992.

16. Rancière, "The Politics of Literature," 10.

17. Rancière, *Dis-agreement*, 29.

18. Ibid., 30; *La mésentente*, 53.

19. Rancière, *Malaise dans l'esthétique*, 39–40.

20. Rancière, *Dis-agreement*, 43.

21. Although Chantal Mouffe's work is squarely situated in the logic of identity and difference, she nonetheless indicates one of the dangers inherent in this logic: "Despite its claim to be more democratic," extreme pluralism "prevents us from recognizing how certain differences are constructed as relations of subordination and should therefore be challenged by a radical democratic politics." *The Democratic Paradox*, 20. Nancy Fraser puts her finger on this problem in her critique of what she calls deconstructive antiessentialism: "Deconstructive antiessentialists appraise identity claims on ontological grounds alone. They do not ask, in contrast, how a given identity or difference is related to social structures of domination and to social relations of inequality." *Justice Interruptus*, 183. She also rejects the pluralist version of multiculturalism, where "difference is viewed as intrinsically positive and inherently cultural": "This perspective accordingly celebrates difference uncritically while failing to interrogate its relation to inequality." Ibid., 185.

22. As we will see, *La haine de la démocratie* nonetheless remains largely within the logic of identity and difference.

23. Rancière, *Malaise dans l'esthétique*, 38.

24. Rancière, *The Politics of Aesthetics*, 12.

25. Rancière, *Malaise dans l'esthétique*, 37.

26. Rancière himself seems to recognize this (see ibid., 37).

27. Rancière, *The Politics of Aesthetics*, 51.

28. Ibid., 51.

29. It is likely that Rancière would reply to this criticism by reminding us that the "proper" of politics is to be "improper" by constantly stirring up the

sediments of the police order. However, we should not be distracted by what has become a common deconstructivist strategy: politics will *never* be so improper that it will throw off its proper harness of *being* improper.

30. Rancière, *La haine de la démocratie*. 7. Rancière's earlier article, "La démocratie criminelle?" remains far superior to the book that eventually grew out of it precisely because he focused on the reconfiguration of the French political imaginary since the dissolution of the Soviet Union rather than venturing into historical generalizations regarding the perpetual disdain for democracy (see *Chroniques des temps consensuels*).

31. See Finley, *Democracy Ancient and Modern* and *Politics in the Ancient World*; Birch, *The Concepts and Theories of Modern Democracy*; and Castoriadis, "Imaginaire politique grec et moderne" and "La démocratie athénienne" in *La Montée de l'insignifiance*.

32. See Finley, *Democracy Ancient and Modern*, 9; Graubard, "Democracy"; Palmer, "Notes on the Use of the Word 'Democracy' 1789–1799"; Dahl, *On Democracy*, 7–9.

33. See Williams, *Keywords*, 14; and Palmer "Notes on the Use of the Word 'Democracy,'" 205: "It is rare, even among the *philosophes* of France before the Revolution, to find anyone using the word 'democracy' in a favorable sense in any practical connection." To take a few poignant examples, Montesquieu and Rousseau both suggest that democracy is against the natural order (see *De l'esprit des lois* I, XI, vi; *Du contrat social* III, iv). Anthony H. Birch asserts that "the founders of the American constitution shared in the generally poor view of democratic government. . . . The Founding Fathers talked of creating a republic, based on representative institutions, not a democracy; the leaders of the French Revolution talked of a republic also; and in Britain people described their system as one of representative and responsible government." *The Concepts and Theories of Modern Democracy*, 45–46. As an example thereof, see the critique of "pure democracy" in *The Federalist Papers* (most notably nos. 9 and 10). The writings of Alexis de Tocqueville, although far from being unequivocal, can be taken as signs of important conceptual and terminological changes, whereby "democracy" was partially revalorized: "To want to stop democracy thus appears to be to struggle against God himself, and nations would but have to accommodate themselves with the social state imposed upon them by Providence." *De la démocratie en Amérique*, 1:61.

34. Moses Finley's historical analysis clearly points to one of the fundamental

problems with Rancière's schematic account of the perennial hatred of democracy: "In antiquity, intellectuals in the overwhelming majority disapproved of popular government, and they produced a variety of explanations for their attitude and a variety of alternative proposals. Today their counterparts, especially but not only in the west, are agreed, in probably the same overwhelming majority, that democracy is the best form of government, the best known and the best imaginable." *Democracy Ancient and Modern*, 8–9; see also Palmer, "Notes on the Use of the Word 'Democracy,' " 203; and Laniel, *Le mot "democracy" aux Etats-Unis de 1780–1856*, 31.

35. To say that one is in favor of democracy today, at least within the Euro-American world, is a moral no-brainer structurally equivalent to statements like "I am for peace" or "I am against child abuse." Such statements are generally devoid of any analytic content and primarily function as social signs, whose message can be literally translated as: "I am a good person like all other good people." The relatively small group of conservatives attacked by Rancière is in fact playing off of this moralization of political categories and sardonically reversing the values by condemning democracy as a form of cultural corruption.

36. We could therefore say the same thing about democracy that Paul Valéry says about freedom: "It's one of those detestable words that have more value than meaning, that sing more than they speak [*C'est un de ces détestables mots qui ont plus de valeur que de sens; qui chantent plus qu'ils ne parlent*]." Quoted in Kerbrat-Orecchioni, *La connotation*, 6.

37. "Subjectivization," at the very least, allows Rancière to underscore the dynamic aspect of politics (see the three definitions of politics in note 5), and it emphasizes the role of subjects in the political process.

38. This confusion is exacerbated by Rancière's tendency to claim that the commonsense use of the term is "confused" (*Le haine de la démocratie*, 101).

39. See Rockhill, "The Silent Revolution"; "Démocratie moderne et révolution esthétique"; "Le cinéma n'est jamais né"; "Recent Developments in Aesthetics."

40. Rancière, *The Politics of Aesthetics*, 61.

41. Ibid., 61.

42. Ibid., 62.

43. There is at least one important qualification to make: Rancière *does* provide a fascinating account of the ways in which art is reappropriated by

various regimes (see, most notably, *L'inconscient esthétique*). This *might* be interpreted as suggesting that the political being of art always depends on its regime. However, even if this is the case, Rancière nonetheless purports to have access to the "political being of art" within each regime rather than recognizing that the *politicité* of art is a concept in struggle, a crossroads of social negotiation.

44. Paraphrasing his own terminology, we might say that he suffers from a *meta-politics of art*.

45. It is interesting in this regard that the story of the film *Lili Marleen* is not significantly different from the story of the song. The project had its origins in the work of two representatives of Papa's Kino. The producer, Luggi Waldleitner, was known for being a conventional member of the establishment, and the screenwriter, Manfred Purzer, had a reputation as a conservative. In accepting to direct the film, R. W. Fassbinder appears to have concluded a devil's pact. However, echoing the theme of the "right to survival" in *Lili Marleen* and many of his other films, he states in one of his interviews, "If someone objects, as some of my friends do, that you shouldn't make films with the money of rightists, all I can say is that Visconti made almost all his films with money from rightists. And always justified it with similar arguments: that they gave him more leeway than the leftists." *The Anarchy of the Imagination*, 61.

46. Some useful reference points in the elucidation of "logics of production" include the work of Pierre Bourdieu and his followers, H. R. Jauss's aesthetics of reception, and Anthony Giddens's theory of the duality of structure.

47. The same thing could be said about Robert. Although he is portrayed as a Jewish resistance fighter deserving of all of the obligatory social credit, he is also depicted as Mr. Mendelsson, the cowardly pawn and eventual perpetuator of patriarchal power. On this and other related issues, see the chapter on *Lili Marleen* in Elsaesser, *Fassbinder's Germany: History Identity Subject*.

48. Since there are no transhistorical, objective criteria in hermeneutics, the distinction between better and worse arguments can only be based on various forms of legitimation through social negotiation. Although this is not the place to develop such an argument, it is important to note that the position I am taking on this issue should not be unduly identified with relativism.

49. See Rancière, "Les nouvelles fictions du mal"; and "Le tournant éthique" in *Malaise dans l'esthétique*, 143–73.

50. In "Le tournant éthique," the reference to *Elephant* is dropped, and the other two films are used as illustrations of the ethical turn in contemporary politics and aesthetics. Juxtaposed with the work of Brecht, Hitchcock, and Lang, these films are taken to be signs of a new "consensual" age in which facts and principles are rendered indistinct in a morass of unbridled wickedness: evil is used to battle evil in a world in which the difference between the innocent and the guilty has dissipated against the backdrop of an original trauma shared by all (the link between September 11, 2001, and the war parade against the "axis of evil" should be clear). It is interesting that Rancière, in what is otherwise one of his most intriguing recent articles, insists on there being "two eras" of cinema, whereas he dedicated a large portion of *La fable cinématographique* to proving that Deleuze's division of film history into two periods was a mistake. Although this is not the place to analyze the relationship between these two claims, it should be noted that his argument in *La fable* focuses on perceived changes in film between the early and the mid- to late twentieth century, whereas his claims in "Le tournant éthique"— which are also made in passing in "Les nouvelles fictions du mal"— concentrate on the differences between film in the latter part of the twentieth century and cinema in the early twenty-first century.

51. There are a number of interesting elements in this film that are situated at the limit of justifiable interpretation. For instance, the letters "DA" in the concrete immediately recall Freud's analysis of a child's "*fort . . . da . . .*" game in *Beyond the Pleasure Principle* and suggest that Dave's childhood game with Jimmy and Sean, unlike the little boy's game described by Freud, was marked by a "Da" that trapped him forever "there" at his last moment of happiness or innocence. Although it is difficult to know with certainty, it seems like this kind of reference, which was not present in Dennis Lehane's novel, would be within the reach of a screenwriter like Brian Helgeland.

52. Jimmy's last name is Markum, and he bears the mark of his debt on his back in the form of a tattooed cross, which recalls the cross in Katie's mother's name: Mari*t*a, or Maria bearing a cross. The other names in the film are equally symbolic, as should be clear from the "good" cop who knows when divine law trumps the rules of the here-and-now (Sean

Devine) and the phantomlike wanderer who cannot keep his deep-seated rage from overflowing (Dave *Boyle*).

53.   In uncritically accepting the auteur policy with all of its limitations, Rancière has placed undue emphasis on the role of the director. He doesn't even mention the fact that the screenplay was based on a novel by Dennis Lehane that was published in 2001 and therefore written prior to the discourse on the axis of evil.

54.   It is significant that Jimmy's daughter was murdered in the old bear cage, just as Dave had been tortured as a boy in a wolf's den.

55.   Like Rancière, I refuse to condone this conception of "justice." However, I think it's important to clearly understand its inner logic and its mystical underpinnings.

56.   The only time the dog is seen is at the very end of the film, when Grace decides to spare him his life, since he is justifiably angry at her for having stolen his bone. A vertical tracking shot receding into the heavens, which echoes the final shot in *Breaking the Waves*, reveals Moses barking toward the sky.

57.   It is, of course, important that this was the first film in Lars Von Trier's trilogy *USA—Land of Opportunities*, since followed by *Manderlay* (2005).

58.   Grace mentions that (like Christ) she doesn't have a family, only a father.

59.   The end of *Dogville* recalls Augustine's account of the earthly city: "But the earthly city will not be everlasting; for when it is condemned to that punishment which is its end, it will no longer be a city." *The City of God against the Pagans*, 638. It would certainly be a mistake, however, to identify the life of the gangsters with the "City of God."

60.   In addition to its religious dimension, there are many other aspects to this film, as visible in the multiplication of references to the Greek world (Jason and the rest of his family), famous fairy tales (Snow White), theater (Brecht) and the "birth" of film (Thomas Edison). However, the spiritual themes developed in *Dogville* are clearly part of a larger project, which includes both *Breaking the Waves* (1996) and *Dancer in the Dark* (2000). In the former film, Von Trier weaves together a comparable story of perverted yet authentic spiritual devotion based on very similar themes: the divine gift, its acceptance, exile and excommunication, the proof of love, the logic of sacrifice, the battle between dogma and truth, and the struggle between the life of the flesh and the life of the spirit. *Dancer in the Dark* is also based on a story of misunderstood devotional sacrifice in which an outsider (Selma, a young Czech working in an

American factory) dedicates herself to saving her son from blindness with a level of commitment (including her devotion to protecting the police officer's secret) that is scarcely understandable to those around her. She finds "salvation" in a parallel world of musicals that allows her to face hardship and eventually capital punishment. The final shot of the film is structurally equivalent to the final shots in *Breaking the Waves* and *Dogville*: a vertical tracking shot ascending into the heavens is doubled by the providential statement "it's only the last song if we let it be."

61. Rancière, "Les nouvelles fictions du mal," 96.

62. Rancière seems to have overlooked the important role played by the high school principal, who punishes John in the beginning and is gunned down by Eric toward the end of the film.

63. Rancière, "Les nouvelles fictions du mal," 96.

64. Diane Keaton, one of the executive producers of *Elephant*, responded to a question about her reaction to the shootings at Columbine with the following description: "My immediate reaction is, why? That's it. Why why why why why why why? I think this movie [*Elephant*], as well as *Bowling for Columbine*, actually tries to deal with the whys of it in its own way. What's interesting to me about Gus's movie is that he's not trying to say, "It's because of *this*!" He forces you to sit there and watch it unfold before you in this amazing way, and you have the responsibility of your own thoughts. You have to sit there with your own fucking thoughts and think about it. That was astonishing, because for me it was something, for Bill it was something else, for Gus it was something else. For me, it was about being a parent, because I'm a parent." Gus Van Sant and Diane Keaton, "Elephant."

65. A similar psychosocial pattern is to be found in the demonization of individual politicians: a single, external cause is isolated as the unique root of all evil. The belligerent and repetitive vilification of Mahmoud Ahmadinejad in the mainstream Western media—I'm writing this in the summer of 2008—is an excellent example of the extreme shortcomings of political monocausality: a president elected by universal suffrage for a four-year term who has no direct control over the armed forces, military intelligence, security operations, or foreign policy (these are all the prerogative of the supreme leader, Ayatollah Ali Khamenei) has been transformed into an evil "dictator" anxious to use nuclear weapons to wage war (even though Iran is still *at least* five years away from having nuclear power, and the Iranian president does not even have the right to declare

war). It is clear that such political monocausality is directly linked to the drumbeat for more war in the Middle East and is part of the "perfect" exit strategy for the debacle in Iraq: it "explains" the failure of the American military in Iraq (it's Iran's fault); it is capable of distracting public opinion from Iraq, which is old news, in the same way that Iraq has thrown a blanket over almost all major media coverage of Afghanistan; it provides for a clearly identified diabolic enemy to fill the shoes of Saddam Hussein; it perpetuates a faulty image of Iran as unjustifiably hostile to the United States and contributes to American amnesia regarding the recent history of Iran (marked perhaps most notably by the 1953 coup organized by the CIA to replace a democratically elected regime with the autocratic Shah). In the case of military action, such ideologically generated monocausality could serve to nourish America's pluto-imperial military-industrial complex. It could also help prevent the emergence of any robust form of democracy in Iraq (which would allow for a Shia majority, most probably with leanings toward Iran), and it could further the cause of the fundamentalists in Iran by providing them a justification for repressive policies while fanning the nationalist fires of a people under attack.

66. "Rencontre avec Gus Van Sant."

67. These aesthetic choices recall the work of another great portraitist of American life and social violence, who was equally fond of referencing *Macbeth* and avoiding facile, one-sided explanations: William Faulkner. The six different trailers for *Elephant*, which are guided by the name intertitles in the film, emphasize the connections to novels such as *The Sound and the Fury* and *As I Lay Dying*.

68. See Van Sant's answer to the question concerning kids' reactions to his film in "Elephant: Interview with Gus Van Sant and Diane Keaton": "I think that kids will probably be the best audience, because I think that they recognize the quote-unquote answers as scapegoats or red herrings. They know, since they live in this situation, that the answer is way more unpredictable. You can say, 'Well, you know, these are the signs to look for. If you look for these signs, you will be safe. Or, if you look for these signs, you can fix it before it happens.' They're smarter than that, I think. They already know they have to do a little more thinking, and that it's less curable than just [watching for] the warning signs. And they live with it. Since they're in high school, they live with this day to day; they live inside of it. When you talk to them, they can play the part of the student who is

just playing up to the adult, pretending they know all the things they should be saying about school shootings, or they can be themselves, and they can just tell you that they're sick of the whole thing—adults don't get it, and it's their own world, and leave them alone, basically."

69. Interview with Gus Van Sant in *Repérages* 42, no. 9–10 (2003): 33. This reference is borrowed from Roï Amit's forthcoming essay, "Trauma-Image: The Elephant Experience," in *Trauma and Memory*. Unfortunately, I have not yet been able to obtain the original interview.

70. It remains to be seen whether Rancière's rejection of ontology and essentialism in his contribution to this collection constitutes a significant shift in his work or is simply an authoritative rejection of certain criticisms of his stance on politics. In assessing his interestingly pragmatic stance at the end of "The Method of Equality," it is important to remember that claiming that something is the case does not necessarily make it so.

13. CINEMA AND ITS DISCONTENTS

1. *La fable cinématographique*, 16; in English as *Film Fables*, 8. In the notes below the French edition will be signaled as *FC* and the English translation as *FF*. Now and again, for the ends of theory, I have slightly modified Emiliano Battista's excellent translation.

2. As shown in *Politique de la littérature*, 52; or in the last chapter of *Malaise dans l'esthétique*. Sustained critical reading is found in Rockhill, "Jacques Rancière's Politics of Perception" and "The Janus-Face of Politicized Art: Jacques Rancière in Interview with Gabriel Rockhill"; and in Rancière's own "Contemporary Art and the Politics of Aesthetics." A productive critical perspective on the aesthetic age, in which art bears witness to what cannot be represented, is found in Sanyal, *The Violence of Modernity*, 207n9. She believes that what Rancière, in *Malaise dans l'esthétique*, calls the "ethical turn" happens to be a highly "depoliticized version of modernism's aesthetic economy." In her eyes, Rancière's criticism of the Frankfurt school's rejection of any art that compromises with "cultural commerce and aestheticized life" when it becomes a mere witness to catastrophe—and not an agent—is a symptom of retraction from critical engagement.

3. It is "a multiplication of texts and readings upon a single surface. From this point of view an intimate relation exists between the image and the

landscape. A landscape is a stratification of texts that permits a multiplicity of readings. . . . I believe that no fundamental difference exists between an image and a text, a text having been for ages received as an image." Michel de Certeau, "Entretien avec Alain Charbonnier et Joël Magny," 19–20. The work is close to what he remarks of the construction of "spatial stories" in Michel de Certeau, *Arts de faire*, 172–74.

4. Such is Marguerite Duras's *India Song* in de Certeau, *La fable mystique*, 48–50.

5. Specialists of cartography, such as Giorgio Mangano, have mobilized the theory in readings of maps that are similar to film criticism, especially in his *Cartografia morale*, 218–27 and *passim*.

6. *Politique de la littérature*, 40.

7. Sergei Eisenstein, "The Cinematic Principle and the Ideogram," 28.

8. Ropars-Wuilleumier, *Le texte divisé*, 32–38; I have reviewed the concepts in the introduction to the second edition of my *Film Hieroglyphs*, ix–xix.

9. *FC* 34; *FF* 25.

10. Ibid. The English version translates *déchaînement* as "explosion." The term seems related to montage inasmuch as it is a concatenation that, contrary to its binding effects, "deconcatenates" or releases (in detonating) montage in its own process. Rancière's contrary reading is visible in the style and choice of terms that run against the grain of the matter he studies.

11. *FC* 36; *FF* 27, emphasis added.

12. *FC* 37; *FF* 28, emphasis added. Eisenstein's essay appears in *Film Form*, 122–49. Rancière grafts the unconscious onto the gloss where Eisenstein speaks of primitive thought. "Inner speech," Eisenstein noted, "is precisely at the stage of image-sensual structure, not yet having attained that lyrical formulation with which speech clothes itself before stepping out in the open, in a dual process: an impetuous progressive rise along the lines of the highest explicit steps of consciousness and a simultaneous penetration by means of the structure of the form into the layers of profoundest sensual thinking. The polar separation of these two lines of flow creates that remarkable tension of unity and form characteristic of true artworks" (144–45).

13. *FC* 37; *FF* 28.

14. *FC* 40; *FF* 30.

15. Ibid.; *FC* 40; *FF* 41.

16. *FC* 12; *FF* 5.

17. This is what Deleuze does in "Qu'est-ce qu'un événement," a pivotal chapter of *Le pli: Leibniz et le Baroque.*

18. *FC* 12; *FF* 6.

19. *FC* 13; *FF* 6. In "La mise à mort de Madame Bovary," a chapter of *Politique de la littérature*, Rancière uses Deleuze's concept of *haeccity* to discern the protagonist's extreme *aisthēsis*. Emma bathes in "a pure flux of sensations" (72–73).

20. Deleuze, *L'image-temps*, 234. It would be worth pursuing the interstice in the context of what Jean-François Lyotard had described (roughly at the same time) as the effect of *parataxis* in the "postmodern" age, at least in *Le post-moderne expliqué aux enfants.*

21. *FC* 146; *FF* 108.

22. *FC* 141; *FF* 101.

23. *FC* 150; *FF* 111.

24. *FC* 155; *FF* 116.

25. *FC* 235; *FF* 185.

26. *FF* 236; *FC* 186, emphasis added.

27. *FC* 237; *FF* 186.

14. POLITICIZING ART IN RANCIÈRE AND DELEUZE

1. See Rancière, "Existe-t-il une esthétique deleuzienne?" in *Gilles Deleuze: Une vie philosophique*, ed. Alliez, 525–36; and Rancière, "Deleuze, Bartleby and the Literary Formula," in *The Flesh of Words*, 146–64. See also the English translation of "Existe-t-il une esthétique deleuzienne?": "Is There a Deleuzian Aesthetics?" However, the translation of this particular text in the present essay is mine.

2. For a detailed consideration of the above, see Rancière, *Dis-agreement.* See also Rancière, *The Politics of Aesthetics.*

3. See Rancière, "The Janus-Face of Politicized Art."

4. Rancière, "What Aesthetics Can Mean," 21.

5. Ibid., 18.

6. Ibid., 19 and 23.

7. Rancière, *The Flesh of Words*, 149.

8. Rancière, "Existe-t-il une esthétique deleuzienne?" 535–36. This is my translation. The original reads: "L'analyse de Deleuze s'inscrit alors dans le destin de l'esthétique comme mode de pensée, dans le destin de l'œuvre

moderne liée à ce sensible pur, en excès par rapport aux schèmes de la doxa représentative. Elle s'établit dans les zones où la pitié—c'est-à-dire la sympathie avec la vie in-individuelle voisine avec la folie, avec la perte de tout monde. Deleuze a affaire avec l'œuvre moderne comme œuvre contradictoire où l'élément pathique, la pensée-arbre ou la pensée-caillou, vient défaire l'ordre de la doxa mais où cet élément pathique est lui-même inclus, racheté dans une organicité et un logos de type nouveau."

9.   Rancière, *The Flesh of Words*, 154.

10. Rancière, "What Aesthetics Can Mean," 28 and 33. See also "Existe-t-il une esthétique deleuzienne?" 533–35.

11. Rancière, *The Flesh of Words*, 162–63.

12. Ibid., 163.

13. Ibid., 164.

14. Rancière, "The Janus-Face of Politicized Art," 53.

15. Rancière, *Politique de la littérature*, 23, my translation. The original reads: "Ce que la littérature oppose aux usurpations de la littérarité démocratique, c'est une autre puissance de signification et d'action du langage, un autre rapport des mots aux choses qu'ils désignent et aux sujets qui les portent. C'est en bref, un autre sensorium, une autre manière de lier un pouvoir d'affectation sensible et un pouvoir de signification. Or, une autre communauté du sens et du sensible, un autre rapport des mots aux êtres, c'est aussi un autre monde commun et un autre peuple."

16. Rancière, "What Aesthetics Can Mean," 32.

17. Rancière, *Politique de la littérature*, 54, my translation. The original reads: "La scène des choses muettes qui sont là sans raison, sans signification, et entraînent les consciences dans leur aphasie et leur apathie, le monde des micro-individualités moins qu'humaines qui imposent une autre échelle de grandeur que celle des sujets politiques."

18. Rancière, "Politics and Aesthetics," 196–97.

19. Rancière, "The Janus-Face of Politicized Art," 65.

20. See, for example, Maria-Benedita Basto's article, "L'écriture dans la colonie."

21. One of the men apprehended for Djaout's murder was quoted as saying, "Il écrivait trop bien, il avait une plume intelligente, il arrivait à toucher les gens." See Geesey, "Exhumation and History," 272. And in the prophetic words of Djaout himself: "Le silence c'est la mort et toi, si tu te tais tu meurs et si tu parles tu meurs alors dis et meurs." Quoted in Isabelle

Constant, "Le roman moderne et le roman du passé dans *L'Invention du désert* de Tahar Djaout," 39.

22. Djaout, *The Watchers*, 90, 94. All subsequent references will be to this edition, and page numbers will be cited in the text.

23. Rancière, *Dis-agreement*, 57.

24. I am thinking here of Jakobson's theory of metaphor. See "Two Aspects of Language and Two Types of Aphasic Disturbances," in *Fundamentals of Language*, ed. Roman Jakobson and Morris Halle, 67–96; and "Closing Statements: Linguistics and Poetics," in *Style and Language*, ed. Thomas A. Sebeok. As Michael Silk points out, Jakobson is one of the first to analyze metaphor at the systemic level of discourse rather than at the unitary level of the sentence. For more on Jakobson's (largely tacit) debt to Saussurian linguistics, see Silk, "Metaphor and Metonymy." To return to the question of Rancière's engagement with Deleuze, Eric Alliez also notes that Rancière analyzes Deleuze's thought almost exclusively through the dual prisms of signification and its attendant dissociation, ignoring its constructivist aspect and the notion of forces in particular. See "Existe-t-il une esthétique rancièrienne?"

25. Deleuze, "To Have Done with Judgement," 134.

26. Deleuze, *Essays Critical and Clinical*, 135.

27. Rancière, *Aux bords du politique*, 117.

28. Deleuze, "Bartleby; or, the Formula," 90.

29. Rancière, "What Aesthetics Can Mean," 32–33.

30. Rancière, *Aux bords du politique*, 116–17. This is my translation. The original reads as follows: "Et cette égalité définit, dessine une communauté, à condition seulement de comprendre que cette communauté n'a pas de consistence. Elle est, à chaque fois, portée par quelqu'un pour quelque autre, une infinité virtuelle d'autres."

31. Rancière, *Dis-agreement* 19, 27, 35, and 42.

15. IMPOSSIBLE SPEECH ACTS

1. At the very start of his writing career, Said translated (with Maire Said) Auerbach's seminal essay "Philology and *Weltliteratur*." Said's *Humanism and Democratic Criticism* contains a slightly revised and expanded version of his introduction to *Mimesis* (85–118).

2. Said, *The World, the Text, and the Critic*, 5.

3. Catherine Gallagher and Stephen Greenblatt cited this method—"the

isolation of a resonant textual fragment that is revealed, under the pressure of analysis, to represent the work from which it is drawn and the particular culture in which that work was produced and consumed"—as the inspiration for the anecdote with which the classic new historicist essay began (*Practicing New Historicism*, 35).

4. Auerbach, *Mimesis*, 557.

5. On Auerbach's transformation into "a legend of the writer in exile," see Lerer, *Error and the Academic Self*, 221, 247, and 250. Emily Apter suggests that Auerbach "resisted Turkey" during his eleven-year residence there and that his "jaundiced depiction of his loneliness in the wilderness really appears to be a distorted picture of what it was like to live and work in Istanbul. . . . Auerbach's self-portrait as a lonely European scholar seems increasingly questionable the more one takes account of the sizeable professional, artistic, and political European community that was well established in Istanbul (and Ankara) by the time he arrived in Turkey in 1936" (Apter, *The Translation Zone*, 48, 50). See also Gumbrecht, " 'Pathos of the Earthly Progress'."

6. Said, *The World, the Text, and The Critic*, 5–8.

7. Mufti, "Auerbach in Istanbul," 98.

8. See also Rancière, *The Flesh of Words*, 71–79.

9. Mufti, "Auerbach in Istanbul," 106.

10. Rancière, "The Politics of Literature," 13. See also Hallward, "Jacques Rancière and the Subversion of Mastery," 35.

11. Auerbach, *Mimesis*, 33–36.

12. Ibid., 31.

13. Ibid., 36.

14. Ibid., 37.

15. Rancière, *The Names of History*, 25.

16. Auerbach, *Mimesis*, 39–40.

17. Rancière, *The Names of History*, 27.

18. Ibid., 25, 18.

19. Ibid., 26.

20. See ibid., 27.

21. Ibid., 27.

22. Ibid., 28.

23. Ibid., 28.

24. Ibid., 29–30.

25. Said, *Humanism and Democratic Criticism*, 99.

26. Apter, "Saidian Humanism," 43. See Damrosch, "Auerbach in Exile," which finds Auerbach projecting himself repeatedly into the authors and characters of the texts through which he sought to write an objective history of the representation of reality. On identity politics, see Said, "Edward Said Talks to Jacqueline Rose," 25: "I've become very, very impatient with the idea and the whole project of identity: the idea, which produced great interest in the United States in the sixties and which is also present in the return to Islam in the Arab world and elsewhere, that people should really focus on themselves and where they come from, their roots and find out about their ancestors—the book and television program *Roots*. That strikes me as colossally boring and totally off the mark. I think that's the last thing that we should be thinking about in a way. What's much more interesting is to try to reach out beyond identity to something else, whatever that is. It may be death. It may be an altered state of consciousness that puts you in touch with others more than one normally is. It may be just a state of forgetfulness which, at some point, I think we all need—to forget."

27. Said, *Humanism and Democratic Criticism*, 91–92.

28. Ibid., 87.

29. Rancière, "Politics, Identification, and Subjectivization," 67.

16. *STYLE INDIRECT LIBRE*

1. Rancière, "On the Theory of Ideology." Originally published as "Sobre la teoria de la ideología." The French text is reprinted in *La leçon d'Althusser*.

2. Rancière, "La scène du texte," 48. A revised version of the text can be found in *The Flesh of Words*.

3. Althusser, "From *Capital* to Marx's Philosophy," 15–16.

4. Rancière, *Mallarmé*, 10, 79.

5. Wordsworth, *The Prelude* [1805] i.15–19. Cited in Rancière, *The Flesh of Words*, 15.

6. Rancière, *The Names of History*, 57.

7. In both *The Names of History* (54) and *Short Voyages to the Land of the People* (75), Rancière gives paradigmatic importance to the following passage from Michelet's *Origines du droit français* (cited from *œuvres complètes*, 3:607): "And yet what were the mother's laments? They alone could say. The very stones cried for them. Ocean himself was moved on hearing

Simonides' Danaë." Stone and calcification play an organizing role in the discussion of Michelet in both these books; the figure of speaking stone is equally important in *La parole muette*, notably 18–20 and 31–35.

8. Rancière, *The Names of History*, 68.

9. For interviews concerning the place of this inaugural work in Rancière's trajectory, see Ewald, "Qu'est-ce que la classe ouvrière? Entretien avec Jacques Rancière"; Rancière, "Histoire des mots, mots de l'histoire"; Panagia, "Dissenting Words"; Guénoun and Kavanagh, "Jacques Rancière."

10. Rancière, "Histoire des mots," 87–88.

11. Ibid., 88, 99; Panagia, "Dissenting Words," 121; Guénoun and Kavanagh, "Jacques Rancière," 14–16. See also *Names of History*, 100, which predates this set of interviews and where the reference is to *To the Lighthouse* rather than *The Waves*. If this group of texts clearly poses a strong distinction between a "realism" that continues the romantic tradition and a "modernism" that breaks with it, Rancière's later discussions of the history of literary aesthetics will largely relativize the distinction.

12. Rancière, *La parole muette*, 115.

13. Rancière, *The Flesh of Words*, 11.

14. A history of the emergence of the notion can be found in Philippe, *Sujet, verbe, complément*, 66–84. An influential use in English can be found in Ullmann's *Style in the French Novel*, 94–120. To my mind, the most rigorous (although highly controversial) delineation of the phenomenon is to be found in Banfield, *Unspeakable Sentences*. Banfield prefers "reported speech or thought" to "free indirect discourse." A consideration of Banfield's technically precise definition points out the extent to which my use of the term here is fundamentally metaphorical; the tense-shifting effect and the anomalous conservation of pronouns and other situation-dependent elements of discourse are absent from the examples I will cite from Rancière.

15. Rancière, *The Ignorant Schoolmaster*, 68–69.

16. Rancière, *The Names of History*, 45.

17. Rancière, *On the Shores of Politics*, 40–42, for all citations given below. The translations have been revised by the author.

18. The inverted parenthetical ("*dit . . . Périclès*") is, however, entirely compatible with the combination of tense and pronoun shift and retention of expressive elements that characterizes the free indirect style.

19. The source Rancière refers to for the argument about the militaristic purpose of the funeral oration is Loraux, *The Invention of Athens*. It is worth

noting that the close relation between the vocabulary and themes of the funeral oration (as a genre, including but not limited to this most famous example) and antidemocratic discourse is one of the major themes of Loraux's book.

20. See Plato, *The Republic* 561c–e, p. 274: "And so he lives out his life from day to day, gratifying the desire of the moment. One day he drinks himself under the table to the sound of the pipes, the next day he is on a diet of plain water. Now he is taking exercise, but at other times he is lazing about and taking no interest in anything. And sometimes he passes the time in what he calls philosophy. Much of his time is spent in politics, where he leaps to his feet and says and does whatever comes into his head. Or if he comes to admire the military, then that is the way he goes. Or if it's businessmen, then that way. There is no controlling order or necessity in his life. As far as he is concerned, it is pleasant, free, and blessed, and he sticks to it his whole life through." Rancière paraphrases: "One day, Plato tells us, he will get drunk to the sound of flutes [*s'enivrer au son de la flute*], the next day he will diet [*fera du régime*]; one day he will do gymnastics and the next day he will be lazy; one day he will go in for politics and the next for philosophy; for a while he will think about war and for a while about business."

21. Plato, *The Republic* 557d: "And I tell you, it's a good place to look if you want a particular kind of constitution.—Why?—Because the liberty it allows its citizens means it has every type of constitution within it. So anyone wanting to found a city, as we have just been doing, will probably find he has to go to a city with a democratic regime, and there choose whatever political arrangements he fancies. Like shopping for constitutions in a bazaar. Then, when he has made his choice, he can found a city along those lines."

22. Aristotle, *Politics* 1294b35–36.

23. Aristotle, *Politics* 1293b34–35.

24. Rancière, *The Philosopher and His Poor*, xxviii.

AFTERWORD

1. Gauny, "Le travail à la tâche," in Jacques Rancière, *The Nights of Labor*, 82. I published a selection of the essays and letters left by Gauny, under the title *Le philosophe plébéien*.

2. Letter from Gauny to Ponty, *The Nights of Labor*, 19.

3. Gauny, "Le travail à la tâche," 81.

4. See Rancière, *The Ignorant Schoolmaster*.

5. See, in this volume, "Historicizing Untimeliness."

6. See, in this volume, "The Politics of Aesthetics: Political History and the Hermeneutics of Art."

7. On this point, I would agree with Yves Citton. See, in this volume, "Political Agency and the Ambivalence of the Sensible."

8. The politics of aesthetics would more accurately be named as a meta-politics: a politics without *dēmos*, an attempt to accomplish—better than politics, in the place of politics—the task of configuring a new community by leaving the superficial stage of democratic dissensus and reframing instead of the concrete forms of sensory experience and everyday life. But, for the sake of commodity, I shall use here the simple expression the "politics of aesthetics."

9. See Rancière, "The Aesthetic Revolution and its Outcomes"; and Rancière, *Malaise dans l'esthétique*.

10. See, in this volume, "Rancière's Leftism."

Bibliography

Alliez, Eric. "Existe-t-il une esthétique rancièrienne." *La philosophie déplacée: Autour de Jacques Rancière*. Paris: Horlieu, 2007.

———, ed. *Gilles Deleuze, une vie philosophique*. Le Pleissis–Robinson: Empêcheurs de Penser en Rond, 1998.

Althusser, Louis. *L'avenir dure longtemps*. Paris: Stock/IMEC, 1992.

———. "From *Capital* to Marx's Philosophy." *Reading "Capital,"* ed. Althusser and Balibar, 15–16.

———, ed. *Lire le Capital*. Paris: Presses Universitaires de France. 1996.

Althusser, Louis, and Étienne Balibar, eds. *Reading "Capital,"* trans. Ben Brewster. London: New Left, 1970.

Amiel, Anne. *Hannah Arendt: Politique et événement*. Paris: Presses Universitaires de France, 1996.

Apter, Emily. "Saidian Humanism." *boundary 2* 31, no. 2 (2004).

———. *The Translation Zone: A New Comparative Literature*. Princeton: Princeton University Press, 2006.

Aristotle. *The Politics and The Constitution of Athens*, ed. Stephen Everson, trans. Benjamin Jowett. Cambridge: Cambridge University Press, 1996.

Auerbach, Erich. *Mimesis: The Representation of Reality in Western Literature*, Fiftieth anniversary edition, trans. Willard R. Trask with a new introduction by Edward W. Said. Princeton: Princeton University Press, 2003.

——. "Philology and *Weltliteratur*," trans. Edward W. Said. *Centennial Review* 13 (1969): 1–17.

——. *Scenes from the Drama of European Literature*, trans. Willard Trask. New York: Meridian, 1959.

Augustine. *The City of God against the Pagans*, trans. R. W. Dyson. Cambridge: Cambridge University Press, 1998.

Badiou, Alain. *Abrégé de métapolitique*. Paris: Le Seuil, 1998.

——. *Being and Event*, trans. Oliver Feltham. London: Continuum, 2005.

——. *Circonstances, 3: Portées du mot "juif."* Paris: Lignes, 2005.

——. *La Commune de Paris*. Paris: Conférences du Rouge-Gorge, 2003.

——. *L'éthique*. Caen: Nous, 2003 [orig. pubd 1993 by Hatier].

——. *Logiques des mondes*. Paris: Le Seuil, 2006.

——. *Manifesto for Philosophy*, ed. and trans. Norman Madarasz. Albany: SUNY Press, 1999.

——. *Metapolitics*, trans. Jason Barker. New York: Verso, 2005.

——. *Polemics*, trans. Steve Corcoran. London: Verso, 2007.

——. *La révolution culturelle: Une déclaration politique sur la politique*. Paris: Conférences du Rouge-Gorge, 2003.

Balibar, Étienne. *Droit de cité: Culture et politique en démocratie*. Paris: Éditions de l'Aube, 1998.

——. "Foucault et Marx: L'enjeu du nominalisme." *Michel Foucault philosophe*. Paris: Le Seuil, 1989.

——. *Les frontières de la démocratie*. Paris: La Découverte, 1992.

——. *Masses, Classes, Ideas: Studies on Politics and Philosophy before and after Marx*, trans. James Swenson. New York: Routledge, 1994.

——. "Vers la citoyenneté imparfaite." *Les Cahiers de la Villa Gillet*, no. 8. Lyon: Circé, 1999.

Banfield, Ann. *Unspeakable Sentences: Narration and Representation in the Language of Fiction*. Boston: Routledge and Kegan Paul, 1982.

Barlow, Tani, ed. "Badiou and Cultural Revolution." *Positions: East Asia Cultural Critique* 13, no. 3 (2005) [special issue].

Barthes, Roland. *Le degré zéro de l'écriture: Michelet, mythologies*, vol. 1 of *Oeuvres complètes*. Paris: Le Seuil, 1993.

——. *Le neutre: Cours au Collège de France (1977–1978)*. Paris: Le Seuil, 2002.

——. *Sur Racine*. Paris: Le Seuil, 1963.

Bensaid, Daniel. *Éloge de la résistance à l'air du temps*. Paris: Éditions Textuel, 1999.

Benveniste, Émile. *Problems in General Linguistics*, vol. 1, trans. Mary Elizabeth Meek. Coral Gables: University of Miami Press, 1971.

Birch, Anthony H. *The Concepts and Theories of Modern Democracy*. London: Routledge, 1993.

Bosteels, Bruno. "Post-Maoism: Badiou and Politics." *Positions: East Asia Culture Critique* 13, no. 3 (2005): 576–634.

——. "The Speculative Left." *South Atlantic Quarterly* 104 (2005): 751–67.

Boys-Stones, G. R., ed. *Metaphor, Allegory, and the Classical Tradition*. Oxford: Oxford University Press, 2003.

Campion, Pierre. "Jacques Rancière et la démocratie: Un livre d'intervention." http://pierre.campion2.free.fr/cranciere—democratie.htm.

——. Review of Jacques Rancière's *Le partage du sensible*. *Acta Fabula: Revue en ligne des parutions en théorie littéraire*. 2000. http://www.fabula.org/revue/cr/17.php. Accessed December 13, 2007.

Castoriadis, Cornelius. "Imaginaire politique grec et moderne" and "La démocratie athénienne." *La montée de l'insignifiance*. Paris: Le Seuil, 1996.

Certeau, Michel de. *Arts de faire*, vol. 1 of *L'invention du quotidian*, ed. Luce Giard. Paris: Gallimard, 1990.

——. "La beauté du mort." *La culture au pluriel*. Paris: Christian Bourgeois, 1980.

——. "Entretien avec Alain Charbonnier et Joël Magny," *Cinéma* 301 (January 1984): 19–20.

——. *La fable mystique*. Paris: Gallimard, 1982.

——. *The Practice of Everyday Life*. Berkeley: University of California Press, 1984.

——. "Practiques quotidiennes." *Les cultures populaires*, ed. G. Poujol and R. Labourie. Toulouse: Privat, 1979.

Chomsky, Noam. "Deterring Democracy in Italy: A Key Case of Thought Control." *Just Response*, 2002. http://www.justresponse.net/deterring_democracy.html, accessed December 13, 2007.

Cingolani, Patrick. "*Eppur si muove!* Classes populaires et structures de classes dans *La Distinction*." *L'empire du sociologue*, by Collectif "Révoltes Logiques."

Citton, Yves. "ConcateNations: Globalization in a Spinozist Context." *Cosmopolitics and the Emergence of a Future*, ed. Diane Morgan and Gary Bantham, 91–117. London: Palgrave Macmillan, 2007.

——. *Lire, interpréter, actualiser: Pourquoi les études littéraires?* Paris: Amsterdam, 2007.

Collectif "Révoltes Logiques." *L'empire du sociologue* (Paris: La Découverte, 1984).

——. "L'ordre économique de la mondialisation libérale: Une importation chinoise dans la France des Lumières?" *Revue Internationale de Philosophie*, 2007, no. 1: 9–32.

Comolli, Jean-Louis, and Jacques Rancière. *Arrêt sur histoire*. Paris: Centre Pompidou, 1997.

Constant, Isabelle. "Le roman moderne et le roman du passé dans *L'invention du désert* de Tahar Djaout." *Études Francophones* 12, no. 2 (1997): 39–54.

Cornu, Laurence, and Patrice Vermeren, eds. *La philosophie déplacée: Autour de Jacques Rancière*. Paris: Horlieu, 2007.

Crozier, Michel, Samuel P. Huntington, and Joji Watanuki. *The Crisis of Democracy*. New York: New York University Press, 1975.

Cusset, François. *La décennie: Le grand cauchemar des années 1980*. Paris: La Découverte, 2006.

Dahl, Robert A. *On Democracy*. New Haven: Yale University Press, 1998.

Damrosch, David. "Auerbach in Exile." *Comparative Literature* 47, no. 2 (spring 1995): 97–117.

Deleuze, Gilles. *Critique et clinique*. Paris: Éditions de Minuit, 1993.

——. *Essays Critical and Clinical*, trans. Daniel W. Smith and Michael A. Greco. Minneapolis: University of Minnesota Press, 1997.

——. *Pourparlers*. Paris: Éditions de Minuit, 1990.

——. *What Is Philosophy?*, trans. Hugh Tomlinson and Graham Burchell. New York: Columbia University Press, 1994.

Deleuze, Gilles, and Félix Guattari. *A Thousand Plateaus*, trans. Brian Massumi. Minneapolis: University of Minnesota Press, 1987.

Derrida, Jacques. *Dissemination*, trans. Barbara Johnson. Chicago: University of Chicago Press, 1983.

——. *Force de loi: Le "fondement mystique de l'autorité."* Paris: Galilée, 1994.

Djaout, Tahar. *The Watchers*, trans. Marjolijn de Jager. St. Paul, Minn.: Ruminator, 2002.

Duroux, Yves. "Jacques Rancière et ses contemporains: La querelle interminable." *La philosophie déplacée*, ed. Cornu and Vermeren.

Eisenstein, Sergei. *The Film Form: Essays in Film Theory*, ed. and trans. Jay Leyda. San Diego: Harcourt, Brace, 1979.

"Elephant: Interview with Gus Van Sant and Diane Keaton." http:// www.aboutfilm.com/features/elephant/feature.htm.

Elsaesser, Thomas. *Fassbinder's Germany: History Identity Subject*. Amsterdam: Amsterdam University Press, 1996.

Esposito, Roberto. *Categorie dell'impolitico*. Bologna: Il Mulino, 1988.

———. *Communitas, origine e destino della communità*. Turin: Einaudi, 1998.

———. *Communitas, origine et destin de la communauté*. Paris: Presses Universitaires de France, 2000.

———. *Nove pensieri sulla politica*. Bologna: Il Mulino, 1993.

———. *Oltre la politica: Antologia del pensiero "impolitico."* Milan: Bruno Mondadori, 1996.

Ewald, François, and Jacques Rancière. "Qu'est-ce que la classe ouvrière? Entretien avec Jacques Rancière." *Magazine Littéraire* 175 (July–August 1981): 64–66.

Farge, Arlette. "L'histoire comme avènement." *Critique* 601–2 (June–July 1997).

Fassbinder, R. W. *The Anarchy of the Imagination*, ed. Michael Töteberg and Leo A. Lensing. Baltimore: Johns Hopkins University Press, 1992.

Fassin, Didier, and Richard Rechtman. *L'empire du traumatisme: Enquête sur la condition de victime*. Paris: Flammarion, 2007.

———. *La fin du soupçon: Politiques du traumatisme*. Paris: Flammarion, 2006.

Faure, Alain, and Jacques Rancière, eds. *La parole ouvrière, 1830–1851*. Paris: Union Générale d'Éditions, 1976.

Finley, Moses I. *Democracy Ancient and Modern*. New Brunswick, N.J.: Rutgers University Press, 1988.

———. *Politics in the Ancient World*. Cambridge: Cambridge University Press, 1983.

Fontenay, Elisabeth de. *Une tout autre histoire: Questions à Jean-François Lyotard*. Paris: Fayard, 2006.

Foucault, Michel. "Pouvoirs et stratégies: Entretien avec Michel Foucault." *Révoltes Logiques* 4 (1977): 89–97.

Fraser, Nancy. *Justice Interruptus: Critical Reflections on the "Postsocialist" Condition*. London: Routledge, 1997.

Freud, Sigmund. *Beyond the Pleasure Principle*, ed. and trans. James Strachey. New York: W. W. Norton, 1961.

Furet, François. *Interpreting the French Revolution*. Cambridge: Cambridge University Press, 1981.

——. *The Passing of an Illusion: The Idea of Communism in the Twentieth Century*, trans. Deborah Furet. Chicago: University of Chicago Press, 2000.

Gallagher, Catherine, and Stephen Greenblatt, eds. *Practicing New Historicism*. Chicago: University of Chicago Press, 2000.

Gauny, Gabriel. *Le philosophe plébéin*. Paris: La Découverte / Presses Universitaires de Saint-Denis, 1985.

Geesey, Patricia. "Exhumation and History: Tahar Djaout's *Les chercheurs d'os*." *French Review* 70, no. 2 (1996): 271–79.

Gernet, Louis. *Droit et institutions en Grèce antique*. 1968; repr. Paris: Flammarion, 1982.

Grandin, Greg. *Empire's Workshop: Latin America, the United States, and the Rise of the New Imperialism*. New York: Metropolitan, 2006.

Graubard, Stephen R. "Democracy." *Dictionary of the History of Ideas*, ed. Philip P. Wiener, vol. 1, 652–67. New York: Charles Scribner's Sons, 1973.

Guénoun, Solange, James H. Kavanagh, and Jacques Rancière. "Jacques Rancière: Literature, Politics, Aesthetics: Approaches to Democratic Disagreement." *SubStance* 93 (2000): 3–23.

——. "Jacques Rancière's Freudian Cause." *SubStance* 33, no.1 (2004): 25–53.

Gumbrecht, Hans Ulrich. " 'Pathos of the Earthly Progress': Erich Auerbach's Everydays." *Literary History and the Challenge of Philology: The Legacy of Erich Auerbach*, ed. Seth Lerer, 13–35. Stanford: Stanford University Press, 1996.

Halimi, Serge. "Un mot de trop" and "Les 'philo-américains' saisis par la rage." *Le monde diplomatique*, May 2000.

Hallward, Peter. "Dialectical Voluntarism." Unpublished paper.

——. "Jacques Rancière and the Subversion of Mastery." *Paragraph* 28, no. 1 (March 2005).

——. "The Politics of Prescription." *South Atlantic Quarterly* 104, no. 4 (autumn 2005): 771–91.

——. "What's the Point: First Notes towards a Philosophy of Determination." *Material Worlds*, ed. Rachel Moffat and Eugene de Klerk, 148–58. Cambridge: Cambridge Scholars, 2007.

——, ed. *Think Again: Alain Badiou and the Future of Philosophy*. London: Continuum, 2004.

Jakobson, Roman, and Morris Halle, eds. *Fundamentals of Language*. The Hague: Mouton, 1956.

Kerbrat-Orecchioni, Catherine. *La connotation*. Lyon: Presses Universitaires de Lyon, 1977.

Lacoue-Labarthe, Philippe. *L'imitation des modernes*. Paris: Galilée, 1986.

———. "Stagings of Mimesis." *Angelaki* 8, no. 2 (2003).

Laniel, Bertlinde. *Le mot "democracy" aux États-Unis de 1780–1856*. Saint-Étienne: Université de Saint-Étienne, 1995.

Lazarus, Sylvain. "Singularité et modes historiques de la politique." *Anthropologie du nom*, 88–94. Paris: Le Seuil, 1996.

Lebovici, Martine. "À plusieurs voix autour de Jacques Rancière." *Mouvements* 44, no. 2 (2006): 172–79.

Lenin, Vladimir I. "Dialectics and Eclecticism." *Collected Works*, vol. 32. Moscow: Progress, 1960.

Lerer, Seth. *Error and the Academic Self: The Scholarly Imagination, Medieval to Modern*. New York: Columbia University Press, 2002.

Lévy, Benny. *Le meurtre du Pasteur*. Lagrasse: Verdier, 2002.

Livy. *Ab Urbe Condita*, books 1–2, trans. B. O. Foster. Cambridge: Harvard University Press, 1988.

Locke, John. 1689. *An Essay concerning Human Understanding*, ed. A. D. Woozley. London: Fontana, 1964.

Loraux, Nicole. *The Invention of Athens: The Funeral Oration in the Classical City*, trans. Alan Sheridan. New York: Zone, 2006.

Lyotard, Jean-François. "L'Europe, les Juifs et le livre." *Libération*, May 15, 1990.

———. *Heidegger and "the Jews,"* trans. Andreas Michel and Mark Roberts. Minneapolis: University of Minnesota Press, 1990.

Mackay, Christopher. *Ancient Rome: A Military and Political History*. Cambridge: Cambridge University Press, 2004.

Mann, Thomas. *Reflections of a Nonpolitical Man*. New York: F. Ungar, 1983.

Marty, Eric. *Une querelle avec Alain Badiou, philosophe*. Paris: Gallimard, 2007.

Marx, Karl. "Contribution to the Critique of Hegel's Philosophy of Law." *Collected Works*, vol. 3, by Karl Marx and Frederick Engels. New York: International, 1975.

———. *The Eighteenth Brumaire of Louis Bonaparte*, trans. Daniel de Leon. Chicago: C. H. Kerr, 1913.

McLuhan, Marshall, and Quentin Fiore. *The Medium Is the Massage*. New York: Random House, 1967.

Michelet, Jules. *Oeuvres complètes*, ed. Paul Viallaneix. Paris: Flammarion, 1973–85.

Milner, Jean-Claude. *Le Juif de savoir*. Paris: Grasset, 2006.

———. "Théorie du nom juif." http://www.mezetulle.net/article-1792627.html, accessed October 26, 2008.

Montag, Warren. "Althusser's Nominalism: Structure and Singularity (1962–6)." *Rethinking Marxism* 10 (1998): 64–73.

Montesquieu, Charles de. *De l'esprit des lois*, vol. 1. Paris: Garnier-Flammarion, 1979.

Mouffe, Chantal. *The Democratic Paradox*. London: Verso, 2000.

Mufti, Aamir R. "Auerbach in Istanbul: Edward Said, Secular Criticism, and the Question of Minority Culture." *Critical Inquiry* 25, no. 1 (autumn 1998).

Nancy, Jean-Luc. *La communauté désoeuvrée*, expanded edition. Paris: Christian Bourgois, 1990.

Noudelmann, François. "La question du nom juif." *Temps Modernes* 627 (April–June 2004).

Osborne, Peter, ed. *From an Aesthetic Point of View: Philosophy, Art and the Senses*. London: Serpent's Tail, 2000.

Palmer, R. R. "Notes on the Use of the Word 'Democracy,' 1789–1799." *Political Science Quarterly* 68, no. 2 (June 1953): 203–26.

Panagia, Davide, and Jacques Rancière. "Dissenting Words: A Conversation with Jacques Rancière." *Diacritics* 30, no 2 (summer 2000): 113–26.

Parsons, Talcott. *The Social System*. Glencoe, Ill.: Free Press, 1951.

Philippe, Gilles. *Sujet, verbe, complément: Le moment grammatical de la littérature française, 1890–1940*. Paris: Gallimard, 2002.

Piven, Frances Fox, and Richard A. Cloward. *Poor People's Movements: Why They Succeed, How They Fail*. New York: Pantheon, 1977.

——. *Regulating the Poor: The Functions of Public Welfare*. New York: Vintage, 1993.

Plato. *Protagoras*, trans. C. C. W. Taylor. Oxford: Clarendon, 1976.

——. *The Republic*, ed. G. R. F. Ferrari, trans. Tom Griffith. Cambridge: Cambridge University Press, 2000.

Rancière, Jacques. "The Aesthetic Revolution and Its Outcomes." *New Left Review* 14 (March 2002).

——. "Après quoi." *Confrontation: Après le sujet qui vient* 20 (winter 1989).

——. *Aux bords du politique*. Paris: La Fabrique, 1998.

——. "The Cause of the Other," trans. David Macey. *Parallax* 4, no. 2 (April 1998): 25–33.

——. *La chair des mots: Politiques de l'écriture*. Paris: Galilée, 1998.

——. *Chroniques des temps consensuels*. Paris: Le Seuil, 2005.

——. "Le concept de l'anachronisme et le vérité de l'historien." *Inactuel: Psychanalyse et culture* 6 (1996): 53–69 [special issue: "Mensonge et vérité"].

——. "Contemporary Art and the Politics of Aesthetics." *Communities of Sense: Rethinking Aesthetics in Practice*, ed. Beth Hinderliter, William Kaizen, Vered Maimon, Jaleh Mansoor, and Seth McCormick. Durham: Duke University Press, 2009.

——. *Courts voyages au pays du people*. Paris: Le Seuil, 1990.

——. "La démocratie corrigée." *Le Genre Humain* 22 (1990).

——. *Le destin des images*. Paris: La Fabrique, 2003.

——. *Dis-agreement: Politics and Philosophy*, trans. Julie Rose. Minneapolis: University of Minnesota Press, 1999.

——. "Élection et raison démocratique." *Le Monde*, March 22, 2007.

——. "The Emancipated Spectator." August 2004. http://theater.kein.org/node/130, accessed December 13, 2007.

——. *The Emancipated Spectator*. London: Verso, 2009.

——. "Esthétique, inesthétique, anti-esthétique." *Alain Badiou: Penser le multiple*. Paris: L'Harmattan, 2002.

——. "Ethical Turn of Aesthetics and Politics," trans. Jean-Philippe Deranty. *Critical Horizons* 7, no. 1 (2006): 1–20.

——. "L'éthique de la sociologie." *L'empire du sociologue*, by Collectif "Révoltes Logiques."

——. "Existe-t-il une esthétique deleuzienne?" *Gilles Deleuze: Une vie philosophique*, ed. Alliez.

——. *La fable cinématographique*. Paris: Le Seuil, 2001.

——. *Film Fables*, trans. Emiliano Battista. Oxford: Berg, 2006.

——. *The Flesh of Words: The Politics of Writing*, trans. Charlotte Mandell. Stanford: Stanford University Press, 2004.

——. *The Future of the Image*, trans. Gregory Elliott. London: Verso, 2007.

——. *La haine de la démocratie*. Paris: La Fabrique, 2005.

——. *Hatred of Democracy*, trans. Steve Corcoran. London: Verso, 2007.

——. "Histoire des mots, mots de l'histoire (entretien avec Martyne Perrot et Martin de la Soudière)." *Communications* 58 (1994): 87–101.

——. *The Ignorant Schoolmaster: Five Lessons in Intellectual Emancipation*, trans. Kristin Ross. Stanford: Stanford University Press, 1991.

——. *L'inconscient esthétique*. Paris: Galilée, 2001.

——. "Is There a Deleuzian Aesthetics?," trans. Radmila Djordjevic. *Qui Parle: Literature, Philosophy, Visual Arts, History* 14, no. 2 (2004): 1–14.

——. "Jacques Rancière." *Entretiens avec "Le Monde" 1: Philosophies*, ed. Christian Delacampagne, 158–66. Paris: Le Monde / La Découverte, 1984.

——. *La leçon d'Althusser*. Paris: Gallimard, 1974.

———. *Le maître ignorant: Cinq leçons sur l'émancipation intellectuelle.* Paris: Fayard, 1987.

———. *Malaise dans l'esthétique.* Paris: Galilée, 2004.

———. *Mallarmé: La politique de la sirène.* Paris: Hachette, 1996.

———. *La mésentente: Politique et philosophie.* Paris: Galilée, 1995.

———. "La méthode de l'égalité." *La philosophie déplacée,* ed. Cornu and Vermeren.

———. *Les mots de l'histoire: Essai de poétique du savoir.* Paris: Le Seuil, 1992.

———. "The Myth of the Artisan: Critical Reflections on a Category of Social History," trans. David H. Lake and Cynthia J. Koepp. *Work in France: Representations, Meaning, Organization, and Practice,* ed. Steven Laurence Kaplan and Cynthia J. Koepp, 317–34. Ithaca: Cornell University Press, 1986.

———. *The Names of History: On the Poetics of Knowledge,* trans. Hassan Melehy. Minneapolis: University of Minnesota Press, 1994.

———. *The Nights of Labor: The Workers' Dream in Nineteenth-Century France,* trans. John Drury. Philadelphia: Temple University Press, 1989.

———. "Les nouvelles fictions du mal." *Cahiers du Cinéma* 590 (May 2004): 94–96.

———. *La nuit des prolétaires: Archives du rêve ouvrier.* Paris: Fayard, 1981.

———. *On the Shores of Politics.* Translated by Liz Heron. New York: Verso, 1995.

———. "On the Theory of Ideology (The Politics of Althusser)" and "Afterword." *Radical Philosophy* 7 (spring 1974).

———. "On War as the Ultimate Form of Advanced Plutocratic Consensus," trans. Lucy R. McNair. *Contemporary French and Francophone Studies: Sites* 8, no. 3 (2004): 253–58.

———. *La parole muette: Essai sur les contradictions de la littérature.* Paris: Hachette, 1998.

———. *Le partage du sensible: Esthétique et politique.* Paris: La Fabrique, 2000.

———. *Le philosophe et ses pauvres.* Paris: Fayard, 1983.

———. *The Philosopher and His Poor,* ed. and with an introduction by Andrew Parker, trans. John Drury, Corinne Oster, and Andrew Parker. Durham: Duke University Press, 2004.

———. "La philosophie en déplacement." *La vocation philosophique,* ed. Marianne Alphant and Kostas Axelos. Paris: Centre Pompidou, 2004.

———. "Politics and Aesthetics: An Interview," by Peter Hallward. *Angelaki* 8, no. 2 (August 2003).

———. "Politics, Identification, and Subjectivization" and "Discussion." *October* 61 (summer 1992): 58–64, 78–82.

——. *The Politics of Aesthetics*, ed. and trans. Gabriel Rockhill. London: Continuum, 2004.

——. "The Politics of Literature." *Substance* 103, vol. 33, no. 1 (2004): 10–24.

——. *Politique de la littérature*. Paris: Galilée, 2007.

——. "La scène du texte." *Politique et philosophie dans l'œuvre de Louis Althusser*, ed. Sylvain Lazarus. Paris: Presses Universitaires de France, 1993.

——. *Les scènes du peuple: Les révoltes logiques, 1975/1985*. Paris: Horlieu, 2003.

——. "Sens et figures de l'histoire." *Face à l'histoire*. Paris: Centre Pompidou, 1996 [exhibition catalogue].

——. *Short Voyages to the Land of the People*, trans. James B. Swenson. Stanford: Stanford University Press, 2003.

——. "S'il y a de l'irreprésentable." *Le Genre Humain* 36 (December 2001) 81–102 [special issue: "L'art et la mémoire des camps"].

——. "Ten Theses on Politics," trans. Davide Panagia. *Theory and Event* 5, no. 3 (2001).

——. "The Thinking of Dissensus: Politics as Aesthetics." Paper presented at the conference "Post-Structuralism and Radical Politics," Goldsmiths College, London, September 16–17, 2003. http://homepages.gold.ac.uk/psrpsg/conference/fidelity/html, accessed October 15, 2007.

——, ed. *Le philosophe plébéien: Gabriel Gauny*. Paris: Maspero, 1983.

——, ed. *La Politique des poètes: Pourquoi des poètes en temps de détresse?* Paris: Albin Michel, 1992.

"Rencontre avec Gus Van Sant." Disc 2. *Elephant*. Collector's edition. DVD. Paris: MK2, 2004.

Rifkin, Adrian. "Il y a des mots qu'on ne souhaiterait plus lire." *Paragraph* 28, no. 1 (March 2005).

Rockhill, Gabriel. "Le cinéma n'est jamais né." *Le milieu des appareils*. Paris: L'Harmattan, 2008.

——. "Démocratie moderne et révolution esthétique: Quelques réflexions sur la causalité historique." *La philosophie déplacée*, ed. In Cornu and Vermeren.

——. "New Developments in Aesthetics: Badiou and Rancière." *New Developments*, ed. Todd May. *The History of Continental Philosophy*, vol. 8. Teddington: Publishing Limited.

——. "The Silent Revolution." *SubStance: A Review of Theory and Literary Criticism* 103, no. 1 (2004): 54–76.

Ross, Kristin. Introduction, *The Ignorant Schoolmaster*, by Jacques Rancière, vii–xxiii.

——. *May '68 and Its Afterlives*. Chicago: University of Chicago Press, 2002.

———. "The Sociologist and the Priest." *Sites* 1, no. 1 (1997).

Rousseau, Jean-Jacques. *Du contrat social*. Paris: Flammarion, 1966.

Said, Edward W. *Beginnings: Intention and Method*. New York: Basic Books, 1975.

———. *Culture and Imperialism*. New York: Alfred A. Knopf, 1993.

———. "Edward Said Talks to Jacqueline Rose." *Edward Said and the Work of the Critic: Speaking Truth to Power*, ed. Paul A. Bové. Durham: Duke University Press, 2000.

———. *Humanism and Democratic Criticism*. New York: Columbia University Press, 2004.

———. *Orientalism*. New York: Vintage, 1979.

———. *Reflections on Exile and Other Essays*. Cambridge: Harvard University Press, 2000.

———. *The World, the Text, and the Critic*. Cambridge: Harvard University Press, 1983.

Sanyal, Debarati. *The Violence of Modernity: Baudelaire, Irony, and the Politics of Form*. Baltimore: Johns Hopkins University Press, 2006.

Sartre, Jean-Paul. *Being and Nothingness*, trans. Hazel Barnes. London: Routledge, 1991.

———. *Situations III*. Paris: Gallimard, 1949.

Schiller, Friedrich von. *On the Aesthetic Education of Man in a Series of Letters*, trans. Reginald Snell. New York: Ungar, 1965.

Sebeok, Thomas A., ed. *Style in Language*. Cambridge: Technology Press of MIT, 1960.

Sen, Amartya. *Inequality Reexamined*. Oxford: Oxford University Press: 1992.

Silk, Michael. "Metaphor and Metonymy: Aristotle, Jakobson, Ricoeur, and Others." *Metaphor, Allegory, and the Classical Tradition*, ed. G. R. Boys Stones. Oxford: Oxford University Press, 2003.

Spinoza, Benedict de. *Ethics*, trans. Edwin Curley. London: Penguin, 1996.

Thiongo, Ngugi wa. *Decolonising the Mind: The Politics of Language in African Literature*. London: Heinemann, 1986.

Tocqueville, Alexis de. *De la démocratie en Amérique*, vol. 1. Paris: Flammarion, 1981.

Ullmann, Stephen. *Style in the French Novel*. Cambridge: Cambridge University Press, 1957.

Van Gunsteren, Herman R. *A Theory of Citizenship: Organizing Plurality in Contemporary Democracies*. Boulder: Westview, 1998.

Van Sant, Gus, and Diane Keaton. "*Elephant*: Interview with Gus Van Sant and Diane Keaton," by Carlo Cavagna. 2003. http://www.aboutfilm.com/features/elephant/feature.htm, accessed September 5, 2008.

Wallerstein, Immanuel. *Unthinking Social Science: The Limits of Nineteenth-Century Paradigms*, 2nd edition. Philadelphia: Temple University Press, 2001.

Weber, Samuel. "Displacing the Body: The Question of Digital Democracy." 1996. http://www.hydra.umn.edu/weber/displace.html, accessed December 13, 2007.

Weil, Simone. *Waiting for God*. New York: Putnam and Sons, 1951.

Williams, Raymond. *Keywords*. Oxford: Oxford University Press, 1985.

Wittig, Monique. *The Lesbian Body*, trans. David Le Vay. New York: Avon, 1976.

Wordsworth, William. *The Prelude* (1805), i.15–19. repr. in *The Major Works*, ed. Stephen Gill. Oxford: Oxford University Press, 2000.

Index

Chateaubriand, François-René de, 278, 283

Chinese Cultural Revolution. *See* Cultural revolution, the

Chomsky, Noam, 153–54, 156,

Cinema, 40, 52–53, 130, 216–25, 227–28; classical, 225; Hollywood, 226; modern, 225

Cinéma 1 (Deleuze), 223

Cinéma 2 (Deleuze), 223

Cinematography, 219, 222

Clarke, Alan, 214. *See also individual works*

Class struggle, 3, 80, 140

Clowen, Richard, 152

Colliot-Thélène, Catherine, 95

Commitment, 195–96, 283; content-based, 195; formal, 195

Committed art, 199, 205, 283. *See also* Politicized art

Communism, 35, 37, 39, 50, 100, 222

Communist party, 34, 41

Community of equals, 48, 50, 116

Comte, Auguste, 96

Consensus, 6, 16, 81, 84–85, 99, 101, 103, 112, 118, 277

Critical theory, 67, 69

Critique of Judgment (Kant), 279

Cultural Revolution, the, 5, 32, 34

Cultural studies, 17–18, 21

Culture and Imperialism (Said), 249

Dance, 92, 134, 232, 235

Daney, Serge, 10, 216

David, Jacques-Louis, 283

Debord, Guy, 130, 144

Deer Hunter, The (Cimino), 206

Degree Zero of Writing, The (Barthes), 195–96

Delacroix, Eugène, 283

Deleuze, Gilles, 2–3, 8, 45, 82, 121, 124, 237–39; art and, 10–11, 233, 285–87; cinema and, 216, 219, 220, 222–27; literature and, 232–35, 244, 246, 285–86; molar and molecular, 129, 132, 134–35, 200. *See also individual works*

Democracy, 35, 37, 50, 76, 81–82, 157, 211; Aristotle and, 73, 270–71; community and, 104, 110, 115; crisis of, 176–77; disorder of, 4; dissent and, 86–87; ethics and, 190, 192; history of, 10, 203–5, 215, 287; incommensurable and, 100–2; literature and, 137, 235–36, 284, 287; mass media and, 135; Plato and, 39, 269–70; theatre and, 148; Thucydides and, 267–68

Dēmos, 37, 61, 65, 77, 102, 110, 112–14, 203, 284. *See also* People, the

Demystification, 265

Deroin, Jeanne, 4

Derrida, Jacques, 66, 70, 77, 80, 82, 99, 101, 189, 283. *See also individual works*

Descartes, René, 70

Dialectic, 31, 37, 38, 42, 83, 276

Dick, Philip K., 25

Dickens, Charles, 220

Diderot, Denis, 133–34, 151. *See also individual works*

Differend, 64

Disagreement, 30, 55, 64–66, 68, 76, 80, 82, 88, 137, 237

Event, the, 4, 21, 23, 27–29, 43–44, 84, 96, 283

Exploitation, 275, 277, 280

Fable cinématographique, La (Rancière), 217–18, 227. *See also Film Fables*

Fabulation, 219, 234

Farge, Arlette, 20

Fassbinder, R. W., 208. *See also individual works*

Faure, Elie, 225

Febvre, Lucien, 26, 263, 267

Fénelon, François, 69, 111

Ferry, Jules, 153

Fiction, 9, 25, 52, 86–88, 230, 242, 251

Film, 3, 60, 209, 212, 217–19, 221, 223–24; criticism, 217; history, 10; studies, 10, 258; theory, 1, 10, 216, 220

Film Fables (Rancière), 9, 223. *See also La fable cinématographique*

Film Form (Eisenstein), 219

Flaubert, Gustave, 56, 155, 197, 217, 222, 225, 263–64

Flesh of Words, The (Rancière), 9, 259

Fontenay, Elisabeth de, 183

Fontenelle, Guy Éder de La, 69

Foucault, Michel, 4, 19–20, 26, 31, 38, 40, 48, 60, 99, 101, 114–15, 163, 259

Fourier, Charles, 79

Freedom, 58, 61, 99–100, 102–3, 113, 268, 274, 277

French Communist Party, 31

French Revolution, 21, 27–28, 111

Freud, Sigmund, 97–98, 217, 219

Freund, Julien, 98

Functionalism, 17–18, 24

Furet, François, 21–22, 27–28, 96, 267

Future of the Image, The (Rancière), 9, 183

Gauny, Gabriel, 4, 25, 263, 273

Genealogy, 21, 199

General Line, The (Eisenstein), 221, 222, 223

Genre, 9, 230, 251, 255, 266

German romantics, 221

Gerry (Van Sant), 213

Giotto, Bondone di, 226–27

Glucksmann, André, 164, 168, 169

Godard, Jean-Luc, 33, 35, 219, 223–27. *See also individual works*

Goethe, Johann Wolfgang von, 278

Gramsci, Antonio, 71

Grand narrative, 28

Greenberg, Clement, 151

Griffith, D.W., 220

Guattari, Félix, 82, 132, 237, 246. *See also individual works*

Gunsteren, Herman van, 104

Habermas, Jürgen, 78, 82, 97, 104, 133

Haine de la démocratie, La (Rancière), 203. *See also Hatred of Democracy*

Halbwachs, Maurice, 18

Hardt, Michael, 124, 142

Harvey, David, 17

Hatred of Democracy (Rancière), 187–88. *See also Haine de la démocratie, La*

Klee, Paul, 135

Knowledge: in Foucault, 115; interpretation of, 59, 62; politics and, 24, 155, 275, 277–78; transmission of, 5, 31–34, 36, 38, 40–43, 46, 48–49, 158–59

Koselleck, Reinhart, 18

Kubrick, Stanley, 214. *See also individual works*

Labor, 3, 21, 89, 260, 277, 279, 280, 285. *See also* Division of labor; Work

Laborer, 277–8. *See also* Worker

Lacan, Jacques, 5, 31, 34–35, 48, 178, 217

Lacoue-Labarthe, Philippe, 145, 157

Lang, Fritz, 182, 210, 219, 227. *See also individual works*

Langue maternelle (Jacotot), 265

Lanzmann, Claude, 227

Laws, the (Plato), 61

Lazarus, Sylvain, 174

Leçon d'Althusser, La (Rancière), 2, 7, 24, 31, 41, 71, 259, 267

Lefebvre, Henri, 19

Lefort, Claude, 99

Leftism, 158, 167. *See also* Speculative leftism

Leibniz, G.W., 84, 122, 124

Lenin, Vladimir Ilyich, 53, 168

Leninism, 41, 49

Letters on the Aesthetic Education of Man (Schiller), 150. *See also On the Aesthetic Education of Man in a Series of Letters*

Letter to d'Alembert on the Spectacles (Rousseau), 132–33

Lévinas, Emmanuel, 189

Lévi-Strauss, Claude, 70

Levy, Benny, 187

Liberalism, 21, 98

Liberty, 16, 45, 63, 89, 91, 108–9, 161, 260, 280, 283

Lili Marleen (Fassbinder), 206–8

Linguistics, 31–32

Lire le Capital (Althusser), 1, 71

Literariness, 236

Literature, 3, 11, 68, 130; agency and, 137–38; Deleuze and, 232–33, 235–36, 238; disciplinary boundaries of, 281, 283–87; the people and, 135, 246; politics and, 196–97, 278–79; world, 249

Literary criticism, 259; discourse and, 11, 197; history of, 1; misunderstanding, 137–38, 236–37; theory and, 1, 70, 140, 281

Litigation, 64–66, 88, 129

Little Red Book (Mao), 34

Livy, Titus, 76, 78–79, 81

Locke, John, 57–58. *See also individual works*

Logos, 61, 63, 74, 77, 83–84, 87, 276, 282

Lyotard, Jean-François, 2, 8, 18, 78, 82, 151, 176–84, 188, 191, 198, 200, 283

M (Lang), 219

Macbeth (Shakespeare), 213

Machiavelli, Niccolò, 95–96, 100

Maeterlinck, Maurice, 217

Magic Mountain, The, (Mann), 98

Malaise dans l'esthétique (Rancière), 9, 140, 172, 177–78, 188, 201–2

Narration, 27, 262, 264

Narrative, 55, 218, 223–25, 228, 255, 273–76, 281

Nation-state, 27

Negri, Antonio, 8, 49, 97, 99, 121, 124–25, 127–29, 134–35, 142

New Testament, the, 253

New Wave, 195, 216

Ngugi wa Thiongo, 144

Nietzsche, Friedrich, 91, 220. *See also individual works*

Nights of Labor, The, (Rancière), 3, 5, 11, 23, 71, 134, 172, 261–63, 267, 273. *See also Nuit des prolétaires, La*

Nouveau roman, 195

Novel, the, 130–31, 238, 263

Nozick, Robert, 8, 108–10

Nuit des prolétaires, La (Rancière), 265. *See also Nights of Labor, The*

Occupation, 275–78

Old Testament, the, 283

Oligarchy, 271

On Cosmopolitanism and Forgiveness (Derrida), 101

On the Aesthetic Education of Man in a Series of Letters (Schiller), 279. *See also Letters on the Aesthetic Education of Man*

On the Shores of Politics (Rancière), 7, 70, 72, 164, 199–200, 202, 246, 267

Ontology, 10–11, 23, 46, 66, 84, 127, 205, 215–16, 223, 286

Opera, 52–53

Oppression, 275

Orientalism (Said), 249

Painting, 234, 283

Paradox of the Comedian (Diderot), 133

Para-politics, 56, 77–78, 103, 197, 287

Paris Commune, 53, 284

Parole muette, La (Rancière), 9, 140, 263, 267, 271

Parsons, Talcott, 27–28

Partage du sensible, Le, 201. *See also Politics of Aesthetics, The*

Partition of the sensible, 58, 81, 120–23, 125, 128–29, 136–39, 199. *See also* Distribution of the sensible; Sharing of the sensible

Patrimony, 60

Pedagogy, 26, 111

People, the, 26–27; in cinema, 260; in classical antiquity, 64–66, 76; democratic claims and, 102–3, 110–12, 115, 119; Diderot and, 133; dissensus and, 236, 247–48; general will, 99; metaphysics and, 87–88; Negri and, 125, 128–29, 131, 135–36; theory and, 41, 45, 51–52; workers' archives, 71, 80, 284, 286. *See also Dēmos*

Pericles, 268–69

Phaedrus (Plato), 281

Philosopher, the, 28, 63, 65, 85, 125, 276

Philosopher and His Poor, The (Rancière), 3, 18, 161, 174, 258, 260, 267, 271

Philosophy, 5–6, 68; of cinema, 216–17, 223; disciplinary hierarchies and, 24–25, 28, 33, 38–39; 229, 259, 281–82; of history, 95; politics

Philosophy (*continued*)
and, 44–45, 58, 82, 87–88, 96–97,
108–9, 226
Piven, Frances Fox, 152
Place in the Sun, A (Stevens), 226–
27
Plato, 3, 9, 35, 83; archi-politics in
77, 103, 162; beauty in, 91; democ-
racy and, 37–40 distribution of
roles in, 142–44, 267, 275–78, 281,
287; education in 48–49, 56;
meta-politics in, 100, 103;
Sophism in, 61–63, 65–66; on
style, 263, 269–71; theatrocracy
in, 146, 151, 153, 156. *See also indi-
vidual works*
Platonism, 47, 100
Plot, 55, 224
Poem, the, 92, 263
Poet, the, 5, 25
Poetic regime of art, 230–31. *See also*
Representational regime of art;
Representative regime of art
Poetics, 4, 230, 232–33, 255, 261, 281;
historical, 267
Poetics (Aristotle), 9
Poetics of knowledge, 4, 281
Poetry, 27, 130, 171–73, 197, 220, 258
Police, 7, 10, 36, 46, 49, 132, 139, 147,
199–200, 287–88; Plato and, 61,
101; in United States, 109, 117, 119
Police order, 6–7, 12, 64, 112–18,
199–200, 203, 243
Polis, 36, 49, 64, 70, 73, 75–78, 80,
88, 96, 103
Political, the, 58, 98–99, 200, 287
Political action, 107, 110, 113–14, 130

Political activity, 64, 113
Political agency, 8, 121, 129, 134, 136,
139
Political community, 63, 98–99,
103–4, 244
Political discourse, 71
Political economy, 69, 75
Political performance, 146–51
Political philosophy, 6–7, 69–70,
72–73, 77–78, 82, 95–97; Anglo-
American, 107–9; Esposito and,
99–101
Political representation, 98
Political science, 281
Political subject, 104, 110, 114–16,
237, 257, 268, 285. *See also* Subject
Political theory, 3, 25, 69, 77, 110,
140, 200
Politicization of art, 172, 206
Politicized art, 195, 283–4. *See also*
Committed art
Politics (Aristotle), 72–74, 79, 271
Politics of Aesthetics, The (Rancière),
9, 89, 183, 235, 237. *See also Par-
tage du sensible, Le*
Politics of emancipation, 8, 42, 46–
47
Politics of Friendship (Derrida), 101
Politics of knowledge, 255, 282
Politics of literature, 218, 235, 237,
278, 285–86
Politique de la littérature (Rancière),
9
Polity, 271
Postcommunist era, 222
Postmodernism, 17
Postmodernity, 67, 69, 82

Contributors and Translators

ALAIN BADIOU is Professor of Philosophy at the École normale supérieure. Recent translations of his works include *Being and Event* (2006), *Ethics: An Essay on the Understanding of Evil* (2002), *Metapolitics* (2006), and *The Handbook of Inaesthetics* (2002). *Logiques des mondes* was published in France in 2006.

ÉTIENNE BALIBAR is Emeritus Professor of Philosophy at the Université Paris X, Nanterre. He is the author of *Politics and the Other Scene* (2002), *Masses, Classes, Ideas* (1994), *We, the People of Europe?* (2003), and, with Immanuel Wallerstein *Race, Nation, Class: Ambiguous Identities* (1992).

BRUNO BOSTEELS is Associate Professor in the Department of Romance Studies at Cornell University. He is the author of *Badiou o el recomienzo del materialismo dialéctico* (2007). His *Badiou and Politics* will be published by Duke University Press. He has published dozens of articles on Latin American literature and culture, on European philosophy, and on political theory. He currently serves as general editor of *diacritics*.

YVES CITTON is professor of eighteenth-century French literature at the University of Grenoble and is a member of the editorial board of the journal *Multitudes*. He recently published *L'envers de la liberté:. L'invention d'un imaginaire spinoziste dans la France des Lumières* (2006, winner of the Rhône-Alpes Book Prize 2007), *Lire, interpréter, actualiser:. Pour quoi les études littéraires?* (2007), and, with Frédéric Lordon, *Spinoza et les sciences sociales* (2008).

TOM CONLEY is Abbott Lawrence Lowell Professor of Romance Languages and Literatures and of Visual and Environmental Studies at Harvard University. A specialist in early modern French literature and film studies, his most notable publications are *Cartographic Cinema* (2006), *The Self-Made Map: Cartographic Writing in Early Modern France* (1997), *The Graphic Unconscious in Early Modern French Writing* (1992), and *Film Hieroglyphs: Ruptures in Classical Cinema* (1991).

SOLANGE GUÉNOUN is Professor of French at the University of Connecticut, where she specializes in seventeenth-century literature, psychoanalysis, and contemporary French thought. She is the author of *Racine: La mélancolie du cygne: entre rature et signature* (2005) and of articles on Michel Foucault and Jacques Derrida.

PETER HALLWARD teaches at the Centre for Research in Modern European Philosophy at Middlesex University and is the author of *Damming the Flood: Haiti and the Politics of Containment* (2007), *Out of this World: Deleuze and the Philosophy of Creation* (2006), *Badiou: A Subject to Truth* (2003), and *Absolutely Postcolonial* (2001).

JOHN HULSEY is a PhD candidate in Romance Languages and Film and Visual Studies at Harvard University.

PHILIP E. LEWIS, Professor Emeritus at Cornell University, is a vice-president of the Andrew W. Mellon Foundation.

TODD MAY is Kathryn and Calhoun Lemon Professor of Philosophy at Clemson University. His seven books are centered on recent French philosophy, particularly the thought of Michel Foucault and Gilles Deleuze. More recently, he has begun to focus on the political thought of Jacques Rancière. He has also been involved in political organizing in civil rights movements, labor struggles, the Palestinian rights movement, gay rights, and other resistance efforts.

GIUSEPPINA MECCHIA is Associate Professor of French and Italian at the University of Pittsburgh. She is the author of *L'écrivain et la communauté: Maurice Blanchot et la politique de 1932 à 1968* (forthcoming) and editor of a special issue of the journal *SubStance* on Italian post-workerist thought (2007). She is currently at work on a book titled *Reinventing the Left: Adventures of thought between France and Italy, from the mid-60s to the 21st Century.*

ERIC MÉCHOULAN teaches French literature at the Université de Montréal. He has published *Le corps imprimé: Essais sur le silence en littérature* (1999) and has coedited *Passions du passé: Recyclages de la mémoire et usages de l'oubli* (2000) and *La vengeance dans la littérature du XVIIᵉ siècle* (2000). His forthcoming books are *De l'immédiateté: Histoire, littérature, esthétique* and *Thinking Revenge and War: The Case of Classical France.* He is the editor of a special issue of the journal *SubStance* on Jacques Rancière, published in 2002.

JEAN-LUC NANCY is Distinguished Professor of Philosophy at the Université Marc Bloch, Strasbourg. Recent publications include *Being Singular Plural* (2000), *Dis:Enclosure: the Deconstruction of Christianity* (2007), *Listening* (2007), and *Philosophical Chronicles* (2008).

ANDREW PARKER is Professor of English at Amherst College. He introduced, edited, and helped translate Rancière's *The Philosopher and His Poor* (2004).

CATHERINE PORTER, Professor Emerita at the State University College at Cortland, is a freelance translator.

JACQUES RANCIÈRE is Professor Emeritus at the Université de Paris VIII, where he held the chair of aesthetics and politics. His most recent publications include *The Politics of Aesthetics* (2006), *The Future of the Image* (2007), *Hatred of Democracy* (2007), and *Politique de la littérature* (2007).

GABRIEL ROCKHILL is Assistant Professor of Philosophy at Villanova University and Director of the Atelier de Théorie Critique at the Centre Parisien d'Études Critiques and the Collège International de Philosophie. He is the author of *Logique de l'histoire: Pour une analytique des pratiques philosophiques* (forthcoming) and co-author of *La teoría crítica en Norteamérica: Política, ética y actualidad* (2008). He is currently co-editing *Technologies de contrôle dans la mondialisation: Enjeux politiques, éthiques et esthétiques*, and he edited and translated Jacques Rancière's *The Politics of Aesthetics* (2004).

KRISTIN ROSS is Professor of Comparative Literature at New York University. Her first book, *The Emergence of Social Space: Rimbaud and the Paris Commune*, has recently been reissued by Verso. Her latest book, *May '68 and Its Afterlives*, has recently been published in French and Spanish translations.

JAMES SWENSON teaches in the French Department at Rutgers University, specializing in eighteenth-century literature and intellectual history. He is the translator of books by Jacques Rancière and Étienne Balibar, and the author of *On Jean-Jacques Rousseau Considered as the First Author of the Revolution*.

TZUCHIEN THO is a graduate student in philosophy at the University of Georgia and the Université de Paris X. He is currently writing a dissertation concerning the conception and reception of Leibniz's work on the philosophical status and structure of infinitesimals. He worked with Zachary Luke Fraser on the editing and translation of Alain Badiou's *The Concept of Model* (2007).

RAJESHWARI VALLURY is Assistant Professor of French at the University of New Mexico and the author of *Surfacing the Politics of Desire: Literature, Feminism, and Myth* (forthcoming).

PHILIP WATTS is Associate Professor and Chair of the Department of French and Romance Philology at Columbia University. He is the author of *Allegories of the Purge* (1999).

Library of Congress Cataloging-in-Publication Data

Jacques Rancière : history, politics, aesthetics /
Gabriel Rockhill and Philip Watts, eds.
p. cm.   Includes bibliographical references and index.
ISBN 978-0-8223-4493-3 (cloth : alk. paper)
ISBN 978-0-8223-4506-0 (pbk. : alk. paper)
1. Rancière, Jacques. 2. Political science—Philosophy.
I. Rockhill, Gabriel. II. Watts, Philip, 1961-
JA71.J277 2009   320.092—dc22
2009005699